See Advertisement on Page 151.

HISTORY AND DIRECTORY

OF

KENT COUNTY,

MICHIGAN,

CONTAINING A

History of each Township, and the City of Grand Rapids;

The Name, Location and Postoffice Address of all Residents outside of the City; a List of Postoffices in the County; a Schedule of Population;
AND OTHER VALUABLE STATISTICS.

COMPILED AND PUBLISHED BY

DILLENBACK & LEAVITT,

COUNTY, HISTORY, DIRECTORY AND MAP PUBLISHERS.

GRAND RAPIDS, MICH.:
DAILY EAGLE STEAM PRINTING HOUSE.
1870.

INTRODUCTION.

The publishers of this work take pleasure in presenting to the citizens of Kent County a book that supplies a long-felt need experienced by business men, and which unites with its utility an amount of truly interesting historical matter. At the same time, they pride themselves upon its originality of design and tasty execution---not being altogether blind, however, to its defects. Doubtless errors will be found, which, to some may seem almost inexcusable; but where they occur the public may rest assured that they are not the result of carelessness on the part of the publishers. It can be safely said that no book of the kind was ever published which was free of errors. In collating the historical matter great care was taken to draw the information from the most reliable sources. As you glance through the history of your township or city, or any township with whose history you claim to be acquainted, do not hastily pronounce statements errors until you are confident that you are correct and the historian wrong; but remember that some one equally as well informed as you, in regard to the general facts, has stated otherwise. In a number of instances, the histories of particular townships have been written by residents, who have taken great pains to collect *facts* into the form in which they appear. To this diversity of authorship may be attributed the repetitions which occur in some of the sketches; similar thoughts in regard to the sufferings and privations of the pioneers being in the minds of all.

The publishers are well aware that a work of this kind, relating, as it does, facts with which purchasers are themselves acquainted, will meet with more or less criticism. Knowing this, they have left no stone unturned which would assist in making the book what the prospectus represented it would be. Besides using every precaution to avoid errors in the matter promised, they have even added to its appearance and utility a very pretty map of the State, which was engraved expressly for this work.

The book purports to contain the name of every man in the county (of twenty-one years of age and upwards) outside of Grand Rapids city, and of every widow owning real estate. The canvassers were instructed to call at every house, and to be as thorough as a census taker.

The names were copied, compared, and arranged in every instance before they were placed in the hands of the printer; and where a question arose in the mind as to the correct name, or mode of spelling, it was referred to the canvasser.

Numerous advertisements have been inserted, but in no instance in a manner that can be made just cause of complaint. The history is complete in itself, and only here and there have advertisements been placed in the directory matter, and even then uniformly on the right hand page. Further, the advertisements are from the best business firms in the county, and if carefully noted, will prove of great value to purchasers.

It has been customary to prepare Directories of cities exclusively, while there has been even greater need of Directories of counties and farming territory. The publishers intend to make this the first of a series of like publications, in this and other States, and, while they hope to increase their facilities for preparing even better books than the present, they trust this will not only meet the present demand in this locality, but be preserved as a book containing an account of the sufferings, trials, and achievements of the pioneers of Kent county.

The generous patronage and cordial co-operation of all classes of the community have fully justified the publishers' reliance on their intelligence and public spirit; and they are under obligations, in every town, to the township officers and old residents for historical and statistical information, always cheerfully furnished.

GRAND RAPIDS, Mich., Nov. 21, 1870.

INDEX TO ADVERTISERS.

GENERAL INDEX.

STATE OFFICERS.

Governor....HENRY P. BALDWIN.
Lieutenant Governor....MORGAN BATES.
Secretary of State....DANIEL STRIKER.
State Treasurer....VICTORY P. COLLIER.
Auditor General....WILLIAM HUMPHREY.
Commissioner of Land Office....CHAS. A. EDMONDS.
Superintendent of Public Instruction....ORAMEL HOSFORD.
Attorney General....DWIGHT MAY.
Member of Board of Education....WITTER J. BAXTER.

COUNTY OFFICERS.

State Senator.. BYRON D. BALL.
Representative 1st District.. JULIUS HOUSEMAN.
Representative 2d District.. SAMUEL M. GARFIELD.
Representative 3d District.. ASA P. FERRY.
Representative 4th District.. NICHOLAS R. HILL.
Sheriff.. JESSE F. WYCKOFF.
Clerk.. DANIEL McNAUGHTON.
Treasurer.. GEORGE YOUNG, Jr.
Register.. WILLIAM G. BECKWITH.
Prosecuting Attorney.. ANDREW J. REEVES.
Dircuit Court Commissioners.. OMAR H. SIMONDS, JAMES B. WILSON.
Coroners.. JOHN BRADY, CHARLES G. HYDE.
Surveyor.. ROBERT S. JACKSON.

Population of Kent County.

FIRST REPRESENTATIVE DISTRICT.

	Pop. 1870.
City of Grand Rapids, 1st Ward	3,483
" " " " 2d "	4,780
" " " " 3d "	3,906
" " " " 4th "	2,781
" " " " 5th "	1,557
	16,507

SECOND REPRESENTATIVE DISTRICT.

	Pop. 1860.	
Wyoming Township	1,237	1,787
Paris "	1,314	1,543
Cascade "	892	1,157
Lowell " }	1,201	1,583
" Village }		1,503
Bowne "	743	1,275
Caledonia "	763	1,599
Gaines "	870	1,205
Byron "	1,039	1,328
		12,980

THIRD REPRESENTATIVE DISTRICT.

Alpine "	1,249	1,446
Walker "	1,430	1,675
Plainfield "	1,240	1,499
Grand Rapids "	8,085*	1,650
Cannon "	1,061	1,126
Ada "	1,116	1,427
Vergennes "	1,344	1,342
		10,165

FOURTH REPRESENTATIVE DISTRICT.

Grattan "	1,127	1,298
Oakfield "	1,078	1,092
Courtland "	947	1,338
Algoma " }	993	1,377
Rockford Village }		582
Sparta Township	939	1,668
Tyrone "	172	730
Solon "	393	911
Nelson "	462	1,102
Spencer "	...	580
		10,678
Total	30,716	50,330

*City and Township.

Post-offices in Kent County.

NAME.	TOWNSHIP.
Ada,	Ada.
Alaska,	Caledonia.
Alpine,	Alpine.
Alto,	Bowne.
Alton,	Vergennes.
Austerlitz,	Plainfield.
Belmont,	Plainfield.
Bostwick Lake,	Cannon.
Bowne,	Bowne.
Burch's Mills,	Algoma.
Byron Center,	Byron.
Caledonia,	Caledonia.
Caledonia Station,	Caledonia.
Cannonsburg,	Cannon.
Casnovia,	Tyrone.
Cedar Springs,	Nelson.
Cody's Mills,	Byron.
Courtland Center,	Courtland.
Edgerton,	Algoma.
Spencer Mills,	Spencer.
Vergennes,	Vergennes.
Englishville,	Alpine.
Fallassburg,	Vergennes.
Gainesville,	Gaines.
Grattan Center,	Grattan.
Grand Rapids,	Grand Rapids City.
Grandville,	Wyoming.
Hammond,	Gaines.
Harris Creek,	Bowne.
Indian Creek,	Walker.
Kelloggville,	Paris.
Lisbon,	Sparta.
Lowell,	Lowell.
Mill Creek,	Plainfield.
Nelson,	Nelson.
North Byron,	Byron.
Oakfield,	Oakfield.
Pleasant,	Alpine.
Rockford,	Algoma.
Sand Lake,	Nelson.
Sparta Center,	Sparta.
Spencer Mills,	Spencer.
Vergennes,	Vergennes.

COUNTY OF KENT.

The county of Kent was organized in the year A. D. 1836. It was at that time very thinly populated, fifteen years only having elapsed since the first white settler placed his foot upon its soil. Rix Robinson came in the year 1821, and remained several years almost entirely alone, trading with the Indians. In 1826, Uncle Louis Campau settled here, and from that time forward the county has been steadily settling up.

The soil of Kent, considered as a whole, is not as good as that of some of its neighbors; however, it possesses some of the finest and most productive farms in the State. Some individual townships in the county possess as much good land as can be found anywhere within a limit of thirty-six square miles. But in the northern part of the county especially, there is much poor land, the timber being chiefly pine.

Its railroad facilities within a few years have become quite good, and, we are happy to say, are still improving. The Detroit & Milwaukee Railroad passes through the entire county, from east to west, having stations at Grand Rapids, Lowell and Ada. The Kalamazoo Division of the Lake Shore & Michigan Southern Railroad comes in from the south, passing through the townships of Byron and Wyoming, and has the following stations: Eagle Mills, Grandville, Scudder and Byron Center, with a northern terminus at Grand Rapids.

The Grand Rapids & Indiana Railroad passes through the entire length of the county, from north to south, and has the following stations: Cedar Springs, Burchville, Edgerton, Rockford, Child's Mills, Whitney, North's Mills and Grand Rapids, thereby opening up the northern part of the county, whence come most of the lumber and logs in this section. This road has recently been completed between Fort Wayne and Grand Rapids.

The Grand River Valley Division of the Michigan Central Railroad comes in from the south, and passes through the townships of Caledonia, Gaines and Paris, with a northern terminus at Grand Rapids. This road has the following stations: Hammond, Paris and Caledonia.

The villages in the county are all small with the exception of Lowell and Rockford; the former having a population of 1503, and the latter 582. Both of these are thrifty, go ahead places, and are rapidly building up.

Grand River enters the county on its east line, and meandering north-westerly and south-westerly, touches in its course eight townships and passes out a little south of a point directly opposite of the place of entrance. At the rapids, in the City of Grand Rapids, it furnishes an immense water power, which has been considerably improved.

Thornapple River forms a junction with the Grand at the village of Ada, the Flat River at the village of Lowell, and the Rouge River at Austerlitz (formerly Plainfield.)

This sketch being intended simply as an introduction, we will leave the more particular history of the county to be treated under the head of the several townships.

ADA.

Ada township is centrally located in the county; being bounded on the north by Cannon, on the east by Vergennes, on the south by Cascade, and on the west by Grand Rapids. It was named,—it is said,—after a highly respected lady by the name of Ada Smith, who then resided in the township.

Unfortunately the records of the township are not now in existence previously to the year 1835, which, however, must have been soon after the date of its organization.

The township of Ada originally embraced a large tract of country, including several of what are now the adjacent towns. It was of Ada as it then existed, that Rix Robinson, Esq., was elected the first supervisor. The first entry upon the records, under date of 1835, is to the effect that Norman Smith was elected supervisor by *one* majority, he receiving in all *thirty-two* votes.

Supposing that he had but one competitor,—as he probably had,—we estimate the whole number of votes *sixty-three.* Just think of it! In an extent of territory where there were at the last election at least *one thousand* votes polled, thirty-five years ago they could muster but *sixty-three.* Picture in your mind the sights of a "town meeting" during those times. Here they come, one by one. from the different points of the compass, hard-working, honest men. It is a gala day with them. They meet perhaps for the first time in months. They go early and stay late. They urge their brief political campaign in their homely way. They *enjoy* as well as perform their duty, and then part for the scenes of stern labor. Thus the times count themselves, each year bringing an increase in numbers, until fourth and fifth sub-divisions count more votes than the original united one.

One of the most prominent of the early settlers was Rix Robinson, Esq., the first white man in the township, and one of the first in the country. For a long time he was engaged in the fur trade with the Indians on Grand River. Alone he traversed the forests, and "paddled his own canoe," surrounded with savages by nature,—and sometimes by deed,—but he remained unmolested by them. The spirit of the natives had already been somewhat subdued by the influence of Christianity, and itinerant missionaries were then laboring among them. A tribe of these Indians remained on sections six and seven of the present township of Ada, until about the year 1860 or '61, when they sold their lands, and removed to Pentwater. During the latter years of their residence on these lands, they cultivated the soil, built respectable dwellings, had well organized schools and comfortable churches. They were of the Roman Catholic faith.

Mr. Robinson, or "Uncle Rix," as he is familiarly called, during his sojourn and life among the Indians, became quite attached to them; so much so that he chose one of their daughters as his partner for life, with whom he now lives. They have but one son, and he is well known throughout Grand River Valley as an energetic business man.

The life of the pioneer is fraught with toil, and peril, and actual suffering. It is pleasant for us to sit by the warm fire on a chilly night, and listen while the grandfather tells of the "dark days," as he once called them, in the history of his experience. We have often heard him repeat the story of the nights he spent in the woods alone, far from any house; of fording streams in winter; of encounters with wolves and other animals; of the poor log house with its stick chimney; of sickness and death in the family, with no attending physician, and so on through the long lists. But we are not the only delighted one. What a change came over the countenance of the aged man as he recounted those scenes! Ah! yes, he was "dreaming a dream of the olden time." All was not sorrow, hardship and suffering. It may have seemed to him at the time that it was nearly all "rainy weather;" but as he now calls up their "shadowy forms," he discovers that

> "Taking the year all around * * * *
> There *wasn't* more night than day."

Then we have passed through the valley of youth and middle age, and have ascended the hill of years, as we look back into the valley through which we have come, we shall discover many more scenes of real enjoyment than of discontent. So it is: whatever may be his experience, wherever he may be, in country, town, or wilderness, with pure mind, and a laudable ambition, every individual has his share of the music of life.

The experience of the pioneers of Ada, was similar to that of other townships; they worked hard, they endured much, and they enjoyed much. They lived a noble life, although it was a life perhaps few of us would choose. They lived a noble life, I say, and did a good work. Every stroke of their pioneer axe sounded a note in the song of a "thousand years."

Among the EARLY SETTLERS of Ada in addition to the one we have already mentioned may be named Edward Robinson, who settled in 1830, Torrey Smith, A. H. Riggs and Edward Pettis in 1836-7, Peter McLean, R. G. Chaffee, Hezekiah Howell, E. McCormick, P. Fingleton, Gurden Chapel, John Findlay and J. S. Schenck, 1840 to 1845.

The principal

RIVERS

in the township are the Grand and Thornapple. Grand River crosses the township from the northwest to the southeast, and is navigable for small crafts. Before the completion of the Detroit and Milwaukee Railroad, steamboats passed up the river as far as Ionia.

Among the

LAKES

"Chase's" is the only one worthy of mention. It is located on sections two and eleven, and contains about one hundred and sixty acres.

THE TIMBER

is mostly oak.

THE LAND

being what is usually termed "oak openings." It is rolling, particularly on either side of Grand River, but becomes nearer level as it recedes from the river.

THE SOIL

is rather sandy, being well adapted to fruit culture. It is well suited also to the production of the different kinds of grain.

The citizens of Kent County appreciate the value of good educational faculties.

No township can be said to be an exception to this statement. The

SCHOOL HOUSES

of Ada are located and numbered as follows: School house No. 1 was erected in 1858, at a cost of $600, on section thirty-four. Material, wood. School house No. 2 is located on section twenty, value, $800. Material, wood. School house No. 3 was erected in 1859. Material, wood. School house No. 4 (fractional Ada, Vergennes and Lowell,) was erected in 1852, at an expense of $200. Material, wood. School house No. 4 was erected in 1867, at an expense of $800; located on section twenty-three. Material, wood. School house No. 6 was erected in 1854, at a cost of $450; on section twelve. Material, wood. School house No. 8 was erected in 1856, at an expense of $800, on section five. School house No. 13 was erected in 1867 at an expense of $1,000, located on section ten. Material, wood.

ADA VILLAGE

was laid out into lots by Dalrymple & Dunn when the Detroit and Milwaukee Railroad was built,—about the year 1858; and although one or more additional plats have been made its growth seems to be quite slow. It is located on sections thirty-three and thirty-four, near the confluence of the Thornapple and Grand Rivers, ten miles, *via* the railroad, from the city of Grand Rapids. It possesses a tolerably good water power, which, as yet, has been but slightly improved. Two good grist mills are situated on Thornapple River, and appear to be doing a good business. One of them is called the "Ada Mills." It was built in 1856, and cost about $15,000. The present proprietors are E. Bradfield & Sons. The other, called the "Kent County Mill of Ada," was built in 1865, at an expense of about $15,000. It is situated at the mouth of the Thornapple, River, and is owned and operated by E. Averill & Co.

The Baptist Church, which, by the way, is the only church in the village, is a substantially built and well furnished brick structure. The village also contains a good school-house, two hotels, three dry goods stores, one drug store, two grocery stores, besides various blacksmith, butcher, cooper and shoemaker shops.

ALGOMA.

Algoma lies north of Plainfield, and is bounded on the north by Solon, east by Courtland, and west by Sparta.

It was first settled by Smith Lapham, from Washtenaw county, in 1843. He settled on the east side of Rouge River, in the southeast part of the township, where he now lives in the midst of the village of Rockford, (formerly called Laphamville.)

He was soon followed by the Hunter Brothers and others, in this corner; but none went farther north or west until 1845, when Joshua Briggs and family, from Yates county, New York, went on the east line of section twenty-five. John Davis and family, from Ingham county, went a mile farther north on the east line of section twenty-four, and Henry Helsel and Henry Shank and families, from Ohio, went up the right bank of the river and settled on section twenty-one. Mr. Helsel now has a fine farm of 280 acres, mostly improved; Mr.

Briggs and his sons have nice farms where they first settled; and Mr. Davis now lives, on an enchanting spot, on the bank of a roaring brook, which leaps and tumbles over a dam close to his cabin door, two miles west of his old home. Mr. Shank is not now a resident of the township.

Benj. Pettingill, and his son B. N. Pettingill, who came from Ingham county, and settled in the southeast corner of the township in 1845, are now living on a good farm on section twenty-six. The Longs and Turners who came in at an early day and settled in this vicinity, have good farms, with nice farm buildings, orchards, &c.

Among other pioneers in this township we would mention the names of Henry Morningstar and sons, John Boyer, John Jacobs, Jacob Ipe and sons, John M. Smith, James Smith, James Barnes, Andrew House, Daniel Youngblood, James Mosher, and Messrs. Emmons, Hull, Bowers and Christy, all within the first ten years. Mr. Emmons was the first settler on the west line, north of the river. Mr. Morningstar and sons were the first to penetrate the forest and settle on the now thickly settled line, one and one.half miles east of, and parallel with the west township line. They were soon followed by John Dome and Daniel Youngblood.

They were then three and one-half miles from Mr. Helsel, who was their nearest neighbor.

This is now one of the finest farming regions of the township. The farm of Mr. John Hull being the largest and one of the best. On the south line are some old, nice farms,'among the largest of which are those of Messrs. Jewell and Bennett.

But we must return to the

ORGANIZATION

of the township under the present name—Algoma—which was given in honor of a steamer of that name then plying on Grand River, between Grand Rapids and Grand Haven.

Algoma was previously attached to Plainfield. The first annual township meeting of Algoma was held in 1849, at which time the following were elected as the

FIRST TOWNSHIP OFFICERS:

Supervisor—Smith Lapham; Clerk—William Thornton; Treasurer—Albert L. Pickett; Justices—Morgan Allen, John H. Jacobs and John Hamilton.

The township meetings have generally been held at the school house, one mile south of the center, known as the Helsel school house, or more commonly as the "Gougeburg" school house. By a majority vote of the electors the place of meeting was changed in 1869, to Rockford village.

PRESENT TOWNSHIP OFFICERS.

Supervisor—H. N. Stinson; Clerk—C. E. Blakeley; Treasurer—Richard Briggs; Justices—Charles G. Hyde, Benj. W. Soule, William Powell, Oscar House.

GENERAL DESCRIPTION.

Pine was the prevailing timber of this township, although very much mixed with beech, maple, oak, etc.

There are some small parcels of land timbered exclusively with beech and maple; but they are small parcels, and few in number; and are situated principally in the west and southwest part.

In the southeast part, near Rouge River, oak prevails; but there are only a few farms in the township which are entirely free from pine stumps. The northeastern part is still almost an unbroken pine forest, with but little other timber.

As may be inferred from the timber, there is a great variety of soil. We were told by one man that he could show as great a diversity of soil on twenty acres of his farm, as could be found in the State. There is scarcely any swampy land in the township.

The south part along the river is very much broken, some of the hills being very steep, and nearly a hundred feet above the level of the land along the streams. This is chiefly a sandy or clay soil, intermixed with stone and gravel. In the remaining portions, those parts which are timbered with beech and maple are usually a fine, rich loam, and the parts which are exclusively timbered with pine are generally sandy.

We commenced our general description by describing the timber, as that has been more valued in the past than has the soil; but as the timber is being rapidly taken off, more interest is now taken in the latter.

At first it was bought in large tracts by speculators, who generally hold it until the pine can be culled, and all of the best taken off; then it is sold out in smaller parcels to actual settlers. At one time, J. B. Chipman, of the State of New York, owned nearly a thousand acres of land, chiefly timbered with pine, in the northeast corner of the township. In 1854, his son, Walter Chipman, a lawyer by profession, came to look at the land, and, becoming enamored of "backwoods life in Michigan," settled here, where he still remains, a much esteemed citizen.

Some years previous to coming hither, Mr. Chipman, being obliged, by a decline in his health, to give up his profession, joined a regiment of soldiers just starting out for our Western coast, and when he was discharged, remained as a pioneer in California. He was a member of the Convention which framed the Constitution of that State when it was admitted into the Union. Returning to New York, he spent some time with his friends, then went to Vermont, where he engaged in teaching for a year, and at last came here as before stated and became a pioneer in this township. I say pioneer, for although the south part had been settled eleven years, the north part was very new when he came. His brother J. B. Chipman, Jr., came on some years later.

Andrew House, who was one of the first settlers of Plainfield, as well as Algoma, owned, at one time, 700 acres of pine land, in the east part of the township.

John Almy, of Grand Rapids, also owned several hundred acres in the north and northwest. These were among the largest tracts, although there were others who owned parcels of considerable size.

STREAMS, LAKES, &C.

Rouge River is the principal stream of Algoma. It flows in on section thirty, from Sparta; thence southeast for a short distance; then northeast, and lastly, south across nearly the whole width of the township, and out, on section thirty-six, into Plainfield. It is a good sized, rather swift-flowing stream, and furnishes plenty of power for the manufacturing now done, with much to spare. This stream is quite extensively used for running pine logs to the various mills below, on this and Grand River.

Cedar Creek comes from Solon, enters the northeast corner of Algoma, flows southwest, to the northeast corner of section sixteen, where it unites with a branch called the Little Cedar, which also comes from the northeast, but further to the south. From here it flows south, and enters Rouge River on section twenty-two. This stream furnishes good water power in two places, which are used. It might be used in various other places.

A spring creek, sometimes known as *Wicked Creek*, about five miles long, rises in the west part of Courtland, flows southeast, crossing sections thirteen and fourteen, and enters Rouge River on section twenty-three. This stream, though but a mere spring brook runs sufficiently swift to furnish power for twelve mills, all of which are within four miles of its mouth; eight of them in this township, and four in Courtland.

A fine spring brook, two and one-half miles in length, rises in the western part of Courtland, flows across the farm of E. H. Penfield on section twenty-five, and empties into Rouge River. This stream is remarkable for its nearly uniform size throughout the whole length, and during the whole year. This uniformity is caused by its being so short that it is hardly affected by heavy rains.

In the northwest part of this township, and on the adjoining sections in the southwest corner of Solon, and the northeast corner of Sparta, are a number of small lakes, among which are the following:

Camp Lake is a long, narrow lake, nearly one mile in length, situated in the west part of Algoma, on sections seven and eighteen. Its outlet is a small stream which flows northwest through sections twelve and one of Sparta, and enters Rouge River.

Long Lake is nearly as large, and lies in the southwesterly part of section thirty-one, in Solon.

Round Lake is smaller, and lies on the line between Algoma and Solon. So also do the two Sand Lakes and Big Lake.

On and near the line of Algoma and Sparta are the two Indian Lakes and Squaw Lake. The outlet of these latter lakes is a small stream, sometimes called Indian Creek, which flows across section one of Sparta, and enters Rouge River from the northeast.

These lakes abound in small fish, such as bass, perch, etc., and an effort is being made to propagate pickerel in some of them.

Marl or Bog-lime has been found on the south side of Big Lake, on the south line of section thirty-two, of Solon, much of which has been burned and used for building purposes in the surrounding country.

The land in this vicinity is rolling, and is said to be good for the production of fruit.

VILLAGES.

Rockford is a flourishing little town of over 500 inhabitants. It is situated on the Rouge River five miles from its mouth, and thirteen miles from Grand Rapids, on the Grand Rapids and Indiana Railroad. It is in the extreme southeast corner of Algoma, on section thirty-six, and includes a small piece of section one of the township of Plainfield. The first settler here was Smith Lapham, previously mentioned as the first settler of the township. He came in the year 1843, constructed a dam across the river, and erected the building now used by Messmore & Watkins as a shingle mill. The mill on the west side of the stream, now used by the same firm, was erected the following year by Hunter Brothers.

In the year 1845 a Postoffice was established here, with S. Lapham as the first Postmaster. The mail being carried by him from Plainfield, once a week, in his pockets, for want of a mail-bag.

In the year 1848, White and Rathbun, of Grand Rapids, opened the first stock of store goods sold here. A grist mill was erected by Chase and Judson, in 1852, which contains three run of stone, and is now owned and operated by Messmore and Watkins.

The village was first platted in 1856, under the name of Laphamville, replatted in 1865, and the name changed to Rockford. It was regularly incorporated by an act of the Board of Supervisors, in June, of the year 1866. It now contains fifteen stores, one livery stable, two meat markets, three shoe shops, two brick yards, one foundry and two or three blacksmith and wagon shops, etc. Also a photograph gallery, a good supply of lawyers and doctors, and last, but not least, we noticed two or three good looking millinery establishments. There are two good frame hotels, one kept by H. N. Stinson, and the other by Smith Lapham; a steam stave factory, owned by Barker and Hyde, which cuts about three million staves and one million heading per year; a sash, blind and door factory, run by water power, and owned by McConnell and Addison, who do a good custom business and ship some work north; beside the grist mill and two saw mills of Messmore and Watkins, before mentioned, and which seem to be doing a good business.

The Baptist Church is a good frame building, 36x60 feet in size. It was erected in 1858.

The Methodist Episcopal Church is also a frame building, 24x60 feet in size, and was erected in 1865.

The schools are on the graded system, consisting of three departments. This is the original district No. 1, of Algoma, and the frame building used for the school, years ago, still stands in the southern part of the village, on an elevation, near the river. This building was about 25x35 feet in size, and when the village began to grow up, an addition, nearly the same size, was built on the rear. Subsequently the wood house was taken for a primary department, and now, these three failing to be sufficient to accommodate the "rising generation," a fine, large brick school house 60x63 feet in size, is being erected at a cost of $20,000. This building is on the original site, which has received some additions and now includes nearly a whole block.

Burchville, situated near the centre of section one, in the northeast corner of Algoma, is a thriving "lumber station," on the Grand Rapids and Indiana Railroad, five and one-half miles from Rockford, and about eighteen from Grand Rapids.

It was platted in 1868, by John S. Weller, of Ann Arbor, and named in honor of his partner, Jefferson Burch, who came here and built the first steam saw mill in 1866. That mill was totally destroyed by fire in 1867, and a new one erected by Mr. Burch on the same site. This mill is now operated by M. L. Whitney and has a capacity for cutting 15,000 feet of lumber and 15,000 shingles per day. It now cuts only about half that amount for want of logs.

In 1867, George R. Congdon & Co., erected a mill of about the same capacity, which was destroyed by fire in June, 1870, with about $100,000 worth of lumber.

It was at that time owned by Isaac Newton & Co., of Grand Rapids, who are now erecting a new mill on the same ground. Newton & Co. have also a small, portable steam mill near by, which cuts 10,000 feet of lumber per day.

Campbell & Stanton have a portable steam shingle mill about one hundred rods west of the station, which cuts 15,000 shingles per day. This mill has been running since October, 1868.

In 1868 a school district was organized here, and a school is kept in a board shanty, although money has once been raised and paid for building a school house. Finding that they were the victims of misplaced money as well as misplaced confidence, the people have voted $910, and let the job to another man, who is to put up a good frame house this summer. It will be 30x36 feet in size, with sixteen feet posts.

The present population is probably about two hundred, including those on Congdon's addition, recently platted, and which includes all of that part of the village lying south of the Little Cedar Creek.

Edgerton is the name of a railroad station about halfway between Rockford and Burchville, and a little more than half a mile from the east line of Algoma. This place boasts a postoffice and two groceries. Andrew House is the present Postmaster. This is near the well known "Porter Hollow," which contains the stream that is noted for so many

MILLS,

which we now will proceed to describe: Going west from the station about a quarter of a mile, we come to the first saw mill built on this stream. It stands on the southwest corner of section thirteen, and was erected in 1846 by Newton Andrews. It is now run by Charles Fox, and cuts 4,000 feet of lumber or 12,000 shingles per day.

Half a mile southwest of this at the mouth of the creek, is the shingle mill of John S. Doty. This was built by Hiram Davis in 1866, and cuts 10,000 shingles per day.

We will now retrace our steps and go up the creek nearly to the railroad, and about one quarter of a mile from the station, where we come to a grist mill and shingle mill, both of which are operated by David Munro. These mills were erected by Harvey Porter, in 1854, and are now owned by Jones and Johnson. These parties also own and operate a saw mill just above the railroad track, which was erected in 1854, by Seth Porter. The grist mill is principally used for custom business, although they ship some flour and feed north. The shingle mill cuts 10,000 shingles per day, and the lumber mill about 10,000 feet of lumber. Up the creek three-fourths of a mile farther, is a shingle mill, capable of cutting 10,000 per day, owned and operated by Seth Porter. A few rods farther east, near the Courtland line are the grist mill and saw mill of Coon & Scarvell. These mills were erected by Dennis Porter in 1862. They are small custom mills; the former making some flour and feed for sale. All of these mills except the second are on section thirteen, and that is on twenty-three.

Two miles west of Edgerton, on the Cedar Creek, near the west line of section twenty-two, Jackson and George Coon are erecting a grist mill, on the site of a saw mill which was destroyed by fire some time ago.

One and a half miles up this creek, on the north side of section sixteen, is the saw mill commonly known as the Morningstar Mill. This mill was erected in 1852, by Norman Ackley, and refitted, and mostly rebuilt, in 1866, by Solomon and Caine, who now own and operate it. Its capacity is about 7,000 feet of lumber, or 14,000 shingles per day.

About one and one-fourth miles farther up the Big Cedar, is a large, steam saw mill, which was erected in December, 1868, by Ammon Fox, who still owns and operates it, cutting 14,000 feet of lumber, or 15,000 shingles per day.

There is a portable detached steam saw mill on the west side of section eleven, on the Little Cedar, erected in June, 1869, by McClure & Kidder. This mill cuts 10,000 feet of lumber, or 15,000 shingles per day. It will be better known as the "Hodag" mill.

This name was given it, from the fact that an unknown and mysterious animal was heard, seen, and even fired at, in the woods near here, some years ago, and as no other name could be found for it, it was called "Hodag," and when the mill was built, this was the name given to it by the people of Burchville.

Jacob Long has a small water power saw mill on the northwest-quarter of section five, near the northwest corner of the township. This mill was built by Zimrod Burnham, in 1860, and cuts about 3,000 feet of lumber per day.

SCHOOL HOUSES.

District No. 2 (fractional with Courtland), organized in 1850, and a small frame house erected, which was used until 1866, when the present frame building was erected at a cost of $500, one half mile east of Edgerton station, on the township line. District No. 3 has a small, wooden frame house, erected in 1852. This school house is one mile south of the centre of the township, and half a mile north of the little collection of houses known as Gougeburg, where a dam was once built across Rouge River and a saw mill erected by C. C. Comstock, of Grand Rapids. The mill burned down, the proprietor failed, and so also did the village, which was springing up around the mill. District No. 4 has a small frame house, which was erected in 1854, on the center of section twenty-nine District No. 6 organized in 1852, and erected a small log house on the south side of section eight. In 1862 the site was changed to the north side of eight on account of a division of the district, and a block house erected the following year, which is still used. District No. 7 has a building called the "House" school house. It is a frame building, and was erected in 1863, on the south part of section twenty-three. District No. 8 organized in 1860, and a log house was erected near the north side of section sixteen, on the farm of Calvin Babcock.

The Good Templars are erecting a frame hall 24x36 feet in size, at the center of section twenty-nine. Estimated cost $300.

ALPINE.

Alpine is one of the west tier of townships, and is bounded on the north by Sparta, on the east by Plainfield, on the south by Walker, and on the west by the township of Wright, Ottawa county. It retains its original form and size, containing thirty-six square miles.

The first settlers were Solomon Wright and family, who came from Wayne county, New York, in the year 1837, and located on the south line, near Indian Creek. The family consisted of the old gentleman and lady and five sons, Benjamin, Solomon, Noadiah, Andrew and Jeremiah, only one of whom remains in the township, and that is Solomon. The old people are both dead, one son lost his life in the recent war, one is living at Lowell, and two are in Walker. In the year 1840 John Coffee and Richmond Gooding came from Ohio, penetrated the forest nearly five miles beyond the Wright neighborhood and settled on section nineteen, near the west line of the township. For years this was considered the "jumping off place," as they called it, there being no settlements north of them, and in fact no house in any direction nearer than three or four miles. About the same time Jacob Snyder—a German—settled on section thirty-five, and another German by the name of John Plattee on section thirty-six, in the southeast corner of the township. A short time before this, Turner Hills and family came from Vermont, and located in the east part of the township, on section thirteen, where, for several years, they were the northernmost settlers. Mr. Hills died many years ago, but the widow and two sons remain in the township.

Among other pioneers who settled in various parts of the township, were Noel Hopkins, Baltas Schaffer, Peter Schlick, James Snowden, Sherman Pearsall, John B. Colton, A. B. Toms, Thompson Kasson, Joseph Hipler, John Ellis, Edward Wheeler, Hervey Wilder, Joseph Bullen, Moses Ramsdell, John J. Downer, Hiram Stevenson, Artemus Hilton, Henry S. Church, Charles Anderson, Francis Greenley, and the Boyds, Denisons, Meads, Brewers, Davenports, and Cordes, all of whom came before 1850; and most of them yet remain to enjoy the fruits of their early labors and sufferings.

Many and varied were the privations endured by these early settlers. We who have never been pioneers cannot fully appreciate the sufferings, the trials, and hardships which were their lot. Think of a journey to Grand Rapids with an ox team, over rough roads, with a grist for the mill; of a return in the night with its many perplexities, now and then losing the indistinct road, with a consequent delay of an half hour; of finding trees blown across the way, preventing further progress until they have been removed by the use of the ax, and so on through the list.

Again imagine the loneliness of a family coming from a thickly settled part of the country, and making a home in the wilderness, with no actual neighbors; with no schools; with no churches; and in fact with no associations except those of their own fireside. Little time can be spared for social intercourse even at home. The round of duties consumes each day but the Sabbath, which is to them indeed a day of holy rest.

We would not wish to be understood to intimate that there are no enjoyments connected with such a life, for downright satisfaction is always the result of manly toil. Situated, as the pioneer is, in an unbroken forest, with every stroke of the ax, and with every effort made toward improvement, he seems to be hewing out a little world of his own. Every acre added to the cleared space adds more than its proportionate amount of pleasure to the soul of the laborer. He looks forward to the time when his broad acres shall be seen clothed with the rich yellow grain of a plenteous harvest. He walks by faith and not by sight. The "sweet bye and bye" is anticipated, and that is what incites him to labor and to endure.

Then again much pleasure is found in the little visits which they are occasionally favored with. That peculiar community of feeling which is the characteristic of persons in depressed circumstances, is enjoyed by pioneers, and early settlers, in an unusual degree. There is a mutual dependence of one upon another, felt by everybody; and this never fails to beget a spirit of friendship between them.

ORGANIZATION.

Alpine was united with the township of Walker, until the year 1847. Its first independent township meeting was held at the School House in the southeast corner of the township, on the 5th day of April, 1847; which resulted in the election of the following named persons as officers: Supervisor, Edward Wheeler; Clerk, C. D. Shenich; Treasurer, Casper Cordes; Justices, Wm. H. Withey, John Coffee, John Colton, and John Tuxbury. The next annual meeting was held at the house of Edward Wheeler, near the center of the township. Soon after this a small log School House was erected on the corner of Mr. Wheeler's farm, one-half mile east of the center, and was used as a place of holding township meetings until about the year 1860, when a nice, frame, Town Hall building was erected on the northeast corner of section twenty-one.

THE PRESENT OFFICERS

of Alpine are Supervisor, Isaac Haynes; Clerk, Hanson Rogers; Treasurer, Charles Dole; Justices, John Coffee, Warren Bailey, Charles Waterman, and Hollis R. Hills.

GENERAL DESCRIPTION.

Alpine—which is said to have derived its name from the supposition of many of the early settlers, who were near the streams, and in the eastern part of the township, that it was chiefly timbered with pine—is very different from what its name would indicate to a stranger. There was, originally, considerable pine along the larger streams, and in the northeasterly corner of the township. At one time, seven saw mills were situated on Mill Creek, and were doing a brisk business; but now there is hardly enough pine left to sustain three.

The source of Mill Creek is Cranberry Lake, which is situated on the line between Kent and Ottawa counties, extending into section six of Alpine. From there to Pickerel Lake on section ten Mill Creek is but a small rivulet. We mention this as the main stream; however there is another branch about the same size, which comes in from Sparta, and unites with the former near the north line of section nine. From Pickerel Lake to its mouth it is fed by several small streams, one of which comes from Downer Lake on the southeast quarter of section ten. The main stream passes about one and one-half miles north of the center of the township, thence southeasterly until it unites with Grand River in the southwest corner of Plainfield. For a distance of five or six miles from its mouth, the water power is sufficiently good for manufacturing purposes. Along this stream is a series of small swamps, extending nearly the whole width of the township from east to west, and bordered on either side by clay bluffs, rising in some places to a height of sixty or seventy feet.

North of this, and extending into Sparta, is a ridge of high, rolling, timbered land, which is as good as can be found in the county, for farming purposes, fruit growing, etc. On the south is a similar ridge, which divides Mill Creek on one side from Indian and Sand Creeks on the other.

One branch of Indian Creek rises near the center of the township, and the other in the western part. These branches unite in the north part of section twenty-eight; thence the stream flows south into Walker, crossing the south line of Alpine near the center.

One branch of Sand Creek rises in the Western part of Alpine, and flows south into Walker, and thence west into Ottawa county. Another branch of the same stream has source in a small lake covering about ten acres, situated on the line between sections twenty-eight and twenty-nine.

Minnie or New Boston Lake is situated on the east line of section twelve, and extends east into Plainfield. The lake and surrounding swamp cover about forty acres. A number of years ago a saw mill was erected on the north side of this lake, and an effort was made to build up a burgh, which was christened New Boston; but like many other enterprises of a like nature it never went much beyond the paper plat.

THE SOIL

of the beach and maple timbered portions of Alpine—which comprise about two-thirds of the township—is generally clay or loam. Indeed Alpine is a township of good land, well adapted to the production of both grain and fruit. The good looking orchards, and the loads of nice apples, peaches, plums, pears, etc., as well as the excellent yields of wheat and other grain, speak for themselves. The soil of the pine timbered portions is sandy, but it grows fair crops when well cultivated and improved. Among the largest and best farms in the township, are those of Solomon Wright, A. Downer, Mrs. James Snowden, Judson Buck, L. N. Dennison, David Herrick, Richmond Gooding, and Eberhard Cordes, each of which comprises two hundred acres or more.

MILLS AND MANUFACTURING ESTABLISHMENTS.

Colton's Saw Mill, built in the year 1845 by Colton and Phillips, situated on the south side of section thirteen, is now owned and operated by Gideon Colton. This mill is capable of cutting nearly a million feet of lumber per year; but on account of the scarcity of pine does a comparatively small business.

The Saw Mill situated on the northeast corner of section twenty-five, commonly called Withey's Mill, is manufacturing large quantities of shingles and some lumber. It is owned and operated by Aaron Leland.

Stonehouse's Steam Saw Mill, situated on the northeast corner of section twenty-five, was erected by John Stonehouse in the year 1868, on the site of an old water power mill owned by him, and which was destroyed by fire in the year 1867. The new mill is turning out large quantities of shingles, also some lumber and lath.

Ellis & Brown's Grist Mill, situated on section thirteen, on Mill Creek, is doing a good custom business.

The Wolverine Pump Works, S. N. Edie, Proprietor, are situated on section thirty-six, one-half mile northwesterly of Mill Creek Post-office. This establishment was erected in the year 1868. It is located on a small branch of Mill Creek, whose waters give it motive power. The shop is furnished with facilities for manufacturing five thousand pumps per annum.

Orrin Gee owns and operates a small Brick Yard on the south side of section thirty-one.

There is a water power Cider Mill situated on Mill Creek, owned and operated by Gideon Colton, which is wo rthy of notice. The mill is so built on the bluff at the side of the stream, that the apples can be unloaded from the wagon into the hopper at the top, where they are ground, below which they are pressed, then barreled and loaded into wagons at the foot of the bluff without necessitating the lifting of a pound.

SCHOOL HOUSES.

District No. 1 is in the center of the township. Its first School House was built on the farm of Edward Wheeler, on the north side of section twenty-two. The present School Building was erected in the year 1861, and is a substantial frame structure. It stands on the south side of section fifteen, one-half mile east of the Town Hall.

District No. 2 has an old wooden building, commonly known as the Coon School House.

District No. 3 (fractional with Wright,) has a nice, brick building situate on the north side of section thirty. It was erected in 1868 at an expense of $1,000.

District No. 4 (fractional with Sparta,) has a small frame house, known as Rouse School House, situated on the north line of section three.

District No. 6 (fractional with Sparta), has a school house in the northeast corner of section five. It was erected in the year 1864, at a cost of about $1200.

The school house in District No. 7 (fractional with Plainfield), known as the Colton school house, situated on the south side of section thirteen, is a neat frame structure. It was erected in the year 1869, at an expense of $950.

District No. 8 has a small, frame house, known as the Pearsall school house, which was erected in 1851, on the northwest corner of section twenty-eight.

District No. 9 (fractional with Plainfield), has a very old building, known as the Withey school house, situated on the northeast corner of section thirty-six.

District No. 10 (fractional with Wright), has a small frame house, known as the Boyd school house, standing on the southwest corner of section eight. It was erected in the year 1856.

District No. 11 has a small, wooden building, which was erected in the year 1855, and used until the year 1869, when the Roman Catholics of the district, with the aid of those of surrounding districts, erected a building of their own at at a cost of $1500, in which they now have a German-English school. The deserted building is situated on the south side of section twenty six, and the new one at the center.

District No. 13 (fractional with Walker), has a nice frame building, known as the Johnson school house. It was erected in the year 1859, and stands on the south side of section thirty-four.

District No. 14 (fractional with Sparta), has a small, frame building, which was erected in the year 1852, and is known as the Englishville school house. It is located on the north side of section one.

District No. 15 (fractional with Walker), has a small, frame building, known as the Monroe school house.

CHURCHES.

The Alpine and Walker Baptist Church is a good frame building, 36x56 feet in size. It was erected in the year 1859 on the south side of section thirty-three, at a cost of probably $2000.

The Roman Catholic Church, situated on the north side of section thirty-four, was erected in the year 1849, at a cost of about $1500. It is a frame structure 26x46 feet in size.

HOTELS.

The Alpine House, which was erected in the year 1867 by M. Crill, is a large, commodious, frame building, situated on the south side of section thirteen on the Sparta Center road. This is located in the midst of a little cluster of houses, sometimes called Coltonville. They have a postoffice known as Alpine, also two or three shops, and not far distant on the same section, are the grist and saw mills heretofore described. The "Brick Inn," erected by Joseph Bettes, in the year 1862, on the site of the old "Log Inn," is now owned and kept by Washington Heath. It is located in the south part of section thirty, on the Newaygo State road.

BOWNE.

Bowne is the southeastern township of Kent County. It is bounded on the north by Lowell, on the east by Campbell, Ionia county, on the south by Irving, Barry county, and west by Caledonia. The surface of the township is rolling in the south part, the western part is mostly timbered openings, while the eastern part is beech and maple land, and is rather level. It is all rich and excellent soil, and well adapted to all kinds of agricultural pursuits. And, although comparatively new, is fast being developed into fine farms. It is watered by the Coldwater, or Little Thornapple, which enters the township on its eastern boundary on section thirty-six, and flows in a westerly direction through the township, leaving its western boundary on section thirty-one. This is a very rapid stream and would afford five or six mill sites within the limits of this township, only two of which are improved. One on section twenty-nine, occupied by Patterson's saw mill, and one on section thirty-six, occupied by Richardson's saw mill. In the western part of the township is a small stream flowing from the north, called Harris Creek, on which Hon. A. D. Thomas has a grist mill with two run of stone, driven by an overshot wheel with a fall of thirty feet. In the eastern part of the township is another small stream called Duck Creek, which affords in the northeast corner of the township water power for a saw mill, owned by Jaspar Kuykendall.

In 1836, Mr. Jonathan Thomas, of Ovid, New York, entered a large tract of land in the southwestern portion of this township, and, in 1837 came on to improve it, bringing with him Mr. Frederick Thomson and family, who still reside in Bowne, Mr. Israel Graves and family, and Mr. William Wooley and family. They came by water to Toledo, and thence to their destination with ox teams, making the trip from Toledo in about two weeks. They proceeded to build houses and clear up the farm now owned by A. D. Thomas. The first house they built, and the first within the town, is still standing, and is preserved by Mr. A. D. Thomas as a relic of the past and as a contrast with the present. It is of logs, about twelve by fourteen feet square, without any chamber, and with only one door and one window and a "shake" roof. Near this Mr. Thomas built two other houses and a small log building for an office for himself. Mr. Thomas was taken sick soon after he arrived, and was sick most of the time until the next winter, when his son-in-law Mr. John Harris came, and they fixed a bed in a sleigh and he started for his home in New York. They made the whole distance with a sleigh, dragging through northern Ohio in the slush and mud. During the first summer, when they got out of provisions, Mr. Thomas, although quite ill at the time, had his bed fixed in a wagon, and taking his whip started his ox team for Kalamazoo. He was obliged to go a few miles beyond there and buy wheat, bring it back to Kalamazoo and have it ground. Mrs. Thomson says there were a great many Indians on the Coldwater when they moved there. They found them good neighbors when they were sober, but when they could get "fire water" they were quarrelsome, and occasioned trouble at times. One came to their house one day when Mr. Thomson was away from home, and sat down in the rocking chair before the fire and rocked himself over into the fire-place, she pulled him out of the fire and he became enraged and attempted to stab her. But when she picked up an axe, and told him she would kill him if he did not leave, he beat a retreat. Another time, a lot of Indians came up on their ponies, when the men were gone, and ordered Mrs. Wooley to get them something to eat. She ran to her door and called to Mrs. Thomson, who went over, she says, as brave as could be, and talked to them. The old chief ordered her to go back to her wigwam and get him something to eat. She obeyed, trembling with fear all the time, and got the best dinner she could under the circumstances, setting her table with the nicest spread and dishes she had. The chief ate his meal alone at her house and seemed much pleased, told her she was a "brave squaw," and that they would not harm them then, but after a certain number of moons they were going to kill all of the whites in the country. The other families that came with them soon became discouraged and went back, and they were left alone, seven miles at first, from any white neighbors. One time Mrs. Thomson remained alone eight days. Mr. Thomson went to Kalamazoo to mill, and while there his oxen strayed away, and before he could find them and get home, eight days passed by. She remained at home until nearly noon the last day, when the suspense became so great she could not bear it any longer, and she started, on foot, for the nearest neighbor's, "Leonard's," seven miles distant. After proceeding about half way she met a white man. He was very much surprised at meeting a woman under such circumstances, and inquired of her where she was going. She told him, and inquired if he had seen or heard of her husband. He told her of his losing his cattle, and that he was on the road and would be along before night, and as it was very warm advised her to either go back or wait until her husband came along, and when she told him "No," she would never stop until she had seen her husband, he said that he was a bachelor, but if he could find a woman who would endure as much and as bravely for him he should certainly marry. They used to see many wolves and bears, but never felt much fear of them. For some years they went to "Scale's Prairie" to meeting, and afterward, when there got to be population enough so that preachers used to come among them, Mrs. Thomson says she used frequently to entertain three or four at a time in their little log shanty, twelve by fourteen feet square.

In the spring of 1838 Messrs. Malcolm and John McNaughton commenced "breaking" on section twenty. They broke up forty acres that year and put it into wheat. In the fall of 1838 Messrs. Roswell Tyler, Norman Foster and J. G. Beach settled at the centre of Bowne. They came from Detroit with teams, *via* Gull Prairie, and were about ten days on the road. Mr. Tyler and another man came through from Jackson on foot, following what was called the Clinton Trail. At this time there were no settlements nearer on the north than Ada and Lowell. Among the other early settlers whose names we have been able to get, we find James H. Truax, Jared Miller, William Stewart, Daniel C. McVean, Abraham Lowe, and Messrs White and Cobb, who settled at different times ranging from 1840 to 1845.

SCHOOL HOUSES.

There are eight school houses in Bowne, all frame buildings, situated on sections 29, 28, 24, 12, 7, 4, 22 and 20. Bowne is well supplied with

POSTOFFICES.

Containing three, viz: Bowne, Alto, and Harris Creek. The Bowne postoffice, James C. Johnson, P. M., is located at Bowne Center. Alto postoffice is situated near the centre of section four, and kept by David M. Skidmore. Harris Creek postoffice, Wilbur S. March, P. M., is on the southwest part of section twenty-nine, near Thomas' Mills.

LAKES.

Foster Lake, on section 24, is a fine sheet of water about a quarter of a mile in length. On the northwest corner of section 23, near the residence of Stephen Johnson, is a small lake called Putnam Lake. A small lake near the centre of section 10, is known as Number Ten Lake. Campbell Lake is a handsome lake, about half a mile in length, on section 19. In the north part of the township are several large swamps, interspersed with small lakes or ponds; one range lying on sections 1, 2, 3, and 4, and one lying on sections 5 and 8.

ORGANIZATION.

The township of Bowne was organized in the year 1848, by the election of the following named gentlemen as the

FIRST TOWNSHIP OFFICERS:

Supervisor—Roswell C. Tyler; Clerk—Daniel C. McVean; Treasurer—Justus G. Beach; Justices of the Peace—Jared Miller, Norman Foster; Assessors—Abijah Poole. John A. Campbell; Commissioners of Highways—Loren B. Tyler, James H. Truax, Asa. R. Tyler. School Inspectors--Jared Miller, William Gibson. Overseers of the Poor—Roswell F. Tyler, John Underwood. Constables—Salmon E. Platt, Henry C. Foster.

TOWNSHIP OFFICERS IN 1870.

Supervisor—Abner D. Thomas. Clerk—Abel Ford. Treasurer—James M. Nash. Justices of the Peace—Stephen Johnson, Benjamin J. Lee, Levi Stone, Henry D. Francisco. Commissioners of Highways—Loren B. Tyler, Henry D. Francisco, William H. Stone. Constable—Oliver A. Stone.

BYRON.

The township of Byron is situated in the extreme southwestern part of Kent county, with Wyoming on the north, Gaines on the east, Dorr, Allegan county, on the south, and Jamestown, Ottawa county, on the west.

The surface of it is rolling, being covered with gently rolling swells and small knolls, with the exception of a swamp which commences on section thirteen and extends in a southwesterly direction into Allegan county. This swamp varies from eighty rods to one mile in breadth, and is mostly timbered with tamarack and cedar. The extreme southwestern part of the township is somewhat broken, but not enough so to injure its value for farming purposes. The soil varies from argillaceous to sandy; but is what is generally known to farmers as either clayey or sandy loam. The surface of some of the creek bottoms is underlaid with marl or "bog lime," while the "big swamp" is a bed of muck, in many places of several feet in thickness. On section twenty-one, on the farm of S. S. Towner, is a small swamp timbered with tamarack, through which the track of the northern branch of the Lake Shore and Michigan Southern Railroad passes, which has several times sunk so as to engulf the road bed. This swamp is probably the site of a lake which has become covered with a coating of vegetable matter of sufficient thickness to support trees of from fifty to sixty feet in height.

This township is composed of what is known as "timbered lands," comprising within its limits nearly every variety of trees known in this climate, viz. the Oak, Elm, Basswood, Whitewood, Sugar and Soft or White Maple, Blackwalnut, Butternut, Sycamore, Pepperage, Beech, White and Black Ash, Hickory and Bitter Walnut, Pine, Cedar and Tamarack. And in some very favored localities a few Hackberry trees are to be found. Of shrubs nearly all that flourish in this State are found, and in the rich hollows of the heavy timbered lands the Paw Paw flourishes to a considerable extent.

Byron is quite well watered by Buck and Rush Creeks, and the springs and numerous small streams that form these creeks. One branch of Buck Creek rises in the extreme southeastern corner of the township, flows a northwesterly direction for some distance, and then north by east until it leaves the town on its northern limits at the center line of section one. Another branch rises in Dorr, Allegan county, and flows northeasterly through the "big swamp" until it forms a junction with the main stream.

About the center of section twenty-six is a small lake called "Mud Lake." Rush Creek rises near the center of the township and flows in a northwesterly direction, leaving Byron very near its northwestern limits.

Go back with me reader for a space of thirty-four years, to the summer of 1836. Byron was then an unbroken wilderness. The ruthless hand of the white man, armed with that terribly destructive weapon, the axe, had never been laid on natures beautiful forest that crowned the hills and shaded the vales. As the God of nature created it so the grand old forest stood. But the axe, the Pioneer's great weapon, as honored as his rifle, was soon destined to be heard in its depths. During the summer of this year Mr. Nathan Boynton located a farm on section five, and selected a place to build a house on a little knoll near the banks of Rush Creek. Mr. Boynton returned to Grandville and was taken sick, but in August or September sent his brothers, Messrs. William and Jerry Boynton to build a house for him. All the guide they had was the section line. This they followed until they came to the line between the present townships of Byron and Wyoming, where they, not knowing that there was a variation in the section lines of the different ranges of townships, lost the line and were sometime finding the place Nathan had selected for his dwelling. Having found the spot they went at work to erect a house. Listen reader while we give you the description Mr. William Boynton gave us. It was built of small logs, such as they could carry and put up, the roof was of small basswood, split in two parts and gutters cut, with an ax, in the flat side. One tier of these was laid with the flat side up and the other with the flat side down, so that the outside edge of the upper tier fitted into the gutter of the lower. The floor and door of the house were made of plank, or as woodsmen usually call them "puncheons," split from basswood trees. The fire place was built of clay, which Mr. Boynton says he mixed by treading with his bare feet, and was built up with small twigs; while the chimney was built of split sticks laid up in the same kind of mortar. This fireplace and chimney were used, and did good service for a goodly number of years. Such was the first house erected in the township of Byron.

Messrs. Jerry and William Boynton soon located farms on sections nine and eight, respectively, and commenced improving their present homesteads, which by their skill and energy they have rendered both attractive and productive. In 1837 Mr. John Harmon settled on section nine. During the same year Mr. Harmon Kellogg settled on section three, and Mr. James B. Jewell on section nine. We cannot find that any one settled in the township in 1838 except Mr. Ella Judson, who during this year settled on section eight. Mr. Judson says that when he built his log house he had to go a distance of four miles for men to help "raise" and only had eight men at that. In 1839 Mr. Larkin Ball settled on section twenty, at which time he was the only man south of the center of the township. Soon after, Peter Goldin settled on the same section. Mr. William Boynton says that four of them cut the logs, carried them, and raised Mr. Goldin's house. This house was standing as late as 1859. During this year Mr. Eli Crossett settled on section seventeen; also Mr. Amelek Taylor on the same section. Mr. Alden Coburn on section seven, and Mr. Benjamin Robinson on section six. During 1840 there was but one new settler in the town, Mr. William Olmstead, who settled on section eight. 1841 went by without any augmentation of the numbers of this sturdy band of pioneers. In 1842 Samuel Hubbel settled on section twenty-eight, Joseph Gallup on section thirty-two, and Henry A. Vannest on section five. Mr. William Boynton says that when they "raised" either Mr. Gallup's or Mr. Hubbel's house, he has forgotten which, they did not get it up the first day, and it was so far to go home that they stayed and camped out over night, and finished "raising" the next day. And all they had for supper and breakfast was roast potatoes.

During the year 1843 Mr. Fox was the only man who settled in the "South Woods." Oliver Harris settled on section fourteen about this time, but we have not been able to fix the exact date.

During 1844 Mr. Ezekiel Cook settled on section thirty-five, Mr. Tuft on section twenty-three, and Messrs. E. R. Ide and James K. McKenney on section twenty.

Mrs. Cook tells us that when they moved into the woods they had no neighbors nearer than four miles, they being the first to settle in the southeast part of the township. And their nearest Post-office was at Grand Rapids, a distance of fourteen miles through an unbroken wilderness. At the time Mr. Kenney moved on his place there was no road from there to Grandville except as he followed the trails that wound around through the woods. Mrs. McKenney says that they moved into their house the 19th day of November, 1844, and that there were neither doors nor windows in the house, and no floor below. They moved into the loft or chamber, and the next day Mr. McKenney was taken sick and was confined to his bed for two weeks. And before he was well enough to build a fireplace and chimney there was two feet of snow. And that during all this time she had to do all of her cooking out of doors by a log fire. Mrs. Tuft says that they moved on their place the last day of December, 1843, and all the signs of a house they had was a small sled load of lumber. Mr. McKenney says that for some time he used to carry his "grist" to Jerry Boynton's, a distance of three miles, on his shoulders, get him to take it to Grand Rapids to mill, and when he returned, carry it home again.

During the year 1845 Messrs. Corkins Barney, Clark S. Wilson and William Davidson settled within the limits of the township. Among the early settlers whose names we have been able to procure are Josiah R. Holden, Bradley Weaver, Daniel Prindle, Carlos Weaver and Prentice Weaver, who settled in Byron from 1846 to 1849. During 1850 and '51 Messrs. Eli Young and James M. Barney settled on section thirty-two. About this time is famous among the old settlers as the "wolf year." Mr. Young says that he killed one within four rods of his door, with his dog and corn cutter. Mr. William Boynton says that frequently, before this time, however, when he was obliged to work at Grandville to get provision for the support of his family, he would work all day, get the proceeds of labor in provisions, and at dark start for home, a distance of about five miles, through the woods, while the wolves were howling all around him and sometimes coming almost within reach of the good, stout cudgel which he carried. Mr. James M. Barney says that during the first summer that he lived on his place he had to keep his cow and calf in a high log pen near his house, nights, to keep them from the wolves. He says that one night, after being kept awake until almost morning, he took his gun just at daylight and sallied forth, determined on vengeance. When he went out the wolves retreated for a short distance. But when he came into a thicket of bushes they surrounded him, and he backed up against a tree, and they kep him there for about two hours, until broad daylight. He shot at them several times, but the bushes were so thick that he did not kill any, although they would come so near that he could hear them snap at each other. The wolves were never very thick after this season, and as they decreased, until about 1856, deer increased and became very thick. Mr. Barney says that he has had during the winter from forty to fifty deer hung up in the woods at one time.

ORGANIZATION.

The first township meeting (the township of Byron then embraced Wyoming also), was held at the house of Charles H. Oaks, in Grandville, on Monday, the second day of May, A. D. 1836. The following officers were chosen, viz:

Supervisor—Gideon H. Gordon. Township Clerk—Isaac A. Allen. Assessors—Eli Yeomans, Ephraim P. Walker and Justin Brooks. Justices of the Peace—Gideon H. Gordon, Robert Howlett and Ephraim P. Walker. Collector—Lorenzo French. Commissioners of Highways—Gideon H. Gordon, Eli Yeomans, and H. Pitts. Commissioners of Schools—Joseph B. Copeland, Sanford Buskirk and James Lockwood. School Inspectors—Gideon H. Gordon, Isaac A. Allen and Eli Yeomans. Overseers of the Poor—Ephriam P. Walker and Justin Brooks. Constables—Lorenzo French and Sanford Buskirk.

At the first general election held at Grandville, November, 1836, the highest number of votes cast for electors tor President and Vice President was twenty.

The following are the present township officers, viz.: Supervisor, William P. Whitney; Township Clerk, Silas L. Hamilton; Treasurer, Samuel A. McKenney; Justices of the Peace, William P. Whitney, James M. Brown, George W. Ewing and Isaac M. Winegar, Jr.; School Inspectors, George W. Ewings and William P. Whitney; Commissioners of Highways, Jerry Boynton, George W. Ewings and John Homrich; Constables, A. A. Palmer and William D. Tibbits.

The whole number of votes cast at the last general election held at Byron Center, November, 1868, was 337.

For the first few years the settlement of Byron progressed very slowly. It required a brave heart and a strong arm to encounter the dangers and hardships consequent to the opening up of a new and heavy timbered country. But gradually the forest yielded to the axe of the pioneer; beautiful fields, thrifty orchards, comfortable dwellings, and well-filled barns have taken the place of the little log cabin and unbroken forest. Byron is now fast becoming one of the foremost agricultural townships in Kent County. With a varied soil, adapted to nearly all of the different branches of husbandry, and especially to fruit growing, and the very best facilities for marketing its produce, its farmers must soon stand among the best. Byron is traversed by two railroads, viz.: the northern branch of the Lake Shore and Michigan Southern R. R., and the Grand Rapids and Indiana R. R. The Lake Shore and Michigan Southern runs north and south through the town, and has two stations on its line, in Byron, viz.: Byron Center and North Byron. The Grand Rapids and Indiana runs north and south through the eastern part of the township, and has one station near the south part of the town. The present population is 1,328.

Mr. George L. Tobey carries on the manufacture of lumber, at his mill, on section twelve, and Rosenberger Bros. & Co. carry on the manufacture of flour, feed, lumber and heading, at the village of Cody's Mills, on section twenty-five.

POST-OFFICES.

Cody's Mills, Byron Center and North Byron.

SCHOOL HOUSES.

Byron has eight school houses, ranging from first-class to indifferent. District No. 1 has a fair wooden house; District No. 2 has one of the finest country school buildings in the county; it was erected in 1858. There is a very good school house at Cody's Mills. The people of this township support their schools liberally.

CALEDONIA.

Caledonia is one of the southern tier of townships of Kent County, and is bounded on the north by Cascade, on the east by Bowne, on the south by Thornapple, Barry County, and west by Gaines. It is traversed from south to north by the Thornapple river which divides it into two equal parts. The banks of the river are high and the country on both sides of the river is high and rolling. On the east side of the river the land is what is known as "openings," the soil being sandy and gravelly with a slight mixture of clay, and is timbered principally with oak and hickory. The soil on this side of the river is especially adapted to wheat and fruit, but produces good crops of all kinds of grain and most grasses. There are several lakes on this side of the river. There is a lake on sections one, two, eleven and twelve, about one mile long, and from eighty to one hundred and sixty rods in width. The shore on the southeast side is sandy and on the northwest side mucky and marshy. Barber's Kake is on sections twenty-five and twenty-six. Tobey's Lake is on section twenty-three. Lovejoy's Lake is on section twelve. The Coldwater or Little Thornapple enters Caledonia on section thirty-six and empties into the Thornapple on section thirty-five. The west side of the river is all "timbered lands," producing all of the kinds of timber that usually grow in this climate on such lands. The surface of most of this part of the town is high and somewhat rolling, with a clayey loam soil, that is well adapted to all kinds of farming purposes, especially to grazing. All kinds of fruits grow almost to perfection on this soil. There are a great many fine farms in this township, and its agricultural resources are being developed very fast.

The Thornapple is a very rapid stream here, and with its high banks is capable of affording a great amount of water power. Mr. Warren S. Hale informs us that there are at least nine chances for water powers, only three of which are developed, within the limits of this township, with a fall at each of from five to eight feet without overflowing the banks at any place. This river is full of picturesque islands, varying in size from one-half acre to three acres. With the rich agricultural country tributary to it, with its unfailing water power, the time must come when this town will be the "Lowell" of Western Michigan, when the busy hum of machinery will be heard from its northern to its southern boundary.

Nestled among the hills on the banks of the Thornapple, in the northern part of the township, is the thriving little village of Alaska, formerly known as North Brownville. It has a very pleasant location and is an active, enterprising place. It contains one dry goods and grocery store, one dry goods, grocery and drug store, one grocery store, one hardware store and tin shop, one flouring mill, two saw mills, one furniture manufactory, which ships a great deal of cabinet work in the white besides finishing for the home market; one carriage and wagon factory and one hotel, besides the usual number of blacksmith shops, boot and shoe shops, &c. There is not a saloon in the place. Surrounded by a rich agricultural country, its growth must be rapid and its future prosperous.

EARLY SETTLEMENT.

Mr. Asahel Kent was the first settler in the township, settling on section thirty-five in 1838. Mr. Kent, and after his death Mrs. Kent, kept a public house, which became famous for its good cheer, all over the surrounding country. A gentleman who lived at that time in New York State, tells us that he used to hear people who had been to Grand River tell about "Kent's Tavern," and when one would return, others who had traveled on this route—the "Gull Trail"—would always inquire after the Kents. Mrs. Kent afterwards married Mr. Peter McNaughton, and the place became equally well known to travelers on the Battle Creek and Grand Rapids stage route, as McNaughton's. And while talking of this subject there are some reminiscences of this stage route that Mr. Edward Campau relates, that we may as well give now, and which will help contrast the mode of traveling in those days with that of the present. Mr. C. says that in 1839, he, then a boy of 14, made the journey with three or four others from Grand Rapids to Detroit, and that they stopped at "Kent's" over night, and he with others of the men had to sleep out in a sort of shed, as the house was so small it would not accommodate them. At this time this was the only house from Ada to "Leonard's," a distance of seventeen miles. About two years after this he commenced to drive stage on this route, and drove for several years. The road at this time wound round through the woods, and it was no uncommon thing to get "stuck" in the mud or to overset. At one time, a very dark, stormy night, they broke an axletree about six miles south of Ada, and the passengers, five or six in number, had to walk through mud and snow to that place, as it was the nearest settlement. At another time Hon. John Ball, Mrs. Thomas B. Church and others were in the stage; they overset in a mud-hole and the passengers were all *landed* (?) in the water. It was quite dark, and Mr. Fred. Church, then an infant, was nearly suffocated before they found him. At another time

6

Hon. Wm. A. Richmond and Hon. Harvey P. Yale were his only passengers, the roads were muddy and badly rutted out and the night dark. Mr. Yale fell asleep and the wheel striking into a deep rut pitched him out into the mud. After a hearty laugh he resumed his place and they labored along. There is a great contrast between travel over that route, and over the different railroad routes, with their elegant passenger coaches, now leading from the Valley City.

To go back to the settlement of Caledonia: Mr. James Minsey settled on section thirty-six in 1838 or 1839. Among the earlier settlers were Orsemus Rathbun, Eber Moffitt, Hiram McNiel, Peter McNaughton, Levi Tobey, John Sinclair, O. B. Barber, John Pattison, Henry Jackson, Wm. H. Brown, and Warren S. Hale. Mr. Lyman Gerrald was the first settler on the west side of the river. Mr. Wm. H. Brown erected the saw mill at Alaska, now owned by L. W. Fisher, in 1848, and the flouring mill now owned by J. W. Boynton, in 1853, and is now one of the proprietors of the Caledonia mills, two miles above Alaska, on section twenty-two. Mr. Orsemus Rathbun is the oldest settler now residing in the township.

Among the incidents connected with the early settlement of the township, showing some of the hardships the pioneers had to endure, we have the following: Mr. Wm. H. Brown, previous to his settlement at Brownsville, but after he located his land, lived at "Scale's Prairie" or Middleville. Having occasion to go there one winter, he started from home in the morning on horseback, intending to return the same day. After making his observations and examining his land about where the village of Alaska now stands, he started for home; night soon came on, and after endeavoring to follow his track for a while he found out that he was lost. He dismounted, and as he had nothing to kindle a fire with, cleared the snow out of a path, with his feet, and some bark from a dry tree, and walked backwards and forwards in it all night. When morning came he mounted his horse and after riding for some time came out at the Green Lake House. His friends had started after him in the morning, expecting to find him frozen to death, and followed his tracks until they found him at Green Lake.

At the mouth of the Coldwater was a great Indian camping ground and burial place. They did not leave here entirely until within a very few years. One of them, old Soh-na-go, or "Squirrel," has been since seen visiting the burial place and the hunting grounds of his fathers, but the "White man's axe" had been there, and it was no longer a home for him.

Caledonia has nine school houses, all wooden buildings, and two churches, viz: The Baptist Church at Alaska, and a Catholic Church on section twenty-five, both wooden structures. There are two hotels in this township, the Alaska Hotel, at Alaska, Wm. H. Lock, proprietor, and the Oak Grove House, O. B. Barber, proprietor, on section twenty-six. There is a saw mill on section twenty-seven, Jacob Brown, proprietor.

The postoffices are as follows.—Alaska, Warren S. Hale, P. M.; Caledonia, O. B. Barber, P. M.; Caledonia Station, Adam B. Sherk, P. M.

The Grand River Valley Railroad crosses the southwest corner of the township and has a station on section twenty-nine.

ORGANIZATION.

The township of Caledonia was organized in 1840 by the choice of the following named officers:

Supervisor—John P. McNaughton. Clerk—Justus G. Beach. Justices of the Peace—Justus G. Beach, Loren B. Tyler, Malcolm P. McNaughton, Asahel Kent. Treasurer—Norman Foster. Assessors—Roswell F. Tyler, Malcolm P. McNaughton, John A. Campbell. Highway Commissioners—Asahel Tyler, Asahel Kent, Norman Foster. School Inspectors—Norman Foster, William G. Wooley. Directors of the Poor—Roswell Tyler, John Campbell. Collector—Roswell F. Tyler. Constables—Roswell F. Tyler, Frederick B. Thompson.

OFFICERS IN 1870.

Supervisor—Adam B. Sherk. Clerk—Daniel S. Haviland. Treasurer—Sherman T. Colson. Justices--Adam B. Sherk, Levi White, Hugh B. McAlister, Elijah V. E. Pratt. Highway Commissioners—John Patterson, David Kinsey, Isaac Stauffer. School Inspectors—Alfred W. Stowe, Levi White. Constables—Fayette McIntyre, Charles E. Emmons, Eliphalet Scott.

CANNON.

Cannon, originally a part of Plainfield, lies northwest of Grand Rapids, having Courtland on the north, Grattan on the east, Ada on the south, and Plainfield on the west.

In the year 1837 the first farm was entered within its territory by Andrew Watson, who came with his family, accompanied by A. D. W. Stout and family, and settled on section thirty, where Mr. Watson and his aged wife yet reside. In the next year came Isaac Tomlinson, Sen., locating upon section twenty-seven, in a beautiful situation commanding an extensive and enchanting view of Grand River and its beautiful valley. In 1839 Wm. M. Miller settled upon section nineteen. Steadily now a tide of emigration set in, rolling the wilderness back by the sturdy energy of the hardy and determined pioneer, swiftly multiplying farms and broadening cleared acres.

Prominent among the new comers in 1840 were James Thomas, on section twenty-seven, Oliver Lovejoy, on section seven, Mr. Rood, and Rev. Mr. Frieze, on section nineteen, the first Minister of the Gospel who took up his residence within the town.

Among the early settlers who bore a conspicuous part in the development and organization of the new town, we would make honorable mention of M. A. Patrick, locating on section twenty-six, and Ebenezer C. Smith, on section twelve, in 1844. About the same time Mr. Samuel Steel located five lots for as many sons, in the near vicinity of Mr. Smith, thus fixing the name of Steel's Corners to a most beautiful and productive part of the town. Mrs. John Hartwell, on section thirty-four, and Demas Hine, on section thirty, settlers of 1845, and James Dockery, on section four, who settled in 1846.

In 1845 a separation from Plainfield was effected, and the township was erected into a separate town, under the name, by a mistake in the Legislature, of Churchtown, assuming its present name, however, in honor of its principal village, at its first town meeting, held to complete its organization, on the first Monday of April, 1846, at the house of C. Slaght, in Cannonsburgh. At that time it had a population of about 290, and the whole number of votes cast were 64. Its present population is 1,126

FIRST TOWNSHIP OFFICERS.

Supervisor, Andrew Watson; Clerk, Henry H. Worden; Treasurer, Lewis D. Dean; School Inspectors, Loyal Palmer, M. A. Patrick; Directors of the Poor, Ebenezer C. Smith, Martin Johnson; Commissioners of Highway, John Hartwell, Cornelius Wample; Justices of the Peace, Harlow T. Judson, John Bishop, Demas Hine, Jared Spring; Constables, Robert Howard, Major Worden, Isaac Tomlinson, Mindrus Whitney.

OFFICERS IN 1870.

Supervisor, Asa P. Ferry; Clerk, Thomas Noy; Treasurer, Charles A. Provin; Justices of the Peace, Nathaniel Steel, James Nesbit, Demas Hine, M. A. Patrick; Highway Commissioner, Wm. C. Young; School Inspector, John C. Chapman; Constables, John S. Baker, John M. Thomas, Charles A. Provin, Henry C. Watkins.

Cannon presents a great variety of surface, soil and productions, being quite hilly and broken along Bear Creek and in the vicinity of Grand River, but in other parts, more gently rolling, or beautifully undulating scenery meets the view. In the southern part there are patches of beech aud maple timber land, with a sprinkling of pine along the streams, but, mainly, the town is oak openings, plentifully interspersed with hickory. Its main staples raised for the market are wheat, wool, corn and apples. Of the former, large quantities are exported, and its rolling lands and dry, healthful climate make its wool growing a success. Lying within the great Western fruit belt, and being blessed with a deep, pliable soil, it is eminently adopted to horticultural pursuits; of this its people are fully aware, and we find in many flourishing orchards. Apples, pears, peaches, cherries and currants abound, while grapes and the small fruits are fast becoming specialities.

Whatever may be said of its business centers, thrift and enterprise mark its rural districts. Comfort smiles from its tasteful dwellings, nestled amid shade and bloom, and an abounding plenty peeps from its well filled and commodious barns. Indigence is scarcely known among its population. All are, to a remarkable degree, independent in worldly goods.

Bear Creek, the exclusive property of Cannon, rises in the northwest corner of the town, on section one, in a large spring having the peculiar power of petrifying all substances that may chance to lie in its waters. The creek, fed by springs all its length, takes its devious way south and southwest, cutting the town nearly in two, debouching in Grand River on section thirty, the southwest corner of the town. This stream, being fed by springs, presents a never failing supply of water, and, running rapidly, gives an opportunity for a number of mill sites, and excellent facilities for manufacturing purposes.

Cannonsburgh, the only business center of any note within the town was founded in 1842, an Indian war trail its main thoroughfare, and the settler's ax the only key that would open the forest gates that guarded its entrance. In 1844 and 1845 its mills were erected by E. B. Bostwick, H. T. Judson architect, and a store opened. As an inducement to permanent settlement, the village was platted in 1845, and Mr. Bostwick, the enterprising business agent of LeGrand Cannon, its proprietor, (an eastern capitalist and large land holder in the town,) was instructed to give a village lot to each resident not otherwise provided for; thus twenty-five lots were given away. The town received the name it now bears in honor of its founder, who testified his appreciation of the distinction conferred by presenting the village with a small ordnance bearing his name and the date. This is treasured as a memento of early times, and used on the 4th of July and other holiday occasions, wakening the echos of memory in many a heart as its thunders reverberate among the hills that completely surround the little village. Cannonsburg is situated upon both sides of Bear Creek. Laterly it has suffered much by fire. It has one store, one grist mill, one woolen mill, with a cider mill attached, one saw mill, one cooper shop, two wagon shops, three blacksmith shops, and one hotel. It has no dedicated place of worship, but the Methodists are about erecting a fine church, to be constructed of wood, 38x60 feet in size, and costing $3,300. It has a Union School House, situated on a picturesque bluff overlooking the town; it is built of wood, two stories high, 34x56 feet in dimension. Two teachers are employed in its schools.

Buenavista is situated on section thirty, near the mouth of Bear Creek. It consists of eight or ten dwelling houses, and the Bear Creek flouring mill, erected in 1848, and now owned by Carey & Horton, of Grand Rapids. There is nothing more to be said of it, save that it is located amidst beautiful scenery, and is something of a wheat mart in the fall of the year.

There are several lakes within the town, but only two are worthy of particular note. Silver Lake, on sections nine and ten, lying just north of and touching the line of the Grand Rapids and Ionia State Road, as its name indicates, is a most beautiful sheet of water, containing about 300 acres.

One mile directly east of Silver Lake we come upon Bostwick Lake, a huge crystal, in emerald setting. No more beautiful scene can well be imagined. Its waters are very cold, evidently emanating from springs, as it has no visible inlet or natural outlet. This was a favorite resort in early days for fishing parties, and parties of pleasure coming from the village often camped on its banks and tarried over night. A huge canoe, fashioned by an Indian, from a white wood tree grown a mile south of Cannonsburgh, was transported with a vast amount of labor to its shores and launched upon its waters. The distance traversed was five miles, occupying two days in the transit, and employing four yoke of oxen. There, in the later years, the settlers on lands adjacent to the lake found the deserted canoe, a monster of its kind, over thirty feet in length. Wind and wave have long since done their works upon it; only a fragrant of it remaining as a relic in the family of S. B. Kutz, formerly of Cannon, now a resident of Rockford. This lake also lies north of the State Road, which bends slightly in passing round its southern shore. It contains about 400 acres.

Ball Hill is a noteworthy eminence on section one. It rises abruptly from the surrounding country, and lifting its lofty tower above the forest trees, is visible for many miles away. It received its name from its long time-owner, John Ball, of Grand Rapids. It is now the property of Mr. Cowen, and planted with apple trees to its very summit.

CHURCHES AND SCHOOLS.

There are eight district schools in the town, and two churches. The First Congregational Church, (Rev. Mr. Eaton, of Lowell, present officiating pastor,) is a wooden structure 36x50 feet in dimensions. It stands upon a little eminence east of and commanding a beautiful view of Bostwick Lake. It has a small Cemetery attached. The First M. E. Church, at Steel's Corners; one mile east, was erected in the same year. It is also built of wood and is a trifle smaller than the Congregational Church.

The number and prosperity of the schools and churches in the town are a reflex of the intellectual and spiritual enterprise of the people, speaking more than volumes of history for their useful and moral lives.

It is worthy of record here, that, of the first six families settling in the town, namely A. Watson, A. D. W. Stout, I. Tomlinson, E. Whitney, Mr. Rood and J. Thomas, both heads of each family are yet living, and four familes still reside in the town.

It is an equally remarkable fact that the first two white children were born in the families of Mr. Stout and Mr. Watson, on the same day, September 27, 1837. Both were daughters, and there was but two hours difference in their birth. The children were named respectively Mary Stout and Jeanette Watson.

May 6, 1842, the great destroyer entered the family of Mr. Isaac Tomlinson and laid low his little daughter, Martha Jane. This was the first death in the town, occurring among the whites.

Most of the early settlers are living yet, but some are dead. Of those who are gone, justice demands that, as in a "roll of honor," should be placed the names of E. B. Bostwick, business agent for Mr. Cannon, who died on an overland journey from the States to California; S. S. Haskins, closely identified with the early history and prosperity of the town, and several years a dealer in dry goods and groceries at Cannonsburgh; Timothy Wetmore, horticulturist, and at one time an efficient Supervisor of the town, and Benj. Davis, also Supervisor for some years, and dying while yet holding that office. These have passed on, but in the prosperity of the people, and smiling fields from the wilderness reclaimed, their works do yet remain.

CASCADE.

Cascade lies in the second tier of townships from the south and east line of the county, and is bounded on the north by Ada, on the east by Lowell, on the south by Caledonia, and on the west by Paris. The Detroit and Milwaukee Railroad passes through this town, entering on the north part of section 12, and following the course of the Grand River Valley through the southwest corner of section 1, crossing section 2 in almost a direct line from southeast to northwest, into Ada, where is located its nearest depot, four miles from Cascade village.

GENERAL DESCRIPTION.

Cascade presents a variety of soil, from light sand and gravel to heavy clay, and is greatly diversified by hills, valleys, streams, lakes, springs and marshes. Grand River flows northwest through sections 12, 1 and 2, into Ada, and the Thornapple—one of the most important tributaries of Grand River--takes its course north through the centre of the township. Entering Cascade from the south on section 24, it flows through 27, 22, 16, 9, 10, 3 and 4 to Grand River, at Ada village. On the east of the Thornapple, a creek rises in section 11, and enters that stream at section 10. Another, one branch of which rises in section 30, Lowell, and the other in section 1, of Caledonia, forms a junction at section 26, in Cascade, and carries its united currents to the Thornapple at 27; furnishing, in its route, water power to a saw mill on section 26. On the west side of the river, a creek rising on section 29, forms a junction with it on section 34. Another having its head on section 19, enters the river at 16. Another, whose source is a large boiling spring on section 6, in its course of two and a half miles attains considerable size, and empties its waters into the Thornapple at section 9. Remains of an old beaver dam were to be found on this creek, quite recently. On the southeast corner of section 14, is found a lake with a greater depth of water than Lake Erie. The aborigines of the country have a singular superstition with regard to this lake; never floating their canoes on its bosom, or eating the fish of its waters, asserting that it is inhabited by an "Evil Spirit," or, as they term it, a "Great Snake." Another lake is also found on the line of sections 4 and 5. Also one in the northwest corner of section 8, matched by one some forty rods directly south.

TIMBER.

This township contains but little pine, which is sparsely scattered along the borders of its streams. The sandy soil is chiefly oak openings; while the gravel and clay bear some fine sugar orchards and are also productive of beech, elm, ash, hickory, and a meager supply of white wood.

MINERAL WEALTH.

Lime is manufactured on section 35. Brick have also been manufactured on section 3, and a bed of red ochre lying on section 9 was used in painting some of the first buildings and the old red school house on that section. This mineral is not considered pure enough to be profitably worked. The soil also shows traces of bituminous coal, copper and iron. The latter ore, manifesting itself in magnetic or mineral springs. One of these, of great power, has been discovered this year, on the farm of James Sutphen, section 26. The water bubbles up from the soil with icy coldness, and flows over a pebbly bed, staining—with brilliant coloring—its stony path. Iron brought in contact with it becomes heavily charged with magnetism. The water has not yet been analyzed.

EARLY SETTLEMENT.

This township was at first a part of the township of Ada. Lewis Cook, a native of New Jersey, is said to have been the first settler within the limits of Cascade. He removed from that State to Seneca county, New York; from thence to Washtenaw county, in this State; from which he came, a pioneer settler to Cascade in 1836. At or near this time also came Mr. Hiram Laraway to this place from New York. His wife being a sister of Mrs. Cook. But, discouraged by the hardships of the wilderness, he soon returned to his native place. In the following year, Edward Linen, a native of Ireland—whose shores he left for America in 1836—settled in Cascade, where he yet resides, a useful, industrious citizen. During the year 1838, and the subsequent year, he was followed by James May, David Petted, John Farrell, James and William Annis, Michael Matthews, Patrick, Christopher and Michael Eardley, all natives of the same country, most of whom yet survive, orderly citizens of their adopted home. In 1838, Frederick A. Marsh, of New York, united in marriage with Olive Guild, a daughter of Joel Guild, one of the pioneer settlers of Grand Rapids—and began domestic life in the unbroken wilderness, one mile north, and west of where Cascade village now stands. Mr. Marsh lived to see the forest yield its place to cultivated fields and comfortable dwellings, and to have a school house erected on his own land. He was killed by a fall from his wagon in 1856. Mrs. Marsh, afterwards Mrs. Walden, survived her husband eleven years, and often spoke of those days, when her nearest neighbors were miles away, and for three months at a time she did not see the face of a white man, except her husband, while a human being passing over the newly cut road was a relief to her intense loneliness. She died at the old homestead in 1867.

Sometime during 1839 or 1840, Mr. Laraway returned to his Cascade possessions, and was frozen to death between that place and Ada, in the winter of 1841. Widow Laraway bravely met the heavy burdens of pioneer life, and trained up three sons and a daughter to lives of usefulness. While the name of aunt Mary Laraway became a household word in the community and a synonym of virtue and piety. She lived to see her children settled in life, and died suddenly in the summer of 1869. Her oldest son is well known as the proprietor of a stonecutting establishment in Grand Rapids.

Peter and George Teeple came to Cascade during these years, joining the settlers on the west side of the Thornapple, while the eastern side was yet unmarked by civilization, but inhabited on and near sections 23 and 26, by a colony of about 350 natives, known, through the adoption of the name of their missionary, as the Slater Indians.

In the year 1841, Peter Whitney, of Ohio, moved his family into that part of Cascade known as Whitneyville, and E. D. Gove, of Mass., selected a site for his future home near the center of the township on sections 22, 15 and 14, to which he brought his family in the summer of 1842. Horace Sears, from New York, and Zerah and Ezra Whitney, (father and brother to Peter) accompanied them in their journey and settled in Whitneyville. Mr. Gove yet resides on the land he first settled, on section 15. But the old homestead on section 21—being the second house built on the east side of the river, in this township—having sheltered children and grand children, was burned in the autumn of 1869. Mr. Sears yet lives in Whitneyville; and Zerah Whitney, elected Justice of the Peace at the first township meeting—now an aged man—resides with his son Ezra on a farm south of Grand Rapids. Another son of Zerah Whitney, Oscar, died at Whitneyville in 1849. And the remaining sons, Peter, Johnson and Martin, now reside in other parts of the county.

In the Spring of 1845, Asa W. Denison, and family, of Mass., (accompanied by a brother, Gideon H. Denison, look ing for a homestead, to which he brought his family the following year,) came to join the settlers on the west side of the Thornapple. Coming in on the State road, from Battle Creek to Grand Rapids, the teams, women and children of the company, were obliged to wait at Ezra Whitney's public-house, for the road to be "chopped out" between that point and the river, theirs being the first teams that passed over the road. At Cascade they forded the Thornapple with their household goods, and found timbers on the ground for the erection of the old Ferry House, (now Cascade Hotel,) which was, at that time, owned by D. S. T. Weller. During that year the house was so far completed as to admit of occupancy, and the first ferry-boat commenced its trips just above where the bridge now spans that stream. D. S. T. Weller then owned the plat of land now occupied by Cascade village, although first purchased by Joel Guild; and it was at that time staked out into lots of one acre each, as the fine fall on the river gave hopes for the speedy erection of mills at that place, some of the most sanguine settlers phophesying that Cascade would outstrip Grand Rapids in the strife for precedence. Mr. W. sold out his property here to W. S. Gunn, in 1846, who held it until after the organization of the township. Mr. Weller ultimately settled in Grand Rapids city, where he remained until he transferred his home to Detroit, in 1869.

During the year 1845, a disease, which our old settlers denominate the black tongue, broke out among the Indians near Whitneyville, reducing their number in a few weeks to about 200 persons. The band now became slowly wasted by disease and removal, until less than fifty remained at the time of their removal to the Indian Reservation in 1856. In the year 1846, another family was added to the few settlers, of the east side of the river;—Jared Strong, the first settler in the forest between E. D. Gove and Ada. The following year a school was opened in a little log house on the river bank, section 27, for the few pupils of that vicinity. Who the young woman was, to whom belongs the rank of pioneer teacher, we have been unable to ascertain, or whether this was the first school taught in the township. It was certainly the first on the east side of the river; and the lumber sawn for the Whitneyville school house, erected in 1848, was among the first work done by the old saw mill, on Sucker Creek, then owned by Peter Whitney. Abont this time, also, the Kalamazoo stage made its trips through Whitneyville—via Ada—for Grand Rapids.

ORGANIZATION.

The first township meeting was held at Whitneyville, April 3, 1848, and the following board of township officers was elected:

Supervisor—Peter Teeple. Clerk—John R. Stewart. Treasurer—Asa W. Denison. School Inspectors—James H. Woodworth, Thomas I. Seeley. Commissioners of Highways---Ezra Whitney, Fred. A. Marsh, Wm. Degolia. Justices of the Peace—Leonard Stewart, Zerah Whitney. Assessors—Thomas I. Seeley, Harry Clark. Constables—Morris Denison, O. P. Corson, Wm. Cook, Peter J. Whitney.

Of the above board, Peter Teeple is yet a respected member of the township. J. R. Stewart, after filling other offices of trust, and teaching for several terms the Cascade school, removed to the city, where he now resides. A. W. Denison, was also a recipient of the various gifts of the voting public, for many years, and died from injury by the kick of a colt, in 1857, aged 52 years, universally mourned by his townspeople. His widow—now Mrs. Johnson—yet lives, and to her are we indebted for much of our information in regard to the early days of Cascade. J. H. Woodworth is now engaged in fruit culture in the north part of the township, near Ada village. Of T. I. Seeley we have known nothing since 1853. Messrs. Whitneys and Marsh, we have spoken of in our preceding pages. Wm. Degolia amassed a fine property, and left the county in 1869. A few months after his removal, his body was brought back for burial. L. Stewart is also with those, who, sleeping, dream not! Harry Clark yet lives, where he first broke ground, a hale old man. Mr. Denison is a thriving farmer on the north line of the township.

About the year 1848, W. H. Chillson came to Cascade and erected a small dwelling house near the hotel; also a log house just across the river, to which, in 1849, Rev. Erie Prince, of Ohio, brought a small stock of Yankee notions and opened a store, or grocery, for those whose nearest trading point was Grand Rapids. Elder Prince deserves more than a passing notice. He soon identified himself with the religious, and educational needs of the young community. He held at one time the office of School Inspector, and, up to the time of his death, worked actively in the Sunday school cause, as Superintendent in the different neighborhoods, now grown around the first nucleus of settlers. Was a picnic or temperance meeting to be looked after, or were chastened hearts called to lay their treasures in the dust, Elder P. was ever found ready to speak the kindly word, pour forth the earnest appeal, or—with tender thought of sympathy—lead the sorrowing mourner to Him, who is the "resurrection and the life." The fathers and mothers of the little ones of to-day remember with affectionate respect the tall, slightly bowed form, the kind face, the searching, yet mild grey eye, and the hand lightly laid on the head, as he passed them with some friendly question, or brief admonition---seed sown in life's morning time! In the autumn of 1853 he was called upon to speak before the Kent County Agricultural and Horticultural Society, at Grand Rapids, October 6th; and his address will be found in the records of the society, for that year. About the year 1856, he donated to the township of Cascade the land occupied by the Cascade cemetery; and there his body lies buried. His grave is shadowed by a young oak, and unmarked—by an explicit clause in his will—by a headstone. He died August 7, 1862, aged 65. In church connection he was a Presbyterian.

We have been unable to learn the precise time that a postoffice was given this township. We think, however, it was established at Whitneyville, soon after its organization. The first Postmaster was Clement White, who held that position with only an intermission of one or two years, until the office was discontinued in 1868.

A postoffice was also established at Cascade in 1854, postmaster Dr. M. W. Alfred, first resident physician. A store was opened the same year at Cascade by Seymour Sage, and William Gardner. When the drumbeat of the Union echoed through our land in 1861, Cascade was not forgetful of her trusts and privileges as a small member of a great country. It is to be regretted that no complete list of those who donned the soldier's uniform has been preserved. We have called to mind eighty volunteers, and the number is probably about a hundred. Of those who never returned we are also unable to give a perfect record. But, from every battle field of the Republic from 1861 to the close of the contest, came back a voice bidding some heart grow chill with pain, yet glow with hallowed pride, for the *souls* that were "marching on!"

CASCADE TO-DAY.

Cascade has been an organized township for twenty-two years, and, according to the census for 1870, has 1175 inhabitants. Children, between the ages of five and twenty, by report of public schools, 1869—416. Votes cast at the last April election—227. Property assessed, real estate, $204,107; personal, $32,317.

The following is the present Board of township officers: Supervisor, Edgar R. Johnson; Clerk, Henry C. Denison; Treasurer, Geo. W. Gorham; Justices of the Peace, Geo. S. Richardson, John F. Proctor, Lawrence Meach, Hugh B. Brown; School Inspectors, E. R. Johnson, Chas. F. Holt; Highway Commissioners, Jonathan W. Sexton, Clinton A. Wood, Chas. M. Dennison; Constables, S. G. Fish, T. J. Hulbert, Miner Spaulding, Warren Streeter.

SCHOOL HOUSES.

Cascade can claim one or two school houses of decidedly fine appearance and convenience. But many of her school buildings are those erected in her infancy, and are wholly inadequate to the demands of the present school population. A movement is being made, however, to remedy this defect in many districts.

Her present number of districts is ten. District No. 10 was organized in 1847. There is a frame house on section 35, built in 1848. District No. 4 was organized in 1847, and built a small frame house on section 9: are now (1870) erecting a fine structure on the same site, on the Cascade and Grand Rapids road, one mile from Cascade village. District No. 1 was organized in 1848, and built a school house in 1849, on section 29, which stood until 1869, when a frame house was erected on the same site. District No. 2 was organized in 1849, and built a small log house on section 10, which yet stands. District No. 12 (fractional district, Cascade and Paris) was organized in 1849, and built a small frame house on section 31, in 1850. In 1867 a good frame house, painted white, and protected by window blinds, was erected. District No. 3 was organized in 1853, and built a frame house on section 14, in 1854. District No. 8 has a frame school house, painted white, built in 1856, on section 8. Fractional District No. 10 (Cascade and Lowell) was organized in 1859, and has a small log house on east side of section 13. District No. 5 was organized in 1857, and school taught in a small log house on south side of section 33; was reorganized in 1860 and log house built in center of section 33. This was burned in 1867, and a temporary building has supplied its place until the present year. A fine house is now in process of erection on section 28. District No. 6 was organized about 1860, and has a nice frame school building, painted white, and fitted with black walnut furniture, on section 26.

CHURCHES.

Only one church edifice has as yet been erected in Cascade. This has been built by the Roman Catholic Brotherhood, and stands on the northeast corner of section 31. It was built in 1856, and cost about $1,000. The building is of wood, with a stone foundation. The society worshiping here was founded by Fathers Decunic and Fizaski. The latter was parish priest in 1849, when the church members were few and worshiped in private houses. Now the church numbers about 47 families, to whom Father Rivers preaches monthly. A Sabbath School is connected with the church. The M. E. Church also has two classes in this township, numbering about 60 members and worshiping in school houses. The United Brethren persuasion have a small charge of about a dozen members. And the "Christians" also hold public worship, but the strength of the order we have not ascertained.

We regret our inability to give the number and membership of our Sunday Schools; though nearly every district has one connected with its regular church worship.

CEMETERIES.

Cemeteries are located on section 31—Catholic. Section 16—Cascade Burial Ground. Section 35—Whitneyville. Section 7—West part of township.

CASCADE VILLAGE.

Cascade village is located on the line of sections 9 and 16, on the west side of the Thornapple river. It contains a Hotel, now owned by DeWitt Marsh, where all township business is transacted; a general store, and Post-office, in charge of E. D. Johnson; flouring and saw mills, owned by H. L. Wise and Jacob Kusterer; a physician's office, occupied by Dr. Danforth; and less than a dozen private residences. The flouring mill is a large, well constructed building, with a capacity for three run of stone. Dr. Danforth is the resident physician, and is making preparations for opening a drug store in connection with his office. His practice is Eclectic.

Gaylord Holt, professor and teacher of music, resides one mile north of Cascade, on the river road. This was also the former home of Hon. H. H. Holt, now of Muskegon, who has represented his district in the State Legislature.

WHITNEYVILLE.

Whitneyville is a point on the old State Road, between Battle Creek and Grand Rapids; and is situated on section 35. A Hotel, erected there in 1853, and familiarly known as the Whitney Tavern Stand, yet opens its doors to the public, under charge of S. F. Sliter. James Sutphen now owns the old Whitney saw mill on section 26.

COURTLAND.

Courtland is bounded on the north by Nelson, on the east by Oakfield, on the south by Cannon, and on the west by Algoma.

Barton Johnson, the first settler of the township, located in May, 1838. He is still a resident, and may be found on the west half of the southwest quarter of section twenty-two. Alexander Dean settled in the township in 1839. He was the first to locate lands, selecting the northeast quarter of section twenty-one. The manner in which this tract came to be located by him is quite amusing. Mr. Dean and fifteen others came into the country to select homes and lands, with the understanding that the right of first choice should be decided among them by lot. So they drew, and lo and behold the lot fell upon—not Jonah, but Alexander, and he therefore exercised the right of first choice by selecting the piece just mentioned.

These sixteen persons located land contiguous to each other, and moving to the township a short time afterward, organized it, and resided there alone for a number of years—or until about the year 1844, or 1845, when they were joined by Horace Colby, Philip Becker, the two Thompsons, and others. The first township meeting was held at the residence of Barton Johnson, in the spring of 1839.

Among the other early settlers of the township were the following named persons: Thomas Addison, John Austin, Sabin Johnson, Benjamin Botsford, David Haynes, Lauren Austin, Iram Barnes, Anson Ensign, Philo Beers, James Kinyon, the Rounds and Hunting families, Zenas B. White, and others.

The present township of Courtland, together with some five other townships, were united under the name of Courtland, about the year 1839. Subsequently Algoma was detached from this organization, and still later by a legislative mistake, Oakfield and Courtland were reorganized under the the euphonious name of Wabasis.

The first officers of the township were: Supervisor, Philo Beers; Clerk, Thomas Addison. The records do not give the names of the persons filling the less important offices.

The

PRESENT OFFICERS,

are, Supervisor, Wm. H. Myers; Clerk, Isaac M. Hunting; Treasurer, Frederick C. Stegaman; Justices of the Peace, Joseph Salkeld, Henry D. Burlingame, Wm. H. Myers, Thomas Addison; Commissioners of Highways, Simon P. Peterson, Ezra Stoner, Jos. Salkeld; Constables, Robert Carlyle, John Peterson, Peter Cudington, Cornelius Richardson; School inspectors, Nelson Graham, Charles H. Carlyle.

THE SOIL

of Courtland is mostly good. The southern part is what is called timbered openings; the northern part is timbered with pine, mixed with hard wood, and the soil is less productive than the southern part. There are many better townships; but yet there is some land within its bounds that cannot be outdone in the production of the staple crops.

There are many fine farms in Courtland, among which are those of Alexander Dean, Joseph F. Hayes, Calvin and Almon Thompson, Philip Becker, Jacob Snyder, Daniel S. Moore, Edward S. Fuller, Nathan D. Saunders, Zenas B. White, Wm. H. Myers, Horace Colby, Robert Cornell and Noah R. Ashley.

THE LAKES.

In this township are few in number. Silver Lake, the largest, is situated on sections twenty-seven and twenty-eight. It is triangular in shape, being about one and one-half miles in length by one half mile in breadth in the widest place. It has fine gravelly banks, and is one of the most beautiful lakes in the county. Johnson Lake, a small, but fine body of water, is situated on the southeasterly portion of section twenty-two. Big and Little Brower Lakes are situated on the southern part of section thirty-four. Both of them are small.

THE SCHOOL HOUSES

are numbered and located as follows: The Round's school house, in district No. 8, is located on the south line of section thirty, is a small, red, frame structure, and was built in the year 1860.

The Stinson school house, in district No. 1, is situated on the south line of section twenty-eight. It is a wooden building, painted white. and was built some twelve years ago.

The Shank school house, district No. 2, is located on the north line of section twenty-nine, near the residence of G. Shank. It is a respectable looking, red, framed structure.

The Graham school house, in district No. 7, a small, frame building, painted white, is located on the east line of seetiou twenty-seven.

The Becker school house, in district No. 4, is located on the south line of section twenty-five. It is a small, white, framed structure, and has been built some fifteen years.

The Smith school house, in district No. 6, is built of logs, and is situated on the north line of section two.

The Courtland Center school house, in district No. 3, is located on the north line of section twenty-two, one-half mile east of the centre of the township. It is a fine, framed structure, painted white, and has been standing but two years.

The Benham school house, in district No. 5, is located on the west line of section nine. It is a framed building, painted red, and was erected in the year 1860.

MILLS.

The Becker Shingle Mill, Jacob Becker, proprietor, is located on the north line of section twenty-three. It was built in the year 1868.

The Davis steam saw and shingle mill combined, is located near the centre of section 10. It was erected in the year 1869. Hiram R. Davis, proprietor.

The Becker saw mill, Garrett Becker, proprietor, is located near the northwest corner of section eight. It was erected in the year 1867.

The Anderson saw mill, John H. Anderson, proprietor, is located near the south line of section 7, on Potter Creek. It was built in the year 1866.

The Porter shingle mill, Dennis Porter, proprietor, is located on Porter Creek, near the centre of section 7. It was built in the year 1868.

The

COURTLAND CENTER HOUSE

is the only hotel in the township. It is situated at Courtland Center, on the southwest corner of section 15. It is a fine, framed structure.

GAINES.

The township of Gaines—town 5 north, of range 11 west—is situated in the southern tier of townships of Kent county. It is bounded on the north by Paris, on the east by Caledonia, on the south by Leighton, Allegan county, and on the west by Byron.

The first settler in this township was Alexander Clark, who located on section 8, in the spring of 1837. He was joined the following autumn by Alexander L. Bouck, who located on section 5, his present homestead, and Andrew and his son, Renssalaer Mesnard, who located on section 17, the place now occupied by Henry Kelley; and soon after by Foster Kelley, Charles Kelley and Joseph Blain, who located on their present homesteads, on sections 4 and 5. Gaines at that time had little to recommend her to the eyes of civilization; being nothing more or less than 36 square miles of wilderness. Yet to the hardy, enterprising pioneers her heavy forests ot beech and maple, and in some localities pine and oak, abundant supply of fresh water, with an average supply ot bear, wolves, deer, wild turkeys, etc., possessed a charm that was irresistable. And the ice once broken the development of her resources was only a question of time.

At this time the only thoroughfare within the limits of the territory of Gaines was a road known as the "Old Gull Road," running a zig-zag course from north to south. And the first settlers seemed for evident reasons to strike for the vicinity of this road. And we now find some of the richest farms in the county near its line. It was afterward straightened as the township became settled, to correspond with the section lines, and became a stage route from Grand Rapids to Kalamazoo, until the completion of the plank road in 1854.

Among the first settlers who still reside in the township, and identified with its organization, growth and prosperity, are Daniel Woodward, Stephen A. Hammond, John E. Woods, Charles B. Keefer, Benjamin Colburn, R. C. Sessions, Jas. Reynolds, William Kelley, John Wolcott, R. R. Jones, William Hendrick, Aaron Brewer, Thomas and Wilmot H. Blain, William Budlong, James M. Pelton, Orson Cook, Peter Van Lew, Eseck Burlingame, James T. Crumback and Bryan Greenman.

Gaines, aside from her agricultural prospects, offered but little inducement to business men. Plaster and Buck Creeks both rise near the center of the township, but were too small during most of the year for mill sites. There was, however, a small water mill erected on the latter stream about the year 1852, by Eseck Burlingame, on section 18, which is still running, and which cut the lumber for some of the first frame buildings in the township.

Most of the settlers of Gaines, as is usual, were poor, having barely means enough to enable them to purchase their land of the government at $1.25 an acre, get their families and household goods transported through the wilderness, and gain a foothold on their farms. But with persistent energy they set to work, and the heavy forests began to disappear. It was soon found to be one of the richest tracts in the vicinity for agricultural purposes, and at the present date is one of the best in the county. The north half of the township is gently rolling, is well watered with springs and small streams. The soil is good and of almost every variety. Apple and peach orchards abound. Pears, grapes, quinces and cherries are cultivated to some extent and with good success.

The southern portion comprises a range of beautiful hills and table lands, admirably adapted to fruit and vine culture, and although not developed to any great extent, has some of the best orchards in the county. The soil is gravelly, with a mixture of clay and loam, and is well adapted to all kinds of grain.

ORGANIZATION.

The first attempt at organization was as a part of Paris, in 1839. Foster Kelley, Joseph Blain, Alexander Clark and Andrew and Renssalaer Mesnard were among the township officers of said organization. In the year 1848, it was organized under the name of Gaines, and the first township meeting was held at the old red school house, on the northeast corner of section 8. Among the laws passed at the first meeting was the following:

"On motion of Orson Cook, it was voted that a tax of two dollars and fifty cents be raised for every wolf killed in the township."

Wolves were rather troublesome neighbors in those days, and the author of the motion probably owed them a grudge for their former depredations. Wolves made frequent visits to the early settlers, and would make the very earth tremble with their howlings and complaints to the intruders of their time-honored homes, and usually levied a tax before morning. And, like the wolves of the present day, were only satisfied with the best quality of mutton. One occupation of the boys and larger girls of that day used to be to fire the old stumps about the place in the evening to scare away the wolves. About the year 1846, there was a wolf who had her beat from this vicinity to Gull Prairie, in Barry county, and was known as the "Gull Prairie wolf," who usually made the round trip once a week. (Better time than the early stages.) The dogs would not molest her, and she seemed to fear neither man nor beast. She had been caught once in a steel trap, and all efforts to entrap her again were for a long time unsuccessful. Even the children, in time, learned to distinguish her voice from other wolves, and were in the habit of listening for her on certain nights. She seldom disappointed them, and made night hideous with her dismal howls. She finally killed four sheep in one night on the premises of Mr. Mesnard, belonging to Mr. Rice. Mr. R. R. Jones, who lived near, requested the owner to leave one of the carcasses which madame wolf had partially devoured, and he did so. Mr. Jones and Orson Cook then held a council of war. It was determined to make one more effort to entrap her. Accordingly two traps were set about the carcass. But on her next visit she contrived to remove the carcass several rods, taking care to avoid the traps. Another council resulted in some more traps. Four were set—placing in the intermediate spaces small pieces of iron, which were left in sight, while the traps were carefully concealed. This time they outwitted her. For after visiting two barns in the neighborhood, and trying to obtain a fresh quarter of mutton, she went and put her identical game foot into one of the traps. Early on the follow ing morning, Messrs. Jones and Cook took the trail in pursuit. They obtained a glimpse of their victim near the present residence of Mr. Blake, on section 15, and, after following her to the vicinity of Duncan Lake, in Barry County, succeeded in getting her headed toward home. They followed and overtook her on section 25, in Gaines. She "caved in," completely vanquished, and submitted to being bound with bark and slung to a pole; our two hunters resolving to carry her back alive the the scene of her recent murders. A thing, by the way, much easier resolved than executed. For they were soon satisfied to leave all but the pelt, for which they received one dollar, and ten and a half dollars in the shape of County and State bounties. They soon after caught a neighbor's boy by the heel, in one of the same traps. A large, good natured specimen of the "Genus Yankee," about twenty years of age, who, anxious to become versed in all the mysteries of woodcraft, was peering about to see how a wolf trap was set. He found out—as well as how one was sprung. His cries soon brought his father to his assistance, and gave the wolf hunters no further trouble.

But the wolves, and their allies the bears and wild-cats, have disappeared. The growth of the township has not been rapid. It could not be expected when we consider the difficulties to be overcome. At the first township meeting only 35 votes were polled. Yet in 1868, at the Presidential election, she polled 252 votes, and her present population (1870) is 1,205. Thrifty farms greet you at every turn; comfortable frame cottages take the place of the log hut of the pioneer; roads on section lines traverse all parts of the township; and, from 36 square miles of wilderness, she has grown in thirty-three years to be an enterprising, thrifty, agricultural town.

The first school was taught in a log house erected by Mr. Clark, on the northeast corner of section 8, about the year 1842. This, in time, gave way to a small frame building, painted red, and known throughout the country as the "red school house," which was succeeded, in 1863, by the present elegant structure on the same site, which takes the name and color of its predecessor. There are, in all, eight school houses in the township—all comfortable frame buildings.

The society of United Brethren built a church on section 28 in 1867, which, although plain and modest, is neat and tasty, an honor to the association and an ornament to the community. It is situated on one of the most elevated points in the township, and can be seen for miles around.

Gaines has been without railroad communication until the present year, (1870) when the Grand River Valley Railroad was constructed through her territory. Hammond Station was established on the farm of S. A. Hammond, on section 11, and a large freight and passenger depot, with telegraph office, erected. Woodward & Buckingham have erected a large grain elevator. W. W. Pierce and Philetus Marsh, Esq., have each a small grocery running, and the place already assumes a business aspect.

FIRST TOWNSHIP OFFICERS.

ELECTED APRIL 3D, 1848.

Supervisor--Peter Van Lew. Clerk—James M. Pelton. Treasurer—Charles Kelley. Justices of the Peace—Joseph Blain, Josiah Drake and Robert R. Jones. Assessors—Foster Kelley and Abraham T. Andrews. Commissioners of Highways—Daniel Rice, Levi M. Dewey and William Kelley. School Inspectors—Renssalaer Mesnard, A. T. Andrews. Poor Directors—Orson Cook, Levi Cheney. Constables—Lorenzo W. Sandford, John E. Guild, Foster Kelley, Daniel Williams.

PRESENT TOWNSHIP OFFICERS.

Supervisor—James M. Pelton. Clerk—George Cook. Treasurer—Morris Freeman. Commissioners of Highways—Chester C. Mitchell, John M. Hanna, William B. Pickett. School Inspectors—Abraham C. Clemens, Aaron C. Bowman. Overseers of the Poor—James M. Pelton, Morris Freeman. Constables—Samuel Zelner, John M. Hanna and Thomas M. Read.

GRAND RAPIDS.

The township of Kent was organized April 4th, 1834. There does not appear to have been any certain limits to the organization, but it is supposed to have embraced all the settlements within the present County of Kent. The records from that time to the present are now in the possession of the township clerk. The division, now called the township of Grand Rapids, received its name in April, 1842.

The first township meeting was held at the house of Joel Guild, April 4, 1834. This house stood on the present site of the City National Bank, and was the only frame building in the county except that occupied as a Catholic church. The officers elected were: Supervisor—Rix Robinson; Clerk—Eliphalet Turner; Assessors—Joel Guild and Barney Burton; Collector—Ira Jones. This is the same election that was referred to in the history of Ada, to be found in another place.

At the time of the organization, and for several years thereafter, the taxes were collected by the collector, and paid over to the supervisor, and disbursed by him. In 1839 a treasurer was elected. The first entry on his book reads as follows: "May, 14, 1839, received of E. W. Davis, supervisor, eight dollars, on the Grand River Bank. Three dollars on the Ypsilanti Bank, one dollar and twenty-five cents on the Bank of Pontiac, and sixty-two cents in specie." Amount of taxes collected the year previous, $174.00. This includes all the taxes collected in what is now Grand Rapids town and city, Ada and Paris. The rapid growth and prosperity of the township will be seen when it is stated that the taxes collected for the year 1869 in Grand Rapids township amounted to $7,763.00.

The first settler within the present limits of the township was Ezekiel Davis, who located on section thirty-four in 1834. He also erected the first house. During the same summer Lewis Reed, Ezra Reed, Porter Reed, David S. Leavitt, Robert M. Barr, settled in the township. James McCrath, George Young, and Simeon Stewart settled in the year 1836. Robert Thompson, John W. Fisk, and

Mathew Taylor settled in the year 1837. Mr. Fisk erected the first hotel, now known as the Lake House.

THE PRESENT OFFICERS

of the township are: Supervisor--Foster Tucker; Clerk--Charles J. Manktelow; Treasurer—Henry B. Davis.

THE SOIL

is of good quality, excepting that in the northeastern part of the township. The land is usually rolling, yet in places is quite hilly. The town is generally adapted to the production of wheat and other grain, and is equally well adapted to fruit culture. There are several small marshes in the town, but the largest and most productive is on section eight, and contains about one hundred and fifty acres. The principal part of it belongs to the estate of Obed H. Foote. Saddle Bag Swamp contains about three hundred acres, and is situated on sections twenty-three, twenty-four, twenty-five and twenty-six. There are a few more swamps, but all of them are small.

There are twelve

LAKES

in the township. The largest is Reed's. This lake is well known to the citizens of Grand Rapids, being a recognized summer resort for pleasure seekers. Grounds have recently been fitted up and tastily laid out with walks by the Grand Rapids Boat Club, which will add greater attraction to the place. On the north side of the lake is the "Lake House," whose present proprietor is Delos Drew, Esq. Boats and fishing tackle are kept by H. B. Miller and John Paul on the south side, for the use of visitors.

The

MINERAL SPRING

excitement which has run so high throughout the State during the past summer, has not passed us by. One of these "Fountains of Youth" has been discovered on the banks of the lake just mentioned, which is supposed to be of considerable medicinal value. The water has been analyzed by Prof. Kedzie, of Lansing, who makes the following report:

SOLID RESIDUE IN A GALLON, 28.326.

CONSISTING OF

Carbonate of lime	11.59
Carbonate of magnesia	10.80
Carbonate of iron	.50
Sulphate of lime	1.49
Common salt	1.50
Chloride of Potassium	.95
Silica	1.10
Organic matter and loss	1.96

Free carbonic acid 17.1-6 inches.

The public

SCHOOLS

in this township are in a flourishing condition, every inhabitant being attached to a regularly organized school district.

Lake school house, in district No. 3, situated on the southeast corner of section twenty-nine, was erected in the year 1859. It is a brick structure, with a bell. The school room is supplied with many of the modern conveniences.

The school house in district No. 8, situated on the southwest corner of section five, was erected in the year 1863. It is a neat, substantial wooden building.

Knapp school house, in district No. 7, situated on section seventeen, is a wooden structure. It was erected in the year 1850.

The school house in district No. 5, situated on section thirty-six, near the residence of James H. Martin, was erected in the year 1852. It is a wooden building.

The school house in district No. 2, situated on section twenty-five, near Perry Hills, is a substantial wooden structure with a bell. It was erected in the year 1869.

The school house in district No. 9, situated on the southwest corner of section eleven, was constructed of wood, in the year 1850.

The school house in district No. 10, located on section ten, was erected in the year 1860. It was constructed of wood.

The Beckwith school house in district No. 11, situated on section sixteen, was erected in the year 1860. It is a very neat, wooden structure.

The school house in district No. 4, situated on Bridge street, on section number twenty-one, was erected in the year 1860. Material, wood.

There are two

HOTELS

in the township. The Powers Hotel, aud the Lake House. The former is situated near the city limits, and is kept by A. Powers. The latter is situated near Reed's and is kept by Delos Drew. Owing to its proximity to the city this township has no postoffice, mill, factory, machine shop, store or church.

GRATTAN.

Grattan, one of the eastern tier of towns, is bounded on the north by Oakfield, on the east by Otisco, Ionia county, on the south by Vergennes and on the west by Cannon. It was originally a part of Vergennes, and was erected into a separate town in 1846. It was largely settled in its southern portion, by emigrants direct from Erin, and in deference to them, the new town was named Grattan, in honor of the great Irish orator, at the instance, and by the influence of Hon. Volney W. Caukin, now a resident of Sparta.

Its first town meeting to perfect its organization, was held on the first Monday of April, 1846, at the house of Converse Close; and the number of votes polled was twenty-three, resulting in the election of the following named gentlemen as its

FIRST OFFICERS.

Supervisor—Milton C. Watkins. Clerk—Volney W. Caukin. Treasurer—Erastus W. Beasom. Highway Commissioners—Thomas J. Morgan, Joshua Fish, Wm. C. Stanton. Justices of the Peace—Samuel H. Steele, John P. Weeks, William Byrne, Luther B. Cook. School Inspectors—Samuel H. Steele, Wm. Beaurmann. Constables—Jedediah H. Wood, Thomas J. Morgan. Overseers of Poor—Luther B Cook, Samuel H. Steele. Assessors—Anthony King, Barlow Barto.

OFFICERS IN 1870.

Supervisor—Oliver J. Watkins. Treasurer—Joseph Tower. Clerk—George D. Wood. Justices of the Peace—Joseph Tower, Oliver I. Watkins, Wm. Daniels. School Inspectors—Asa W. Slayton, George C. Adams. Constable—Thomas M. Henry. Commissioners of Highways—Wm. C. Slayton, Thomas M. Henry.

The number of votes polled at the last town meeting was 240.

By the census returns, the town has now a population of 1,298.

Although the surface is quite broken in consequence of its extraordinary network of lakes, there are no ranges of hills, nor prominent highlands in the town, and its soil is remarkably uniform, adapting it to the mixed husbandry of the country, and especially rendering it the best wheat growing portion of the county. Its wool interests are more than an average, and its productions of hay, corn, oats, potatoes, and neat stock are very fair. Apples, pears, peaches, cherries, currants and grapes, are a universal success, and much attention is being paid by some to the cultivation and improvement of choice varieties of fruits. Prominent among these stands Asa W. Slayton, and it well repays a lover of rural beauty, and horti cultural enterprise, and success, to visit his pleasant and tasteful home, situated on section 22, south of the Grand Rapids and Ionia State road.

Formerly, considerable attention was paid to the raising of hops, and some years the returns for this crop reached as high as $10,000, but the reduction of prices has ruined the hop interest here, as in many other places.

Mainly, the town is heavily wooded with oak and hickory, but sections 25 and 36, and a portion of sections 5 and 35, are rich timber lands.

There are no less than twenty-four lakes in this town, covering an area of from 36 to 300 acres each, besides a host of smaller lakes or ponds; but six demand especial notice. Nagles, or Murray's Lake, lies on sections 33 and 34 in Grattan, and extending more than half across section 4 in Vergennes, is the largest of these, and is remarkable for its peculiar shape, being nearly divided in two by a long, narrow, promontory of land owned by Mr. W. Fullington.

Crooked Lake, lying on sections 20, 21 and 29, is one mile long, quite irregular in shape, and is noted for its Islands. Round Lake, a pretty sheet of water, on section 21, is one half mile long, and about the same in width, and contains about 80 acres. This lake and Crooked Lake discharge their waters through Seely Creek into Flat River.

Slayton Lake is another small, but beautiful sheet of water, lying on section 23. It takes its name from one of the early settlers whose residence is near its shore.

Musk-Rat Lake, on sections, 4, 5, 8 and 9, is one mile and a half long, and about one-fourth of a mile wide, on the average. It contains about 230 acres, and is bountifully stocked with fish. The kinds caught in it are black, rock and silver-bass, pickerel and muskelonge.

Pine Island Lake, lying on sections 3 and 10, one mile and a quarter long, and three eights of a mile wide, is the most beautiful of them all. Pine Island, from which the lake takes its name, lies on its bosom like a gem on the wave. The far sweeping lake with its picturesque shores and forest crowned isle, as seen from the home of Mr. Converse Close, near it, fixes the gaze of the beholder like some enchanted scene, of which we sometimes dream.

Grattan has no water course of any note, except Seely's Creek, the outlet of nine of its principle lakes. It is an insignificant stream, averaging no more than two rods wide, yet, with its numerous, and inexhaustible fountains, supplying water power sufficient for three grist mills and one saw mill, in its short course of half a dozen miles. It takes its rise in a small lake on section 15, just north of the State Road, three fourths of a mile east of Grattan Center, running north one and one quarter miles, through Pine Island Lake, west one and one quarter miles through Musk-Rat Lake, south-east one and one quarter miles through Wolf Lake, where it appears as a small stream running thence due east, passing within 60 rods of its source, and debouching in Flat River, at the village of Smyrna, in Ionia county. It was named after Munson Seely, a young hunter, who, in early days camped upon its banks and pursued the chase through its adjacent forests.

In 1850, Edward Bellamy and Nathan Holmes, brothers in-law, formed a partnership, and erected a grist mill upon the stream, near its embouchure from Wolf Lake, on section 16. This was the nucleous of Grattan Center. The mill is now owned by J. A. Adams & Bros. This place is the only business center in the town. It has twelve or fourteen dwellings, one hotel, one cabinet shop, one wagon shop, one cooper shop, two blacksmith shops, one paint shop, one drug store, two dry goods stores, and a fine new church. (Baptist, C. C. Miller, Pastor.) It was erected in 1868. It is built of wood, painted white, costing $5,400.

The Grattan Union School House, a white, two story, frame building, with two departments, is located here, on a beautiful eminence just east of the village. The Metropolitan Cheese Factory, is located just west of here, and its enterprising proprietor, Capt. B. Madison, is opening up an apparently prosperous business for himself and the farmers for miles around, by this new branch of industry. Grattan Center is situated in a fine rural district, and its proprietors are wide-awake and enterprising, but altogether too far away from railroads for their own convenience, or comfort. Within the past year, the place has suffered a severe loss in the sudden death of its esteemed citizen W. L. Atkins, a long time merchant, and efficient business man of the town.

As early as 1848 the Catholics erected a small church in their cemetery, on section 32, dedicated to St. Patrick. In ten years their congregation had become much too large for the seating capacity of the house, and it was moved upon section 31, and converted into a School House, and a new and commodious edifice erected on an eminence one fourth of a mile west of the old site.

This building, while undergoing repairs, was accidentally burned in 1868. Immediately, scores of teams were put upon the roads hauling lumber preparatory to the building of a new church, which is now in process of erection, and when completed will be an honor to its builders, and an ornament to the town. It is 136 by 50 feet in size; has a tower 168 feet high, and is lighted with massive windows of stained glass, which show with pleasing effect.

The congregation is very large, and their annual pic-nic for the benefit of the church has become an "institution" of Grattan. It is noted for its tastefully arranged, and bountifully supplied tables, and the hosts that congregate. Father Rivers is closely identified with the early history and prosperity of this people, but J. P. McMannus is now the resident priest.

Besides the Union School, Grattan has but four district school houses, but, as would at first seem, its educational interests are not neglected, as it is completely surrounded by fractional districts.

In 1843, the first settlement was made within the limits of the town, by Dennis and John McCarthy, on section 30, and Richard Giles, on section 32. In 1844, Luther B. Cook built the first house north of Seely's Creek, on section 12. The same year, William Smith, also settled on section 12. Converse Close, on section 11; Jared Watkins, on section 13; Henry Green, on section 13; Anthony King, Alanson King on section 1; Volney W. Caukin, on section 9; Michael Kennedy, on section 19; and William McCarthy, on section 30. Prominent among the settlers of 1845, we may mention John P. Weeks, located on section 25; Orson Nichoson, on section 2; William Byrnes, on section 27, and Anson Green, on section 14. In 1846 Russel Slayton, located on section 14, and Dudley Newton, on section 17. Among the settlers of 1847, we find Martin Mason, located on section 23. Of these old settlers, most reside where they first located, but Anthony King, Russel Slayton and Orson Nichoson, are dead. Marshal King, son of Alanson King, born December, 1844, is supposed to be first white child born in the town. The first death occurred in the fall of 1846, in the family of a Mr. Springer, then living on section 15. Isaac Springer, an interesting little boy of five years, was the first victim, but in less than 18 months, five of the family were laid side by side, and now sleep on the very spot where the Union School House stands.

There are many interesting personal experiences incident to the early settlement of a new country, which the limits of this work will not permit us to record, but the circumstanees attending the first wedding in this town are so peculiar, we may not omit to mention it here. A widely known, and highly esteemed couple, still residents of the town, wished to get married, but there was no functionary in that part of Kent, vested with authority to perform the ceremony. A well known Justice of Ionia county, chanced to be visiting at the house where the parties were, and their dilemma was made known to him. Of course he had no jurisdiction in Kent, but the county line was only half a mile away, and a walk through the forest, was proposed and agreed to. The Justice took his stand in Ionia county, and the bride and bridegroom, protesting they would not leave the town to be married, joined hands just over the line, and in the presence of a few friends, gathered beneath the grand old oaks, on the pleasant afternoon of July 28, 1844, the twain were made one to their own gratification and the gratification and amusement of their friends here, as elsewhere.

In those early days, the settler, with his axe, cut the way for his future home, and in the absence of stores, grist mills and saw mills, supplied, by his own ingenuity, the actual necessities of himself and family. To-day, all the conveniences of civilized life are at his hand, and the well cultivated farms, and the more than ordinary wealth displayed in dwellings and out buildings, are highly significant of the sobriety, enterprise, and consequent prosperity of the people.

Grattan has not only maintained an honorable position in the county, but has also made its record among the dignitaries of the State. Of its first set of officers, Hon. Volney W. Caukin has once represented the Twenty-ninth District, at Lansing, and Hon. Milton C. Watkins, its first Supervisor, has been Representative, also Senator in the State Legislature, and now holds an appointment under the United States Government.

LOWELL.

This township lies north of Bowne, and south of Vergennes. It is one of the eastern tier of townships in Kent county, being bounded on the east by Boston, Ionia county, and on the west by the township of Cascade.

Its soil, timber and productions are greatly diversified. The soil of the south half is mostly clay or loam, lies very high, and is generally level and well adapted to farming purposes, and on account of its elevation, an excellent fruit section.

The north half is considerably broken; by Grand River, which crosses the township from east to west, at an average distance of one mile from the north line, and Flat River, which comes in from Vergennes, on the north, and enters Grand River about one and one half miles west from the county line, of Kent and Ionia counties. The river bottoms, from half a mile to a mile in width, are heavily timbered with elm, ash, soft maple, etc., and when cleared make good meadow lands. Next back of these bottoms, on either side, rise the sand and clay bluffs, which line these streams throughout the greater part of their course in the county. In some places they rise to the highth of nearly 200 feet, and are usually covered with oak, some time quite heavy, but in other places only what is commonly known as "openings," the timber being light, and the ground covered with a small growth of oak, interspersed with hazel, and other shrubs. These bluffs, somewhat broken by many small brooks which come in from both sides, extend back an average of about a mile on each side, which, on the north side brings us about to the township line, and on the south to the high level tract before mentioned. This latter is partially watered by some small lakes, the largest of which is Pratt Lake, covering about 300 acres on the north part of section 25, near the east line of the township, and about three miles south of Grand River. It is named in honor of William Pratt, who settled on the north side of it about the year 1850. Barcis, or McEwing Lake, on the east part of section 32, is nearly one mile in length, but quite narrow, its greatest width being less than 80 rods. It extends from the northeast to southwest. On the northwest corner of the same section is a pond of about ten acres, called Morse Lake. Between them, and on the south part of the same section, is a small lily pond, hardly to be called a lake. Stoughton Lake is a small lake of 4 or 5 acres, near the center of section 35, and has a tamarack swamp of about 20 acres on the east of it. There is also a small lake of 3 or 4 acres, and a swamp of about 15 acres on the south side of section 22. A swamp of some 300 or 400 acres lies west of Pratt Lake, on section 26. On the south side of section 33, and extending over the line into Bowne, is a fine marsh of about 40 acres. From Pratt Lake and the swamp already mentioned, to this marsh is a ravine through which is a stream of water in wet seasons, but which dries away in ordinary weather, leaving the lake without any visible outlet. The people along the line have recently petitioned the County Drain Commissioner to open this natural water course deep enough to form a living stream, to the south line of Lowell township, from which it would flow into a small stream which runs to Thornapple River. Aside from the sources already mentioned, and some few smaller ponds and swamps, water can only be obtained in this part of the township by digging a depth of 50 to 100 feet. The timber of this southern part was originally sugar maple and beech, interspersed with very large red and white oaks. This township is well supplied with stone for building purposes, and in some parts they are used to some extent for fencing, especially in the northwest corner of the township, and various other places north of Grand River. Fine gravel beds also abound throughout the north part, and the soil is quite gravelly along the road leading down the river from Lowell village.

PIONEERS.

In the year 1829, Daniel Marsac came from Detroit, and went among the Indians in the vicinity of the present village of Lowell, as a trader, although a regular trading post was not established until 1831, when Mr. Marsac built a log hut on the south side of Grand River, near the present site of J. Kopf & Co.'s extensive chair works.

What changes a few years have made! When Mr. Marsac first pitched his tent within the borders of Kent county, then an almost unbroken wilderness, the only roads were the Indian trails, and the only means of navigation was the canoe, or "dug out," as it is sometimes called; or, for more extensive transportion, a raft made of poles, or small logs, fastened together. We do not need to speak of the railroads and other facilities for travel now, as the reader can easily compare the present with the past.

In the spring of 1835, a family by the name of Robinson, numbering in all 44 persons, set out from the State of New York, and arriving at Detroit, embarked on a small vessel for Grand Haven *via* Mackinaw. On the 7th day of June of that year they reached the mouth of Grand River, and, putting their household goods, etc., on rafts, and "paddling their own canoes," made their way up the river and settled in Kent and Ottawa counties, principally the latter, in the vicinity of Blendon. These were only a part of the Robinsons. Rix Robinson had been trading with the Indians at Thornapple—now called Ada—for several years previous to this, and had one son by the squaw whom he had taken for a wife soon after he came there. A year later, in 1836, another brother, named Lewis, came with his family and settled on the west bank of Flat River, in the south part of what is now the village of Lowell. He was soon followed by Rodney, a brother from the Blendon settlement, who remained one year with Lewis, and then removed up the river into the present township of Vergennes, where he and another brother, Lucas, have made good farms. Philander Tracy—a relative of the Robinson family, who now resides at Grand Rapids, and is generally known as Judge Tracy, also came from the State of New York, and was for some time with Lewis Robinson. The timber for their first log hut was cut two or three miles up Flat River, and floated down by the help of Indians, who were always friendly to those who used them well.

There were good and bad Indians, as well as good and bad whites. One Indian, named Negake, who was not, however, a member of either of the tribes then occupying this portion of the State, but a renegade from some Eastern tribe, who had taken up his abode with the Pottawotamies, caused the whites some trouble, and was reported to have killed one of the Government Surveyors some years previous, when an attempt was made to survey and throw into market all lands up to the 43 degree of latitude, which parallel cut across a bend in the river in this township, and took a strip about a mile in width on the north side, to which survey the Indians objected. Subsequently the river was made the frontier line, and no lands north of the river were put into market until August, 1839.

A tract of land lying on the east side of Flat River, was set apart as University lands. In 1836, Luther Lincoln, from Grand Rapids, formerly from the south part of the State, where he had been quite a wealthy man, came and settled on a small lot of this University land, and built a log house, which was afterwards used by Don A. Marvin, as a tavern. Mr. Lincoln and Rodney, and Lucas Robinson, helped the Indians to fence in a tract of about 100 acres, on the east side of Flat River, and about one mile from Grand River, for a planting ground, to prevent any trouble on account of their letting their cattle run at large on "Uncle Sam's Domain," as the cattle would have been likely to destroy their crops, and this would naturally have led to hostilities.

Mr. Rodney Robinson states that the Indians were usually good neighbors, and even Mr. Lincoln—whose mind was somewhat wandering, and consequently led him into some trouble with the early white settlers, always got along finely with the Indians, and when, on account of some "unpleasantness" with the whites he was obliged to leave this point, he went up the river a long distance and erected a saw mill, right in the midst of the Indian country. They were often employed to work for the early white settlers, and generally well paid, although it was usually best to pay them in provisions and other necessaries, rather than in money, for, if they got money, many of them would go off to places where they could get liquor, and come home drunk, when they would be quarrelsome and dangerous neighbors, until the fire-water and its effects were gone. No liquor was allowed to be sold to them in this vicinity if the settlers could prevent it, although itinerant traders would sometimes undertake to sell it to them in order make it easier to cheat them in their trades.

In 1837, Charles Newton, Matthew Patrick, Samuel P. Rolf, Ira A. Danes, William Vandeusen and Mr. Francisco—nearly all of whom were from New York, settled along the north side of Grand River, on the old Grand River Road, from two to five miles west of Flat River. This road came from Ionia, by the way of Fallassburg—at which point the first bridge was built across Flat River, in 1840, previous to which the river was forded—and passed about two miles west of the mouth of the river, thence along down Grand River, near the side of the bluffs.

The following bit of school romance is introduced without any apology: In 1837 the people of this vicinity organized a School District, including all the settlers on Flat River, and being the only School District between Grand Rapids and Ionia. They erected a log school house in 1838, in the north part of the present village, on the west side of Flat River, and employed Miss Caroline Beard, from New York State, to teach the first school that summer. The following winter the district furnished a cook-stove and provisions, and Miss Beard lived in the school house and kept the school. Caleb D. Page, who had taken up a piece of land near the Fallassburg of later days, took matrimony into his head and Miss B. to his heart, and the bonds of wedlock were entered into by this couple in the school house.

In 1839, William B. Lyon and Ransom Rolf, also from New York, settled on the same road, near those previously mentioned. At the time of the sale of lands in this tract, (previously mentioned as occurring in August, 1839) the Indians attempted to enter and hold the land they had been tilling, under the pre-emption laws, but, as the agent knew nothing about whether the red man could hold land by those laws, the matter was referred to the General Land office, and, while waiting the decision, Philander Tracy attempted to gain possession by erecting a small hut on it, and sowing the field to oats, which were destroyed by the Indians. His papers which had been granted were afterward revoked, and, although the decision was that Indians could not enter lands in their own name, they lent money to a Frenchman by the name of Nontah, and he bought the land, and afterward, failing to pay back the money, he gave them a deed of it.

The lands were afterward found to be a part of the " University Grant," and so also was the land taken by Lincoln. When Mr. L. left here, he sold his claim to Daniel Marsac, who, in 1847, platted it under the name of " the village of Dansville," which name it retained until about the year 1855. In 1850 Mr. M. sold his claims to Edwin Avery, of Ionia, who then paid the State and obtained a complete title to the same. John B. Shear and some others, came in about the year 1844, and settled in or near the present village of Lowell. In December, 1846, Cyprian S. Hooker, formerly from Connecticut, came from Saranac, Ionia county, where he had been a pioneer and almost the only settler. Mr. Hooker erected the first framed house in the township, which was also the first in the village. His lumber was brought from Saranac. He commenced his house on the 18th day of December, 1846, and on the ensuing Christmas moved into it with his family. This would be called quick work even in these days of steam and electricity. Said house is the one now owned and occupied by Robert Marshall. In 1847 Mr. Hooker erected the grist mill on the east side of Flat River, now owned and since enlarged by William W. Hatch, who erected another large mill on the west side of the river in 1867. When Mr. H. first erected his mill it was run by an overshot water-wheel—water being brought by means of a race, a distance of about 40 rods from the Island in Flat River. In 1849, Mr. Hooker constructed the dam across the river just below Bridge street. In 1849, the first sermon ever preached in Dansville, was delivered at the house of C. S. Hooker, Esq., by Rev. S. S. Brown, a Congregational Minister. Mr. Hooker also had the job of building the first frame school house in the village, which was the first in the east part of the county. It was built in 1850 and stood on the present M. E. Church site. Soon after this a Sunday School was established by the agent of the Congregational Union Society.

The Lowell post office was established about the year 1848, and took its name from the township, which was organized about this time, and which seems to have been named on account of its prospects as a manufacturing point, although the village was still called Dansville. After Mr. Avery bought Mr. Marsac's claim, he added some territory to the original plat, making in all about 100 acres. In 1854 Messrs. Richards & Wickham platted nearly 100 acres on the west side of Flat River, which they named

LOWELL.

About the same time Chapin & Booth's addition to the village of Dansville was platted, containing about 30 acres, and lying on the east of the original plat, but within a year, by common consent, the whole village was called Lowell, since which the following additions have been platted, and called Additions to the Village of Lowell; *Fox's Addition*, lying north of R. & W.'s plat on the west side Flat River, containing 52 acres, platted by James S. Fox. *Lee's Addition*, on the north of Avery's plat, east of Flat River, containing 48 acres, platted by Peter Lee in 1868. *Snell's Addition*, on the west and south of R. & W.'s addition, containing about 50 acres, platted by Mrs. Caroline Snell in 1869. *Ellsworth's Addition*, lying north and east of Lee's addition, contains 60 acres, 20 of which are within the present corporate limits of the village of Lowell, and the remainder in the township of Vergennes, platted by A. M. Ellsworth in 1870.

An act to incorporate the Village of Lowell passed the State Legislature in 1859, but for some reason the village was not then organized. It was re-enacted March 15, 1861, and the organization completed in the summer following.

FIRST VILLAGE OFFICERS.

President—Cyprian S. Hooker. Recorder—Charles A. Blake. Treasurer—Simeon Hunt. Marshal—J. Chapman. Assessor—Cyrus Hunt. Trustees—William W. Hatch, J. B. Shear and Arvine Peck.

PRESENT VILLAGE OFFICERS.

President—Morris R. Blodget. Recorder—John Huggins. Treasurer—Clark M. Devendorf. Marshal—Robert Marshall. Trustees--L. B. Lull, John C. Scott and Simeon Hunt.

The village proper now contains 1,503 inhabitants, according to the census of 1870. During the past four years some fine brick buildings have been erected, among which are the large two story block on Bridge street, west of the river, containing five stores below, and a large hall and offices above; Lee's Block, two story, which contains two stores and a hall above; King's Block, now used by Joseph Amphlett as a carriage factory, and Graham's Block, three story, containing two stores, printing office and other offices, and which was erected almost entirely by Mr. Graham with his own hands. Besides the brick stores there are some very good wooden buildings. The village contains in all between 30 and 40 stores, besides the usual number of meat markets, restaurants, etc. There are two hotels: The Clifton House, part brick, kept by Charles Morse, and the Franklin House, a large frame building, kept by C. C. Parks.

MANUFACTURING ESTABLISHMENTS.

Hatch & Craw's grist mills are two large framed mills containing three run of stone each, and capable of grinding 50,000 barrels of flour per year, besides doing a large custom business. Water power.

The Lowell Woolen Mill, erected by Blodgett Brothers, in 1867, is a good, framed building, now owned by M. R. Blodgett, and does about $20,000 worth of business per year. Water power.

Wilson, Gardner & Co. have a steam planer, sash, door and blind factory, erected in 1868, and are doing a good custom and shipping business.

Avery & Johnson have a planer and sash, door and blind factory, which is doing an extensive custom business, and shipping largely both east and west.

This factory runs by water power, and was erected in 1868, on the site of their mill which was destroyed by fire the previous year. In connection with this mill is a machine for the manufacture of wooden eave troughs—a new invention of Mr. E. W. Avery.

FORT'S WESTERN MEDICINE MANUFACTURING COMPANY.

E. M. Fort, the patentee of these medicines, commenced business a few years since on borrowed capital, paying therefor at the rate of 15 per cent. interest. Many of our readers will remember having seen his pleasant face on the streets of the various towns and villages of Kent county, when he was selling his remedies at retail. The business had increased so rapidly and become so popular in Lowell, that in March, 1870, some of the leading capitalists of the town joined him, and established the above-named stock company with a chartered capital of $100,000, making Mr. Fort the secretary and business manager, with the assistance and advice of a board of directors. Since that time they have branched out, and are rapidly introducing it in the adjoining states, and money invested in the company's stock must prove exceedingly profitable. Parties who know best, think it will soon pay a dividend of 30 per cent. as the sales are already immense and largely on the increase; these preparations being acknowledged to be among the best medicines in the market, their popularity having gained for them the endorsement of the widely known and popular drug house of Farrand, Sheley & Co., of Detroit, generally admitted to be the largest wholesale drug house in Michigan, who have purchased a large amount of the capital stock of the company, and are acting as their agents for Detroit.

Boyce & Nash have a shop for the manufacture of agricultural implements, axes, etc., making about 150 dozen axes per year, and manufacturing in all about $6,000 worth per year.

Joseph Amphlett's carriage factory is quite an extensive establishment, turning out about 100 carriages and wagons per year.

CHURCHES.

The Methodist Episcopal church building is a fine brick structure 40x60 feet in size, completed and dedicated in 1859. It stands on a little rise of ground on Bridge street, east of the business part of the village. Cost over $8,000, including furniture. Near this is the unpretending Baptist church, which is a good, little framed building, erected in 1859. During the present season this church has been tastefully fitted up and newly painted. The Congregational church on the west side of Flat River is a good looking, framed building, 40x56 feet in size, erected in 1858 at a cost of $2,500. There are also two or three church societies and a Masonic Lodge and a Good Templar's Lodge, which meet in halls.

SCHOOLS.

There is a good, framed school-house 36x54 feet in size, and two stories high, which was erected in 1862 at a cost of about $2,000. It is being repaired the present season, but is small for the size of the district, which takes in quite a large extent of territory, and a larger building will soon be required. There is one ward or branch school in connection with this district, which is the old district No. 1, of the township of Lowell. This branch school is located on the south side of Grand River, in the vicinity of the Detroit and Milwaukee Railroad depot, where a village called Segwun was platted by William Chesebro, about the time the railroad was built, but which is seldom known by that name.

MILLS AND FACTORIES.

On the above-mentioned plat is the steam saw mill of C. T. Wooding, erected in 1866 by Knapp & Tucker, and capable of cutting 20,000 feet of lumber per day; also, the cider and vinegar manufactory of E. R. Peck, erected in 1869, and capable of grinding 18,000 bushels of apples per year. In this vicinity is also quite a collection of small houses, mostly occupied by laborers in the above-named establishments and on the railroad. Near at hand and a little east of the depot is the extensive chair factory of John Koph & Co., which has a small cluster of pleasant looking buildings around it, and has withal an appearance of thrift and neatness. This building was erected in 1858, by Seth Cogswell, and the machinery is run by an overshot waterwheel, water being obtained from a small spring brook which rises about two miles south and comes in through a gorge in the hills.

About a mile distant is the large grain cradle and bed bottom factory of E. W. Tucker. His first mill was a three-story frame building 30x40 feet in size, erected in 1862, in connection with which is a new mill or shop 35x50 feet, erected in 1868. In the one item of grain cradles they have facilities for manufacturing 1,200 dozen per year, besides bed-bottoms and harvesting implements, such as hay-rakes, etc. This is also run by an overshot water-wheel. From 20 to 60 hands are employed.

At the head of this stream, and about two miles south of the depot, is a fine bed of marl, on the farm of Alexander McBride, from which Mr. McB. has manufactured $4,000 worth of lime within the past four years.

THE GRAND RIVER NURSERIES.

N. P. Husted, proprietor, are situated about five miles southwest of the Lowell depot. He commenced planting in 1862, putting out about 40,000 apple trees, 40,000 peach trees, and other stock, since which time he has been gradually increasing until now he sets 300,000 apple and 300,000 peach and other stock every year. Besides this he is giving considerable attention to ornamental stock. The nurseries now cover 130 acres, all closely planted, and the amount of sales is nearly $50,000 per year. From 30 to 60 hands are employed. He is also turning his attention to orchard culture, having at present 1,000 four-year old peach trees, over 500 apple trees, 400 pear trees, 200 plum trees, and 4,000 grape vines; also, a good assortment of small fruits. The soil is a clay loam, which is well adapted to the growth of hardy, sound, nursury stock and profitable orchard culture. There are now over 15,000 orchard trees in the immediate vicinity, all of which have been set within a few years. Peaches have borne well every year.

EARLY SETTLERS SOUTH OF GRAND RIVER.

Among the pioneers in this part part of the county was George Post, who came from Connecticut in 1842 and settled on the northwest corner of section 23, at the crossing of the territorial road from Portland to Grand Rapids, and the one from Battle Creek *via* Hastings, to the trading post then established by Daniel Marsac at Lowell. He was the first, and for three years the only settler south of the present line of the D. & M. Railroad, within the township. In 1843, Mainard Chaterdon, with his wife and family of three sons and three daughters, came from Calhoun county, Michigan, (formerly from the state of New York), and went nearly to the southwest corner of the township, on section 31, where his widow and the three sons and one of the daughters still live, and have nice farms. In 1848–9, Harrison Wickham, Peter Hornbrook, Charles Gordon, Mr. Monk, and Mr. Montague settled in the south and southwest part of the township, followed in 1850 to 1854 by John Brannan, William Pratt, John Yeiter, Jacob and Christian Loyer, George Acker, Jacob Yeiter, James Easterby, James Wallace and William Proctor, most of whom were from Ohio, and of Dutch descent, and nearly all of whom are now wealthy farmers, having good farms and buildings.

ORGANIZATION.

The township of Lowell was organized in 1848, being previously a part of the township of Vergennes, which originally included all of the east part of the county. The first township meeting was held at the house of Mr. Timothy White.

FIRST TOWNSHIP OFFICERS.

Supervisor—Cyprian S. Hooker. Clerk—Timothy White. Treasurer—Henry Church. Justices—C. S. Hooker, Daniel McEwen, Samuel P. Rolf and Ira A. Danes.

PRESENT TOWNSHIP OFFICERS.

Supervisor—Robert Hunter, Jr. Clerk—John Huggins. Treasurer—Webster Morris. Justices—Robert Hunter, Jr., Simeon Hunt, Joseph W. Sprague and Matthew Hunter.

NELSON.

The township of Nelson is one of the northern tier of townships, and is bounded on the north by Pierson, in Montcalm county, on the east by the township of Spencer, on the south by Courtland, and on the west by Solon.

Twenty years ago this township was an unbroken wilderness where wild animals made their homes but little molested by man, and twenty years is a short time in which to make a history. But the stalwart men who are now cutting down its forests and converting the timber into lumber, while at the same time fitting the soil for the growth of grains and fruits are doing a good work, which, if it offers few salient points for the historian, is still of immense value to mankind. If he who causes a blade of grass to grow where there was none before is a public benefactor, the world must owe much to those who open the wilderness to the uses of man.

We are informed that William H. Bailey was the first white settler in Nelson, having settled there in 1851, some time in July of that year. He still resides in the township on section 8. We are glad to have sold him a copy of this history, and have no doubt he will feel a justifiable pride when he reads the long list of residents who now point him out as that honored individual "the oldest inhabitant." Mr. John S. Jones moved into the township during the same year, and is said to be the second settler. He now resides on section 33.

Among the early settlers, although we did not learn the date of their coming, were John M. Towns, Josiah Towns, N. R. Hill, D. B. Stout, H. M. Stanton, George Stout, Andrew Stout, Riley Smith, Samuel Punches, Joseph M. Clark, Andrew S. Tindall, John N. Tindall, John Dean, Elisha Dean, H. D. Streeter, Thomas Almy, Mr. Ream and his two sons, Bradford Bailey, James Bailey and Joseph Wood.

Wm. C. Benjamin, a bachelor, came to this town several years ago with a "pocket full of rocks," from California, purchased a fine farm, and improved and beautified it. He also repented of this lonely state, married an intelligent lady and became the father of two children. Last summer, at the close of harvesting, in which he had worked hard, he committed suicide by cutting his own throat,—it is supposed in a fit of temporary insanity. This sad tragedy cast a gloom over the entire community where he lived.

ORGANIZATION.

Nelson was organized as a township by the Board of Supervisors on the 13th day of October, 1854, and the first township election was held at the house of Charles H. Leake on the first Monday of April, 1855, George Hoyle, John S. Jones and George N. Stoddard, being Inspectors of Election. The following were the

FIRST TOWNSHIP OFFICERS.

Supervisor—George Hoyle. Clerk—George N. Stoddard. Treasurer—Charles H. Leake. Justices of the Peace—Samuel Punches, Simpson Anderson, Cyrus Stillwell, Harlow H. Stanton. Commissioners of Highways—Smith Barrett, Harlow H. Stanton, Moses E. Ross. School Inspectors—Harlow H. Stanton, Ithiel R. Smith. Constables—Bradford Bailey, Josiah D. Townes, Amos Bessey, Peter D. Buck. Overseers of Poor—Church Bailey, Joseph Wood.

From this election we take a step of fifteen years and present the names of the

PRESENT TOWNSHIP OFFICERS.

Supervisor—Mindrus H. Whitney. Clerk—Brownell S. Simmons. Treasurer—David B. Stout. Justices of the Peace—Brownell S. Simmons, Mindrus H. Whitney, Jason R. Squires. Commissioners of Highways—Jason R. Squires, Stephen Ferner, Nathaniel Hughey. School Inspectors—Orlon Smith, Nicholas R. Hill. Constable—William A. Dean.

GENERAL DESCRIPTION.

Pine timber predominates in this township, and in the northeast corner there are many large cedar and tamarack swamps. But the soil, although in many places light, as the presence of pine denotes, is still very productive, where, as is generally the case, beech, maple and other hard wood trees are mixed with the pine. For fruit raising this town promises to be one of the best in the county. Its streams are Black Creek, in the northern part of the township, and Little Cedar and Big Cedar, in the western part. Pine Lake is a fine sheet of water, covering some 100 acres on sections 26 and 35.

SCHOOL HOUSES.

The school house in District No. 1, known as the Clark School House, is located in the center of section 8, and is a fine framed building, painted white.

The school house in District No. 2, is a plain framed structure, standing near the northwest corner of section 20. It was built in 1869.

The school house in District No. 3, a large white, framed building, was erected in 1869. It stands on the southeast corner of section 23.

District No. 4, has a good, white, framed school house on the west line of section 34. It was erected in 1867 and is known as the "White Dove" school house.

The Cedar Springs school houses, used for a graded school, are described in the history of

CEDAR SPRINGS,

which village is located partly in this township and partly in Solon, its description being given under the latter head.

OAKFIELD.

Oakfield, formerly a part of Courtland, lies twenty-one miles northeast of Grand Rapids, having Spencer on the north, Eureka, in Montcalm county, on the east, Grattan on the south, and Courtland on the west.

The first settlement was made within its territory, June 5th, 1838, by Hon. Wm. R. Davis, who located on section 19. There seems to have been no one save himself and family to break the solitude of the wilderness, till June, 1839, when Mr. Isaac Tower, Stephen S. Tower and William Thornton, (ex-Sheriff of Kent county,) with their families, moved in, and become comparatively near neighbors to the hitherto lonely pioneers. Stephen S. Tower and Mr. Thornton locating on section 29, and Mr. Isaac Tower on section 30. There were no more settlements till April, 1842, when Thomas Crinnion located on section 18, and David J. Gilbert on section 19, in September of the same year. In 1844, Sheldon Ashley selected a beautiful home on section 36, and in 1845, three brothers, Harry, Giles and Erie McArthur, located respectively on sections 33, 32 and 34. Morris Hart, section 8; Nathaniel W. Mack, section 12; John Davis, section 32; Levi White, section 21; James Elstley, section 31; William Peterson, section 20, and Benjamin Potter, section 21, may be mentioned as among the settlers of 1846 and 1847.

At one time the town was organized under the name of Wabasis, but by subdivision of the territory, was again incorporated with Courtland, and finally permanently organized under the name of Oakfield, through the influence of Sheldon Ashley, in March, 1849. Its first town meeting was held the first Monday of April, 1849, at a little log school house in district No. 1, on section 29. This was the first school house in the town, but the log cabin was replaced in 1852, by a frame structure thirty-six by twenty-six feet in size. This is the famous No. 1, that has educated, and sent forth more, and better teachers, than any other district school in the county. It is known as the White Swan School. Oakfield has six other district school houses: noteworthy among these is the Horton School House, a large frame edifice, painted white. It was erected in 1868, and is used as a church, as well as for school purposes. It is located on sections 17 and 18, just across the road from the Horton Cemetery, beautifully situated on the southwest corner of section 8. There is no Union School in the town; but its educational interests are, and have always been of paramount importance in the minds of its people. Its first school was organized with but six scholars—all the children then in town and kept in a private house, with Miss Sarah Davis, now Mrs. Almon Thompson of Courtland, as teacher. When a school house was finally erected, Mr. Harry McArthur was installed as teacher, and to his earnest labors many, not only in this town, but in adjacent towns, owe much of their advancement in knowledge.

CHURCHES.

Religious societies among the people of Oakfield have reached a highly ad vanced, and truly enviable position, if we may be allowed to judge of moral status by success, and pecuniary prosperity. It has three very fine church edifices, and all its places of worship are well attended.

The First Baptist Church of Oakfield, is a fine frame structure, located on section 36. It was built in 1863, and has a fine bell. It cost about $2,200, and the honor of its erection is largely due to Shelden Ashley, one of the oldest inhabibitants of the town. C. C. Miller is the present pastor.

The Second Baptist Society of Oakfield was organized in April, 1865, with some 40 members, under the ministration of Rev. C. C. Miller, pastor, and Stephen S. Tower, Henry Rich, Thomas Jones, Nathan R. Squiers and William R. Jones, Trustees. The house belonging to this Society—the Second Baptist Church, ot Oakfield—a fine frame building, dedicated January 14, 1868, stands upon on acre of ground purchased from the farm of Robert Olmsted, in the southeast corner of section 19. It is 36 by 56 feet in size, and has a tower 95 feet in height, which is furnished with a very fine toned bell that cost $400. The whole cost of the church was $4,150, of which the citizens of the City of Grand Rapids generously donated over $500. It has an organ, and an excellent choir under the efficient leadership of Mrs. Samuel Tower. Rev. C. C. Miller, is the pastor.

The First Methodist Episcopal Church, of Oakfield, is also a very fine frame building, located on the south line of section, 9, one fourth of a mile away from the Second Baptist Church.

The total cost of its erection closely approximated $4,500. It was dedicated April 14, 1869, and is yearly supplied by the circuit with a pastor.

The physical geography of this town presents us with a rolling surface, quite frequently broken with lakes and ponds, with a soil much too sandy in the northern part, but a rich clay loam in the more southern portions, peculiarly adapting it to wheat culture, wool-growing, and dairying, besides the ordinary production of corn, oats, potatoes and buckwheat.

Of wheat, large quantities of excellent quality, annually find their way from this town to the markets east and west; and as to wool, Oakfield has some of the best flocks, and carries some of the finest clips to the factories, of any town in the county.

The dairy is receiving more and more attention, and pays exceedingly well, where care and capital are expended.

Horticulture is in its infancy here as in many other towns; but on some farms it has received a share of attention, and the returns in apples, pears, peaches, grapes, cherries, currants and strawberries, show that Oakfield, in fruit raising, may become a peer of her successful sister towns. The timber is mainly oak; but, scattered over the town, there were some fine groves of pine, which are fast being decimated by the lumbermen's axe and saw.

On sections 1 and 2 there is a very fine bed of marl lime, so pure as to be cut from the bed in squares, dried and placed immediately in the kiln for burning. To facilitate the mining of this bed, a chain of lakes on sections 1, 2 and 11 were drained. Their natural outlet was through Stack's Lake, which emptied into Black Creek; but, by dint of engineering, an outlet was effected into Wab-ah-see Creek, from the head of the Horse Shoe—a large lake on section 2—which is thus rendered nearly dry. Of this marl deposit George and John Banks are proprietors.

Besides the above, there are several small

LAKES

that demand but a passing notice. Of such is Scram's lake, and Addis' lake closely connected with it, lying on sections 17, 18 and 19; the Zeigenfuss lake on sections 11 and 14—the outlet from which forms the north branch of Wab-ah-see Creek; and also a number of little lakes on sections 33 and 34, the principal of which is Flat-Iron Lake near the residence of Harry McArthur, Esq. But Long Lake, about one-half mile long, and one-eighth wide, situa'ed on section 34, cannot be thus lightly passed by, for on its frozen surface in March, 1843, occurred the first death among the whites of this township. Orin Gilbert, brother of Rev. D. Gilbert, in endeavoring to reach his brother's house from Cook's Corners, was overcome by fatigue and cold, and perished on this lake. Soon after Tahanah, an Indian, in passing on the trail, discovered him lying on the snow. The wily Indian did not approach him, but, after circling several times around the prostrate form to make sure that he was dead, sped away to convey the sad intelligence to his friends. Ever after, the Indians called this "Dead Man's Lake."

Wab-ah-see, or Wabasis, as the white people call it, is much the largest lake of the town, or even of the county, being two miles long. It is very irregular in shape, but it is said to average nearly one mile in width. It has excellent fishing grounds, and at certain seasons of the year—though they are caught at no other time, and even then, are only found in particular places—whitefish are caught in considerable quantities. How they come there no one can tell, and where they disappear to is equally a mystery.

The Wab-ah-see abounds with pickerel, and a gigantic specimen of this variety of fish has frequently been seen by seekers of the finny spoil, so immense in its dimensions as to excite almost as much wonder as the periodical appearing of the fabulous sea-serpent. Wab-ah-see projects into sections 29, 33 and 34, but lies mainly on sections 27 and 28. It was named after the Indian chief Wab-ah-see (White Swan), who fell under the displeasure of his people for selling their lands, and also (as they supposed) for secreting and retaining the gold for the purchase. To obtain this, they deferred his death, and banished him to the shores of this beautiful and romantic lake. By some the gold is supposed to be hidden on its shores, and many have sought for it by torchlight and by sunlight, with equal lack of success. Failing to extort money, and maddened by the loss of their hunting grounds, the big chief, Ne-ogg-ah-nah, with almost fiendish subtlety, induced Wab-ah-see to go beyond his limits, and, in a drunken frolic, killed him with a firebrand. His broken skull is now in a museum in Connecticut, having been sent there by Mr. Hall, of Plainfield.

The Oakfield grist mills, containing two run of stones, erected in 1864, is located upon section 15, on Wabasis Creek, the outlet of the lake, which becomes quite a stream, emptying into Flat River in Montcalm county.

The first saw mill in town was built by John Davis, about the year 1846 or 1847. It was located on Beaver Dam Creek, a small stream running into Wab-ah-see Lake. Three times it was swept into ruins by the freshets, and as often repaired, or rebuilt, by the indomitable perseverance of its owner. But at last, patience and capital alike gave out, and a steam mill was erected in its stead. That has since been dismantled, and desolation now reigns where sterling enterprise once presided. No inhabitant of Oakfield and adjacent to towns, who may read these pages, shall be allowed to forget, for lack of a record here, the history ot the old mill on Beaver Dam Creek, or the vicissitudes of its cheery and brave-hearted owner, who snapped his fingers in the face of the jade, Fortune, when she made faces at him, and went whistling away to the tune of "Old Ragged," despite all adversity. (The foregoing quaint cognomen will be understood by every old-time business man of Kent county.)

The Lillie Steam Shingle Mill was built in 1861, on section 3. It was burned on the 17th of April, 1868, and rebuilt in the same year. The Addis Shingle and Cider mills are located on the northwest quarter of section 20, and were built in 1869; John Addis, proprietor. The Oakfield shingle mill is located on Wab-ah-see Creek, adjacent to the grist mill spoken of above. Near these mills a little village, consisting of a store or two, a blacksmith shop, and half a dozen dwellings, has sprung up within a few years. This is the only business center in the town.

FIRST TOWNSHIP OFFICERS.

Supervisor—Thomas Spencer. Town Clerk—Harry McArthur. Treasurer—Harry Osgood. Justices of the Peace—Thomas Spencer, Harvey D. Pond, David J. Gilbert, Wm. M. Gould. Constables—Nathan H. Gould, Giles McArthur, William Chapman, Jesse Stewart. Commissioners of Highways—Benjamin Morey, William Peterson, Cyrus B. Thomas. School Inspectors—John Davis, Lafayette Knight. Overseers of the Poor—Sheldon Ashley, Harry Osgood.

PRESENT TOWNSHIP OFFICERS.

Supervisor—Wm. R. Davis. Clerk—Azariah V. Rowley. Treasurer—John Ashley. Justices of the Peace—Henry Watson, Oliver R. Lewis, John Ashley, George Cathey. Commissioners of Highways—Henry E. Rowley, Chester A. Lillie, Rufin Caukin. School Inspectors—Wm. H. H. Davis, Henry E. Rowley. Constables—John W. Gilbert, Henry E. Rowley, Edward Jones.

The town has now a population of 1,092. Of the old settlers, and men who took an active part in the organization of the town, Isaac Tower and Morris Hart, are dead; also Thomas Spencer, the first Supervisor of the town, who was torn in pieces by the machinery in a mill, in Montcalm county, in the spring of 1867.

The first marriage in the town was solemnized by Rev. James Ballard, August 2nd, 1840. Bride—Miss Hannah Tower, daughter of Isaac Tower; bridegroom—Zenas G. Winsor, now of Grand Rapids.

The first birth among the whites, was Wm. H. H. son of Wm. R. and Electa M. Davis. Born April 24, 1840.

Among other first things occurring in the town, was the first bear killed, by John, and his brother, Wm. R. Davis, present member of the State Legislature, from the Fourth Representative District, and present nominee for the same position. Returning late one afternoon, in the summer of 1842, from mowing on a marsh on Crinnion Creek, in the north part of the town, William riding a horse, and carrying some game he had caught through the day, John on foot, equipped with a fine rifle, and closely followed by a faithful dog, were surprised and delighted when within two miles of home, by the discovery of a huge black bear. The dog gave instant pursuit, closely followed by the brothers. Frightened by the baying of the dog, the bear was soon treed. The brothers were quickly upon the spot, William, anticipating bruin a speedy victim to his brothers unerring aim; but what was their chagrin, on examining the rifle, to find that in the hurry of the pursuit, their last cap had been lost from the gun. Here was a dilemma; but necessity is said to be the mother of invention, and she did not belie her character in this case. The only expedient was to send William one and one half miles away, to Mr. Crinnion's, the nearest house, for caps, if they could be found, otherwise for fire, while John and the dog kept watch by the bear. Mounting old Dutch, his horse, and furiously flourishing his whip, William was soon lost to sight, returning in a very short time, not with gun and caps, however, but a burning brand from Mrs. Crinnion's fire-place. He found bruin a few rods from where he left him, in another tree, and John and the dog still watching. It was already dusk; what was to be done, must be done speedily. Powder was poured into the tube, and John, a splendid marksman, took aim, while William stood by with a live coal, ready to apply at the word fire, which soon came, William asserts, in a trembling voice, but whether John's voice trembled, or William's ears, has not been decided to this day; however, that the sharp crack of the rifle rang through the forest depths, and that the bear lay dead at the foot of the tree, are verities not to be disputed.

David J. Gilbert built the second frame barn and dwelling in the town; Isaac Power having built a frame barn in 1840, and William Thornton a frame house in 1841. In future time, posterity may open its eyes with wonder, asking "of what, then, were other dwellings made?" and it is therefore well to record that, in the early days, the woodman's ax was his only saw mill, and the forest, with its treetops waving many feet aloft in the breezes, his only lumber-yard; consequently his house was made of rough logs rolled one above another, his floor of logs, his roof of pieces of the same, called "shakes;" his fire place was composed of sticks and clay; his fire of huge logs stood on end and walked across the floor, a side at a time, and rolled to their place with a hand-spike. The doors were rude oaken planks split from the heart of some huge forest giant, and as for windows—some houses had very small holes in their sides which passed by that name, and some had none.

The only means of transportation, either for business or pleasure, was the lumber wagon, or sled, drawn by the patient ox, whose rate of speed might be three miles an hour in good going; and many a party of pleasure, clad in homespun and homemade garments, and seated on the straw in the bottom of the wagon or sled, as the case might be, has been borne thus slowly over the devious roads leading from one cabin to another, and have found ample time to enjoy themselves by the way, sure of a hearty welcome at the end of their ride, who now live in stately dwellings, dress in costly raiment and ride in fine carriages, after dashing steeds timed to many a mile the hour. But not a whit the lighter are their hearts now, than then; fortunate indeed are they, if, in the trials and perplexities of life they have not grown sad. Then, men broke ground, and civilization came after. Now, the log cabin is an institution of the past, and the hardships of frontier life, a tale that is told. Now the *iron rail* pushes its way into distant gorges, and unbroken forests, and on the coming railway train man follows, bringing with him all the comforts and appliances of civilized life.

In these days of easy and speedy transportation and mechanical improvements, teeming fields are won from the wilderness in a few months; palatial residences rise, and cities spring up as if by magic, almost surpassing the fabled oriental stories of the olden time.

The people of this town are noted for industry, sobriety and hospitality. There is but one place in the town where strong drinks are sold.

Oakfield responded nobly to the call for volunteers, in the late rebellion, sending her bravest and her best to the front, and many of her noble boys lie buried in known and unknown graves, in southern soil. Many suffered the untold horrors of southern prisons. Prominent among these was Chyler B. Davis, made prisoner at Gettysburg, July 3, 1863, who endured all forms of hardships, in all the Southern prisons from Belle Isle to Andersonville, for 17 months, when he was paroled, a mere walking skeleton, and finally discharged at Fort Leavenworth, Kansas, in June, 1865. He recovered, as by a miracle from his long suffering, and starvation, and is now farming in this town.

PARIS.

The township of Paris is situated in the second tier of townships from the south line of the county, and is bounded on the north by Grand Rapids, on the east by Cascade, on the south by Gaines, and on the west by Wyoming. Being situated so near the City of Grand Rapids, which is a market for all its produce—and being traversed by the Grand River Valley Railroad, it is, so far as convenience is concerned, an exception to the general location of townships.

Paris is next to the oldest township in the county. As long ago as the year 1833, Barney Burton, Edward Guild, Joel Guild, Daniel Guild, and James Vanderpool located within its present limits. Benjamin Clark and Abram Laraway, settled in the year 1835; Jacob Patterson, Miner Patterson, James Patterson, Orleans Spaulding and Philanzo Bowen, in the year 1836; Nicholas Carlton in the year

1837; Hiram H. Allen in the year 1838. Among the other early settlers were De Witt Shoemaker, Clinton Shoemaker, Robert Shoemaker, Alvin H. Wansey, Jared Wansey, James Ballard, Stephen Hinsdill, Abram Laraway and Robert Barr. We would here also make special mention of "Captain Davis," as he was familiarly called, who was the father of Ezekiel W. Davis, commonly known as "Judge." He settled in the township in the year 1834, and remained a resident up to the time of his death, which occurred some twenty-five years ago.

The trials and hardships undured by the pioneers of those days seem to have been unusual. Nearly all of the settlers were poor, and consequently were unable to relieve the unequal distress of the less fortunate among them. The lots of some were peculiarly distressing. Orleans Spaulding, who was before mentioned as having settled in the year 1836, informs us that, in the month of June, 1837, he was afflicted with sore eyes, and that for six years he was thereby unfitted for labor. During three years of the time he was totally blind, and that, too, while his family was dependent upon the productions of their little farm for a living.

But there were trials of a general nature which had to be endured at this period, occasioned by the "hard times," or "wild cat times," as they were commonly called. Many of the new settlers had but a small part of their farms cleared, and and a still smaller part cultivated, and consequently were obliged to buy their provisions. Those who had been in the country longer, and had larger improvements, raised a few bushels of wheat more than was required for their own use, but they could sell it neither for money, nor for groceries. Usually it could be given in exchange for "shelf goods" as they were called, provided no more than fifty cents per bushel was charged.

While wheat was selling at only fifty cents per bushel, flour was selling at $15 per barrel, pork $36 per barrel. potatoes $2 per bushel, and butter fifty cents per pound.

We are informed by Mrs. Burton, that when she commenced keeping house in the township, on what is now the Garfield farm, she had no neighbors on the south nearer than Gull Prairie, none on the east nearer than Ionia, and none whatever on the west. Uncle Louis Campau, Joel Guild and Jonathan F. Chubb, were the only residents of Grand Rapids. Rix Robinson was in the township of Ada, trading among the Indians.

Mr. Burton built the first log house in the township of Paris, and erected the first barn the county. He also erected the first frame house in the township, upon the site of the present fine residence of S. M. Garfield.

The following incident illustrates the condition of the country at an early day: when Mr. Burton was on his way from Gull Prairie to Grand Rapids, one night he and his few companions halted as usual, spanceled their horses, and took their rest. In the morning, the horses belonging to Mr. Burton were nowhere to be seen, so he started out in search of them. He wandered about in the thick woods for several hours, without success, and finally turned about with the intention of returning to the camp. He traveled until the sun was low in the west, and no camp could be found. Night came on, and he rested himself, a lost man in a dense forest. The experience of the succeeding day was similar to that of the first; and it was not until the third day that he reached a settlement. By following a creek which he found in his wanderings, he reached the Thornapple river, tracing which to its mouth brought him to what is now the Village of Ada. Thence he proceeded to Grand Rapids where he found the settlers quite excited over the fact of his disappearance, which had been reported by his companions; Mr. Campau having already dispatched a number of Indians in the direction he supposed Mr. Burton would be, to search for him.

At one time in the winter of the years 1835 and 1836, the cries of what was supposed to be a man were heard in the vicinity of Mr. Burton's residence. He was answered, horns were blowed, and other noises made to attract his attention, with no result. About the same time a grey horse came to the residence of Abram Laraway, not many miles away, which none of the settlers claimed. Early in the spring a saddle was found by Robert Barr in the woods not far away. Still later the body of a man was found on what is now called the Penny property, in the Third Ward of the City. Its appearance indicated that death had taken place some months previously. A few dollars in money, a watch, and some papers were found on his person, the latter indicating the name of the man to have been Moore. Nothing further was ever ascertained in regard to the matter. He probably lost his way in the pathless woods, wandered about for several days, perhaps lost his horse, and finally starved to death; or, overcome with weariness sank down to rest, and perished by the excessive cold.

In the year 1835 or 1836, a man by the name of Sizer was shot by an Indian, near Plaster Creek, on what are now the premises of Henry Allen. At that place on the creek was a deer lick, which, of course, was watched by the early settlers as well as by the natives. The parties concerned in the affair to which we refer were both looking for deer, the one not knowing of the presence of the other. As the white man was moving about in the bushes, the eye of the Indian caught a glimpse of his white shirt bosom, which he mistook to be a spot upon a deer about to run. A second more, and the white man fell dead, with a bullet through his heart. You can imagine the terror of the Indian when he discovered what he had done, as he supposed his own life must pay the forfeit.

It seems to have been the custom of the Indians to demand a life for a life. We were informed by an old settler that, at one time, while a little Indian girl was taking care of an infant white child, near what is now the city, she accidentally let it fall from her arms upon the ground, and it was taken up dead. The Indians took the girl with the intention of executing her; but upon the earnest solicitation of Uncle Louis Campau, and Joel Guild, and the offer of an amount of money for her life, she was spared.

In this instance the Indian went immediately to the missionary named Slater, who lived on the west side of the river, told him all, and gave himself up. Mr. Slater advised him to go back, arouse the whites and tell them what had he done; and assured him that he would not be punished. He did as he was advised, and the affair there ended.

When Benjamin Clark came into the township, in 1835, he selected a piece of land on section twelve, located upon it, and has ever since made it his home. When he settled, no one was living in that part of the township, except Alexander Clark. He says he came all the way from Morau's residence near Reed's Lake, to Abram Laraway's, without seeing a house.

James Patterson came into the township in 1836, via a road on the east side of Thornapple River, which he followed to Ada. There he found John W. Fisk keeping tavern in the wilderness. His cattle swam the river, while himself and family and team were ferried across on a scow owned by Mr. Fisk. From there he took a southwesterly course through swamps, streams, and woods, without the least sign of a road, a distance of six miles to his new home. On his route thither he saw only one settler, and he had but just located.

When Hiram H. Allen settled in the township in the year 1838, there was but one regular thoroughfare through it, and that was the old Gull Prairie, or Kalamazoo road. N. O. Sargeant had just previously established a line of stages between Kalamazoo and Grand Rapids. Mr. Allen says he took a trip through Cascade in 1838, and found but very few settlers. From the Patterson settlement on sections 12 and 13 to Cascade village, there were no passable roads for teams.

During the first few years of early settlement there was no regular camp of Indians in the township. Occasionally they would pitch their tents for a few days on their hunting and fishing excursions, but the first regular colony was formed about the year 1840, on or near section 33. They lived there for several years, but when the county became more thoroughly settled, they sold their lands and left.

ORGANIZATION.

The township of Paris—which then included Gaines—was organized in the year 1839, and the first town meeting was held at the house of Hiram H. Allen, which resulted in the election of the following officers:

Supervisor—Joel Guild. Clerk—Hiram H. Allen. Treasurer—Robert Barr. Assessors—Stephen Hinsdill, Foster Kelley, Joseph H. Blain. Justices of the Peace—H. H. Allen, Hezekiah B. Smith, Barney Burton, Alexander Clark. Commissioners of Highways—Joseph Blain, Jacob Patterson, John Kirkland. School Inspectors—James Ballard, Renssalaer Mesnard, Joseph K. Palmer. Directors of the Poor—Andrew Mesnard, Daniel Guild. Collector—Jacob Patterson. Constables—Jacob Patterson, Joseph J. Baxter, Palmer Allen.

SOIL, TIMBER, ETC.

The soil of Paris as a township, is quite good. To be sure it has its poor land as well as other townships; but considered as a whole, it is considerably above the average. The soil in the southeasterly and central parts is heavy clay, while in the northerly and westerly parts it is sandy.

The timber in the southeasterly and central parts is quite heavy; that in the northerly and westerly parts light, and what might be called oak openings. In the southwesterly part of the town is some pine, in places mixed with elm, black ash, etc.

There are many good farms in Paris, among which may be mentioned those belonging to T. S. Smith, on section 27; Stark Le Fever, on section 35; Seeley S. Buck, on section 34; Isaac D. Davis, on section 29; Philanzo Bowen, on section 28; Abram G. Shear, on section 21; Oscar S. Shafer, on section 23; James Patterson, on section 12; Miner Patterson, on section 13; S. S. Bailey, on section 13; Myron

Richards, on section 10; John H. Ford, on section 2; S. M. Garfield, on section 7; John D. Alger, on section 7; Joel Simonds, on section 7.

Some of the best residences in the township are those owned by T. S. Smith, Myron Richards, S. M. Garfield, John D. Alger, and Riley Cole. The orchard on the premises of John H. Ford, is the most thrifty and extensive of the many we saw in the township.

SCHOOL HOUSES.

The first school-house erected in the township stood on the corner of the northeast quarter of section 7. It was used for many years, but was finally removed, and the present building erected in 1857. There are several fine school-houses in the township. The Godwin school-house standing on the old plank road, a short distance beyond the Godwin tavern, is a good brick building, and an ornament to the locality. The school-house on the southwest corner of section 10, built of brick, presents a fine appearance, and exhibits the enterprising character of the inhabitants in its vicinity; also, the frame school-house situated near the northeast corner of section 34. We mention these as being particularly good, while, in fact, all of the school buildings in the township are above the average character.

COUNTY POOR HOUSE.

The county farm and poor-house are located in Paris, on section 16. The farm contains 104 acres or thereabouts, and has the appearance of being well worked.

At the time the farm was purchased by the county, a log house was standing on it, which was used for a number of years as a poor house. It was removed in 1860, and the present frame building erected in its stead. Several additions have been made to it, until now it is a large structure. The present keeper is John Otis.

MILLS.

The Bostwick Grist and Saw Mills were erected many years ago, on Plaster Creek, on the east line of section 17. Four dams were constructed at different times, but in each instance they were carried away. The mills were run at intervals, but never for any great length of time, and were finally abandoned.

The Tanner Mills, situated on the southeast corner of section 20, were operated for a number of years; but are now among the things of the past.

THE PRESENT OFFICERS

of Paris, are: Supervisor—Samuel M. Garfield. Clerk --John Steketee. Treasurer —Everett Hurd. School Inspectors—John H. Ford, Gilbert G. Bailey. Justices of the Peace—Hiram H. Allen, Abram C. Barclay, Seeley S. Buck, John H. Ford. Commissioners of Highways—G. G. Bailey, Mason L. Shafer, Bester Brown. Constables—Abram T. Cook, Thomas H. Foster.

PLAINFIELD.

Plainfield lies north of Grand Rapids, east of Alpine, south of Algoma, and west of Cannon, and has a population of 1,499.

It was settled in 1837; and in 1838, when it was organized, comprised within its limits, several townships of land, that eventually organized into separate towns, under their respective names of Algoma, Courtland, Cannon, etc.

It was named for the many plains within its borders, that, swept clean by the annual Indian fires, presented their wild, but beautiful acres to the admiring gaze of the settlers. Its first township meeting to complete its organization, was held on the first Monday of April, 1838, at a rude log school house on section 23. There is no record of the number of votes cast; but at its last town meeting, the number of votes polled was 220.

FIRST TOWNSHIP OFFICERS.

Supervisor—Zenas G. Winsor. Clerk—Ethiel Whitney. Assessors—Daniel North, Andrew Watson, George Miller. Highway Commissioners—A. D. W. Stout, Warner Dexter. School Inspectors—Zenas G. Winsor, Ethiel Whitney, Cornelius Friant. Collectors—Damas Francisco, Henry Godwin. Poor Masters —Jacob Francisco, Jacob Friant. Justices of the Peace—Daniel North, Samuel Baker, Zenas G. Winsor, George Miller. Constables—James Francisco, Henry Godwin, Ezra Whitney.

OFFICERS IN 1870.

Supervisor—Hollis Konkle. Treasurer—James Crawford. Clerk—Edwin A. Morris. Justice of the Peace—George S. Curtis. School Inspectors—George H. Outhouse. Highway Commissioners—Joseph C. Upson. Constables—Caleb E. Carr, Gilbert Dickerson.

Plainfield presents many variations in soil and surface. High bluffs along Grand River, and the Rouge, present the beholder with many magnificent outlooks, over lowland, water course, hillside and plain, rarely excelled; and no more beautiful spot can well be found, than the little prairie set in hills, lying on the Grand Rapids and Ionia State Road, just north and east of the little village of Plainfield, where, for many years was the home of the Hon. Harry C. Smith, now a resident of Grand Rapids.

There is a troublesome amount of stone in some portions, and some sand along the western line; but, as a general thing, the soil is a rich clay loam, rendering this a first class agricultural town.

Its timber is mainly oak, with some beech and maple, and considerable pine along its western borders.

Its principal productions are, wheat, wool, corn, oats and potatoes, all of which it exports in fair quantities; but most of wheat, wool, and corn. Its rich intervals of grass lands, its numerous spring brooks, and clear and rapid watercourses, peculiarly adapt it to dairy purposes; but no especial attention is paid, as yet, to this healthful and lucrative branch of husbandry.

It also lies within the great western fruit belt, and where the altitude is favorable, gives splendid returns of apples, peaches, cherries, currants, and the small fruits generally; but in the bottom lands, and low situations, the returns are by no means sure, the frosts destroying the peaches, and the winters killing the trees. It presents many fine locations for vinyards, and the hardier varieties of grapes ripen nicely here; but nothing worthy of note is being done in this branch of horticulture.

There are several inconsiderable lakes in the town, but only two are worthy of note, namely: Scott's Lake, lying on section 17, about three-fourths of a mile long, and half a mile wide, quite deep, and well stocked with fish; and Crooked, or Dean's Lake, on sections 33 and 34, one mile long and half a mile wide. It has an Island of one acre, is generally shallow, and quite destitute of fish. These lakes are adjacent to no highway, hence are only visited by fishing parties, or hogs seeking aquatic sports. But for what it lacks in lake views, it makes ample amends in river scenery.

THE RIVERS.

Grand River, the Owash-te-nong of the redman, enters its borders by its eastern boundary, at the northeast corner of section 36, reaches the highest northern point at the exact center of section 23, where the bridge on the Grand Rapids and Ionia State Road, crosses its stream; then it sweeps away to the southwest—its banks adorned on either hand with billowy maples, and grand old elms, that have shed their leaves for centuries on its waves, leaving the town by its southern line, on the southeast quarter of section 31.

The Rouge River, so called from the peculiar tint of its waters, enters the town from the north, on the west half of section 1, and runs southwesterly, debouching in Grand River, on the line of sections 22 and 23.

The G. R. and I. R. R. entering the town on section 1, and leaving it near Plumb's mill, on section 31, crosses this stream six times within two miles, hence, as may readily be seen, it is very crooked in its course, and being very rapid, presents vast facilities for manufacturing purposes.

In 1840, Gideon H. Gorden erected on section 15, the first mill placed upon the stream. It is only a saw mill now, and owned by Mr. Watters, of Grand Rapids, but then it had a small grist mill attached, and there the settlers and Indians carried their corn to be ground.

In 1848, a saw mill was erected by Roberts and Winsor, on section 2, at a point then called Gibraltar. It is now owned by H. B. Childs & Co., who erected in its near vicinity, a paper mill in 1866, which was destroyed by fire in 1869, but rebuilt the second year by the enterprising proprietors. It is on the line of the G. R. and I. R. R. and the place is now known as Child's Mills Station.

In 1850, a saw mill was erected by Robert Konkle some forty rods from the mouth of the Rouge. It is now owned by Tradewell & Towle. Save the above, no use is made in this town of the immense water power of the stream, amply sufficient to drive a continuous chain of machinery, several miles in extent.

Mill Creek runs through the southwest corner of the town, and as early as 1838, a saw mill was erected on this stream on section 31, by Daniel North. It is now owned by Eli Plumb, who erected a flouring mill at the same place, in 1866. It lies on the line of the G. R. & I. Railroad, and is known as North's Mills Station. There is also a railway station at Belmont, about six miles northeast of Grand Rapids. It lies in the midst of a fine farming district, and has a large hotel, kept by Mr. Post, for the accommodation of parties of pleasure; otherwise, it possesses no particular advantages or attractions.

Plainfield village is a very small place, at the foot of the bluffs on section 23. It was the old ferrying post, when a ferryboat was the only means of communication —if we except the Indian canoe—between the two banks of the Grand River. It has a sunny site, and a pleasant outlook up and down the river.

Plainfield has ten district school-houses, but its Union school interests are merged at the present with Rockford, in Algoma, and the same may be said, in a measure, of its church interests. It has but one church edifice, which belongs to the Episcopalians. It is picturesquely situated on the bluff above the village of Plainfield, is a wooden structure 30x60 feet in size, is painted brown, and has a tower sixty feet high. It was erected in 1852. Its officiating clergyman was Rev. Mr. Van Antwerp, of Grand Rapids. It has no pastor at the present time.

Among the early settlers, we find, in 1837, George Miller, Esq., located on section 23; James Clark, on section 24; Thomas Friant, on section 24; and Warner Dexter, on section 14. In 1838, Cornelius Friant, on section 24; Zera Whitney, on section 15; Gideon H. Gordon, on section 15; and Daniel North, on section 31; and in 1844 Samuel Post settled on section 8, while his father, Jacob Post, and seven other sons, settled about the same time.

In 1835, Samuel Gross made his way with his family, by the aid of his axe, to a home on section 2; and in 1846 Chester Wilson settled on section 12.

The first family on the ground was Mr. George Miller, and the deprivations which fell to their share was the common lot of all who made their homes in this new land, at that early day. Grand River was the only thoroughfare and means of communication with the outside world, hence the settlers depended mainly on what they raised, and their own ingenuity, to prepare it for food. Pork, if imported, was $60 per barrel. The nearest flouring mill was sixty miles away, and the bread eaten in the family of Mr. Miller, for eighteen months, was ground in a coffee mill.

In the fall of 1838, the first birth occurred among the whites, in the family of Mr. Miller, a twin girl and boy, living but a short time, making the first deaths, also, among the settlers; and the greatest delicacy loving friends were able to offer Mrs. Miller during her confinement, was boiled wheat.

In the winter of 1838, the accidental shooting and subsequent death of Mr. Peleg Barlow, who had come to seek a home, but had not located, cast a saddening gloom over the little band of pioneers.

Although the lands were being surveyed and rapidly located, they were not in market, and it was no uncommon thing to see white men and Indians tilling their corn in the same fields, in amicable proximity to each other. But in the fall of 1839 the great land sale came off, when the settlers secured their claims, and the red man vanished from the scene, leaving naught *in memoriam* but the bones of his dead, on section 23, where the burial mounds, worn by the attritions of the plow, are fast being leveled with the surrounding country.

Of those who bore a conspicuous part in the settlement and organization of the town, Warner Dexter, James Clark, Thomas Friant, Daniel North and Gideon H. Gordon are dead; but by their tireless energy, they helped to open up a township possessed with natural resources of wealth, surpassed by none in the country. Smiling vineyards should terrace its sunny slopes, and teeming factories line the rapid flowing Rouge, for fabulous wealth lies hidden there, awaiting the fiat of combination and enterprise, surer to the seeker than in the golden gorges of the mountains that lean against our western skies.

SOLON.

This township lies in the north part of the county, between Algoma on the south and the township of Ensley, of Newaygo county, on the north; with Tyrone on the west, and Nelson on the east.

It was first settled in 1854. Some of the residents claim that a Mr. Beals, who is not now a resident of the township, was the first settler, and others that J. M. Rounds, who now resides in Algoma, was in advance. They were soon followed by John and Martin Hicks, from Indiana; also Robbins Hicks, from Ohio. In 1856 and 1857 the Jewells, Smiths, Roys and Whispels came, followed in 1858 by Ansel Rogers. J. D. Watkins, now a resident of Alpine, settled on section twenty-six in 1855.

ORGANIZATION.

This township was attached to Algoma (and called north Algoma) until 1857, when it was organized as a separate township, under the name of Solon. The first annual meeting was held at the house of Walter Rowe, one mile south of the center.

FIRST TOWNSHIP OFFICERS.

Supervisor—Edward Jewell. Clerk—John E. Roys. Treasurer—John D. Watkins. Justices—Andrew Fluent, Munson Robinson and Obadiah Smith.

For several years the annual township meetings were held at the school house of district No. 2. In 1865 the place of meeting was changed to Cedar Springs—where they are now held.

PRESENT TOWNSHIP OFFICERS.

Supervisor—Benj. Fairchild. Clerk—John Thetge. Treasurer—Wm. Johnson. Justices—John Thetge, C. B. Ford and J. D. Clark.

GENERAL DESCRIPTION.

The elevation of Solon is probably as great as any township in the county, it being nearly on the divide between Grand and Muskegon rivers. It is comparatively level, and, in the eastern part, somewhat swampy.

The timber is chiefly pine throughout the whole township, being interspersed with some grand old oaks in some parts, and in others with beech and occasionally a little maple.

The farms are generally new, with but small improvements. The farms of M. H. Clark, Jewell, and one or two others might be mentioned as exceptions to this. Fruit does well on this pine land wherever orchards have been set. The south-eastern part of the township is the most thickly settled, while nearly the whole of the northwest quarter is an unbroken forest.

LAKES, STREAMS, ETC.

In describing the lakes and streams of this township we will commence at the north.

First, then, there is a small lake on the north line of section four, lying partly in the township of Ensley, Newaygo county. This is sometimes called Lampman Lake. On the Kent county map, published in 1863, there was a large sized stream marked as the outlet of this lake, but we failed to find any such stream. It has no outlet. One and a half miles east of this, on the northwest corner of section two, is a large, flowing spring, known as Crandall's Spring. which is the source of the west branch of Duke Creek. The stream flows southeasterly through three lakes, known as the Chain of Lakes; the first being on the line of sections two and three, (chiefly on three); the next near the center of section two; and the third on the south line of two and partially on seven. This stream then flows a little east of south, to the north part of section twenty-four, where it unites with the east branch, which rises in Jordan Lake, on section one, flows out into Nelson, where it receives some additional water, and again enters Solon at the southeast corner of section twelve. At the junction of these two streams Wellman & Co. constructed a dam in 1856, at a cost of $1,000, with the intention of erecting a large saw mill, which, however, was never built. From this point Duke Creek flows in a southwesterly direction across the township. and passes out on section thirty, into Tyrone. It is fled by several small streams, the largest of which comes from a small lake near the center of section fourteen, (for which we heard no name), and flows into the main creek on the north side of section twenty-eight. This stream has been much used for running logs to the Rouge, and thence to Grand River.

There is a small lake on the north line of section fifteen, known as Mud Lake, which has no outlet.

The size of these seven lakes varies from ten to one hundred acres each.

Cedar Creek rises in Nelson, flows across the southeast corner of Solon, and southwest into Algoma, in the history of which it will be mentioned at greater length.

In the southwest corner are Long Lake, and some smaller ones, which will be farther spoken of in connection with the lakes in the northwestern part of Algoma.

THE VILLAGE OF CEDAR SPRINGS

was platted in 1859, and probably will be incorporated at the next session of the State Legislature.

It is situated twenty miles northeast from Grand Rapids, by the G. R. & I. Railroad, and lies about half in Solon and half in Nelson, one mile from their south line.

The first settler here was Robbins Hicks, who came in 1855, and was previously mentioned as one of the early residents of Solon. He now resides with his family in the northeast corner of the township.

There were but few inhabitants and but a very limited amount of business in Cedar Springs until 1867, when the railroad was completed to that point. This immediately infused life into the place, and it continued to grow rapidly as long as it was the terminus of the railroad north, which it was for nearly two years. Since that time, although it has not grown as rapidly, and business has not been quite as good in some respects, still it is steadily progressing, and new enterprises are being engaged in.

A line has been surveyed the present season, for a railroad from this place to Muskegon, in connection with a road projected from Greenville hither, which, in connection with the road now running from Lansing to Ionia, and the one being constructed from Ionia to Greenville, would make a continuous line from the lake shore to our state capital, directly through Cedar Springs.

We are informed by Mr. Fairchild, who, by the way, is wide awake on railroad matters in that vicinity, and in fact on matters of every kind connected with the growth and prosperity of the village, that the Continental Improvement Company contemplate building a branch railroad from this place to Newaygo. A state road passes through here from Grand Rapids to Big Rapids; also, one from here to Muskegon.

A Flour-Barrel, Stave and Heading Factory has been erected the present season, by Richards & Sharer, which seems to be doing a good business, cutting 20,000 staves and 10,000 headings per day, besides circling fitty to seventy-five barrels per day for their own use, in packing the heading which they ship.

The village contains six Steam Saw Mills, which cut in the aggregate 50,000 shingles and 50,000 feet of lumber per day. These mills have all been erected since 1866, and are severally owned and operated by the following gentlemen and firms: W. L. Barber & Co., Byron Prentiss & Co., Mr. Slawson and J. H. Shaw, all of this place; and Isaac Newton and Chauncey Pelton, of Grand Rapids.

It also contains about twenty stores, three or four restaurants, three hotels, kept respectively by Benj. Fairchild, J. S. Tisdell, and C. W. Denison, one livery stable, four blacksmith and several other shops, such as wheelright, cooper shops, etc.

The Baptist Society have a very good frame church, 36x60 feet in size, which was erected in 1868, at a cost of about $4,000.

The Methodist Episcopal Society are erecting a nice, frame structure, in size 40x70 feet, which is to be finished in good style, with stained glass windows, and a spire one hundred feet high. This will be the best church building north of Grand Rapids, and will cost from $5,000 to $6,000.

The Masonic Order have a nice little Hall, tastefully fitted up for their accommodation. There are also two or three halls for public meetings, the largest of which is a new one christened Union Hall, just completed by Paine & Manly. The Post-office is kept at present by Mr. H. C. Russell, in his drug store. A weekly newspaper, called the *Wolverine Clipper*, is published by Maze & Sellers.

The schools are on the graded system, and consist of three departments, which are kept in three buildings, for want of a good Union School House.

MILLS.

Outside of the village there are a number of mills, which cut a large amount of lumber and shingles.

We will first mention that of George French, of Rockford. This is a steam saw mill, capable of cutting 10,000,000 shingles and 2,000,000 feet of lumber per year, and stands on the southwest corner of section twelve. It was erected by Mr. French in 1868.

We next come to a first-class steam saw mill, on the north line of section one, which was erected in 1869, on the site of one built the year previous and destroyed by fire. Capacity of this mill, 20,000 feet of lumber and 16,000 shingles per day. Proprietor, John B. Wagner.

A small, Water-power Saw Mill is to be erected the present year, on the northeast corner of section twenty-eight, on Duke Creek, by Lewis S. Hancock. This is intended to be used as a lumber and shingle mill.

Andrew J. Fluent has a Portable Steam Shingle Mill, on the west side of section twenty-two, which cuts 15,000 shingles per day.

The Portable Steam Saw Mill, situated on the south side of section ten, is capable of cutting 10,000 feet of lumber and 15,000 shingles per day. The lumber mill is owned and operated by H. Morse & Co., and the shingle attachment by C. A. Tower & Co.

The Portable Steam Saw Mill of Willard Barnhart, set up in May, 1870, on the west side of section thirteen, is capable of cutting 10,000 feet of lumber per day.

Solomon Ipe's Portable Steam Shingle Mill, on the south side of section twenty-three, was erected by him in 1866, and cuts 14,000 shingles per day. It will be noticed that every mill now running in this township is run by steam, although good water power could be obtained on almost any section which now has a mill.

SCHOOL HOUSES.

District No. 1 was organized in 1858, and a small frame house erected, which was used until 1860, when a good frame building was erected at a cost of $600. It is located one and one-half miles west of Cedar Springs, on the north side of section thirty-five.

District No. 2--Solon Center—was organized in 1858, and a small log house erected. In 1869 a nice frame building was erected on the southeast corner of section sixteen, at a cost of $700.

This School House is really an ornament to the district, and, in fact, to the township, showing, as it does, that the people of Solon are wide awake, and understand the effect of good educational advantages on the growth and prosperity of a new country, and are willing to provide for the comfort of their children.

We mention this house more particularly because it stands in a much newer portion of the township than the one previously mentioned.

District No. 3 (fractional with Nelson) was organized in 1860, and a small log house was erected, which still stands on the west side of section thirteen, near the residence of A. B. Fairchild. This district is about to raise money for a new house, to be built on the same site, at a cost of $600 or $700.

District No. 4 (fractional with Algoma) was organized in 1869. In the spring of 1870, a nice little frame house was erected at a cost of $250, located on the southwest corner of section twenty-nine, four and one-half miles west of Cedar Springs, on the C. S. & M. State Road.

District No. 5 was orgrnized in 1866, and a small frame house erected the same year on the west side of section eleven, at a cost of $180.

There are many older townships which can erect large churches and other public buildings, but fail to do as well for their school interests as this "backwoods" township of Solon.

SPARTA.

This is one of the western tier of townships, adjoining Chester, Ottawa county, on the west, and Algoma on the east, and lying between Alpine on the south, and Tyrone on the north.

This township was first settled in 1844, when Lyman Smith—now residing at Grand Traverse—settled on section 25, near the southeast part. Very soon after, Norman and Edwin Cummings went on section 34, on the south line, and commenced chopping on the farm now owned by Norman. So far there was no house (worthy of the name) in the township—they only having small shanties.

In a short time, Lewis W. Purdy came from Genessee county, settled on the southwest corner of section 28, and erected the first log house in the now thickly settled township of Sparta. Mrs. Purdy was the first white woman in the township. In January, 1845, Joseph English and family came direct from England, and went just over the line on section 36, in the southeast part of the township.

Mr. English, although unable to read or write when he came to Sparta, being a man of great perseverance, succeeded, in the course of a few years, in erecting a large steam saw mill, which drew quite a number of men, who bought lots and erected small houses, thereby making a little village, which was called Englishville. This mill being destroyed by fire, Mr. English moved to Laphamville, now known as Rockford, which was then considered about dead.

By buying some of the mills and renting others, he succeeded in getting control of nearly all of the mills on Rouge River, from which he shipped a large quantity of lumber to Chicago; but owing to a decline in prices, he failed to make it pay, and was obliged to give up in that quarter, but not until he had—by his great energy and venturesome spirit—infused new life into the whole lumbering district of Rouge River.

He afterwards, with his sons, erected a water mill on the north part of his farm, which is now run by his sons, William, Joseph and Richard. The post office still known as Englishville, is about all that remains to remind us of the once flourishing little Ville, which will probably again revive, if the Grand Rapids and Newaygo Railroad, which has been surveyed, is constructed, and a station established there.

In the spring of 1845, Mr. Cummings—the father of Norman, Edwin and Nelson Cummings—came with his family to the place where the sons had previously began.

The parents are long since dead, but the three sons still remain on the south line, one in Sparta and the others in Alpine, where they have large farms with good buildings, as the fruits of their early labors in pioneer days.

Mr. Lyman Smith and Mr. Purdy did not long remain residents of Sparta, but the marks made by them still remain.

In June, 1845, John Symes, Elihu Rice, and Anthony Chapman, met in Alpine, while on their way to settle in Sparta. They were strangers, but soon found, by comparing descriptions, that the lands which they had respectively bought or pre-empted, all lay adjoining, and, going on the principle that "in union is strength," they, after some consultation, decided on the course they would take; and the next morning Rice and Symes started from the house of Joseph English to underbrush a road from there west, along the present town-line of Alpine and Sparta. Meanwhile Chapman had returned to Mill Creek for provisions. After cutting west to the section corner, now known as Rouse's Corners, they turned north, and followed the line between sections 34 and 35. Toward night they were beginning to think of returning to the house of Mr. English, but at that moment they heard a wagon approaching, and on waiting for it to come up, found it was Chapman, who had come with supplies. They now built a fire by the side of a log, and camped for the night, with the wolves howling around them while they slept; and in the morning completed their road to what was to be their homes.

Mr. Rice's land was on section 27, and Mr. Symes' and Mr. Chapman's on 26. Three trees were found on the line of Symes' and Chapman's land which would do for three corner posts of a shanty; and by putting in one post, and the use of a few boards which had been brought along from Mill Creek, a shelter was soon formed, to which the families were taken the next day, where they lived together until houses were erected. About this time David B. Martindale, who now lives just east of Sparta village, settled on section 36.

During the following fall and winter, Hiram H. Meyers settled east of Rouge River, on section 24, and was soon followed by his father and family from Canada. This family took a large tract of land in the east part of Sparta, where they have engaged quite extensively in lumbering, especially Hiram, John and Myron Balcom near the centre of the township, and William Blackall and family southwest of the center. Myron Balcom is now in Missouri, and John, commonly known as Deacon Balcom, is now living in the village of Sparta. William Blackall has long been laid beneath the sod; but his sons, Benjamin and Charles, still remain.

We neglected to mention Mr. Clark Brown, who came from the state of New York, early in 1845, and is still living on the farm where he first commenced, on the south line of section 33.

In 1846, J. E. Nash, from Massachusetts, settled where he now lives, one mile east of the center of the township.

Among other early settlers who were pioneers in various parts of the township, were the Spangenburgs, Amidons, Bradfords, Hinmans, McNitts, Taylors, Stebbins', R. D. Hastings, and Ira Blanchard, most of whom still reside in Sparta. Hon. Lyman Murray settled in Sparta at an early day, but soon removed to Alpine.

ORGANIZATION.

Sparta was organized very soon after it was settled. The first annual meeting was held in April, 1846, at the house of Clark Brown, on the south line of the township, at which time there were only eleven votes cast. As the full ticket requires sixteen officers, there could not have been much opportunity for a choice.

The present township of Tyrone was attached to Sparta from the time it began to be settled, until 1855.

FIRST TOWNSHIP OFFICERS.

Supervisor—Lewis W. Purdy. Clerk—John M. Balcom. Treasurer—Myron H. Balcom.

At a subsequent annual election, John M. Balcom was elected to the office of Constable by one vote.

The township meetings are now held at the school-house in the village of Sparta.

OFFICERS IN 1870.

Supervisor—Volney W. Caukin. Clerk—Ervin J. Emmons. Treasurer—Charles C. Eddy. Justices—A. B. Cheney, Volney W. Caukin, Albert Finch.

GENERAL DESCRIPTION.

The general surface of Sparta is high and rolling, and it contains but little waste land.

There are several small swamps in various parts of the township, but none of much account, except in the north and northwest parts.

On sections 2 and 3 is a swamp of some extent, requiring the services of the Drain Commissioners. Also a series nearly or quite connected, extending west across sections 4 or 5, and passing off into the south part of Tyrone. There are two quite extensive swamps which commence on the west part of section 6, and run west into Chester. Between them is the ridge, well known to those accustomed to travel the G. R. & Newaygo State Road, as the Hog-back Hill. The highest hills and deepest valleys are in the northwest; still it contains some as nice farming lands as are to be found in the township.

The timber is mostly beech and sugar-maple, with some pine in the northeast and southeast parts. There is some hemlock interspersed with the pine in the northeast. The soil is generally a rich loam, suited to the production of wheat, corn, oats, grass, potatoes, etc. Nearly all kinds of fruit which can be raised in the county, do well here.

Among the large farms of Sparta, we would mention that of Mrs. John Manly, in the southwest part of the township, which contains 280 acres, and that of Elias Darling, farther north on the same road, containing 320 acres. The large farm of Moses Bradford is now divided between his sons, Jason and Perry. The farm formerly owned by Nathan Earl, is now owned by his son-in-law, Charles M. Chapman. Norman Cummings has 240 acres on the south township line, which is, however, in two separate parcels.

STREAMS.

Rouge River is the principal stream of Sparta, entering it on section 1, from Tyrone, and passing south and southeast through the east tier of sections; thence out into Algoma, from the east part of section 25. It is used for running logs, having been cleared for that purpose nearly twenty years ago, through this township.

Ball Creek, which has also been considerably used for logging, enters Sparta from Tyrone, near the central part of the line, and flows in a southeasterly direction across sections 3, 2 and 11, into Rouge River, of which it is the principal branch from this township.

Nash Creek, formed by several small branches from the west, flows through the central part, and empties into Rouge River on the southeast corner of section fourteen.

Symes Creek rises in the southern part of the township, and flows northeasterly into Rouge River, on the southwest corner of section twenty-four.

A small stream, sometimes known as the River Jordan, comes in from Alpine, and flows in a northerly direction across sections twenty-five and twenty-six, and empties into Rouge River near the center of the latter section.

Two small streams empty into Rouge River from the northeast, on section one, being the outlets of a chain of lakes in the west part of Algoma. These streams have also been used for running logs.

VILLAGES.

The village of Sparta, not yet incorporated, is a flourishing little town of about 200 inhabitants, located on Nash Creek, one mile east of the geographical center of the township, and 15 miles from Grand Rapids. This place was first settled by J. E. Nash, in 1846, and for some time known as Nashville. It now contains a Post-office, known as Sparta Center, two churches—Baptist and Methodist Episcopal—both of which were erected in 1866, at a cost of about $3,000 each, a good steam saw mill, five stores, two blacksmith shops, and one wagon shop; also a very good hotel, known as the Sparta House, and kept by John M. Balcom. But as yet no graded school building has been erected, although it is greatly needed. A small, frame, district school house, erected in 1849, is the only public school building in the place. A good select school is kept during the winter months by Mr. Amherst Cheney. The steam saw mill already mentioned, is now owned and operated by Wm. Olmsted and Sons. It has a planing machine attached; also one run of stone for grinding flour and feed.

LISBON VILLAGE,

on the west line of Sparta, is sixteen miles from Grand Rapids, on the Grand Rapids and Newaygo State Road. It was first settled by John Pintler, who came here from the State of New York, in 1846. In 1848 a Mail Route was established from Grand Rapids to Newaygo, with a Post-office at this point, under the name of Pintler's Corners, Mr. Pintler being the first Postmaster. In 1859 the name of the office was changed to Lisbon. The first goods sold from a store in this place were by Miner Atherton, in 1855. In March, 1869, it was regularly incorporated as a village, including half a mile each way from the northwest corner post of section 30. It will be noticed that this includes half a section—or, more properly, two quarter sections—from the township of Chester, Ottawa county; but, as the village is under the jurisdiction of Kent county, we will include the whole in our History and Directory.

This village now contains nine stores, three blacksmith shops, two wagon shops, one hotel, a good, two-story frame school house, and three good sized frame churches; also a good steam grist mill, and a saw mill.

The Hotel is a good, frame building, owned and kept by Lorenzo Chubb.

The Graded School building, erected in the summer of 1869, is a good, substantial frame structure, two stories high, 36x46 feet in size, and cost $2,700.

SPENCER.

The township of Spencer is situated in the norteast corner of the county, and is bounded on the north by the township of Maple Valley, Montcalm county, on the east by Montcalm, Montcalm county, on the south by Oakfield, and on the west by Nelson.

The first white inhabitant of Spencer was an old trapper, by the name of Lincoln. He had a shanty on the bank of the lake of that name, and there he lived, Boon like, for a number of years.

The first regular settler of the township was Cyrus B. Thomas, who located in the summer of 1846. Henry Stroup, the second settler, located in January, 1848. Both of these settled on a plain in the southeastern part of the township, near the Oakfield line; and, for a number of years, were the only actual settlers. Matthew B. Hatch, the present Supervisor of Spencer, and one of the earliest settlers, came to the township in 1853. In the list of early settlers may also be mentioned the names of S. B. Cowles, B. G. Parks, Jacob Van Zandt, Wm. H. Hewitt, Wm. T. Parshall, Daniel Haskins, the Cooper family, and others.

The township of Celsus was organized in the year 1861, and the first township meeting was held on the first Monday of April, in the same year, at the residence of Thomas Spencer. Matthew B. Hatch, Thomas Spencer, and Shepard B. Cowles, acted as inspectors of election. The election resulted in the choice of the following named persons as

FIRST TOWNSHIP OFFICERS.

Supervisor—Freeman Van Wickle. Clerk—Henry A. Freeman. Treasurer—Daniel Haskins. Commissioners of Highways—Wm. W. Hewitt and Freeman Van Wickle. Justices—Wm. W. Hewitt, Edwin D. Clark. School Inspectors—Hiram Conse and Alfred Hulburt. Constables—Wm. H. Smith, Geo. McClelland, Henry Strope, and Darius Gray.

The name of the township was subsequently changed to Spencer, in honor of Thomas Spencer, one of the early settlers.

PRESENT OFFICERS.

Supervisor—Matthew B. Hatch. Clerk—Aaron Norton. Treasurer—Beriah G. Parks. Justices—Warren F. Getman, Samuel Van Wickle, Avery J. Sutton, Edward H. Smith. Commissioners of Highways—Edwin Wilson, John Moran. School Inspectors—Wm. B. Powell, Shepard B. Cowles. Constable—Joseph DeGraw.

THE SOIL

of Spencer is, as might be supposed, rather poor, the timber being principally pine. There are, however, some pieces of good land, which it pays to cultivate. There are some fine farms within its limits, among which are those owned by M. B. Hatch, Owen D. Cooper, Beriah G. Parks, Edward H. Smith, Fayette Hough, and Wm. Rittinger.

Spencer is inconveniently located, having no railroad within its limits, and no railroad station within a number of miles; nevertheless, it is fast settling up, and everything indicates that a few years will greatly increase its population and wealth. The first

LUMBERING

establishment, on Black Creek, was commenced in 1853. During the year 1870, one million feet were run out of that stream. The Van Wickle saw mill is located on the same creek, near the south line of section twenty-five. It was built in the year 1856: H. Van Wickle, proprietor. The Powell steam saw and shingle mill, combined, is situated on the bank of Lincoln Lake, on section twenty-seven. It was built in 1867: Wm. B. Powell, proprietor. The Parks steam saw mill, near the center of section seven, was built in 1868: E. H. Gibbs, proprietor. The Griswold steam saw and shingle mill, combined, is located near the southwest corner of section twenty-nine. It was built in the year 1868: Jabes W. Griswold, proprietor. The Spencer Mills, from which the Post-office and settlement derived its name, was built in 1855, by Thomas Spencer, near the southeast corner of section twenty-seven. It was burned in the year 1861.

BLACK CREEK

is the principal stream that flows through Spencer. It enters from the northwest, and passes southeasterly through the township. It is of sufficient width and depth to float logs, and a number of millions of feet are run out every year. It has several small tributaries, among which are Clear and Butternut Creeks.

Among the

LAKES

in this township, Lincoln is the largest. It is a fine sheet of water, situated a short distance east of the center of the township, and is nearly one and one-half miles in length, by one-half mile in width. Cooper Lake, in the easterly part of section thirty-five, is a narrow strip of water, surrounded by a marsh. There is a lake in the southwesterly part of section thirty-four, composed of two distinct sections, connected by a narrow neck. Conjointly they are about one-half mile in length. North of Lincoln Lake is an assemblage of small lakes, extending through the township into Maple Valley, in Montcalm county.

Our list shows but three

SCHOOLS

in Spencer. The first is held at the Griswold School House, in fractional district No 1. The building is a fine, wooden structure, painted white, and stands near the southwest corner of section twenty-nine. It was built in 1869. The second is held at the Hatch School House, in district No. 3. This is a substantial wooden building, is located at the center of section seventeen, and was built in 1867. The third is held at the Mill School House, in regular district No. 1. The building is a fine, slate-colored wooden structure. It was erected in 1861.

The only

POST-OFFICE

in Spencer is in the southeast corner of section twenty-seven. Oliver P. McClure, Postmaster.

TYRONE.

This is the northwest corner township of Kent county, lying north of Sparta, and west of Solon; and being bounded on the north by Grant township, Newaygo county, and on the west by Casnovia, Muskegon county.

Tyrone was first settled in 1849, by Mrs. Louisa Scott and family, who went in to board workmen on the State Road then being made on the west line of this township, by John Brooks, of Newaygo, who had the contract from the State. The family were deprived of the father, by insanity, a short time after going into the woods; but, owing to the great perseverence of Mrs. Scott, they remained, and have succeeded in building up a good home, and making a fine farm on section thirty-one, in the southwest part of the township. In 1850 Lot Ferguson, from Hillsdale county, went about one mile farther and settled on the southwest part of section nineteen, where the Casnovia House now stands. Alfred Bonner settled on section thirty, but remained only a short time.

In 1852 Jacob Smith, from Cleveland, Ohio, and Harlow Jackson, from Branch county, Mich., settled one mile east from the state road, and a mile north from the township line, on the present state road from Cedar Springs to Muskegon. There was not a white settler east of them nearer than Greenville.

In 1853 John Thompson came into the same neighborhood, from Tioga county, New York, and about the same time, Joseph Kies came from Hillsdale county, Mich., and settled near Mr. Fulkerson.

In 1855 Uriah Chubb, who had been living for a few years in Chester township, Ottawa county, settled on the west part of section thirty, and Leander Smith, from Otsego county, New York, went into the Jackson neighborhood.

About this time Asa Clark and family, from Steuben county, New York, penetrated the forest northeast from Sparta Center, or Nashville, as it was then called, and built their cabin on section thirty-six, in the southeast part of the township. Here they had no neighbors, except those who came for a few months at a time to cut pine logs along the river; and during the war they were the only regular settlers in the east part of the township.

James Blackall, from Sparta, also went on section thirty-two in 1855. From that time to the commencement of the war there were many additions, and since the war its population has increased very fast.

ORGANIZATION.

This township was for some time attached to Sparta.

In 1855 it was organized as a seperate township, under the name of Tyrone, the first annual meeting being being held at the only school house, which stood on the west line, near the residence of Mrs. Scott. The township meetings are still held in the same school district, the house now used being about a mile north of where the old one stood.

FIRST TOWNSHIP OFFICERS.

Supervisor—Uriah Chubb. Clerk—Albert Clute. Treasurer—Harlow Jackson. Justices—Patrick Thompson, Albert Clute, and Uriah Chubb.

PRESENT TOWNSHIP OFFICERS.

Supervisor—James M. Armstrong. Clerk—Harlow Jackson. Treasurer—B. S. Treadway. Justices—J. M. Armstrong, U. Chubb, L. V. Hoag, and David Clark.

GENERAL DESCRIPTION.

About three-fourths of this township is timbered with pine, which extends along the Rouge River in the east, and across the north part in connection with the great Muskegon belt. The southwest portion is timbered with beech and maple, interspersed with some pine throughout nearly the whole extent—there being but two sections (thirty and thirty-one) which had none. The pine timbered portions here, as elsewhere, are principally sandy, while the beeech and maple timbered part is mostly clay soil, or rather a clay loam, which makes excellent farming land. This township is high and rolling, and is a good fruit region.

There are no very large improvements yet; those of Messrs. Smith, Jackson and Hemsley, one mile from the south line, and about the same distance from the west line, are probably the largest. Mr. Daniel Hanson, and others, a mile north, are making a good start, and, juding from present appearances, will soon have splendid farms. The same may also be said of H. C. Wylie, and others, east of those first mentioned. On the west line the land is divided into smaller parcels, with one or two exceptions. Mr. Edward Hayward has a nice, large farm lying partly in this township and partly in Casnovia.

STREAMS AND LAKES.

Rouge River is the principal stream of Tyrone. It rises in Rice Lake, in the township of Grant, Newaygo county, about three miles north of the township line, enters Tyrone about one ond one-half miles west from the northeast corner, flows a little east of south, and then flows out near the southeast corner into Sparta. It is fed by several small streams, among which Duke Creek, which flows through Solon and comes in from the northeast on section thirty-six, is the largest. Ball Creek rises in several small streams in the west part of the township, flows southeast, and passes out into Sparta near the middle of the township line.

A curiosity may be found on this stream, on the farm of H. C. Wylie on section thirty-three, which is worthy a description.

It is no more nor less than an old Beaver Dam. This dam was about sixty rods long and rose to a hight of three, four, and even five feet in some places. It was built in a zig-zag form, the sections being uniformly about two rods in length. It must have been built a long time ago, for large trees are found growing on the embankment. Where the pond was, the timber has been killed by the flowing, leaving nothing but a marsh. This pond had apparently covered from ten to fifteen acres, and perhaps more. The remains of trees, cut down by those curious and wonderful animals, have been found there, showing plainly the prints of their teeth in the wood. The stream has broken through in three places. The river, and these creeks, have been much used for floating pine logs.

South Crockery Creek, in the southwest part of the township, rises in Sparta, flows northwest through two small lakes, on section thirty-two, thence across thirty-one and out into Muskegon county, on the west.

There is a lake of about twenty acres on the line of sections seventeen and eighteen, the outlet of which flows southeast across the township into Rouge River. Another, nearly as large, near the center of section twenty-two, also has a small stream flowing from it to Rouge River.

There is considerable wet, swampy land, in the northeast part of the township, and a few small swamps in various other parts; but none ot any great extent.

CASNOVIA CORNERS

(not incorporated) is nearly as much ot a village as some which have been platted and incorporated many years. It was first settled by Lot Fulkerson (before mentioned) in 1850. Mr. Fulkerson was the first to open his doors for the accommodation of travelers, and soon put out his sign, and kept a regular country tavern. In a short time his little one-story log cabin became too small for the accommodation of his guests, and he therefore erected a good frame building for that purpose, which was afterwards kept by Mr. Mizner, and later by Mr. Heath, who erected a large hall adjoining. These buildings are now owned and kept by Mr. John Tuxbury, formerly of Alpine.

In 1853, a post office was established, with Daniel Bennett, who lived just over the line, as postmaster. The first store goods were sold by H. Hamilton, in May, 1862.

There are now four stores, a blacksmith shop, etc.; also, a steam saw mill, which was erected in 1864, now owned by Patterson Brothers. They are doing a good, fair business, and have pine enough within reach to run the mill twenty years.

Asher and Robert Post have a portable steam saw mill three miles north of here; also one on the west line of the township.

SCHOOL HOUSES.

District No. 1, (fractional with Casnovia) was organized in 1853 with nine scholars in attendance at school. A small log house was erected and used until 1861, when the present frame building was erected at a cost ot about $500. The former stood on section 31, and the latter stands on the west side of section 30, near the residence of Mr. Chubb.

District No. 2, (fractional with Sparta), erected a frame house worth about $400, in 1863. This house stands on the northwest corner of section 36, and is commonly known as the Clark school house.

District No. 3, (fractional with Casnovia), erected a small frame house in 1864, on the southwest corner of section 6, known as the Murray school house.

District No. 4, was organized in 1861, and a nice frame house was built, worth $500, the following year. It stands on the southeast corner of section twenty-nine, and is known as the Leander Smith school house.

District No. 5, was organized in 1868, and a good frame house erected at a cost of $500, known as the Ross' school house. It stands on the northeast corner of section nineteen.

District No. 6 was organized in January, 1870. It has four scholars in summer, and about twenty in winter—being in the midst of a pine country, which brings in the people in winter, and drives them out in summer. This district has no school house yet, school being held in the house of Mr. L. R. Burch. It has been chiefly sustained by Mr. B. thus far, at a cost of $50 per term.

District No. 7, was organized in 1870. A house is to be erected on section twenty-two or twenty-seven at a cost of about $500.

Tyrone has no churches, and only one hotel, besides the one mentioned, situated at the Corners, in the village of Casnovia.

This other hotel is generally known as the Block Tavern, being made of hewn logs, and stands on the Cedar Springs and Muskegon state road. It is now kept by Allen Cumings. Mr. L. V. Hoag, and others, are quite sanguine of getting a Post-office established here soon, and building up a village. This is nearly twenty miles from Grand Rapids, and Casnovia is about twenty-two miles from the same. The Cedar Springs and Muskegon state road crosses this township on the section line, one mile from the Sparta line. The surveyed route of the C. S. & M. R. R. runs nearly parallel to the state road, and very near it. The surveyed line of the G. R. and Newaygo R. R. also crosses this township, and strikes Casnovia Corners.

VERGENNES.

Vergennes is bounded on the north by Grattan, on the east by Keene, Ionia county, on the south by Lowell, and on the west by Ada.

Sylvester Hodges, the first white settler in the township, came from the State of New York, in the year 1836. He transplanted the first apple trees put out in the township of Lowell, also assisted in building the first house where the village of Lowell now stands. The trees referred to, may now be seen standing on a lot owned by Mrs. Caroline Snell, near the bank of Flat River, a short distance from the road leading from the village to the D. & M. Railroad depot.

The township of Vergennes was organized in the year 1838. The first township meeting was held on the second day of April, of the same year, when the following persons were chosen as

FIRST TOWNSHIP OFFICERS.

Supervisor—Rodney Robinson. Clerk—M. Patrick. Assessors—Lewis Robinson, T. I. Daniels, John M. Fox. Collector—Porter Ralph. School Inspectors—Everett Wilson, Lewis Robinson, George Brown. Directors of the Poor—Everett Wilson, Chas. Newton. Commissioners of Highways—Lucas Robinson, Henry Daines, P. W. Fox. Constables—Porter Ralph, A. D. Smith, O. H. Jones, Jas. S. Fox.

We are informed by Benj. Fairchild, Esq., that at this time there were only about nineteen families in the township. This gentleman, who went there during the year 1838, says that, as he passed through the township of Lowell, on his way from Canada, he counted but three houses. For several years the farmers in that vicinity were obliged to take their grist to Ionia, to Grandville, or to Kalamazoo to be ground. Considering the poor roads which the scattered community were then tormented with, and the bridgeless streams which must be crossed, such journeys doubtless seemed quite uninviting.

Reader, have you ever traveled through a new country? If you have, you can understand the meaning of the expression, "poor roads," "horrid roads." You who have not, I would advise to take a trip into the northern part of the State of Michigan immediately after a heavy rain. A trip of that kind will benefit your health as much as a voyage on the lakes, during rough weather.

The entire county was then a howling wilderness. Grand Rapids could boast of but half a score of houses, with most of them owned by one man; and two stores, one kept by "Uucle Louis," and the other by a man named Watson.

Among the early settlers may be mentioned the following: Silas S. Fallass, who settled in the year 1838, J. Wesley Fallass, in 1839, Lucas Robinson, in 1837, Thompson I. Daniels, in 1837, James Wells, in 1842, A. R. Hoag, in 1842, Sylvester Hodges, in 1836, James S. Fox, 1836, William P. Perrin, in 1837, Alexander Rogers, in 1837, Alanson K. Shaw, in 1839, Emery Foster, in 1837, Newcomb Godfrey, in 1838, Amos Hodges, in 1838, Eliab Walker, in 1838, Christopher Misner, in 1838, Morgan Lyon, in 1838, Benjamin Fairchild, in 1838, John Branagan, in 1837, Alfred Van Deusen, in 1838, Adam Van Deusen. in 1840.

THE SOIL

of Vergennes is mostly heavy; yet along the banks of Flat River we found some quite light and sandy. The greater portion of the township consists of what might be called oak openings. We noticed a belt of timbered land extending south from Eagle or Horse Shoe Lake, one and one-half miles wide, and four miles in length, reaching into sections twenty and twenty-one; also a short strip of timbered land on the west side of the same lake.

The township is well watered by Flat River, and numerous little tributaries, through the easterly and central part, and Honey Creek, which passes through three sections on the westerly tier.

THE PRESENT OFFICERS

of the township are: Supervisor—J. W. Walker. Clerk—John L. Covert. Treasurer—James Casey. Justices—Joseph S. Jasper, J. L. B. Kerr, Dennis Driscoll, John L. Covert. Constable—John Hull.

The site now occupied by

THE VILLAGE OF FALLASSBURG

was settled upon about the year 1840, by the family or families from which it derived its name.

The two mills and the hotel therein situate were erected before the present thriving village of Lowell had commenced to be built up. Fallassburg Grist Mill, situated on Flat River—a three-story wooden building—was erected in 1840: Proprietor, J. Wesley Tallass. Hecox's Saw Mill, situated here, is an old, wood colored, three-story building. The upper part is occupied as a chair manufactory. It was erected in 1839: Proprietor, Charles Hecox.

Fallassburg supports one store, which has been in operation for many years; and the building was erected before any similar structure in the village of Lowell. The village school house, located in the easterly part of the burgh, is a fine wooden structure, painted white. It was built in the summer of 1867.

FLAT RIVER

passes into Vergennes from the east, three-quarters of a mile south of the northeasterly corner of the township, when it curves and passes back into Ionia county, at a point about three-quarters of a mile south of the place of entrance. It re-enters on section thirteen, and, meandering southwesterly, passes out near the quarter post, on the south line of section thirty-five. It forms a junction with the Grand at the village of Lowell.

THE LAKES

in Vergennes are nearly all small. Eagle, or Nagle, or Horse Shoe Lake, projects a short distance into the town. Eagle was once the most familiar name. It was thus christened, after a bird of that species, which built its nest in a large oak, on an island or peninsula in the lake. From its resemblance to a horse shoe it sometimes passes by that name. It has an outlet called Lake Creek, which is a tributary of Flat River.

Odell Lake is situated near the center of section twenty-nine. It is fifty rods in width, and has an average depth of thirteen feet. The lake and surrounding swamp cover about eighty acres.

Cole's Lake, situate on the east half of section thirty, is a shallow sheet of water, covering about ten acres. Miller's Lake, situate on the west half of section twenty-nine, is quite deep, and covers four or five acres.

Long Lake, situate on section nineteen, is a fine body of water, about three quarters of a mile in length, with an average width of thirty rods. It is frequented by pleasure-seekers in both summer and winter.

Vergennes has good educational facilities. Its

SCHOOLS

are well organized, and are supplied with competent teachers. The school buildings are generally good, though not costly, and present a tidy appearance.

The Valley School house, situate on the south part of section twelve, is a plain, wooden structure. It was once white, but the elements have produced their usual effects upon it, until now it presents a wood-colored appearance.

Bailey School house, situate on the northeast corner of the northwest quarter of section twenty-nine, is a plain, white, wooden structure. It was built in 1855.

The school house at Fox's Corners is a beautiful, new, wooden building, is situate on an eminence at the southeast part of section twenty-seven, and was built in 1870. The McPherson school house is situated on the northeast corner of the southeast quarter of section eighteen. It is a white wooden building, built in 1861.

The Aldrich school house, situate at the center of section nine, is constructed of logs, is quite old, and, to all appearance, is becoming unsafe. The people of the district intend to build a new one ere long.

The Kelsey school house, situate on the northeast corner of section thirty-two, was erected in 1852. It is a red wooden building.

Barto school house, situate on the northeast corner of section two, is a plain, white, wooden structure. It was built in the year 1856. The Godfrey school house, situate on the south half of the southeast quarter of section two, is an old red wooden building. It was built about twenty-five years ago.

The Water's school house, situated on the northwest corner of section twenty-three, is a neat wooden structure, painted white. It was built in 1868.

There are two

CHURCHES

in Vergennes, outside the village of Fallassburg. The First Methodist Episcopal church is situated on the southwest corner of section twenty, within a short distance of Long Lake. It is a substantial wooden building, painted white, and has a capacity to seat three or four hundred persons. The present pastor of the congregation who worships there, is the Rev. Charles Chick. The First Christian Church of Vergennes, situated at the southwest corner of section two, was built in 1868, and is a substantial wooden structure, painted white. The Wesleyan Methodists in this vicinity also hold their meetings in the same building.

There are two grist

MILLS

and one saw mill in Vergennes, outside the village of Fallassburg. The Foster grist mill is situated on Flat River, on section twenty-six. It is a three-story wooden structure, painted white. Proprietors, T. W. Fox & Co.

Alton grist mill is situate on the northeast corner of section ten, on Wood's Creek. It is a two-story wooden building, used exclusively for mill purposes: Proprietor, Thomas B. Woodbury.

Ring's Saw Mill and Wagon Shop, are situated on the northwest corner of section ten, on Wood's Creek. The mill contains one upright saw. Proprietor, Edmund Ring.

There are

BLACKSMITH SHOPS

at the following places: Northwest corner of section twenty-nine; northwest corner of the southwest quarter of section fifteen, (Lewis Smith, proprietor); and northwest corner of section thirty-four.

WALKER.

Walker is in the western tier of townships, being bounded on the north by Alpine, on the east by Grand Rapids township and city, on the south by Wyoming, and on the west by Talmadge, Ottawa county. It was originally six miles square; but, owing to the course of Grand River, which has become the established eastern and southern boundary, it is now quite irregular. The corporation of the city also takes five and one-fourth sections out of the southeasterly part.

The division line between the township of Grand Rapids and Walker, was formerly what is now Division street, in the city; therefore, a list of the early settlers of Walker would include those who located west of that line. However, as the history of the city will be made a special theme, in this we will refer to that part only which lies within what are now the bounds of Walker.

In the year 1836 Samuel White, then a man fifty years of age, came with his family from Canada, and settled on section twenty-three. He had five sons and several daughters, one or two of whom were married. The family purchased of the Government about six hundred acres of land on sections ten, fourteen, fifteen and twenty-three. Mr. White built the first frame barn west of Grand River; and soon after this, with the assistance of his sons, Milo and James, erected a saw mill on Indian Creek, on the north side of section fifteen. Mr. and Mrs. White are still living on the old homestead, and can now count a family of over sixty children, grand children, and great grand children, notwithstanding the loss of one son in the Mexican War, and one in the recent War for the Union.

Later in the year 1836, Jesse Smith, who was also from Canada, settled on Bridge street, about two miles west of the river. He had a large family of sons and daughters, some of whom were married, and who settled in different parts of the township. One of the elder sons, Benjamin, commenced at an early day on the south side of section ten, where he built a small grist mill and machine shop on Indian Creek. The parents are now deceased, and the family scattered.

During the same year, a Frenchman, by the name of John J. Nardin, who had served in the French army under Napoleon the First, came from Detroit, with a large family, and settled in the southern part of the township, west of where the Eagle Plaster Mills now stand. The parents are still living on the old farm, while near them reside two sons, John and George, and two daughters, Mrs. Roger Atkinson and Mrs. James Sawyer. Late in the same year Zelotis Bemis and Robert Hilton went still further south, and located on the north bank of the river, two or three miles below the plaster mills. A portion of the Bemis farm, now owned by John N. Butterfield, was formerly an "Indian Planting Ground." Soon after he settled, Mr. Bemis commenced raising wheat quite extensively, the harvestlng of which furnished employment for some of those that came a year or two later.

The following named persons settled in the township soon after those just mentioned: Henry Helmka, Wm. W. Anderson, Joseph Denton, John Hogadone, and Harvey Monroe, from Canada; John Harrington, of Vermont, and Patrick O'Brien, Stephen O'Brien and James Murray, from Ireland. The family of Edisons also came at an early day, and settled on what is now Bridge street, of which family John Edison is now the only representative on that street.

There are many others who could hardly be classed as first settlers, but who are known as old residents; among whom are Thomas McMan, David Waters, Wm. C. Davidson, Jonathan Blair, Martin Wheeler, Bernard Courtney, and Quigley, in the south part; Samuel Westlake, the Schermerhorns, Phillips, Escotts, Burds, Samuel Corporon, Thomas Cotney, Asa Pratt, Thales Dean, Daniel Stocking, and the Armstrongs, near the central part; the Matthews, A. C. Bailey, Samuel Root, Miner Johnson, John Miller, Peter Huwer, Andrew Loomis, Tenny, the Chappells, Fullers, Tabors, Covell, and Dean in the north; and Palmerlee, Tryon, Berry Wait, Devendorf, and Lamoreaux, in the west.

ORGANIZATION.

The first township meeting was held in the month of April, 1838, at the Mission School House, which stood on the west bank of Grand River, near the present jail site. The records indicate that this was the only school house then in the township, for it was spoken of as "the School House of Walker."

THE FIRST OFFICERS

of the township were: Supervisor—Lovell Moore. Clerk—Isaac Turner. Treasurer—Harry Eaton. Justices—Robert Hilton, Isaac Turner, Ira Jones and Isaiah Burton.

About three years after the organization of the township, a log school house was erected on the north side of section twenty-two, and the township meetings were, for a time, held there. Alpine was detached from Walker in the year 1847; for a year or two previous to which time the meetings were held at the Simond's School House, and afterwards at the center. In the year 1867 a nice brick building, in size 26x36 feet, was erected on the north side of section twenty-two, for a Town Hall.

THE PRESENT OFFICERS

of the township are: Supervisor—Ezra A. Hebard. Clerk—Henry O. Sehermerhorn. Treasurer—George Weaver. Justices—Thomas Healey, Nathan Earle, Bernard Courtney, and Daniel Schermerhorn.

GENERAL DESCRIPTION.

The soil ot Walker is strangely diversified. On the east and south, along Grand River, is a tract of low land, from eighty rods to a mile in width, extending from the northeast to the southwest corner of the township, which is underlaid with a strata of lime stone, lying from two to ten feet below the surface. Above this is a gravelly loam, which, in some parts, is filled and covered with large boulders. Back of this is a series of hills and sandy bluffs, rising to a height of fifty or sixty feet. The sandy belt also extends diagonally across the township from northeast to northwest, and varies in width from one-half to two miles. The original timber of the former was elm, black oak, soft maple, hemlock, cedar, etc., and of the latter, pine and oak.

We next come to what is commonly called timbered land; the timber being chiefly beach and sugar maple, with considerable valuable oak interspersed through some portions. This timbered land extends throughout the remainder of Walker, and northwest into the adjoining townships of Ottawa county. The soil of the northwestern portion is chiefly clay, with some small parcels of rich, black, sandy loam. The face of the country is gently undulating, with but few hills and swamps.

Walker is as thickly settled as any township which contains no village. The southeasterly part is mostly divided into small lots, containing from five to forty acres, and which are usually devoted to market gardening and fruit-growing. The westerly and northwesterly part is devoted principally to farming purposes. In that locality are to be seen some quite large, as well as fine, farms. Stephen O'Brien owns two hundred and eighty acres, situated south of Bridge street, two miles west of the plaster quarries, two hundred acres of which is in a good state of cultivation. Mr. O'Brien informed us that he raises from nine hundred to one thousand bushels of wheat per year, besides other general crops; and that he has sold as high as one hundred tons of hay as the result of one year's yield. P. F. Covell, N. C. Wright, and Daniel Schermerhorn, near the center; Haines Edison and B. F. Woodman, in the northern part of the township; and McCarthy and Davidson in the southern part, have farms containing from one hundred and sixty to two hundred and sixty acres each. Peaches, apples and other kinds of fruit are raised in abundance on the sandy belt, and on most parts of the clay land. The low lands along the river produce good crops of grass and grain.

The greatest elevation in the township is the high rolling swell of land extending from section thirty-two in the southwest, passing through the central part, broken by Brandy Creek, near the residence of William Dunnett, continuing northward on the west of Indian Creek, and afterwards crossing the line into Alpine. On the highest part of this ridge, near the center of section nine, is a lake covering about four acres, situated in the middle of a swamp of about twenty acres. This lake is about one hundred feet above the level of Grand River, and has no visible outlet. Poles have been run down sixty feet without striking any solid bottom.

There is a swamp of about one hundred acres on Bridge street, three and one half miles west of the river, lying mostly on section twenty-nine. There is also one about the same size in the sourthern part of section six. We found one of rather small dimensions on section eight; also, one on section thirty-four. There are other small swamps in different parts of the township, some of which are being drained and cultivated, and are fast becoming rich meadow land. In all, there are, probably, about four hundred acres of swamp land in the township.

Of the streams in Walker, Indian Creek, formerly known as Indian Mill Creek, is the most important. It derived its name from a mill which was erected near its mouth by the Indians, or for them—we have not learned which—many years ago. (The site of this mill was near the present junction of the Detroit & Milwaukee with the Grand Rapids & Indiana Railroad, on section thirteen.) The source of the stream is in Alpine. It enters Walker from the north, near the present location of the Indian Creek post office, and passes through sections ten, fifteen, fourteen, and thirteen, and unites with Grand River near the D. & M. Railroad bridge. There was once considerable pine along its banks, and during the first ten years of the early settlement of the township, five saw mills were erected. In the year 1850, three of them remained. Now, the pine is very nearly gone; and at the time we went through the township (May, 1870), but one of the mills was running.

Brandy Creek, which is a branch of Indian Creek, rises on section sixteen, and flowing north easterly, enters the latter on the south side of section ten.

Black Skin Creek—so-called after an Indian chief of that name—rises in the southern part of the original township, and flowing south alongside the planting ground before mentioned, enters Grand River on the south side of section five.

Sand Creek flows through the northwesterly part of the township, and passes out into Ottawa county on the west.

There are several other small creeks in the township, but none demanding special notice.

RAILROADS.

Walker is crossed by three railroads. The Detroit & Milwaukee passes through the northern part of the township; the Kalamazoo, Allegan & Grand Rapids division of the Michigan Southern runs through the southeasterly part; and the Grand Rapids and Indiana runs parallel with the river through the northeasterly part.

MILLS AND MANUFACTURING ESTABLISHMENTS.

In the year 1845, Joseph Bullen erected a saw mill on the eastern part of section 4. It is run by an overshot waterwheel; the water being conveyed from the pond on Indian Creek, near the residence of Solomon Wright, in Alpine, a distance of nearly ninety rods. The mill possesses the facilities for sawing one million feet of lumber per year; but on account of the scarcity of pine, it does a mnch smaller business. The mill also contains one run of mill-stones for grinding "feed," etc. The present proprietors are McNitt & Wilder.

The plaster mills and quarries on section thirty-four, two and one half miles below Bridge street, in the side of the bluff near the river, are on the east part of section thirty-four. Plaster was first discovered here by R. E. Butterworth, of Grand Rapids, who then owned the land. He opened the first quarry in the year 1852, which was operated under the superintendence of Bernard Courtney. This is the mine now known as "Plaster Cave," or "Hovey's Cave," and is operated by the Eagle Mills Plaster Company. They have large mills and extensive works for grinding the rock for land plaster, and also for the manufacture of stucco.

SCHOOL HOUSES.

The school houses of Walker are generally good, although, perhaps, not quite equal to those of some other townships, nor quite as good as should be expected of a wealthy class of inhabitants near a city of the size of Grand Rapids.

District No. 4, commonly known as the "Walker Center" district, was organized in 1841, and then included a territory of about fifteen square miles. Their first house was a log building, and stood on the north side of section 22; the next was a small wooden building standing at the original geographical center of the township, on the northeast corner of section twenty-one. This building was used until 1867, when a nice frame building was erected at a cost of $1,000. This is the best school house in the township.

District No. 7—Bridge street—has a good wooden building, which was erected in the year 1860. Cost, $400. It is located on the south side of section twenty-two.

District No. 8 was organized in the year 1845. A log house was built, which was used until the year 1858, when the present frame structure, which is generally known as the O'Brien school house, was erected at a cost of $400. Location, south side of section twenty-nine.

District No. 2 is the oldest district now in existence in Walker. A log building was first used. The present frame building was built in the year 1860, at an expense of about $300. Location, near south side of section thirty-three. This district is about to be divided to form a new one in the vicinity of the plaster mills.

District No. 3 has a small frame building on the northeast corner of section nineteen, near the residence of Henry C. Hogadone.

District No. 12 has a small frame house on the north side of section seventeen, near the residence of A. T. Liscomb.

District No. 6 was organized about the year 1840, and a small frame building erected, which was used until 1858, when a large frame house was erected at a cost of $700. This house is located on the south side of section three, and is commonly known as the Simonds' school house.

District No. 11 was organized in the year 1850, and a small frame house built on the west side of section twelve, known as the Wait school house.

In District No. 5, the first school house was built on the farm of Andrew Loomis, on the southwest corner of section six. The present building—a small frame structure—stands on the northeast corner of section seven.

There are several fractional districts, partly in Walker, of which the school houses are in the adjoining townships.

CHURCHES.

Walker contains none yet, but one is being built by the Wesleyan Methodist society, on the southeast corner of section two, which is to be a wooden building 28x44 feet in size. The estimated cost is $1,500 to $1,600.

HOTELS.

The Walker House, owned and kept by Solomon Pierce, was erected in the year 1856, by N. C. Wright. It is a three-story frame building, and stands on the north side of section ten, four miles from the city.

WYOMING.

Wyoming is one of the western tier of townships of Kent county. It is bounded on the north and northwest by the city of Grand Rapids and the township of Walker, on the east by Paris, on the south by Byron, and on the west by Georgetown, Ottawa county.

The soil of this township is diversified, a portion of it, extending from the northern, northeastern part of the township in a southwesterly direction, with a breadth of about two miles, and a length of about five miles, has a gravelly soil, timbered with burr and white oak. It is now principally under cultivation, and is especially adapted to wheat growing. Adjoining this, on the westerly side, are the Grand River bottoms, varying in width from one-fourth to one-half of a mile; and on the east is a large swamp and open marsh. Parts of this swamp are densely timbered with cedar and pine, with an occasional island hemlock and maple. East of this is a large tract of sandy openings, timbered with white and yellow oak. The soil is light, but affords a fair quality of farming lands. South of this is Buck Creek, with its bottom lands; adjoining which on the south is a strip of pine, of about one mile in width, extending from the south line of the township in a north, northwestery direction, to within about two miles of its western border. South of this is a strip of beech and maple land, varying in width from one mile at its eastern extremity to three at its western.

Buck Creek enters Wyoming from the south, about the center of section thirty-six, and flows northwesterly, entering Grand River on section seventeen. This stream affords three good mill sites within the township, which are occupied as follows: One by Fisher's Saw Mill, David Fisher, proprietor, on section twenty-seven; another by Dewey's Saw Mill, on section twenty-one, Egbert Dewey, proprietor; and the third by the Wyoming Flouring Mill, at Grandville, H. O. Weston, proprietor.

Plaster Creek enters Wyoming from the east, on section twelve, and flows northwest, leaving the township just before it reaches Grand River.

There are numerous small spring brooks throughout this township, one of which, entering it from Paris, on section one, and flowing west into Plaster Creek, affords water power for running the plaster mills.

THE VILLAGE OF GRANDVILLE

is located in the western part of this township, on the left bank of Grand River, and contains a population of about 300. It contains five dry goods and grocery stores, two drug stores, two blacksmith shops, one wagon shop, one boot and shoe store, and one harness shop. It has two churches; one Cangregational, which was erected about the year 1855, and a Methodist Episcopal, now nearly finished. The first Congregational Society was organized at Grandvillee in 1838, and Rev. James Ballard was the first pastor. The Grandville Union School House, erected in 1867, is a very fine building. It is thirty feet in width, by sixty in length, with a transept sixteen by thirty feet in size, has two stories above the basement, and is surmounted by a tower. The cost was $10,000.

David Tucker built the first frame house in Grandville. It stood a little north of the present residence of H. O. Weston.

PLASTER.

The existence of gypsum beds, on Plaster Creek, was known to the Indians at the time when the first white settlers came to this township, and gave the stream its name. A portion of the rock was exposed in the bed of the creek at the site of the first plaster mill, where George H. White & Co.'s works are now located. Douglass Houghton, State Geologist, visited the place in 1838, and gave the first published account of the deposits. Prior to that time the 80 acres of land on section two, on which the plaster was found, had been purchased by Mr. Degarmo Jones, of Detroit, with a view to its mineral worth.

The first mill for grinding plaster was built in the winter of 1840-1, by Mr. Daniel Ball, of Grand Rapids. It was driven by a large water wheel, and contained but one run of stone. The last remains of this building, in use until a few years ago, were torn down in 1869. Mr. Ball leased the bed of Mr. Jones, and paid him in plaster, delived in Detroit *via* Grand River and the lakes. Mr. Henry R. Williams bought the lease of Mr. Ball in 1843, and during the same year built an addition to the works, putting in another run of stone for custom flouring. Mr. James A. Rumsey entered these works in 1842, and has been connected with the business since that time, being now employed as foreman by George H. White & Co. The plaster produced for the first four years found a market principally at Detroit, but by dint of wise exertions on the part of the proprietors, who sold it, and often gave it away to farmers for trial, its use as a fertilizer became quite general in the southern part of the State. It was often conveyed on sleighs for use on farms, from 30 to 100 miles distant. George H. White & Co. now own the 80 acres on which the first mill was built, and land adjoining, to the amount of 425 acres in all, of which about 300 acres is underlaid with plaster. The stratum now quarried is 12 feet in thickness, and is overlaid with from 12 to 16 feet of earth, and in places by a stratum of partially decomposed plaster, known as the "seven foot course." The following is the estimated product of these works from 1852 to the present time:

From 1842 to 1850	500 tons yearly
" 1850 " 1860	2,000 " "
" 1860 " 1864	3,000 " "
" 1864 " 1868	8,000 " "
During the year 1869	12,000 tons.
" " " 1870	probably 12,000 tons.

They have a water mill with one run of stone capable of grinding two tons per hour, and a steam mill with two run of stone that grind four tons per hour, and storage for 4,000 tons of ground plaster. Their capital is sufficient to supply all the present or future demands of the trade. The works are located half a mile south of the city limits, on the Grand Rapids & Indiana Railroad, having easy access to all other railroads leading to the city, and also to Grand River.

SAW MILLS.

The Saw Mill of David Fisher is located on section twenty-seven. It contains two saws, one upright and one circular, and cuts about two and one-half million feet per annum. Egbert Dewey carries on the manufacture of lumber and lath at his saw mill on section twenty-one. The mill contains six saws, and cuts about one million two hundred thousand feet per annum.

H. O. Weston carries on the manufacture of flour at the Wyoming Mills, at Grandville. This mill has three runs of stone, and has a capacity of about fifty barrels of flour per day. It was erected by Egbert Dewey, about the year 1856.

These mills are all driven by water power, and are located on Buck Creek.

David Fisher carries on the manufacture of lime, from marl, or bog lime, near his saw mill, affording an excellent lime for mason work, and a good fertilizer. Mr Carpenter also carries on the manufacture of the same kind of lime on section three.

RAIL ROADS.

Wyoming is traversed by three railroads. The Grand River Valley Railroad crosses the northeast corner of the township. The Grand Rapids & Indiana runs across the township, from north to south, near the center line of the eastern tier of sections, and has a station near the center of section thirty-six. The northern branch of the Lake Shore & Michigan Southern Railroad runs north and south through this township, very near its center line, and has a station near the center, called Grandville Station.

EARLY SETTLERS.

As near as we can learn from the memory of the early settlers, Mr. David Tucker was the first settler in Wyoming, he having settled at Grandville in 1832. During the same year Gideon H. Gordon settled at Grandville. In 1833 Luther Lincoln, Joseph B. Copeland, Hiram Jenison, and William R. Godwin settled at Grandville, Jonathan F. Chubb on section four, Myron Roys on section nine, and Henry West on section twenty. During 1834 Roswell Britton, Julius C. Abel,

Ephraim P. Walker, Abraham Bryant, and Josiah McCarthy settled at Grandville, Robert Howlett, and George Thomson on section nine, and Alvah Wanzy on section one. Charles H. Oaks, Joseph A Brooks, Thomas H. Buxton, and Manly Patchen settled at Grandville in 1835, and during the same year, Ransom Sawyer, and Richard Moore on section nineteen, and Justus C. Rogers on section fourteen, and Eli, and Erastus Yeomans also came to Grandville. In 1836 Hiram Osgood, Orrey Hill, Nathan White, Charles Wheeler, Dwight Rankin, James Lockwood, Jacob Rogers, Charles J. Rogers, Leonard Stoneburner, and Mr. Fetterman located at Grandville, and in different parts of the township. Among the settlers of 1837 and 1838, we find the names of Lewis Moody, Chase Edgerly, Col. Hathaway, William Butts, James P. Scott, Jotham Hall, Savoy R. Beals, Cyrus Jones, Cyrus Marsh, Horace Wilder, and James McCray. Edward Fekin was also one of the earliest settlers. Of these, the first settlers of this township, forty-seven in number, only thirteen are now living in Wyoming, viz: Myron Roys, Joseph B. Copeland, Thomas H. Buxton, Richard Moore, Justus C. Rogers, Dwight Rankin, Erastus Yeomans, Eli Yeomans, Charles J. Rogers, Leonard Stoneburner, Lewis Moody, Horace Wilder, and Edward Fekin. Of the others, some few have removed, but the greater part are deceased. Savoy R. Beals and Cyrus Jones had resided in this county some time before settling in Wyoming.

Grandville was one of the first settlements in Kent county; and, for a number of years, one of the largest places. One of the first saw mills, if not the first, (except one built on Indian Mill Creek for the Indians,) was built near the site of the Wyoming Mills, by Messrs. Ball and Wright, in 1834. This mill, after passing through various hands, was destroyed by fire many years ago.

In 1834 Gideon H. Gordon built a saw mill on section seventeen. This mill afterwards fell into other hands, and finally rotted down. During this year Messrs. Britton and Brown also built a saw mill on the site of Dewey's mill, on section twenty-one. It was afterwards torn down to make room for the mill which now occupies the site.

In 1835 Mr. Fetterman commenced to build a saw mill at the mouth of Rush Creek, just within the limits of Wyoming, and afterwards sold it to Geo. Ketchum, who completed it, and also put in a run of mill stones for grinding grain. They were the first ever run in Kent county, and were twenty or twenty-two inches in diameter.

Mr. Gideon H. Gordon, during the same year, built a saw mill on section twenty-seven, on the site of Fisher's Mill. It was afterwards burned. Josiah Burton also built a saw mill on the site of Rumsey's Plaster Mill, in 1836.

Ketchum and McCray built the first furnace and machine shop on Grand River, at Grandville, in 1837. Horace Wilder says that in 1837, under the direction of Mr. McCray, he melted and cast the first iron ever cast in Kent county.

During 1837–8 George Ketchum built, and put in operation, the first flouring mill at Grandville. This mill was burned in 1843, and was never rebuilt. In 1838 the State authorities commenced to bore a salt well at the marsh, on section three, about where the railroad bridge of the L. S. & M. S. R. R. now crosses Grand River. The work was under the charge of Dr. Douglas Houghton, State Geologist. During this year a dwelling house, boarding house, blacksmith shop, and stables were erected, a dock built, tower erected, and curb sunk to the rock, and a steam engine set and made ready for the next year's operations. The next year the job of boring the well was let to Hon. Lucius Lyon, of Detroit, who bored to the depth of 700 feet, when the shaft broke, and the drill, with a portion of the shaft, was left at the bottom of the well. The work was then abandoned and the buildings left to decay.

George Ketchum also built a Gang Saw Mill, at an early day, in what is now Georgetown, Ottawa county, on the site of Jenison's flouring mills.

INCIDENTS OF EARLY SETTLEMENT.

Justus C. Rogers came to Kent county in 1835. He walked from Detroit to Chicago, and from there back to Grand Rapids. At that time the only public conveyance across Michigan was a lumber wagon stage, and walking was preferable to riding in it over the roads as they were then. In the spring of 1836, Mr. Rogers built a small frame house on the site of his present residence, on section fourteen, and in September of the same year there came a tornado which took it up from the foundation and carried it about one rod. When it struck it ended over, so that the south end of the frame lay to the north, and the whole building a wreck. Some of the roof boards and shingles were carried more than a mile, and the woods were strewed with them for quite a distance. Mr. Roger's family had not yet arrived, and he was absent from home at the time. The course of the tornado was from southwest to northeast, and the next building in its course was a log house, on section six, of Paris, which was occupied by Cyrus Jones and family. This it blew down, to within three or four logs of the ground, but luckily none of the inmates were seriously injured, although none of them escaped without some bruises.

Erastus and Eli Yeomans came to Grandville in 1835. They came from Pontiac on foot, *via* the Shiawassee trail, and had to ford all the streams. Dwight Rankin came with a wagon in 1836, by way of Gull Prairie, and was nine days coming from Detroit to Grand Rapids. When they forded the Coldwater they got "set," and were an hour or two getting through.

A pole boat called the Cinderella, was launched at Grandville in June, 1837, and Mrs. Rankin says the occasion was made one of general rejoicing. All the people around were invited, and the boat was poled up and down the river, while they had music and dancing on board. Mr. Lewis Moody came to Grandville in the spring of 1837, but did not bring his family until November. They, with others, came by Green Lake, and were six days getting through. They had four ox teams, and four wagons, and were frequently obliged to put the four teams on one wagon. Just at dark of the fourth day, they came to the outlet of Green Lake, and found the poles that composed the bridge afloat, and were about two hours getting across; and it was raining all of the time. When they reached the Green Lake house, they found some three or four others there before them, but they had none of them had any supper, and all they could muster towards it were some potatoes and onions that the people who kept the house had, and some venison that one of the travelers had. Mrs. Moody told them she could furnish bread, and they made out a supper that relished well, tired and hungry as they were. The next night for supper they had nothing but bread; and the same, in a very limited quantity, for breakfast. Mr. Moody says the Fourth of July, 1837, was the "liveliest" Fourth he ever saw. The steamboat, "Gov. Mason," made her trial trip from Grand Rapids to Grandville. Dr. Scranton was to deliver an address on board of the boat at Grandville, but, as it was very lengthy, when he was but partly through, some one blowed the whistle, and the crowd cheered and broke up. There were four liberty poles raised at Grandville that day, but at night none of them were standing. Mr. M. says that when they first began to carry the United States mail from Grandville to Grand Haven, they used to tie it up in a pocket handkerchief. Mr. Leonard Stoneburner relates the following story, which Mr. E. B. Bostwick told of one of the mail-carriers, an Irishman. He started from Grandville late, and did not get to the lumber camp, where he was to stay all night, until after dark. Just before he got through, Mr. Bostwick, who was but a short distance behind him, heard an owl cry out, "Tu who-o, who-o," and the Irishman answered, "Me name is Jemmy O'Nale, sure, and I carry the mail."

Ebenezer Davis, now of Wyoming, was one of the early settlers of Kent county, having settled at Grand Rapids in 1836. Mr. Davis says that in the spring of 1837, there was a scarcity of flour; and for three weeks there was none to be had at Grand Rapids, and almost everybody lived on sturgeon. The first supply of flour came from Jackson, down Grand River, on a flat boat. Mr. Wilder, and others at Grandville, say that in 1838, they had no flour at Grandville, except some which was said to have been sunk in Lake Michigan. After knocking the hoops and staves off, the flour retained the shape of the barrel, and had to be cut to pieces with an axe, and pounded up. That summer was very sickly, and most of the time this was all that could be had for sick or well. Mrs. McCray says she made bread for her husband, of the same flour, when he was very sick, and for a long time they could get no butter; but finally Mr. Myron Roys, who kept bachelor's hall on his place, and had two cows, made some for them. Mrs. McCray says that, when she hears people complain of hard times and hard fare, now, she always feels like seeing them have a slight trial of those times.

Hiram Jenison says, that, when he came to Grandville in 1834, there was no settlement between Grandville and Grand Haven, and but two families at Grand Haven: Messrs. Ferry and Throop. Ottawa was at that time a part of Kent county. He went to Grand Rapids once to attend an election.

At the time Mr. Roys settled in Wyoming all of the opening lands were entirely free from bushes, and, except the trees, were almost like the prairies. Mr. Roys says that, the first summer he was in Michigan, he worked for Mr. Wright, at the mill, and the woman who was there to cook for them became homesick, and went back to the settlements, and they put him in cook. He would cook meat, beans, etc., as well as any of them, but making biscuit and bread puzzled him. He used to put saleratus into sweet milk, until one night his cow laid out, and the milk soured. He was in trouble; but, finally, concluded to put his saleratus into the sour milk, mixed it up and baked it, and found that he had learned to make biscuit.

FIRST TOWNSHIP OFFICERS.

The township of Wyoming was organized in 1848. Wm. R. Godwin was the first Supervisor; Joseph Blake, Clerk; Chase Edgerly, Treasurer; Erastus Yeomans and Roswell Britton, Justices of the Peace; Nicholas Shoemaker, Dwight Rankin, and James B. Jewell, Commissioners of Highways; Luther D. Abbott and Justus C. Rogers, School Inspectors; L. D. Abbott and J. C. Rogers, Overseers of the Poor; Wm. Richardson, J. A. Britton, C. J. Rogers, and H. N. Roberts, Constables.

At the general election, Nov. 1st, 1848, the whole number of votes cast was 101. At the general election in 1868, there were 344 votes cast.

PRESENT TOWNSHIP OFFICERS.

Supervisor—William K. Emmons. Clerk—Adelbert H. Weston. Treasurer—John V. D. Haven. Justices of the Peace—William H. Galloway, Alexander Mc-Inroy, Cyrus Freeman, Augustine Godwin. Highway Commissioners—Daniel Stewart, Augustine Godwin, Cyrus Freeman. School Inspectors—W. K. Emmons, W. H. Galloway. Overseers of the Poor—Cyrus Freeman, James Jewell. Constables—Charles L. Moody, W. L. Galloway.

CITY OF GRAND RAPIDS.

Grand Rapids is located on Grand River --the largest inland stream in the state —about forty miles from its mouth, and at the head of navigation. Its site is one of great natural beauty, lying on both sides of the river, between the high bluffs that stand nearly two miles apart, and from whose summits the eye takes in a beautiful panorama of hill, vale and river, with all the streets of the busy city laid out like a map at the feet of the beholder.

Grand River at this point runs nearly south, but soon after leaving the city resumes its general westerly direction. On the west side of the river, the ground is nearly level back to the bluffs; on the east side, there were smaller hills between the bank and the bluffs, the leveling of which has cost, and is yet to cost, large sums of money. The east side bluffs, once an ornament to the town, are now marred with deep cuts and unsightly excavations, which may be likened to constantly open sores on the face of nature. But the sores are likely, we must add, to be soon healed, and covered by a crown of comfortable homes, with church spires shooting up from their midst to point the way to the home above.

In writing this sketch, we are not compelled to go to ancient books and dusty files for the record of how the town has grown; for its founder is still alive, and a large proportion of its early settlers. What we write is derived from their lips, and if we fail to mould it into the symmetrical form of legitimate history, we beg some allowance to be made to the live elements that compose it, which will persist in sticking out like the hands and feet of a class of vigorous boys, and will not easily be folded smoothly down like a "preserved specimen."

We have no knowledge of the first white man who visited the rapids on Grand River, called by the Indians the Owashtenong. An Indian village had long existed here—of the Ottawa tribe—before any white men came here to reside. The history of this village, of its chiefs and warriors, of its forays and defences, its councils and treaties, is lost in oblivion from human knowledge, and only written in the books of the Recording Angel.

In 1821, Isaac McCoy—who was appointed by the Board of Managers of the Baptist Missionary convention for the United States, to labor in Illinois and Indiana—visited Gen. Lewis Cass at Detroit, to lay before him the claims of that society, and the needs of Indian tribes of Michigan Territory. The general received him cordially and gave him $450, in goods, for the benefit of his mission at Fort Wayne.

At the Chicago treaty of the same year, through the influence of Col. Trimble, of Ohio, the Pottawattomies agreed to give one mile square of land, to be located by the President, in consideration of the promise of the government to locate thereon a teacher, and a blacksmith, for the instruction and aid of the Indians; the government agreeing to appropriate $1,000 each year for that object. A similar arrangement was afterwards made with the Ottawas, the government agreeing to maintain a teacher, a blacksmith and a farmer, at an expense of $1,500 per year.

Detroit at that time contained only a few hundred inhabitants, and the whole territory of Michigan was a vast wilderness, with only here and there an oasis of a fort or trading post. On the west side of Grand River, and on what is now the Fifth Ward of the city of Grand Rapids, stood, at that time, a collection of 50 or 60 huts, Kewkishkam being the village chief, acknowledging the control of Noonday, chief of the Ottawas.

On the 28th of June, 1822, Mr. McCoy went from Fort Wayne to Detroit, for the purpose of securing the privileges of the Chicago treaty, the war department having placed the matter under the control of Gen. Cass. Gen. Cass commissioned Charles C. Trowbridge to make definite arrangements with the Indians for the sites of the missionary stations. The site for the Pottawattomie station was established on the St. Joseph River, and that of the Ottawas on the Rapids of Grand River. Mr. McCoy visited Grand Rapids in 1823, accompanied by a Frenchman named Paget, and one of his Indian pupils, for the purpose of putting matters into operation at the contemplated station among the Ottawas; bnt was unable to make any satisfactery arrangement, and soon returned to Carey, as the Pottawattomie station was called. In the fall of the same year he had a blacksmith shop set up at Kalamazoo, but only a little was done with it, so far as we can learn, and it was afterwards removed to Grand Rapids.

Some time in 1824, as near as we can learn, Rev. L. Slater, Baptist missionary, and a blacksmith, and one or two other white workmen, came to Grand Rapids and commenced work. The winter proved a very hard one, and supplies had to be sent them on horseback before spring. Mr. Slater erected a log house for himself, and a log school house—the first buildings ever put up in the county.

Religion having let a ray of light into the wilderness, Commerce, her necessary handmaid, was not long in following. The first white settler of Grand Rapids, who came here to found a business and make himself a home, was Louis Campau, an Indian trader. Mr. Campau is still alive, and well known to all the older residents of the city, who honor and respect him as a venerable pioneer and true gentleman. His portrait may be found in the City Directory for 1870, thus making his face familiar to those who, from their short term of residence, had not made his acquaintance. Mr. Campau was born in Detroit, in the year 1791. His ancestors were French, and came to Detroit before the war of the Revolution. He had but few advantages of early education, but made his own career with a clear head, a strong right arm, and an honest purpose. In the fall of 1814, he went to Saginaw to trade with the Indians, at which place he remained for ten years, before removing to Grand Rapids.

Mr. Campau came to Grand Rapids at the solicitation and under the auspices of William Brewster, of Detroit, who was very extensively engaged in the fur business in rivalry with the American Fur Company, and who furnished him with all that he needed to carry on his business. Mr. Campau afterwards opened trading posts and established his agents at Muskegon, Manistee, Kalamazoo, Lowell, Hastings, and Eaton Rapids. He had no trouble with the Indians, but found them friendly and peaceable. They were uniformly honest, and could be trusted with goods, never failing to pay as soon as they had the ability. The currency of that time was—fur. And this was all the Indian had to exchange for the products of civilization.

From 1826 to 1833, Mr. Campau's only white visitors were traders like himself, with a few occasional travelers. He cut down the timber from a few acres of ground to let in the sunlight, but did not attempt any extensive improvements. His brother, Toussaint, then only a youth, was with him most of the time, and helped carry on the business. Toussaint Campau is still a resident of Grand Rapids, and not much burdened with the weight of years.

In 1833, the pioneers of civilization, of whom we may call Mr. Campau the forerunner and scout, began to find their way to Grand Rapids. A land office was opened at White Pigeon in that year, and Louis Campau and Luther Lincoln were the first purchasers. Mr. Campau bought a tract of land in what is now the city of Grand Rapids, and Mr. Lincoln took up a portion of the site of the present village of Grandville.

In the spring of 1833, Mr. Samuel Dexter came to Ionia with a colony of 63 persons from New York, cutting a road through the woods from Pontiac, which was afterwards known as the Dexter trail—and he laid out what is known as the Dexter Fraction in this city. Several of this company afterwards became residents of Grand Rapids and vicinity. Louis Campau, who carried a quantity of goods up the river in batteaux for Mr. Dexter, brought back with him Mr. Joel Guild, carrying his household goods free. He sold Mr. Guild a lot, adjoining the one on which the City National Bank building now stands, for twenty-five dollars. On this lot Mr. Guild erected, during the next summer, a small frame house, which was the first frame building erected in the city, unless, possibly, we may except a building which Mr. Campau erected, just across the street, for a store, and which was completed about the same time. Mr. Guild came from Paris, Oneida county, New York, and brought with him his family, consisting of a wife and seven children. Three of those children are still living: Mrs. Baxter, Mrs. Burton, and Consider Guild; the two former in this city, both widows, but both loved and honored by a large circle of friends, for their useful and consistent lives. The latter now carries on a farm in Ottawa county.

Joel Guild, soon after his arrival, was appointed Postmaster, and held that position for some time, being succeeded by Darius Winsor. Mail was brought once a month from Gull Prairie, on the backs of Indian ponies. Postage was two shillings on a letter, and the ties of friendship had to be pretty strong to support a regular correspondence. A gentleman who came several years later, says that the fifty cents a month required to pay postage on his letters, and the replies of his sweetheart in New York, proved a fearful drain on his pocketbook.

Grand Rapids in 1833, contained but a few acres of cleared land on either side of the river. The Indians had three or four acres cleared on the west side, just below where the bridge of the Grand Rapids and Indiana Railroad now stands, and about as much more on the east side, along what is now Waterloo Street. The timber in that part of the city lying between Fulton and Lyon Streets was mainly oak, and the soil light and sandy. Prospect Hill, (where are the present residences of Dr. Shepard and Deacon Haldane,) which is now nearly removed, was an elevation of remarkable beauty, but in many places so steep that a wagon could not be drawn up without much difficulty.

But the tide of emigration was now fairly set in this direction, and in the next four years Grand Rapids became quite a village.

Eliphalet Turner, whose death occurred this fall, (1870), came in 1833; also Ira Jones, who survived Mr. Turner but a few days. During the same year came Jonathan F. Chubb, with his wife and two children. Mr. Chubb located and improved a beautiful farm between here and Grandville—the same now occupied by Mr. A. N. Norton—but, in a few years, sold out, moved into the city and opened an agricultural store on Canal street. He died several years ago, but his son, A. L. Chubb, is now one of our most active business men.

Rev. Mr. Barrigau, afterward Bishop of the Lake Superior region, also came as a missionary among the Indians, and a church building was commenced on the west side of the river—a small, framed structure. Mr. Campau wanted the building on the east side, and eventually carried his point, hiring Barney Burton to move it across the river on the ice. Mr. Barrigau did not succeed to suit him, and did not remain long.

A saw mill was erected on Indian Creek, about just above Wonderly & Co.'s mammoth mill, some time during the same year.

In the fall of 1833, Mr. Slater kept a school on the west side of the river, and every morning sent an Indian across with a canoe for the white children on the other side.

Among the settlers of 1834, were Richard Godfroy, who set up a store to trade with the Indians, Robert Barr, Louis Morau, and Lovell Moore, Esq. The first marriage in Grand Rapids occurred in 1834. Mr. Barney Burton and Harriet Guild were the happy pair.

The first town meeting was held in 1834, (see history of Grand Rapids township). It was held in the house of Joel Guild, and the whole number of voters was nine.

In the fall of 1834, Mr. Campau commenced a large frame building, which now exists as the upper two stories of the Rathbun House. During the year 1835, Edward Guild and Darius Winsor moved down the river from Ionia, and quite a large number of settlers arrived, among whom were Hon. Lucius Lyon, Jefferson Morrison, Antoine Campau, James Lyman, A. Hosford Smith, Demetrius Turner, William C. Godfroy, Dr. Wilson, Dr. Charles Shepard, and Julius C. Abel. Dr. Wilson was the first Doctor. He was furnished with a medicine case and a set of instruments by Louis Campau, and commenced practice among a population of about 50 souls. Julius C. Abel was the pioneer lawyer, and grew rich out of the misunderstandings of the growing town. James Lyman and Jefferson Morrison set up stores and commenced trading. In the same year, N. O. Sargeant purchased an interest with Lucius Lyon in the Kent Plat, and came on with a posse of men to dig a mill race. Judge Almy and wife came at the same time, with Mr. Sargeant. Among the men in his employ was Leonard G. Baxter. The entrance of that number of men was an interesting and exciting event in the little town. The workmen came into the place with their shovels and picks on their shoulders, to the inspiriting notes of a bugle in the hands of one of their number—Crampton by name, now living in Ada—who afterward blew the same bugle on the first steamboat that ascended above the Rapids. Old Noonday thought they were enemies, and sent Mr. Campau an offer of assistance to expel the invaders.

About this time, Martin Ryerson, then a promising boy sixteen or seventeen years old, came here as a clerk in the employ of Richard Godfroy. He has since become one of the leading lumbermen in Chicago, and is now traveling in Europe with his family. Among other young men who came here, and remained for some time, were Lyman and Horace Gray—the latter a Major in the Fourth Mich. Cav. during the Rebellion—and Andrew Robbins. Rev. Andrew Vizoisky also came in 1835, and, for seventeen years, was pastor of the Catholic flock in this city. Mr. Vizoisky was a native of Hungary. He received his education at the Catholic institutions of learning, in Austria, under the patronage of the Hungarian Chancery. From these sources he obtained that profound knowledge of ancient literature, and of the history and doctrines of the Holy Catholic Church, which distinguished him even in a Brotherhood of world wide reputation for erudition. He came to the United States in 1831. By the appointment of the Bishop of Detroit he officiated three years in St. Clair County. Thence, in 1835, he removed to the Grand River Mission. His ministry in Grand Rapids was marked by unsurpassed devotion, and the most gratifying success. No road was rough enough, and no weather inclement enough, to keep him from the post of duty. To the poor he brought relief; to the sick, consolation; and to the dying, the absolvatory promises of his office. He died January 2nd, 1852, at the age of sixty years; having lived to see a handsome stone church edifice erected on Monroe street, two years previous to his death, and filled with a numerons and prosperous congregation.

1836 witnessed the advent of a large number of new settlers, and the mania of speculation possessed the town. Lots were held at almost as high prices as they will bring to-day. If a man bought a piece of land for $100, he immediately set his price at $1,000, and confidently awaited a purchaser. The currency was inflated, and "wild cat money" in abundance supported these fictitious values. Every man got largely in debt, and every man lived to rue the indiscretion, long and bitterly.

Among those who came in 1836, were Hon. John Ball, William A. Richmond, John W. Pierce, Philander Tracy, Ebenezer W. Barnes, Isaac Turner, A. B. Turner, George C. Nelson, James M. Nelson, Warren P. Mills, George Young, Robert Hilton, Billius Stocking, Abram Randall, William A. Richmond, Truman H. Lyon, William Haldane, Loren M. Page, Charles H. Taylor, Jacob Barnes, William Morman, David Burnett, K. S. Pettibone, Asa Pratt, Samuel Howland, J. Mortimer Smith, Hezekiah Green, George Coggeshall, John J. Watson, George Martin, Myron Hinsdill, Stephen Hinsdill, Hiram Hinsdill, and Harry Eaton. Mr. Eaton, in 1840, was elected Sheriff of the county. His death occurred in 1859.

Roswell Britton, of Grandville, was the first Representative in the State Legislature from this section. His district comprised Kent, Ottawa, Clinton, and Ionia counties. The State Constitution had been adopted only the year before—1835. Major Britton was succeeded in 1837 by John Almy; in 1838, by John Ball; in 1839, by Noble H. Finney; and in 1840, by C. I. Walker.

Hon. John Ball, who has contributed not a little to the growth and prosperity of the town, is a native of Hebron, N. H., and afterward resided in Lansingburg and Troy, N. Y. He graduated at Dartmouth College in 1820, and afterward practiced law in Troy. He came here as a land operator, and has since devoted more of his time to real estate business than to law. He took A. D. Rathbone into partnership with him in 1840, who continued in that relation for about a year. In 1844 Solomon L. Withey became his partner, and the firm was known as Ball & Withey. Afterward George Martin became a partner, and the firm was Ball, Martin & Withey. Afterward it was Ball, Withey & Sargeant. It is now Ball & McKee.

Myron Hinsdill erected the National Hotel in 1836, and it soon after went into the hands of Canton Smith.

John W. Peirce, the pioneer dry goods man of Kent, came here with the late Judge Almy, and assisted that gentleman in surveying and platting that portion of the city now comprising so much thereof as lies under the bluffs. He erected the dwelling on Ottawa street in 1842, and resided therein until, within the last few weeks, (Oct. 15, 1870) he removed into his new and elegant residence, corner of Bronson and Kent streets—having occupied the old mansion for nearly twenty seven consecutive years. He is one of the gentlemen who had an abiding faith in Kent, and the Rapids in general, and by great and and unwearied perseverance has become comfortably off in this world's goods, and, by his enterprise, added many new buildings to this growing city. Mr. Peirce says that he counted all the frame buildings in Grand Rapids when he came, and there were just thirteen. His book store was the first one in the State, west of Detroit.

John J. Watson came from Detroit, and erected, in 1836, a very large store-house, about where the skating rink now stands. It was, in the course of time, moved up the river, and became a part of W. D. Foster's old wooden store.

George Martin, previously mentioned among the settlers of 1836, was a graduate of Middlebury College, Vt. He was for a number of years County and Circuit Judge of this county, and, at the time of his death, was Chief Justice of the Supreme Court of Michigan.

In 1836, Richard Godfroy built the first steamboat on Grand River, and called it the "Gov. Mason." The first boat, however, other than the batteaux of the traders, was a pole boat called the "Young Napoleon," constructed for Mr. Campau by Lyman Gray.

The "Gov. Mason" was commanded by Captain Stoddard. It only had a short existence, being wrecked off the mouth of the Muskegon River in 1838. Captain Stoddard died a number of years ago, in Barry county.

We have mentioned Judge Almy as one of the pioneers of the place. His genial disposition, most corteous manners, and unbounded hospitality, added to a physique at once commanding and noble, made him a representative gentleman in the early days. He was a civil engineer and practical surveyor, of eminence, and was in charge, in 1837-8, of the improvement of the Grand and Kalamazoo Rivers; was a member of the State Legislature, and one of the County Judges. He was also a lawyer by profession, but did not practice any after coming to Michigan. Few men, dying, have left behind them the reflection of a better spent life than John Almy's.

The late George Coggeshall emigrated, in 1836, to this place, from Wilmington, N. C., with his family, and invested his means in Kent. He erected the frame house, on the corner of Bridge and Kent streets, now occupied by the distinguished

Homeopathic physician, Dr. Charles Hempel, and which has been somewhat modified from its primitive appearance. Mr. Coggeshall was a man of many sterling qualities, and was a firm believer in the future of that once impassable quagmire, "Kent," which is now a part of the most populous ward in the city.

Among those who came here in 1837, were Israel V. Harris, Rev. James Ballard, Leonard Covell, G. M. McCray, William A. Tryon, L. R. Atwater, William I. Blakely, A. Dikeman, H. K. Rose, John F. Godfroy, Gaius S. Deane, Henry Dean, C. P. Calkins, James Scribner, and Col. Samuel F. Butler.

The first banking establishment was the Grand River Bank, established in 1847, Judge Almy being President, and Lucius Lyon, Cashier. It lasted a couple of years, and issued bills which were considered good, but finally succumbed to the hard times, and left its promises to pay, a dead loss in the hands of the holders.

Another bank, called "The People's Bank," was started during the same year, under the auspices of George Coggeshall, with Louis Campau for President, and Simeon Johnson for Cashier. The institution failed to secure cash and *nails* enough to comply with the State Banking Law, and was soon wound up; John Ball being appointed Receiver.

For several years succeeding 1837, this was a very "blue" place. Folks were terribly poor, and real estate was hardly worth the taxes. A good many French mechanics, who had been attracted here by the rapid growth of the town, were thrown out of employment, and left in disgust.

A little steamboat, called the "John Almy," was built in 1837, to run above the Rapids. It went up the river as far as the mouth of Flat River,—Crampton waking the echoes with his bugle,—but, alas! sunk before it completed its trip, and rotted away in the bed of the river.

A. Dikeman opened the first watchmaker and jeweler's establishment, in 1837, on Monroe street. It was kept up by him until 1867, and since that time by his son, E. B. Dikeman, whose store is now on Canal street.

Among the settlers of 1838, we may mention W. D. Roberts, John T. Holmes, Esq., Amos Roberts, C. W. Taylor, Erastus Clark, J. T. Finney, and Solomon Withey and his sons, S. L., William, and Orison.

The Bridge Street House was built in 1837, and first kept by John Thompson; subsequently, it was kept by Solomon Withey, who was succeeded by William A. Tryon and Truman H. Lyon—the last two still living in this city.

Amos Rathbun, Ira S. Hatch, Damon Hatch, W. M. Anderson, G. B. Rathbun, and F. D. Richmond, came in 1839. R. E. Butterworth, Heman Leonard, John W. Squier, and Silas Hall, came in 1842.

THE ROCHESTER OF MICHIGAN.

The following description of the place and its prospects appeared in the first newspaper ever printed in Grand Rapids, and was headed "The Rochester of Michigan." We quote it entire, as it appeared in the editorial columns of the *Grand River Times*, Tuesday, April 18, 1837:

"Though young in its improvements, the site of this village has long been known, and esteemed for its natural advantages. It was here that the Indian traders long since made their grand depot. It was at this point that the missionary herald established his institution of learning—taught the forest child the beauties of civilization, and inestimable benefits of the Christian religion. This has been the choicest, dearest spot to the unfortunate Indian, and now is the pride of the white man. Like other villages of the west, its transition from the savage to a civilized state, has been as sudden as its prospects are now flattering.

Who would have believed, to have visited this place two years since, when it was only inhabited by a few families, most of whom were of French origin, a people so eminent for exploring the wilds and meandering rivers, that this place would now contain its twelve hundred inhabitants? Who would have imagined that thus rapid would have been the improvement of this romantic place. The rapidity of its settlement is beyond the most visionary anticipation; but its location, its advantages; and its clime, were sufficient to satify the observing mind, that nothing but the frown of Providence could blast its prospects!

The river upon which this town is situated is one of the most important and delightful to be found in the country—not important and beautiful alone for its clear, silver like water winding its way through a romantic valley of some hundred miles, but for its width and depth, its susceptibility for steam navigation, and the immense hydraulic power afforded, at this point.

We feel deeply indebted to our Milwaukee friends for their lucid description of the advantages to be derived from a connection of the waters ot this river with those of Detroit, by canal or railroad. A canal is nearly completed around the rapids at this place, sufficiently large to admit boats to pass up and down, with but little detention. Several steamboats are now preparing to commence regular trips from Lyons, at the mouth of the Maple River, to this place, a distance of sixty miles; and from this to Grand Haven, a distance of thirty-five or forty miles; thence to Milwaukee and Chicago.

Thus the village of Grand Rapids, with a navigable stream—a water power of twenty-five feet fall—an abundance of crude building materials—stone of excellent quality—pine, oak, and other timber in immense quantities within its vicinity, can but flourish—can but be the Rochester of Michigan! The basement story of an extensive mill, one hundred and sixty by forty feet, is now completed; a part of the extensive machinery is soon to be put in operation. There are now several dry goods and grocery stores—some three or four public houses—one large church, erected, and soon to be finished in good style, upon the expense of a single individual, who commenced business a few year ago, by a small traffic with the Indians. Such is the encouragement to Western pioneers! The village plat is upon the bold bank of a river, extending back upon an irregular plain, some eighty to a hundred rods, to rising bluffs, from the base and sides of which some of the most pure, crystal like fountains of water burst out in boiling springs, pouring forth streams that murmur over their pebbly bottoms, at once a delight to the eye and an invaluable luxury to the thirsty palate.

New England may surpass this place with her lofty mountains, but not with her greatest boast, purity and clearness of water. Our soil is sandy and mostly dry. The town is delightful, whether you view it from the plain upon the banks of the river, or from the bluffs that overlook the whole surrounding country. To ascend these bluffs you take a gradual rise to the height of a hundred feet, when the horizon only limits the extent of vision. The scenery to an admirer of beautiful landscape is truly picturesque and romantic. Back east of the town is seen a widespread plain of burr oak, at once easy to cultivate and inviting to the agriculturist. Turning westward, especially at the setting of the sun, you behold the most enchanting prospect—the din of the ville below—the broad sheet of water murmuring over the rapids—the sunbeams dancing upon its swift gliding ripples —the glassy river at last losing itself in its distant meanderings, presents a scenery that awakes the most lively emotions. But the opposite shore, upon which you behold a rich, fertile plain, still claims no small amount of admiration. Near the bank of the river is seen the little, rude village of the more civilized Indians—their uncouth framed dwellings—their little churches, and moundlike burying places. The number and size of the mounds which mark the spot where lies the remains of the proud warrior, and the more humble of his untamed tribe, too plainly tell the endearment of that lovely plain to the native aborigines, and how quick the mind will follow the train of association to by-gone days, and contrast these reflections with present appearances. Thus we see the scenes of savage life, quickly spread upon the broad canvass of the imagination—the proud chieftain seated, and his tribe surrounding the council fires—the merry war dance—the wild amusements of the 'red man of the forest,' and as soon think of their present unhappy condition; the bright flame of their lighted piles has been extinguished, and with it has faded the keen, expressive brilliancy of the wild man's eye! Their lovely *Washtenang*, upon which their light canoes have so long glided, is now almost deserted!

It is from this point, too, that you can see in the distance the evergreen tops of the lofty pine, waving in majesty above the sturdy oak, the beech, and maple, presenting to the eye a wild, undulating plain, with its thousand charms. Such is the location, the beauties, and the advantages of this youthful town. The citizens are of the most intelligent, enterprising and industrious character. Their buildings are large, tasty, and handsomely furnished—the clatter of mallet and chisel—the clink of the hammer—the *many* newly raised and recently covered frames—and the few skeleton boats upon the wharves of the river, speak loudly for the enterprise of the place! Mechanics of all kind find abundance of employ, and reap a rich reward for their labor. Village property advances in value, and the prospect of wealth is alike flattering to all! What the result of such advantages and prospect will be, time alone must determine.

But a view of this place and its vicinity, where we find a rich and fertile soil, watered with the best of springs, and enjoying as we do a salubrious climate, a healthful atmosphere, and the choicest gifts of a benign Benefactor, would satisfy almost any one that this will soon be a bright star in the constellation of western villages. Such, gentle reader, is a faint description of the place from which our paper hails—from which we hope will emenate matter as pleasing and interesting as the town is beautiful and inviting."

A NOTED INDIAN CHIEF.

The following graphic sketch, from the pen of C. W. Eaton, we quote entire: "We have been told many good anecdotes of Meccissininni, the young chief of the Grand River Indians, in an early day, by an old resident of this place. Meccissininni was called the Young Chief, and old Black Skin the Old Chief; although Meccissininni was not a very young man, being 45; but, according to the custom of the Indians, a young brave that marries the Chief's daughter is made Chief, and called the Young Chief. He was an eloquent orator, a very proud, haughty Indian, and "wanted to be like his white brethren," as he often said. He always dressed like his white brethren, and you might often see him on a hot day in the summer carrying an umbrella, when there was no sign of rain—to keep from being tanned, probably.

He was one of the band of Chiefs that went with Louis Campau, Rix Robinson, and Rev. Mr. Slater to Washington to make a treaty relative to selling their lands on the west side of the river, which was consummated in 1835. While in Washington, Gen. Jackson wished to make him a present of a good suit of clothes, and asked him what kind he would prefer. He said as General Jackson was Chief of his people, and he was Chief of the red men, he thought it would be appropriate if he had a suit like his. The General ordered the suit. It was a black frock coat, black satin vest, black pantaloons, silk stockings, and pumps; but the best of the thing was, Gen. Jackson wore at that time a white bell-crowned hat, with a weed on it, being at the time in mourning for his wife. The unsuspecting Indian, not knowing that the weed was a badge of mourning, had one on his hat also, which pleased Gen. Jackson and his Cabinet not a little. He was much delighted with the warm receptions he received in the different cities on his return home.

After he returned, a council met to hear the nature of the treaty, where Meccissininni distinguished himself as an orator, in his portrayal of the treaty. They sold their lands, and the treaty provided for their removal west of the Mississippi, in a certain number of years; where lands were given them. Several of the Chiefs were opposed to the treaty; but Meccissininni was in favor of their removal, and made an eloquent speech in support of it. In his remarks he said that for his part he had rather remain here, and be buried where his forefathers were; but, on his people's account, he had rather go west of the Mississippi, as his people would become debased by association with the pale faces.

In 1841 he was invited to a Fourth of July celebration. The dinner was served up near the present site of Ball's Foundry, where, after the oration, and refreshments, the cloth was removed and regular toasts drank. Meccissininni was called upon for a toast, and responded as follows:

"The pale faces and the red men—the former a great nation, and the latter a remnant of a great people; may they ever meet in unity together, and celebrate this great day as a band of brothers."

Our narrator relates an incident which occurred while he was keeeping a grocery and provision store on the west side, opposite the Barnard House, where the old ferry was located. Meccissininni said he wanted to get trusted for some provisions, and would pay at the next Indian payment. When he returned from the annual payment, he was asked to settle his bill. He told the provision vender that he must put it on paper, send it to his home, and he would pay it. He said he wished to do business like white people. So our friend made out his bill and repaired to the Chief's house, and was ushered in with all the politeness imaginable. He promptly paid the bill, and signified his wish to have it receipted. After showing him all his presents, and donning his suit which Gen. Jackson had presented him, he brushed his hair back and imitated the walk of the General, taking long strides back and forth across the room; and also mimicked that of the Vice President, Martin Van Buren, by stepping short and quick. Having passed an hour very pleasantly, he took his leave, with a polite invitation from Meccissininni to call again.

About the year 1843, he was attacked with a disease of the lungs, which, after a short illness, terminated his existence, at the age of fifty. He lived and died a professor of the Catholic faith, under the spiritual guidance of the late Rev. Mr. Vizoisky. He was followed to his last resting place by a large concourse of the citizens of Grand Rapids, together with his own tribe."

INDIAN MOUNDS.

The Indian burying ground on the west side, in the Fifth Ward, which the denizens of the village of Kent found in 1833, remained, with its rude enclosure, the wonder of all strangers, until about the year 1850, when it had gradually disappeared under the power of decay, and the avarice of man. In this mound—small portions of which yet remain—the sainted priest, Vizoisky, had consigned to their final rest the bones of many a converted Ottawa, who had been taught to say his Pater Noster and Ave Maria, and perform his daily Matins in the tiny church, that for years was the spiritual home of that good and devoted Catholic priest.

BRIDGES.

The first bridge that spanned Grand River was a narrow foot bridge, built by James Scribner and Lovell Moore, in 1843. E. H. Turner and James Scribner built the first wagon bridge in 1845. The first toll bridge, on Bridge street, was finished in 1852, and for the first year did not pay the expenses of running it. Now there are three in the city, all of which are fine, covered bridges, and pay large dividends. Pearl street bridge was completed in 1858, and Leonard street bridge in 1859. On the sixth day of April, 1858, Bridge street bridge took fire and was utterly destroyed. A foot bridge was at once commenced, and completed by April 10th. During the interval between the destruction of the bridge and the completion of a new one, the steamer Nebraska ran back and forward as a ferryboat.

GAS.

The Grand Rapids Gas-Light Company was incorporated in 1857, and in November of that year the stores on Monroe street were lit with gas for the first time. Gas-pipes were not extended across the river until 1869.

PLANK ROAD.

The plank road from this city to Kalamazoo was completed in 1854, previous to which, stages were two days in going from one town to the other. The plank road enabled them to make the trip in one day. W. H. Withey was the proprietor of the first line of stages on the new road. This road was of immense importance to the rising city, and, until the completion of the Detroit and Milwaukee Railroad in 1858, it was the avenue by which nearly all visitors from the east approached the city. The author has counted as many as 170 teams in one day, coming to the plaster mills in this city and Wyoming township. Many of these teams brought loads of corn and pork for the supply of the Grand Rapids market, which then, as at the present time, furnished immense quantities of those staples to the lumbermen in this vicinity and farther north. In 1869, the toll-gates were abolished, and now the planks are fast breaking up and becoming a nuisance, and in many places are entirely taken up.

NEWSPAPERS.

The first newspaper, called the Grand River *Times*, was started by George W. Pattison in 1837, and the first number published April 18th, of that year. Several copies of the first number are still extant, having been printed on cloth with a view to their preservation. Uncle Louis Campau has one of these sheets, which was presented to him by the editor, with his name printed on the margin. Mr. Pattison was assisted, as editor, by Noble H. Finney. The press on which this paper was printed was drawn up the river from Grand Haven, on the ice, by a team of dogs. It was purchased the winter previous at Buffalo, by Judge Almy. At Detroit it was shipped for Grand Haven on the steamer Don Quixote, which was wrecked off Thunder Bay, and the press taken around the lakes on another boat. Some years after, the paper passed into the hands of James H. Morse, who published a neutral paper for several years. The political department was divided equally between the Whigs and Democrats. Articles were written on the Democratic side by Simeon M. Johnson, C. H. Taylor, Sylvester Granger, and C. I. Walker, and on the Whig side by George Martin, Wm. G. Henry, E. B. Bostwick, and T. W. Higginson. Finally Mr. Johnson was employed as editor, and in 1841 changed the name of the paper to *Enquirer*, after the *Richmond Enquirer*, which was his favorite paper. In 1843, E. D. Burr became a partner, and hoisted the Democratic flag, with the name of John C. Calhoun for President. In 1844, it supported James K. Polk, and published a campaign sheet called *Young Hickory*. After this the paper was published by Jacob Barnes, as agent, with T. B. Church, as editor. Then C. H. Taylor became partner, and was the editor.

In March, 1855, A. E. Gordon started the *Daily Herald*, which was the first daily paper published in Grand Rapids. This was followed in 1856 by a daily from the *Enquirer* office, Taylor & Barnes, proprietors, J. P. Thompson, editor. In a short time the two papers were merged in the *Enquirer and Herald*, Gordon & Thompson, publishers. Mr. Thompson, now assistant editor of the *Eagle*, left the *Enquirer and Herald*, and, associated with Charles B. Benedict, establised a semi-weekly paper called the *Grand Rapids Press*. Gordon continued the *Enquirer and Herald* until it was closed under a mortgage held by H. P. Yale. It was resurrected by N. D. Titus, who afterwards took in Fordham as a partner, and called the *Democrat*. M. H. Clark soon after obtained an interest in the paper. Titus went out, and Mr. Clark continued it, with a Mr. Burt as partner. After Mr. Burt left, C. C. Sexton and Robert Wilson had an interest in it, and finally Dr. C. B. Smith. The *Democrat*, under the able management of Mr. Clark, now boasts one of the finest printing establishments in this part of the state, and is a large, well filled, handsome and prosperous paper.

The *Eagle* was commenced as a weekly, December 25, 1844, (the press and type arriving in time to print tickets for Henry Clay), by A. B. Turner, with George Martin and Charles F. Barstow as nominal editors. Early in 1848, Ralph W. Cole was associate editor. In 1851, James Scribner became a partner, but, being a Democrat, had nothing to do with the editorial department. Mr. Scribner's interest was purchased by A. B. Turner in the fall of 1852. Immediately after the defeat of Scott in 1852, the *Eagle* abandoned the Whig organization and advocated a new one, which assumed the name of Republican at the Jackson convention, in July, 1854. Mr. Turner started a daily May 26, 1856, with telegraphic dispatches by stage from Kalamazoo. He was assisted during the Fremont campaign by Albert Baxter, who continued on the paper until 1860. After that time L. J. Bates, now of the *Detroit Post*, assisted him until 1865, when Mr. Baxter returned. Mr. E. F. Harrington has had an interest in the *Eagle* since 1865. Mr. J. P. Thompson came in September, 1869, as another assistant. No man in Grand Rapids has shown more persistent energy, often under the most discouraging circumstances, than has Aaron B. Turner, and he is now at the head of a profitable business, and in prosperous circumstances: his printing office being one of the best in the state.

In 1857-8, C. W. Eaton and W. S. Leffingwell published, for a year, a small monthly, called the *Young Wolverine*, to a file of which we are indebted for some interesting facts. They were then typos in the *Enquirer and Herald* office. P. R. L. Peirce's exceedingly comical "Rhythmical History of Grand Rapids, More or Less," in choice doggeral, appeared in this little sheet.

In 1857, Thomas D. Worrall started the *Great Western Journal*, a weekly paper whose high sounding name did not save it from a final collapse in a short time. Several other newspapers have risen and died out since that date.

The *Vrijheids Banier*—Banner of Liberty—a paper printed in the Holland language, is published weekly from the *Eagle* building, by W. Verburg.

The *Times*, daily and weekly, C. C. Sexton, proprietor, was started a few months ago, and has achieved a large circulation.

A weekly paper, called the *Pioneer*, is printed in the German language.

COURT HOUSE.

For several years, the question of the location of the Court House and County offices agitated the Board of Supervisors at almost every session from 1851 to 1861; and it is not clear that it is yet definitely settled. The first building erected for court purposes, was on the square, directly in front of Mr. A. B. Judd's present residence. It was a wooden structure, two stories high, with an imposing cupola in the center of the roof. The second story was used for a court room, and also for religious meetings. The lower floor for a jail, and jailor's residence. In this primitive edifice, Judges Pratt and Whipple of the Circuit, assisted by Side Judge Almy, deceased, E. W. Davis, and P. Tracy, both yet living, expounded and interpreted the law, which was being "practiced" by George Martin, A. D. Rathbone, Sylvester Granger, E. E. Sargeant, and others not now living, and by T. B. Church, John Ball, J. T. Holmes, J. C. Abel, C. P. Calkins, J. S. Chamberlain and S. L. Withey, who are still on *terra firma*. Those were high old days for the law, and, had not the records of the county been burned in

January, 1861, some rare information could have been obtained from them; but much of this is still in the head of a gentleman still living amongst us, who was for fourteen years clerk of the county, and who personally knows more of the days we write of than any other man in the city, and can recall with photographic exactness a hundred incidents of peculiar interest, touching those palmy days of Grand Rapids, which we hope he may some day find it convenient to give the public.

HON. LUCIUS LYON.

Among the number of those who contributed not a little to the "opening up" of the future of this city, was the Hon. Lucius Lyon, one of the proprietors, with the late Hon. Charles H. Carroll, of that part of the city called the Kent Plat. Believing that salt could be made here, and knowing that this section indicated, geologically, saline springs, he, in 1841, commenced sinking a well on the west bank of the canal, above the big mill, which, after many difficulties and embarrassments, became a supposed success, and the manufacture of salt was, in 1843–4 and 5, prosecuted with considerable spirit, by means of boiling and evaporation. But it failed of being profitable, owing to the difficulties in keeping out fresh water which diluted the brine. We believe Mr. Lyon expended upwards of $20,000 in this experiment, and his profits were nothing. Subsequently, in 1858 to 1864, Messrs. Ball & McKee, J. W. Winsor, W. T. Powers, C. W. Taylor, and the late James Scribner, with others, renewed the effort to make salt, and several wells were sunk, and several thousand barrels made, but East Saginaw had, in the meantime, found the "Seat of Empire," and, from superior and purer brine, soon demonstrated that she was " master of the situation, and our people could not compete with her, and the works in this city gradually went the way of all unprofitable enterprises.

JUDGE WITHEY.

Hon. Solomon L. Withey was born in St. Albans, Vermont. He came to this city in 1838. After studying law for some time he was admitted to the bar, and became the law partner of Hon. John Ball in 1844. He was also, for several years, law partner of Hon. George Martin, afterwards Chief Justice of the Supreme Court of Michigan—now deceased. In 1848 he was chosen Judge of Probate for Kent county, and held that office for four years. In 1860 he was elected State Senator, and served during the regular session, and two extra sessions called to meet the exigencies of the rebellion. Upon the organization of the Western District of Michigan, in 1863, he was appointed by President Lincoln to the honorable position of United States District Judge thereof, in which capacity he has since served. In 1869 he was tendered an appointment as Judge of the United States Circuit, comprising the States of Michigan, Ohio, Kentucky, and Tennessee, which, after due consideration, he declined. He is President of the First National Bank of Grand Rapids, and enjoys, to a remarkable degree, the respect and confidence of the public.

W. D. FOSTER.

W. D. Foster came to Grand Rapids, from Rochester, N. Y., in the year 1838. He started a small "7x9" store, at the foot of Monroe street, in 1845, keeping a general assortment of tin whistles, patty pans, skimmers, pie plates, and such like, cutting and hammering them all out, and soldering the same with his own hands, there not being business enough to warrant having a journeyman. He did quite a thriving trade for several years, gradually, by great industry, economy and perseverance, accumulating and adding to his slow gains, until, having been prospered, as such men will be, he has become the foremost man in the hardware line in Western Michigan, owner of a large brick block, five stories high, filled from top to bottom with his own merchandise; and not to know Wilder D. Foster is to acknowledge one's self unknown. He employs men by the dozens, and his trade is measured annually by tens of thousands. Mr. Foster has had several partners. The firm for a time was Foster & Parry, then Henry Martin and Martin Metcalf became his associates, and it was W. D. Foster & Co. Afterward it was Foster, Martin & Metcalf, then Foster & Metcalf, and, since 1862, W. D. Foster alone. He built his present block in 1868. "Live and let live," has ever been Mr. Foster's motto, and, if the gratitude of hundreds to whom he has lent substantial assistance in time of need, is worth anything, he is rich in something better than earthly stores.

HON. P. R. L. PEIRCE.

Probably no man has been more intimately connected with public affairs in Kent county, during the past twenty years, than Hon. P. R. L. Peirce, a native of Genesco, N. Y., or Peter Peirce, as he is familiarly called by half the men in the county. It is possible that some men in the county work harder than Mr. Peirce, and that some man may get off more jokes, but entirely improbable that any other man works as hard and says as many funny things as he does. He came to Grand Rapids to reside in the year 1840, from Detroit, and studied law in the office of Judge Martin, along with Hon. S. L. Withey, acting as Deputy County Clerk in 1842–3. In 1853 and 1854, he was City Clerk, and, in 1854, he was elected Clerk of Kent County, which office he held during a period of fourteen years. He was generally conceded to be as good a County Clerk as any in the State, and was always in high favor with the Judge and members of the bar. The young lawyers regarded him almost as a father, and men from all parts of the county came to him with their grievances, sure of sympathy, and assistance if it lay in his power. During the past eighteen years he has contributed largely to the city press, on various topics of personal and local interest to the community, and is a walking encyclopedia of useful information with regard to all that has transpired in the county since he came here. He enjoyed great popularity with the soldiers during the rebellion, and has worked steadily for their interests at all times. In 1868 he was elected State Senator, in which capacity he has proved one of the most influential men from this part of the State. He is now assistant to Hon. William A. Howard, in the Land Office of the Grand Rapids & Indiana Railroad, for which position his rare clerical skill renders him peculiarly fitted.

HENRY R. WILLIAMS.

Among those who are worthy to be mentioned as having contributed not a little to the growth of this city, was the late Henry R. Williams. Mr. W. came to Grand Rapids in 1841, from Rochester, N. Y., and entered into business with

Warren Granger, of Buffalo, N. Y., and occupied one of the Nelson stores, on the corner of Canal and Bronson streets—being now a portion of the Bronson House. The firm of Warren, Granger & Co. were engaged in merchandising, flouring and boating, and Mr. Williams built up a splendid reputation as a prompt, efficient, and reliable business man. He was once a candidate for Congress against Hon. Samuel Clark (lately deceased). His genial companionship, and earnest endeavors to open up this once wild section, endeared him to all of the then denizens; and the "old settlers" recall his memory with feelings of uniform kindness and pleasure. He died some twelve or fifteen years ago. In his lifetime, he built the elegant stone residence on the hill overlooking Bronson street, now owned by Mr. O. S. Camp.

REV. DR. CUMING.

Any history of this city would be imperfect without a brief reference to Rev. F. H. Cuming, D. D., who died in 1863. Doct. Cuming came here from Ann Arbor (and Rochester, N. Y.) in 1843, and took charge of the Episcopal Church. He was a man of large business capacity, of indomitable energy, and a wonderful perseverance, and, outside of his immediate pastoral labors, he gave much of his time to the various enterprises of a local and public nature, calculated to advance the growth and redound to the interest of the city. He had many tempting offers to go to various cities, where his vast capacity could have a larger field of usefulness, but he declined them all, for he had great faith in the future of this city and county, and ventured the prognostication that persons were then born who would live to see a population of 30,000 inhabitants here. Doct. Cuming erected the substantial residence (on the hill between Bridge and Bronson), now occupied by his esteemed widow and family, and was eighteen years rector of the Episcopal Church, erecting, with the aid of his flock, the large stone edifice on Division, at the head of Pearl street, now occupied by St. Mark's congregation.

REV. JAMES BALLARD.

One of the pioneers who has made his mark in the valley City, is the Rev. James Ballard, a native of Charlemont, Massachusetts, who graduated at Williams College, and, after residing for some time in Vermont, found his way to this city in 1837. He was pastor of the Congregational Church for ten years, and, during that time, exhibited such zeal and enterprise as will forever associate his name with the history of that society. The old Congregational Church building, in use until about a year ago, was, through his efforts, purchased of Mr. Louis Campau, and Mr. Ballard walked seventeen hundred miles, through the Eastern States, and appealed to the churches there to assist him in buying a Catholic Church building, for the use of a Protestant society. When he had raised the greater part of the sum required, he came home and mortgaged his own property to pay the remainder. (The old church was built by Mr. Campau, in 1837, and, until the last stick of it is in ashes, it will be a monument to the noble, religious zeal of Louis Campau, the Catholic, and James Ballard, the Protestant. Mr. Campau sold it because his business affairs required the use of a part of the money which it cost, and the Church was not able to refund it.) When the church changed hands, the Catholics reserved the iron cross which surmounted the cupola, and, in removing it, a man lost his life.

Mr. Ballard, as mentioned hereafter, has been, at different times, principal of both the Union Schools in this city. He still resides here, as active as ever, and is now State Agent for the Freedmen's Aid Society, in which capacity he is, as usual, doing a good work. He is also very extensively known for his labors in the Sunday School cause.

GRAND RAPIDS IN 1846.

Prof. Franklin Everett, in the City Directory for 1865, thus describes the infant city of twenty-four years ago:

"We will step back about twenty years to the time when I first saw the village in the wilderness. Then, forty acres was about the extent of the place. Division street might be said to bound civilization on the east, Monroe street on the south, Bridge street on the north, and the river on the west. There were scattered buildings, only, outside of those limits. A wing dam ran half way across the river, and furnished water power for three saw mills, two grist mills, and some minor works. Irving Hall, Fanuel Hall, Commercial Block, Backus' Block, corner of Canal and Bronson streets, and Peirce's Franklin Block, were the stores *par eminence*—the last two "clear out of town." Sinclair's store, where Luce's Block now is, was the business stand fartherest up Monroe street—"too far out of town to do business." Canal street was the muddiest hole in all creation. A two foot side walk, supported on posts, kept the pedestrians out of the mud. It must be borne in mind that this street has been filled from five to ten feet. Where Fitch & Raymond's carriage shop now is, and around there, was a fine, musical frog pond; and there was another, (which by the way is not now altogether filled), north-west of there. The stumps were in the street, and the houses were all one story. Our communication with the outside world was by the Battle Creek stage. People came to church with ox teams. They came to worship God—not, as we go now, to show dry goods. There were no fashionables; men and women dressed plain, and almost all had the ague. Every cow had a bell on, of course; hence we lacked not for music. Wood was one dollar a cord, and a drug at that. Wheat, fifty cents a bushel; corn, twenty-five cents; venison, half a cent a pound; pork and beef three cents; young ladies were scarce and in active demand. Mr. Ballard was preaching in the Congregational Church, and got his living by farming. The Episcopal Church was the building, since much improved, opposite Fitch & Raymond's shop. The Catholics used a dwelling house for a chapel. The Methodists had their present house. We had no fashionable churches or christians. Poor people could go to meeting and be considered decent; and I observed that people spoke of the sermons more than the dresses. It was an out-of-the-way, stirring, primitive place, with warm hearts and energetic heads."

THE PRESENT CITY.

On the first day of June, 1870, Grand Rapids contained, according to the United States census, 16,507 inhabitants, and is therefore the second city in the State, in population. It contains fifteen hotels, twenty dry goods stores, upwards of fifty groceries, eight hardware stores, nine drug stores, twelve clothing stores, sixteen boot and shoe stores, six photograph galleries, seven watchmaker and jewelers' establishments, seven printing offices, three book-binderies, upwards of fifty lawyers, upwards of forty physicians, fourteen dentists, six banking houses, eight machine shops, five flouring mills, four breweries, six furniture manufactories, three large brick manufactories, one fanning mill manufactory, one file manufactory, one mammoth box factory, one file manufactory, one axe factory, two hub factories, two marble cutting establishments, one organ factory, two woolen mills, seven planing mills, eight saw mills, one immense factory for the manufacture of Water's patent barrels, fourteen wagon and carriage manufactories, etc., etc. The traveler can approach or leave the city by railroad, in six different directions, and several new roads are contemplated, and will soon be constructed.

A street railway extends from the depot of the Detroit & Milwaukee Railroad, the full length of Canal and Lyon streets, a distance of over two miles.

WAR RECORD.

Grand Rapids was behind none of her sister cities in her support of the government during the late civil war. The Third and Eighth infantry regiments had their rendezvous here, and the Second, Third, Sixth, Seventh and Tenth cavalry regiments; all of which were largely filled by volunteers from this vicinity. Each and all did credit to the city and State on many well fought fields.

SCHOOLS.

That portion of Grand Rapids which lies upon the east side of Grand River, and south of the Coldbrook district, was, in the year 1849, organized under the school law then existing, as School District No. 1, of the City of Grand Rapids. The stone building which stood on the hill, known as the "Central School," was erected in the autumn of 1849. The first school in it was opened in 1850, under the supervision of Mr. Johnson, with four assistants. Mr. Johnson was soon after succeeded by Rev. James Ballard, who had charge of the school about three years, when he was followed by the late Prof. Edward Chesebro. After Prof. Chesebro resigned, on account of illness, his brother, George Chesebro, was Superintendent for a short time, when Prof. Danforth took the place, with Prof. Edwin Strong, as Principal of the High School department. Prof. Danforth remained about three years, and was succeeded, in 1863, by Prof. Strong, who has since filled the place to the complete satisfaction of all.

In 1867, the stone building having become too small to accommodate the greatly increased attendance, and as it was thought unsafe by reason of defective walls, the present edifice was commenced. It was completed and the old building removed in 1868. Having a commanding site, its tower 137 feet high, it is the first object that attracts the eye of a stranger on entering the city, and the last he sees when leaving it. The cost of the building was about $50,000.

Primary No. 1, is a commodious and nicely arranged brick building, on the corner of Division and Bridge streets, and cost about $15,000.

Primary No. 2, is on South Division street. It is a frame building with a brick basement, and has cost about $5,000.

Primary No. 3, is located on Fountain street, east of Prospect, and is a large wooden structure.

Primary No. 4, is situated on the corner of Wealthy Avenue and Lafayette street. This building was completed in 1869, is of brick, and cost $12,000.

The West Side Central School building was erected in 1855, and during the summer of 1869, thoroughly overhauled and re-arranged.

In 1869, a brick school house was begun in the Fifth Ward, which, when completed, will cost about $15,000. A part of it is now in use. Prof. S. Montgomery is Superintendent of the West side schools.

GRAND RAPIDS BUSINESS COLLEGE AND TELEGRAPHIC INSTITUTE.

The Grand Rapids Business College and Telegraphic Institute, Swensberg & Robbins, proprietors, has been in successful operation for the last five years, and, during that time, has educated several hundred young ladies and gentlemen. We can safely say that no similar institution in the northwest is more favorably regarded, or offers better advantages to students, who desire a thorough business education. Prof. C. G. Swensberg, who gives his whole time to the school, with able assistants, is one of the finest penmen and most accomplished teachers in the west. The large and commodious rooms of this institution are located in Luce's Block, Monroe street.

CHURCHES.

There are, in this city, twenty church buildings, and two more in process of erection. The finest among these are the Congregational, Methodist Episcopal, Episcopal, Presbyterian, Catholic (new), True Reformed, Second Reformed, and Universalist churches. Anything like a satisfactory history of the different societies would far transcend the limits of this sketch.

RAILROADS.

The first train of cars entered Grand Rapids on the tenth day of July, 1858, at 4:30 P. M.; the Detroit & Milwaukee Railroad Company having that day completed their road to the long expectant and previously isolated city. This was one of the most important events, as touching the development of the town, that we have to record, and let in at once a new tide of enterprise and capital.

The next road that led out from the place was a section of the Grand Rapids & Indiana Railroad, from here to Cedar Springs, on which regular trains commenced running on the twenty-third day of December, 1867. Through trains commenced running on this road, to Fort Wayne, Indiana, on the tenth day of October, 1870; opening a new market for our manufactures, which promises to prove of great importance to the leading branches of industry.

The first train of cars on the Kalamazoo, Allegan & Grand Rapids Railroad, now a division of the Lake Shore & Michigan Southern Railroad, arrived on the first day of March, 1869.

Regular trains commenced running on the Grand River Valley Railroad, now a branch of the Michigan Central, on the seventeenth day of January, 1870.

MANUFACTURING ESTABLISHMENTS—PLASTER.

F. GODFREY & BROS.'

plaster works are situated in the city, on the Grand River, and convenient to all the railroads for shipping. They have 100 acres of plaster land. The stratum of plaster is about twelve feet thick, exposed by removing the earth above it, and furnishes 35,000 tons per acre. F. Godfrey discovered plaster at this point in 1859, and works were erected in 1860, the product for that year being about 1,000 tons. From this amount the yearly product has steadily increased until 1869, in which year they quarried 12,000 tons. They have one water mill and a steam mill, each with two run of stone, and can grind in the two mills 80 tons of plaster in ten hours, or 160 tons in 20 hours. Their calcining works are very extensive, being sufficient to manufacture 260 barrels of calcined plaster per day, and their capital is amply sufficient for all their purposes.

THE WEST SIDE OF GRAND RIVER.

The first plaster discoveries on the west side of Grand River were made by Mr. R. E. Butterworth, an English gentleman of culture and enterprise, now proprietor of one of the principal machine shops and founderies in Grand Rapids. He purchased 162 acres of land, now owned by the Grand Rapids Plaster Company, in 1842. His knowledge of geology led him to think that his land contained plaster rock, and he made repeated borings to ascertain the fact. In 1849 he discovered plaster near the present site of the Eagle Mills, and erected a plaster mill in 1852. In 1856 he sold to Hovey & Co. for $35,000.

EAGLE MILLS.

Hovey & Co. bought their property in 1856, and built their mill during the summer of 1857. The first year they mined about 2,000 tons. The business steadily increased until 1860, when the Grand Rapids Plaster Company was organized and the firm of Hovey & Co. merged in that. The amount of plaster quarried and sold by them prior to 1869 was about 98,000 tons, and for 1869 the total was about 18,000 tons. They have now increased their facilities, so that they can grind 200 tons of land plaster in 20 hours, and have the power to double their capacity if they choose. They have just completed and put in running order a new engine of 200 horse power, and have facilities for loading from 40 to 50 cars per day. They have also recently put in one of the Illinois Pneumatic Gas Company's machines for lighting their quarry and mill. The quarry is under a low bluff, aud is widely known as the great plaster cave, being about five acres in extent and covered with from 20 to 75 feet of earth and rock. The stratum is about 12 feet in thickness. The Lake Shore & Michigan Southern Railroad (Kalamazoo Division) runs through their mill yard, connecting with other railroads leading into the city.

EMMET MILLS.

These mills are owned by C. H. Taylor, B. F. McReynolds, P. R. L. Peirce, and L. G. Mason, under the firm name, however, of Taylor & McReynolds, who own about 40 acres of plaster land, which will work out about 35,000 tons per acre. They bought the property three years ago, and have mined for the past three years an average of 10,000 tons per year. Their works were trebled in extent during the year 1870, and can manufacture 200 tons of ground plaster in 22 hours, and 20,000 barrels of stucco per year. Their location is on Grand River, near the city limits, and on the line of the Lake Shore & Michigan Southern Railroad (Kalamazoo Division), and they quarry under the hill the same as the Eagle Mills. The product of this mill for 1870 will be about 10,000 tons.

The companies above named, together with Geo. H. White & Co., mentioned in the history of Wyoming, are all that are engaged in plaster mining in Grand

Rapids and vicinity, and the aggregate capital now engaged in this business is about $400,000. The total of the production of plaster in and near Grand Rapids, up to the close of 1869, was about 277,000 tons, and the aggregate value thereof has been $1,248,000. The total of the production of 1869 was about 50,000 tons. Plaster has been found at Grandville, seven miles below Grand Rapids, on Grand River, and also at points two and three miles above Grand Rapids, and it is probable that many good quarries may be opened in the future, should the demands of the trade require it. The beds now worked are practically inexhaustible.

C. C. COMSTOCK'S MANUFACTORIES.

Mr. C. C. Comstock is one of the leading manufacturers in Grand Rapids. He has two saw mills, a pail and tub factory, planing mill, and sash, blind and door factory. His principal manufactories are situated on the east side of Canal street, between Mason and Newberry streets, occupying, with the yard for piling staves and lumber, drying houses, etc., sixteen lots, 50x100 feet each. The principal building is of brick, and 220 feet in length, averaging 45 feet in width, three stories high, is covered with a durable tin roof, and is divided by fire walls and iron doors into six apartments. In the other buildings and the old pail factory, 45x100 feet, and two stories high, a full set of pail machinery is running. In another building, 22x70 feet, ten saws are run, cutting pail and tub staves and bottoms. On the grounds are nine dry kilns, either built or lined with brick, the largest quite expensive, and fire proof, beside a number of large buildings for drying, storage, etc. The number of men in his employ is about 50, and it requires an outlay of nearly or quite $150,000 per year to carry on his business.

NELSON, MATTER & CO.

It would be hard to find in this part of the West a more complete establishment for the manufacture and sale of furniture, than that of the above named firm, in this city. Their manufactory at the foot of Lyon street is 68x90 feet in size, four stories high, and full of the most improved machinery for turning, sawing and carving the numerous styles of furniture which they manufacture. Their storehouses on Huron street are 54x68 feet in size, and four stories high, and their elegant sales rooms, 29 and 31 Canal street, are 54x80 feet, and occupy three floors. They employ, constantly, about 90 workmen, and ship their manufactures to all parts of Michigan, to Illinois, to Wisconsin, Minnesota, Iowa, Missouri, Nebraska, Kansas, Ohio, and Pennsylvania.

GRAND RAPIDS MANUFACTURING COMPANY.

The above named company have their works on Water street, west side, and their office in Ball's new block, Canal street, and are extensively engaged in the manufacture of agricultural implements and machinery. They make, among other things, large numbers of Sulky Rakes, and of the Buckey Saw Machine; employing from 30 to 40 men. The sales rooms of the company, in Ball's block, are 22x 100 feet in size, and occupy four floors ot that elegant building. The business was first established by the late J. F. Chubb, in 1850, and went into the hands of the present company about a year ago. Mr. A. L. Chubb has been connected with the works ever since they were started, and is now President of the company.

EMPIRE ORGAN COMPANY.

The Empire Organ Company is one of the manufacturing institutions which reflects credit on the city. It was first established in Kalamazoo, in 1867, and removed here last April. The excellence of the musical instruments which they send out, achieves for the makers success, esteem and patronage, which other manufacturers have not been able to acquire in years. Mr. Piggott has had a long experience in this branch of manufactures, and there is not a more thorough master of the art of making reed instruments than he. Their instruments have taken the first premium in competition with the Smith's American, Mason & Hamlin, and Estey organs. Their factory and music store is located at 65 Monroe street, and occupies three floors, employing several first-class workmen. The firm consists of George Piggott and A. F. Burch. Mr. E. A. Baird is traveling agent.

WM. HARRISON.

One of the largest manufacturing establishments in the city is the lumber wagon manufactory of Wm. Harrison, occupying two buildings, one on Front street, west side of the river, and the other on Mill street, east side. Mr. H. commenced the manufacture of wagons in the building situated on the west side of the river, fourteen years ago. His business becoming very extensive he finally found it neecssary to occupy a second building, devoting the one on this side of the river to machinery work, and the other to hand work. The latter building is a large, stone structure, 40x80 feet in size, three stories high. The former is 50x70 feet in size, and is two stories high.

Mr. Harrison has about 35 men constantly in his employ, and has turned out during the past year 700 wagons. He is doing a large wholesale business throughout this State, and sends some of his wagons as far as Texas. They are sold, in large numbers, in the States of Missouri, Kansas, Nebraska, Minnesota, and Iowa. He does not confine himself to the wholesale trade, however, but does a large retail business. Everybody has heard of "Harrison's wagons," and very many in this vicinity, and elsewhere, can testify to their strength and durability.

BUTTERWORTH & LOWE'S FOUNDRY AND MACHINE SHOP.

Located near the foot of the east side canal, in the very heart of the city, are the Foundry and Machine Shops of Butterworth & Lowe. Long years ago a portion of the site on which they stand was occupied by Uncle Louis Campau's Indian trading post. These works were first started by James McCray, since deceased, in 1843. In 1844, Mr. Daniel Ball became a partner. In 1851, Mr. McCray died, and the business was carried on by Mr. Ball, in company with G. M. and S. B. McCray—sons of the first proprietor. Mr. Ball finally bought out their interests, and, in 1856, admitted Mr. R. E. Butterworth as a partner. Mr. Butterworth, two years later, bought out Mr. Ball, and was sole proprietor until 1869, when he admitted his present partner, Mr. James Lowe, recently from near Manchester, England. Mr. G. M. McCray is now principal foreman. These works are among the oldest and largest in western Michigan, and occupy, with foundry, machine shops, blacksmith shops, agricultural shop, pattern shop, storehouses, etc., over half an acre of ground; giving employment to from fifty to sixty hands.

BERKEY BROS. & GAY.

Berkey Bros. & Gay have one of the most extensive furniture manufactories in the Western States. Their factory is situated on the east side canal, near Bridge street, and is 50x140 feet in size, with four floors. On the corner of Kent and Hastings streets they have two warehouses for shipping and storage purposes, each 35x100 feet in size, and three stories high. Their retail rooms are situated at No. 43 Monroe street, occupying three floors, each 25x90 feet in size, in one block, and two of about the same dimensions in an adjoining building. They are now making, and keep on hand, some of the finest upholstery work, lamberkins and cornices, manufactured in the country. During the past year they have shipped about $150,000 worth of furniture of their own manufacture, and their trade extends not only over our own state, but into New York, Pennsylvania, Ohio, Indiana, Illinois, Wisconsin, Iowa, Minnesota, Nebraska, Kansas, Missouri, and Colorado. They employ as many as 120 men in and about their establishment, and keep on hand some 1,500,000 feet of walnut and other valuable lumber.

EMPIRE GANG SAW MILLS.

Among the most important manufacturing establishments in Grand Rapids are the extensive steam saw mills of Wonderly & Co., situated on the west side of Grand River, between Leonard street Bridge and the track of the Detroit & Milwaukee Railroad. This enterprising firm, thoroughly acquainted with the lumber business in Pennsylvania, commenced operations here in the latter part of October, 1869. Since that time they have erected one of the most extensive saw mills in the State, capable of cutting 15,000,000 feet per season, and manufactured, up to November 1st, 1870, over 8,000,000 feet of lumber. Their main building is 50x116 feet in size, two stories high, and has engine and boiler rooms attached. The machinery is run by two engines of 150 horse power. A gang of saws, in which twenty-eight saws can be run when necessary, converts the largest log into boards in a few minutes, it being first trimmed on two sides by a five foot circular saw. The lumber is distributed in the yard by means of some 4,500 feet of horse-railway, elevated about ten feet from the ground. A railroad track extends to the yard, which, with about 1,000 feet of track between the different lumber piles, gives easy access to all railroads extending from the city. Their logs are procured on Rouge River, Flat River, Fish Creek, and their tributaries, where they have a supply of pine timber that will last for many years. Their booms hold about 2,000,000 feet of logs at one time. They ship immense quantities of lumber to southern Michigan, Indiana, Ohio, Kentucky, and some to Pennsylvania, competing successfully with Chicago dealers. In connection with the saw mill is a large planing mill, containing two heavy flooring and matching machines, a surfacing machine, patent siding mill, circular re-sawing machine, etc. J. H. Wonderly and D. E. Little, both young men, compose the firm.

THE MICHIGAN BARREL COMPANY

have recently erected an immense factory near the depot of the Detroit & Milwaukee Railroad, in which they have one of the largest steam engines in Western Michigan. They manufacture the "Water's improved barrel," bail, salt and grease boxes, and all kinds of rim work, employing a large number of men and boys, and shipping their manufactures to nearly all parts of the union. The building which they occupy is vast in its proportions, and admirably arranged throughout.

(SEE OPPOSITE PAGE.)

Directory of Kent County,

INCLUDING ALL THE TERRITORY OUTSIDE OF GRAND RAPIDS CITY.

In the following list the figures and names following the names of individuals, indicate the number of the section upon which the person resides, the name of township, and post-office address, in the order mentioned.

A

Abbott Mrs. Juliana, 13 Algoma, Edgerton.
Abbott John Henry, 13 Algoma, Edgerton.
Abbott Ezra R., 1 Bowne, Lowell.
ABBY SYLVESTER, Cedar Springs.
Abby Sylvester, 35 Solon, Cedar Springs
Abel Myron, 14 Vergennes, Lowell.
Abel Carlos A., 36 Wyoming, Grand Rapids.
Abraham Edson, Lowell.
Abraham James, 36 Cannon, Cannonsburg.
Abrams Delos, Lowell.
Abram Patrick, 1 Ada, Cannonsburg.
Ackley Edward, 33 Paris, Grand Rapids.
Ackley Samuel L. Village Cedar Springs
Ackerson William, 8 Grand Rapids.
Ackerson C., 8 Grand Rapids.
Ackert Peter A., 32 Nelson, Cedar Springs.
Ackert Oliver C., 15 Grattan, Grattan Center.
Ackert George T., 15 Grattan, Grattan Center.
Acker Theodore, Rockford.
Acker Geo., 35 Lowell, Lowell.
Adams John, 3 Courtland, Courtland Center.
ADAMS ALANSON R., 1 Oakfield, Greenville.
ADAMS FRANK D., 16 Grattan, Grattan Center.
Adams George C., 16 Grattan, Grattan Center.
Adams John A., 16 Grattan, Grattan Center.
ADAMS JOHN H., 34 Tyrone, Sparta Cen.
Adams J. B., Lowell.
ADAMS DANIEL, Sparta Center.
Adams James, — Cannon, Cannonsburg
Adams Seymour H., Lowell.
Adams Wm. W., 23 Gaines, Hammond.
ADAMS JAMES W., 25 Byron, Cody's Mills.
Adams H. S., Lowell.
Adams John P., 6 Cannon, Rockford.
Adams Marcellus, 28 Tyrone, Casnovia.
Adams Marcellus W., 29 Byron, Byron Center.
Adams James, 34 Walker, G. Rapids.
Addison Albert, 23 Courtland, Courtland Center.
ADDISON THOMAS, 23 Courtland, Courtland Center.
Addison Robert, 23 Courtland, Courtland Center.
Addison Robert, Rockford.
ADDIS GEO. W., 20 Oakfield, Oakfield.
ADDIS JOHN, 20 Oakfield, Oakfield.
Afton Charles, 27 Tyrone, Sparta Cen.
AKERLY BENJ. N., 4 Cannon, Rockford.
Abbey Henry, 30 Alpine, Indian Creek.
Albert Martin, 11 Alpine, Alpine.

Albee N. F., 19 Tyrone, Casnovia.
Albright Gideon D., 30 Paris, Grand Rapids.
Albright Isaac, 5 Byron, Grandville.
Albright John, 31 Wyoming, Grandville.
Alcorn Joseph, Lowell.
Alcorn John, Lowell.
Alcumbrack Daniel, 20 Grand Rapids.
Alcumbrack Alonzo, 27 Vergennes, Lowell.
Alderman Erastus D., 24 Lowell, Lowell.
Aldrich Harmon, 32 Tyrone, Casnovia.
Aldrich Marvin, Lowell.
Aldrich Lyman, Lowell.
ALDRICH JAMES, 16 Bowne, Alto.
Aldrich Cyrus, 24 Grattan, Grant.
Aldrich Henry, 35 Grattan, Alton.
Aldrich Hiram, 23 Vergennes, Vergennes.
ALDRICH AURILLA, 24 Vergennes, Fallassburg.
Aldrich Marshal, 2 Vergennes, Alton.
Aldrich Julius, 9 Vergennes, Alton.
Aldrich Edward, 26 Byron, Cody's Mills.
ALDRICH WILLIAM, 9 Vergennes, Alton.
Allen Robert T., 35 Gaines, Caledonia Station.
Allen Samuel, 16 Lowell, Lowell.
ALLEN SYLVESTER, 30 Plainfield, Mill Creek.
Allen Laban, 20 Courtland, Courtland Center.
Allen Hiram H., 19 Paris, Grand Rapids.
Allen Isaac, 27 Courtland, Courtland Center.
Allen Wright C., 19 Paris, Grand Rapids.
Allen William, 23 Plainfield, Austerlitz.
ALLEN ASA M., Rockford.
Allen L. W., 3 Walker, Indian Creek.
ALLEN THOMAS W., 1 Solon, Sand Lake.
Allen Ebenezer, 27 Algoma, Rockford.
ALLEN CHAS. B., 6 Cannon, Rockford.
Allen Laban, 29 Cannon, Austerlitz.
ALLEN VOLNEY, 3 Oakfield, Spencer Mills.
Almy Alonzo, 28 Nelson, Cedar Springs
Almy Thomas, 28 Nelson, Cedar Springs.
Almy William, 28 Nelson, Cedar Springs.

Alden Scott, 2 Courtland, Courtland Center.
Alden Avery E., Alaska Village.
ALDEN ELIJAH D., Alaska Village.
Alden John S., Alaska Village.
Alden Avery E., Alaska.
Alexander Willard, 31 Vergennes, Lowell.
Alexander Nelson W., 14 Wyoming, Grand Rapids.
Alexander Charles, 14 Wyoming, Grand Rapids.
ALGER LOUIS J., 12 Vergennes, Lowell.
Alger John L., 7 Paris, Grand Rapids.
Alger John D., 7 Paris, Grand Rapids.
Allen Joseph W., 3 Walker, Indian Creek.
Allen James, 28, Lowell, Lowell.
ALLEN WM. T., 29 Gaines, Cody's Mills.
Allen William G., 7 Cascade, Grand Rapids.
Allen Mrs. Mary A., 20 Courtland, Courtland Cen.
Allen Henry, 16 Paris, Grand Rapids.
Almy Alphonso W., 5 Walker, Indian Creek.
Althen Charles, Lowell.
Ames John, 4 Ada, Ada.
Ames B., 18 Grand Rapids, Grand Rapids.
AMES WALTER C., 24 Wyoming, Kelloggsville.
Amidon Caleb, 9 Sparta, Sparta Center.
Amidon Wiliard, 16 Sparta, Sparta Center.
Ammerman Nelson, 30 Cannon, Austerlitz.
Ammerman David, 22 Plainfield, Austerlitz.
AMMERMAN NELSON, 1 Plainfield, Austerlitz.
Ammerman Elisha, 23 Cannon, Cannonsburg.
Ammerman David, 1 Plainfield, Rockford.
AMOND GODFREY, Cedar Springs.
Amond Joseph, Cedar Springs.
Amon John, 20 Caledonia, Caledonia Station.
Amphlett Joseph W., Lowell.
Amsden L. Miles, Lowell.

A. L. SKINNER. GEO. S. WARD.

SKINNER & WARD,

General Insurance

AND

WAR CLAIM AGENTS,

Office up stairs, City National Bank Building,

Post Office Drawer, 2281. GRAND RAPIDS, MICH.

Dr. AIKIN,

Office, No. 11 Canal Street, - - Grand Rapids,

(First stairs north of Sweet's Hotel.)—Attends to Cases in All Branches of His Profession, curing hundreds where "old school," one-pathy, inexperienced, ignorant "root and herb, or Indian" doctors fail. ☞Terms favorable to all. Consultation, Free.

No idle pretensions or imposture, no flattering or experiments, no injurious drugs, but careful examination and the most reliable treatment—the best remedies approved by science and experience—which may cure YOU, though discouraged and hopeless.

Specialties:—Diseases of the Eye and Ear, Throat, Lungs and Heart, Liver and Kidneys, and all Chronic, Constitutional and Blood Diseases.

Skillful attention given to all cases in Surgery.

Asthma, Catarrh, Rheumatism, Neuralgia, Epilepsy, Scrofula, Piles, Dropsy, Dyspepsia, &c., cured.

LADIES out of health, assured of easy, safe cure.

Cancers and Tumors removed without the knife.

☞INFALLIBLE REMEDIES—Surest and quickest known for all Private Diseases of both sexes, young and old. The worst cases of Stricture and Chronic Venereal diseases quickly relieved. No Mercury used.

Travelers supplied with medicines at short notice.

To YOUTHS AND MEN: The *only* perfect *cure*, permanent and reliable, for Seminal Weakness, Nervous Debility, Impotence, etc. Worth $1,000 to the unfortunate. No quackery or deception. The fullest guarantee given. *All Business Strictly Confidential.*

☞In all special, important cases, stop unreliable or useless treatment, and consult Dr. Aikin at once. Call, or send postage for circulars and questions. (Hours 8 to 8.)

Address, N. J. AIKIN, M. D.,
Grand Rapids, Mich.

P. O. Drawer, **2091.**

J. S. CROSBY. M. S. CROSBY.

CROSBY & SON'S

GENERAL

Insurance and Real Estate Agency,

13 Canal Street,

GRAND RAPIDS, MICH.

Capital Represented, $73,178,105.38.

Agents "Mutual Benefit Life Insurance Co."

Amstice James, Cedar Springs.
Amy Samuel, 14 Courtland, Courtland Center.
Anderson M. B., 1 Byron, Grand Rapids.
ANDERSON JOSEPH, 29 Bowne, Harris Creek.
Anderson John, 32 Lowell, Alto.
Anderson John A., 8 Gaines, Gainesville.
ANDERSON PETER, 20 Courtland, Rockford.
Anderson Duncan, 16 Vergennes, Vergennes.
ANDERSON DONALD, 16 Vergennes, Vergennes.
Anderson Christian, 17 Grattan, Grattan Center.
Anderson Andrew, 16 Sparta, Sparta Center.
Anderson William, 16 Sparta, Sparta Center.
Anderson John, 16 Sparta, Sparta Cen.
ANDERSON CHARLES, 39 Alpine, Englishville.
Anderson Joel, Lisbon.
ANDERSON JOHN H., 7 Courtland, Edgerton.
Anderson Isaac, 20 Oakfield, Oakfield.
Ankney Michael, 26 Gaines, Hammond.
Ankney Jonathan, 35 Gaines, Cody's Mills.
Annis Solomon, Lowell.
Annis Alexander C., 18 Nelson, Cedar Springs.
Annis Richard, 30 Cascade, Cascade.
Annis Solomon, Lowell.
ANNIS WILLIAM, 28 Cascade, Cascade.
Annis Wallace, Lowell.
Annis Alson, Lowell.
ANNIS JAMES, 1 Alpine, Englishville.
ANNIS MRS. GRACE, 28 Cascade, Cascade.
Anna Nicholas, 32 Byron, Byron Center
Ansalmann John, 27 Alpine, G. Rapids.
Antor Adam, 10 Alpine, Alpine.
Anway Ira, 11 Tyrone, Sparta Center.
Apet George, 9 Courtland, Courtland Center.
Apple Andrew, Lisbon.
Apsey John, 35 Cascade, Alaska.
APTED A. M., 34 Walker, G. Rapids.
Arbour James F., 28 Alpine, G. Rapids
Arbour M. T., Rockford.
Arbour B. P., 28 Alpine, Grand Rapids.
Armstrong Riel, Cedar Springs.

Anderson Joseph, 20 Oakfield, Oakfield.
Anderson Thomas, 32 Lowell, Alto.
Anderson Goram, 7 Sparta, Lisbon.
Andrews James H., 34 Grattan, Alton.
Andrews Alva H., 34 Grattan, Alton.
Andrews Norman, 10 Gaines, Hammond
Andrews Samuel, 1 Plainfield, Rockford.
Andrews Oliver, 25 Courtland, Courtland Center.
ANDREWS WILLIAM, 6 Bowne, Alto.
Andrews John A., 34 Grattan, Alton.
Andrews Lewis P., 28 Algoma, Rockford.
Andrus Lemon, 29 Oakfield, Oakfield.
ANDRUS CHARLES W., 1 Alpine, Englishville.
Andrus Mrs. Sarah, 1 Alpine, Englishville.
Anderson Jacob, 7 Sparta, Lisbon.
Anderson Alexander, 16 Vergennes, Vergennes.
ANNABLE GEORGE, 6 Cannon, Rockford.
Angel Heber, 32 Lowell, Alto.
ANGELL ABIAH, 7 Caledonia, Alaska.
Angell Amasa, 18 Oakfield, Oakfield.
Armstrong George W., 20 Cannon, Cannonsburg.
Armstrong Charles, 21 Cannon, Cannonsburg.
ARMSTRONG JAMES, Cedar Springs.
Armstrong Jesse B., 20 Cannon, Cannonsburg.
Armstrong James M., 30 Tyrone, Casnovia.
Arnold Alonzo J., 29 Wyoming, Grandville.
Arnold Abram H., 25 Nelson, Nelson.
Arnold William, 21 Grand Rapids.
ARNOLD DARIUS C., 8 Gaines, Gainesville.
Arnold James, 19 Spencer, Nelson.
Arnet William, 4 Gaines, Grand Rapids
Arndt Jacob W., 26 Walker, G. Rapids.
ARSNOE NELSON, 18 Plainfield, Alpine.
Arsnoe James, 24 Alpine, Mill Creek.
ARSNOE PETER, 24 Alpine, Alpine.
Arsnoe Charles, 24 Alpine, Alpine.
Arthur John, Village Cedar Springs.
Artin Thomas, 26 Grand Rapids.
Aschenbrenner Fred., 23 Alpine, Alpine

ASHLEY SHELDON, 1 Grattan, Ashley.
Ashley Calvin, 35 Cannon, Cannonsburg.
ASHLEY NOAH R., 28 Courtland, Courtland Center.
ASHLEY CHARLES, 2 Grattan, Ashley.
ASHLEY ABNER, 1 Grattan, Ashley.
ASHLEY JOHN, 36 Oakfield, Ashley.
Ashmore Samuel, 5 Walker, Indian Creek.
ATHERTON SYLVANUS, Lisbon.
Atherton George, 19 Sparta, Lisbon.
Atkinson Roger, 23 Walker, G. Rapids.
ATKINS JOHN P., Lisbon.
ATKINS WM. J., 16 Grattan, Grattan Center.
Atkins Horace G., 16 Grattan, Grattan Center.
Atkins Guy H., 16 Grattan, Grattan Center.
Atkins Mrs. W. L., 16 Grattan, Grattan Center.
Atwood William, 14 Vergennes, Lowell.
Auble Milo C., 26 Paris, Grand Rapids.
AUBLE ISAAC E., 30 Cascade, Grand Rapids.
Auble William, 30 Cascade, G. Rapids.
AUSTIN LAUREN, 15 Courtland, Courtland Center.
Austin Phineas, Rockford.
Austin Nelson F., 16 Plainfield, Belmont.
Austin J. J., Rockford.
Austin John, 21 Courtland, Courtland Center.
AUSTIN L. H., 14 Solon, Cedar Springs
Austin Isaiah W., 33 Paris, G. Rapids.
AUSTIN DAVID C., Rockford.
Austin Henry J., 7 Sparta, Lisbon.
AUSTIN AMOS, Rockford.
Austin Lewis, 6 Lowell, Lowell.
Austin Russell, 33 Oakfield, Grattan Center.
AUSTIN GEORGE, 4 Grand Rapids.
Austin Reuben S., 1 Plainfield, Rockford.
Austin Lumas, 6 Lowell, Lowell.
Austin Philip, 12 Plainfield, Rockford.
Averill E., 34 Ada, Ada.
Averill Levi F., 7 Walker, G. Rapids.
Avery H. W., Lowell.
Avery Wm. H., Rockford.
Avery Robert, 30 Cannon, Austerlitz.
Avery Edward, Lowell.
Avery Earl W., Lowell.

Auble George, 35 Paris, Grand Rapids.
Auble Andrew J., 9 Cascade, Cascade.
Auger Lewis, 27 Vergennes, Lowell.
Augustine Rinaldo, 5 Alpine, Lisbon.
Austin John, Lowell.
Austin Henry, 10 Lowell, Lowell.
Austin Leonard C., Rockford.
Austin Orville, 17 Lowell, Lowell.
Austin Charles E., 17 Lowell, Lowell.
Avery Robert, 19 Spencer, Nelson.
Avery George, Lowell.
Avery Mrs. F. R., Lowell.
Avink Amber, 14 Paris, Grand Rapids.
Avink Aaron J., 24 Paris, Grand Rapids
AYERS AUGUSTUS, 19 Tyrone, Casnovia.
AYLESWORTH WILLIS, 22 Cannon, Cannonsburg.

B

Babcock Calvin, 16 Algoma, Rockford.
Babcock Charles A., 16 Algoma, Rockford.
Babcock Benj. F., Sparta Center.
Babe James, 33 Cascade, Alaska.
Babe James, 4 Caledonia, Alaska.
BACON JOHN, 10 Grand Rapids.
Bacon Elisha D., Village Cannonsburg.
Bacon B. F., 1 Alpine, Englishville.
BACON RICHARD, 22 Tyrone, Casnovia.
Bacon Horace L., 22 Tyrone, Casnovia.
Bacon Rufus, 3 Grand Rapids.
BACON S. S., 17 Grand Rapids.
BADGLEY JOHN, 21 Plainfield, Belmont.
Bahre William, Lisbon.
BAIL J. W., 30 Tyrone, Casnovia.
Bail F. A., 30 Tyrone, Casnovia.
Bailey Bradford, Cedar Springs.
Bailey W. J., 35 Solon, Cedar Springs.
RAILEY WARREN, 1 Alpine, Englishville.
Bailey Mrs. R., 35 Algoma, Rockford.
BAILEY MRS. NANCY, 2 Alpine, Englishville.
BAILEY H. L., 1 Alpine, Englishville.
BAILEY CHARLES, 1 Alpine, Englishville.

BAILEY ARTHUR, 1 Ada, Ada.
Bailey Murray, 1 Ada, Ada.
Bailey Harvey K., 34 Algoma, Rockford.
Bailey Otis, 20 Vergennes, Vergennes.
Bailey Wm. K., 24 Cannon, Cannonsburg.
Bailey Benjamin, 35 Bowne, Bowne.
Bailey John, 35 Bowne, Bowne.
Bailey Bradford, 30 Nelson, Cedar Springs.
Bailey Emerson, 23 Bowne, Bowne.
Bailey Sanford H., 19 Nelson, Cedar Springs.
Bailey Gideon, 15 Nelson, Sand Lake.
BAILEY WM. H., 8 Nelson, Cedar Springs.
Bailey Gilbert G., 14 Paris, G. Rapids.
Bailey Freeborn F., 13 Paris, G. Rapids
Bailey Joseph C., 19 Nelson, Cedar Springs.
Bailey Mary, 17 Nelson, Cedar Springs.
BAILEY SMITH, 20 Vergennes, Vergennes.
Bailey Joseph S., 14 Paris, G. Rapids.
Bailey Ansil E., 14 Paris, G. Rapids.
Bailey Wm. L., 2 Walker, G. Rapids.
Bainbridge Thomas, 21 Byron, Byron Center.
Baldwin Henry, 29 Courtland, Rockford.
Baldwin William, Bockford.
Baldwin Edward, 18 Vergennes, Vergennes.
Baldwin James L., Jr., 18 Vergennes, Vergennes.
BALDWIN JAMES L., 18 Vergennes, Vergennes.
Baldwin William, 2 Cannon, Rockford.
Baldwin James H., 23 Cannon, Cannonsburg.
Baldwin James A., Village Cannonsburg.
Ball J. S., Lowell.
Ball Wm. N., Lowell.
Ball, Allen P., 13 Alpine, Alpine.
BALL SILAS, 13 Alpine, Alpine.
BALL NATHAN A., 32 Byron, Byron Center.
Ball Benton W., 29 Byron, Byron Cen.
Ball Nathan P., 29 Byron, Byron Cen.
Ball Mrs. Huldah C., Grandville.
Ballard Charles L., 35 Sparta, Englishville.
Ballard Lyman S., 35 Sparta, Englishville.
Ballard Benjamin, 3 Walker, Indian Creek.

Bainbridge John, 9 Gaines, Hammond.
BAINBRIDGE WM. R., 9 Gaines, Hammond.
Baker William, 15 Byron, Byron Center
Baker Isaac, 13 Plainfield, Rockford.
Baker Alonzo, 36 Caledonia, Middleville, Barry County.
Baker John, 12 Vergennes, Lowell.
Baker Nathan N., 20 Paris, G. Rapids.
Baker Lorenzo, 36 Caledonia, Middleville, Barry County.
Baker Zelken, 1 Wyoming, G. Rapids.
Baker George R., 12 Vergennes, Lowell.
Baker John C., 34 Bowne, Fillmore, Barry County.
BAKER JOHN, 3 Plainfield, Rockford.
Baker William, 3 Plainfield, Rockford.
Baker John, Village Cannonsburg.
Baker George R., 12 Vergennes, Alton.
Baker John C., 12 Vergennes, Alton.
Baker Eunice, 29 Cannon, Austerlitz.
Balcom George B., Lowell.
BALCOM JOHN, Sparta Center.
Bale Henry, 16 Grattan, Grattan Center
Baldwin Edward, 29 Courtland, Rockford.
Ballard O. T., 22 Plainfield, Belmont.
Ballard Sherre H., 35 Sparta, Englishville.
BALFOUR JAMES, 9 Sparta, Lisbon.
Bammaerlin Lewis F., 30 Plainfield, Mill Creek.
BAMMAERLIN REINHARDT F., 30 Plainfield, Mill Creek.
Banks John, 1 Oakfield, Greenville.
Banks George, 1 Oakfield, Greenville.
Bannister Willis, 31 Nelson, Cedar Springs.
Barber George W., 27 Caledonia, Caledonia.
Barber James M., 27 Caledonia, Caledonia.
BARBER GEORGE, 19 Gaines, Gainesville.
Barber M. C., Lowell.
Barber Leonard, 9 Grand Rapids.
Barber J. H., 11 Lowell, Lowell.
Barber Alfred, 24 Lowell, Lowell.
Barber Alfred, 24 Lowell, Lowell.
Barber William R., Lowell.
Barber Martin, 13 Lowell, Lowell.
Barber Wallace, 9 Grand Rapids.
Barber Robert, Lowell.

BARBER OSCAR B., Postmaster at Caledonia.
BARBER A. A., Lowell.
Barber Asahel, 3 Cannon, Rockford.
Barber Robert, Lowell.
Barber William, 12 Wyoming, Grand Rapids.
Barbin Raine, Lowell.
Bardeen Lewis, 30 Oakfield, Oakfield.
Baragar James, 22 Wyoming, Grand Rapids.
Baragar Theodore, 22 Wyoming, Grand Rapids.
Barr Axtyl Y., 8 Paris, Grand Rapids.
BARR GUILD, 7 Paris, Grand Rapids.
Barr R. M., 28 Grand Rapids.
Barr George R., 25 Grand Rapids.
BARR REUBEN, Cedar Springs.
Barr Thomas B., 6 Lowell, Lowell.
Barringer Marcus, 28 Algoma, Rockford.
Barringer David, 28 Algoma, Rockford
Barigan Dennis, 10 Courtland, Courtland Center.
Barringer John, 28 Algoma, Rockford.
Barrett George, Alaska.
Barrett Smith, 7 Nelson, Cedar Springs.
BARRETT HIRAM A., 9 Grattan, Grattan Center.
Barnes Mott, 4 Courtland, Courtland Center.
Barnes Thomas, 32 Bowne, Harris Creek.
Barnes Augustus, 25 Grattan, Smyrna, Ionia County.
Barnes E. P., 17 Grand Rapids.
Barnes Iram, 25 Nelson, Cedar Springs.
Barnes James, 23 Plainfield, Austerlitz.
Barnes John, 29 Grand Rapids.
Barnes John M., 24 Algoma, Edgerton.
BARNES T. D., Lisbon.
Barnes Reuben, 21 Sparta, Sparta Cen.
Barnes Iram C., 16 Oakfield, Oakfield.
Barnes Ely, 25 Byron, Cody's Mills.
Barnes Jacob, 23 Walker, G. Rapids.
BARNEY CORKINS, 18 Byron, Byron Center.
Barney James M., 32 Byron, Byron Center.
Barney Simon Z., 32 Byron, Byron Cen.
BARNUM WM. W., 30 Paris, Grand Rapids.
Barnum Franklin H., 31 Paris, Grand Rapids.
Barnum Franklin, 25 Wyoming, Kelloggville.
Barkman James, 19 Algoma, Sparta Center.

Barrett Henry J., 34 Tyrone, Sparta Center.
Barrett Charles L., 27 Tyrone, Sparta Center.
BARRETT JOHN, Alaska.
Barry James, 36 Grand Rapids.
Barrows George H., 36 Sparta, Englishville.
Barrows Asahel, 32 Plainfield, Grand Rapids.
Barrows Corydon, 24 Cascade, Cascade.
Barrows Abner, 2 Cannon, Bostwick Lake.
Barris Ransom, Alaska.
BARRIS WILLIAM, 2 Caledonia, Alaska.
Barris Ransom J., Alaska Village.
Barras Charles, 22 Cascade, Cascade.
Bareis Jacob, 32 Lowell, Alto.
Barris Byron B., 2 Caledonia, Alaska.
Barnard Ezra P., 30 Oakfield, Oakfield.
Barnard James, Lowell.
Barnard William, 30 Oakfield, Oakfield.
BARNARD JAMES F., Lowell.
BARNARD STEPHEN P., 33 Grand Rapids.
Barkley Wm. H., 32 Cannon, Austerlitz.
BARKLEY CHARLES, 29 Grand Rapids, Grand Rapids.
Barkley Wellington, Village Cedar Springs.
Barkley Byard, 15 Ada, Ada.
Barkley Harvey, 28 Lowell, Lowell.
BARCK JOHN H., Alaska.
BARCLAY ABRAHAM C., 24 Paris, Grand Rapids.
Barker John W., Rockford.
Barker J. W., Rockford.
Barker R. W., Rockford.
Barker Thomas N., Rockford.
Barker I. Irving, Rockford.
Barker Nelson, 30 Wyoming, Grandville.
Barker T. Newton, Rockford.
Barker Isaac, Rockford.
Barker Mason A., 30 Wyoming, Grandville.
Barker Charles L., 29 Cannon, Austerlitz.
Bartlett Jonah, 5 Nelson, Sand Lake.
BARTLETT HORATIO N., 17 Cascade, Cascade.

BARTLETT GEO. E., 36 Lowell, Lowell.
Barto Barlow, 35 Grattan, Alton.
Barton John, 23 Spencer, Spencer Mills
Barton Elliott, 23 Spencer, Spencer Mills.
Barton Silas, Jr., 22 Spencer, Spencer Mills.
BARTON GEO. W., 26 Spencer, Spencer Mills.
Barton Silas, 23 Spencer, Spencer Mills.
Bash George, 1 Bowne, Alto.
Bassinger Winfield, 32 Vergennes, Lowell.
Bassett Almon, 26 Grattan, Grant.
Bassett Ezra, Village Cedar Springs.
Bassett Frederick, Sr., 20 Gaines, Gainesville.
Bass Wm. S., 1 Sparta, Sparta Center.
Bassett George, 6 Byron, Grandville.
Bassett Mrs. Phebe, 20 Gaines, Gainesville.
BATCHELTER JOHN T., 12 Solon, Cedar Springs.
Bates Alfred G., 29 Bowne, Harris Creek.
Bates B. F., 17 Grand Rapids.
BATES EDWARD, 15 Grand Rapids.
Bates George, 21 Oakfield, Oakfield.

Beach Richard W., 19 Grattan, Grattan Center.
Beach Mrs. Rosanna, 1 Ada, Ada.
Beach Samuel, 16 Ada, Ada.
BEACH VALENTINE, 32 Cannon, Cannonsburg.
BEACH WM. A., 12 Bowne, Bowne.
Beach Wm. H., 1 Ada, Ada.
Beach Warren, 22 Ada, Ada.
BEAK GEORGE, 29 Grand Rapids.
Beals Abram E., 13 Courtland, Oakfield.
Beals Edward, 13 Wyoming, Grand Rapids.
Beals Mrs. S. R., 15 Wyoming, Grand Rapids.
Beals William S., 16 Spencer, Spencer Mills.
BEAMER JOHN H., Alaska.
BEAR TIMOTHY C., 2 Caledonia, Alaska.
Beard Linsan, 5 Cascade, Cascade.
Beard Linsan, Jr., 5 Cascade, Cascade.
Beard Nelson, 5 Cascade, Cascade.
BEARDSLEY WILLIAM L., Village Cannonsburg.
Beardslee Abram, 25 Oakfield, Greenville.

Bates Nathan, 15 Grand Rapids.
Bates P. E. F., 17 Grand Rapids.
Bates Seth C., 24 Grattan, Grant.
Bates George R., 8 Gaines, Gainesville.
Bateman Caleb L., 24 Caledonia, Alaska
Bauchamp Anthony, 13 Algoma, Edgerton.
BAUCHAMP JOSEPH, 13 Algoma, Edgerton.
Bauchamp William, 13 Algoma, Edgerton.
Bawn Truman, 10 Grand Rapids.
Baxter Bernard, 22 Cascade, Cascade.
Baxter Eber H., 22 Cascade, Cascade.
Baxter Milo, 22 Cascade, Cascade.
Baxter Ormon, 22 Cascade, Cascade.
Baylis Thomas M., 14 Solon, Cedar Springs.
Bayle Henry, 31 Lowell, Alaska.
Beaber Joseph, 31 Byron, New Salem.
Beach Admiral, 1 Ada, Ada.
Beach Benjamin, 22 Ada, Ada.
Beach Mrs. Laura, 31 Paris, Grand Rapids.
Beach Mary H., 32 Cannon, Cannonsburg.
Beach Orrin, 22 Ada, Ada.

Beardslee John C., 34 Nelson, Cedar Springs.
Beatty Hamilton, 26 Courtland, Courtland Center.
Beatty William, 26 Courtland, Courtland Center.
BECHTEL BENJAMIN H., 28 Paris, Grand Rapids.
Bechtel Ephraim, 32 Caledonia, Caledonia Station.
Beckwith Charles W., 23 Vergennes, Fallassburg.
Beckwith Elijah, Rockford.
Beckwith Edgar L., 15 Vergennes, Lowell.
Beckwith Geo. H., 15 Vergennes, Lowell.
Beckwith Lysander, 22 Grand Rapids.
Beckwith Peter, 21 Grand Rapids.
BECKWITH WM. G., 16 Grand Rapids, Grand Rapids.
Becker Daniel, 13 Walker, Grand Rapids.
Becker Garrett, 8 Courtland, Courtland Center.
Becker Jacob N., 16 Oakfield, Oakfield.

Becker Philip, 36 Courtland, Courtland Center.
BECKER THEODORE W., 27 Courtland, Courtland Cen.
Beckley Everett A., 8 Cascade, Cascade.
BEEBE GUIRDEN F., South 6 Walker, Grand Rapids.
Beebe Rans, 34 Ada, Ada.
Beech Frank, 14 Grand Rapids.
Beede Franklin, 31 Walker, Grand Rapids.
Beehler George, Lowell.
Beer John, 13 Walker Grand Rapids.
BEERS JOHN H., 35 Vergennes, Lowell.
Beeton John, 22 Vergennes, Lowell.
Begrow Charles, 31 Caledonia, Caledonia Station.
Begrow Henry, 29 Caledonia, Caledonia Station.
Behler John, 34 Lowell, Alto.
BEHLER LEONARD, 34 Lowell, Alto.
BELKNAP ANSEL, 32 Vergennes, Lowell.
BELKNAP CHARLES, 6 Byron, Grandville.
BELKNAP CHARLES E., 24 Sparta, Sparta Center.
Bence Geo., Cedar Springs.
Benewa Lucy, 11 Gaines, Hammond.
BENEWA JACOB, 11 Gaines, Hammond.
Benedict Edgar R., Cedar Springs.
Benedict E. R., Cedar Springs.
Benedick Eli S., Lowell.
Benedict J. O.. Cedar Springs.
Benedict Julius O., Village Cedar Springs.
Benedict Luther, Rockford.
Benham Frederick, 9 Courtland, Courtland Center.
BENHAM FERNANDO, 8 Courtland, Courtland Center.
BENHAM FRANCIS, 8 Courtland, Courtland Center.
Benham John, 7 Bowne, Alto.
Benham Mrs. Lorain, 9 Courtland, Courtland Center.
Bennett George B., Lowell.
Bennett Geo., 24 Courtland, Courtland Center.
Bennett Harmon, 14 Courtland, Courtland Center.
Bennett Harmon, 13 Courtland, Courtland Center.
Bennett Horace T., 19 Paris, Grand Rapids.

Belknap James A., 24 Sparta, Sparta Center.
Belknap Joshua, 6 Byron, Grandville.
Bellows Ezra, 7 Cannon, Rockford.
Bellows Edmund C., 15 Cannon, Cannonsburg.
Bellows John D., 34 Courtland, Rockford.
BELLOWS LYMAN O., Alaska.
Bellows Simeon, 34, Courtland, Rockford.
Bell C. C., 5 Grand Rapids, Grand Rapids.
Bell E. B. 5 Grand Rapids.
BELL C. E., 5 Grand Rapids, Grand Rapids.
Bell John, Sparta Center.
Bell Robert H., 11 Lowell, Lowell.
Bellamy William, 17 Cascade, Cascade.
Bement H. H., Rockford.
Bemis Charles E., Rockford.
Bemis Charles, 2 Plainfield, Rockford.
Bemis Henry, 2 Plainfield, Rockford.
Benaway Chas. H., 14 Caledonia, Alaska.
Benaway Minard P., 14 Caledonia, Alaska.
Bennett John, 14 Courtland, Courtland Center.
BENNETT JOHN S., 21 Alpine, Grand Rapids.
Bennett Jonathan, Cedar Springs.
Benjamin Lewis, 11 Lowell, Lowell.
Benjamin William C., 24 Nelson, Nelson.
Benjamin Stephen H., 24 Ada, Ada.
Bennett Albert C., 21 Alpine, Grand Rapids.
Bennett Amelius A., 4 Lowell, Lowell.
Bennett Adelbert, Rockford.
Bennett Benjamin, Burch's Mills.
Bennet Charles, 22 Courtland, Courtland Center.
BENNETT CLARK L., 4 Lowell, Lowell.
Bennett E. B., Lowell.
Bennett Edward L., 22 Vergennes, Lowell.
Bennett Frances E. W., 4 Lowell, Lowell.
Bennett Morris 36 Alpine, Grand Rapids.
BENNETT PERRY 14 Courtland, Courtland Centre.

Bennett Mrs Sarah, 14 Courtland Courtland Center.
Bennett Lyman 14 Courtland Courtland Center.
Bennett Wm. H. Village, Cedar Springs
BENNETT WILLIAM 34 Ada Ada.
Bennett William H. Algoma, Rockford.
BENTON JAMES, 21 Alpine, Indian Creek.
BENSON PETER, 34 Nelson, Cedar Springs.
Bentley Alvin, 20 Grand Rapids.
Bentley Abisha, 24 Vergennes, Fallassburg.
Bepka Joseph, 20 Plainfield, Austerlitz.
BERGY EMANUEL, 35 Bowne, Fillmore, Barry County.
Bergy Isaac, 30 Caledonia, Caledonia.
Bergy Peter, 30 Caledonia, Caledonia.
Bergin J. S., Lowell.
BERGER HENRY R., South 5 Walker, Grand Rapids.
Berger W., 34 Walker, Grand Rapids.
BERKEY PETER, 25 Paris, Grand Rapids.
Berry Arthur, 33 Lowell, Alto.
Berry Caroline, 10 Oakfield, Oakfield.
Bickford Alonzo T., 33 Oakfield, Grattan Center.
Bickhart Jacob, Cedar Springs.
BICKNELL CHESTER C., 36 Solon, Cedar Springs.
Biddinger George, 34 Cascade, Alaska.
BIDDLEMAN HIRAM, 27 Sparta, Sparta Center.
Biddleman Simeon P. F., 27 Sparta, Sparta Center.
Bietwork William, 1 Wyoming, Grand Rapids.
Bigford Thomas, 18 Grattan, Grattan Center.
Bigler William, 12 Oakfield, Greenville.
Biggers John, 12 Lowell, Lowell.
Billings Calvin, 8 Sparta, Lisbon.
Billings Ezra, 13 Plainfield, Austerlitz.
Billings George, Cedar Springs.
Billings Mrs. Mary Ann, 18 Sparta, Lisbon.
Bills C. S., Lowell.
Bingaman Benj. F., Alaska.
Birch Alfred, 11 Vergennes, Lowell.
Birch Edwin, 11 Vergennes, Lowell.
Bird Edward, 9 Courtland, Courtland Center.
Bird John, 3 Grand Rapids.

Berry Edward, 33 Tyrone, Sparta Cen.
Berry Henry, 13 Wyoming, G. Rapids.
Berry John, 9 Cannon, Cannonsburg.
Berry John, 1 Walker, Grand Rapids.
Berry Justus, 1 Cannon, Bostwick Lake.
Berry Lester, 18 Grattan, Grattan Cen.
Berry Matthew, 13 Wyoming, Grand Rapids.
Berry Peleg, 10 Paris, Grand Rapids.
BERRY SIDNEY, 29 Grand Rapids, Grand Rapids.
Besard David, 33 Wyoming, North Byron.
BESSEY L. F., 9 Nelson, Sand Lake.
BEST JONATHAN, 16 Walker, Grand Rapids.
Betterly Albert, 5 Alpine, Lisbon.
Betterly Adelbert, 5 Alpine, Lisbon.
BETTERLY LEWIS, 5 Alpine, Lisbon.
Bettes Henry, 31 Sparta, Lisbon.
Bettes James, 31 Alpine, Indian Creek.
Bettes Joseph, 5 Sparta, Lisbon.
Bettes William E., 5 Sparta, Lisbon.
Bettes Gilbert, 31 Sparta, Lisbon.
Betzler Joseph, 32 Caledonia, Caledonia Station.
Bevins David W., 7 Cascade, Cascade.
Bird Joseph F., 18 Courtland, Courtland Center.
Bird Patrick, 3 Grand Rapids.
Bird Peter, 17 Grand Rapids.
BIRDSALL WM., 34 Alpine, Indian Creek.
Bisby George, 26 Vergennes, Lowell.
Bisbee John, Cedar Springs.
Bishop Christian, 2 Wyoming, Grand Rapids.
Bishop Edmund B., 13 Oakfield, Greenville.
Bishop Frederick, 2 Wyoming, Grand Rapids.
Bishop Loomis K., 24 Cannon, Cannonsburg.
BISHOP WM. F., 27 Solon, Cedar Springs.
Bissell Arnold, 32 Spencer, Cedar Springs.
Blackall Abraham H., 20 Sparta, Lisbon.
Blackall Benjamin, 29 Sparta, Lisbon.
Blackall Charles, 20 Sparta, Lisbon.
Black Andrew, 34 Courtland, Rockford.
Black John, 29 Algoma, Rockford.
BLACK JAMES, Cedar Springs.

Black John, 7 Paris, Grand Rapids.
Black William J., Rockford.
Black William, Cedar Springs.
Blackley Aaron, 18 Courtland, Edgerton.
Blackstone Cassius, 29 Vergennes, Lowell.
Blackmer Richmond, Cedar Springs.
Blackman Lorenzo D., 17 Sparta, Lisbon.
Blackshiel Richard, 23 Byron, Byron Center.
BLAIN CHARLES H., 5 Gaines, Grand Rapids.
BLAIN GEO. W., 17 Gaines, Grand Rapids.
Blaine George, 20 Byron, Byron Center.
Blain Joseph, 5 Gaines, Grand Rapids.
Blain John, Lowell.
Blair John D., 36 Ada, Lowell.
Blain Joseph R., 5 Gaines, G. Rapids.
Blair Nathan, 17 Lowell, Lowell.
BLAIN NORMAN B., Lowell.
BLAIN OSCAR W., 18 Gaines, Gainesville.
Blain Thomas, 18 Gaines, Gainesville.
BLAIN WILMOT H., 29 Gaines, Gainesville.
BLANCHARD WALTER D., 4 Courtland, Courtland Center.
Blanchard Edwin W., 12 Oakfield, Greenville.
Blanchard Charles N., 21 Oakfield, Oakfield.
Blanding Charles, Lowell.
Blanding Alex. H., 32 Vergennes, Lowell.
Blanding Daniel S., 29 Vergennes, Lowell.
BLANDING NOAH P., 32 Vergennes, Lowell.
Blass Charles, Lowell.
Blauvelt John W., 19 Sparta, Lisbon.
Bliss Adelbert F., Rockford.
Bliss Albert, 5 Lowell, Lowell.
Bliss Curtis, 21 Bowne, Bowne.
Bliss Edward, 6 Cannon, Rockford.
Bliss Wm. J., Rockford.
Blobet John, 29 Sparta, Lisbon.
Blodget Alvin, 33 Algoma, Rockford.
BLODGETT CHAUNCEY, 33 Paris, Grand Rapids.
Blodgett Heman, Alaska.
Blodgett M. R., Lowell.
BLOMSTROM CHARLES E., Lisbon.
Blomstrom C., Lisbon.
Blood Abel, 33 Alpine, Indian Creek.

Blair Edwin M., 23 Solon, Cedar Springs.
BLAIR JONATHAN, South 6 Walker, Grand Rapids.
Blaisdell Wm. R., Lowell.
Blake Joseph, 35 Algoma, Rockford.
BLAKE JOSEPH, Grandville.
BLAKE SAMUEL P., 15 Gaines, Hammond.
Blakeny Dwight, 26 Courtland, Courtland Center.
Blakeny Edward, 26 Courtland, Courtland Center.
Blakeslee Alex., 29 Lowell, Lowell.
Blakeslee Enos L., 14 Lowell, Lowell.
Blakeslee Daniel C., 28 Lowell, Lowell.
Blakeley Buel, 19 Algoma, Sparta Cen.
Blakeley Charles E., Rockford.
Blakely Egbert, 12 Alpine, Englishville.
Blakeley Moses, 30 Algoma, Sparta Center.
BLAKELEY R. L., Rockford.
BLANCHARD IRA, 19 Sparta, Lisbon.
Blanchard Orrin D., Lisbon.
Blanchard Riley, 17 Alpine, Pleasant.
Blood Hiram W., 36 Sparta, Englishville.
BLOOD ISAAC D., 22 Ada, Ada.
BLOOD J. M., 4 Walker, Indian Creek.
Blood Mrs. Mary, 4 Walker, Indian Creek.
Blood Putnam, 33 Alpine, Indian Creek.
Blood Zachariah, 36 Sparta, Englishville.
BLOSS CHARLES A., Sparta Center.
Bloss David, 32 Paris, Grand Rapids.
Bloss Henry, 20 Gaines, Gainesville.
Bloss Volney, 15 Sparta, Sparta Center.
Blough Jacob, 24 Bowne, Lowell.
Blount Walter, Rockford.
Blush Christian, 20 Tyrone, Casnovia.
BLUSH RODOLPHUS, 20 Tyrone, Casnovia.
Boardman Arthur F., 2 Grattan, Ashley.
Boardman William, 2 Plainfield, Rockford.
Bodell Benjamin, 20 Tyrone, Casnovia.
Bodell Henry, 20 Tyrone, Casnovia.
Bodell Jacob, Lowell.
Bodell Michael, 20 Tyrone, Casnovia.

Boden Anthony, 23 Paris, Grand Rapids.
Boden Joseph L., 23 Paris, Grand Rapids.
Bogardus Henry H., 36 Wyoming, Grand Rapids.
Bogardus Jacob, 19 Wyoming, Grandville.
Bohlen John, 23 Alpine, Alpine.
Bohn John A., 27 Walker, Grand Rapids.
Bohlen Michael, 23 Alpine, Alpine.
Boice Albert, 14 Solon, Cedar Springs.
BOICE LUTHENIUS S., 27 Caledonia, Caledonia.
Bolan James, 27 Grand Rapids.
Bole George W., Village Cedar Springs.
Bolgar John, 3 Grand Rapids.
Bolhuis Lanowert, 25 Byron, Cody's Mills.
Bolt Adolphus E., 26 Cascade, Alaska.
BOLT LOUIS J., Sparta Center.
BOLTER LEWIS, 24 Lowell, Lowell.
Bolzar Dennis, 17 Plainfield, Austerlitz.
Bomas Peter, 29 Grand Rapids, Grand Rapids.
Bond B. F., 34 Sparta, Englishville.
Bonser John, 20 Lowell, Lowell.
Bonma Oats, 17 Wyoming, Grandville.
BOUCK ALEXANDER L., 5 Gaines, Hammond.
Bouck Oscar, 5 Gaines, Hammond.
Bouck Theodore, 5 Gaines, Hammond.
Bouck William, 25 Bowne, Fillmore, Barry county.
Bouchard Edward, 14 Paris, Grand Rapids.
Boughton Israel, 17 Wyoming, Grandville.
Boughton Ira, 1 Alpine, Englishville.
Bovie Peter D., Burch's Mills.
Bowen Amos, 25 Lowell, Lowell.
Bowen Elijah, 25 Lowell, Lowell.
Bowen Orange, 26 Spencer, Spencer Mills.
Bowen Jehiel, 26 Spencer, Spencer Mills.
BOWEN MERRICK, 29 Gaines, Cody's Mills.
BOWEN PHILANZO, 28 Paris, Grand Rapids.
Bowers Benjamin, 8 Algoma, Rockford.
Bowers Henry, 8 Algoma, Rockford.
Bowler James, 4 Algoma, Rockford.
Bowler Richard, 19 Grattan, Cannonsburg.
Bowman Aaron C., 28 Gaines, Grand Rapids.

Bouter James, 31 Alpine, Indian Creek.
Bookey James, Village Cannonsburg.
Boomer Moses, 23 Vergennes, Fallassburg.
Boorom A. J., 6 Sparta, Lisbon.
Boorom A. W., 6 Sparta, Lisbon.
Boorom Darius, 18 Sparta, Lisbon.
Boorom Lewis, 17 Sparta, Lisbon.
Booth Andrew, 22 Vergennes, Lowell.
Booth Andrew, 34 Vergennes, Lowell.
Booth Edwin, 34 Ada, Ada.
Booth E. J., Lowell.
Booth Henry W, 1 Lowell, Lowell.
Boquette Wm. H., Village Cedar Springs.
Boss Charley, 25 Gaines, Caledonia Station.
Boshoven Peter, 29 Grand Rapids.
BOSWORTH H. J., Lowell.
Botsford David, 13 Courtland, Courtland Center.
Botruff Adam, 16 Algoma, Rockford.
Botruff Isaac J., 16 Algoma, Rockford.
Botruff Samuel S., — Tyrone, Sparta Center.
Botruff William, 16 Algoma, Rockford.
Bowman Absalom, 15 Courtland, Courtland Center.
BOWMAN BENJ. B., 32 Gaines, Cody's Mills.
Bowman Charles, 32 Grand Rapids.
Bowman Elias, 28 Gaines, Grand Rapids.
BOWMAN ELIAS C., 27 Gaines, Caledonia Station.
Bowman Gabriel W., 25 Courtland, Oakfield.
Bowman Jacob W., 30 Oakfield, Oakfield.
Bowman Jacob, 27 Caledonia, Caledonia Station.
BOWMAN JOSEPH C., 35 Gaines, Grand Rapids.
Bowman Levi, 34 Caledonia, Caledonia Station.
Bowman Nelson B., 30 Oakfield, Oakfield.
Bowman Owen C., 27 Gaines, Grand Rapids.
BOWMAN SOLOMON, 4 Caledonia, Alaska.
BOWMAN WENDELL C., 35 Gaines, Grand Rapids.

Boyce Wm., Lowell.
BOYD GEORGE, 17 Alpine, Pleasant.
Boyd James, 17 Alpine, Pleasant.
Boyd Samuel G., 19 Courtland, Rockford.
BOYER DAVID, 21 Plainfield, Belmont.
Boyer George, 14 Bowne, Lowell.
Boyer John, 28 Algoma, Rockford
BOYER JOHN W., 4 Plainfield, Belmont.
Boylon Cornelius, 6 Vergennes, Cannonsburg.
BOYLON CORNELIUS, 21 Grattan, Grattan Center.
Boylan Larry, 31 Wyoming, Grandville.
BOYLON THOMAS, 7 Ada, Grand Rapids.
BOYNTON JEREMIAH W., Alaska, Village.
BOYNTON JERRY, 9 Byron, North Byron.
BOYTON LEVI S., 29 Grand Rapids.
BOYNTON PHILIP W., 10 Caledonia, Alaska.
BOYNTON WILLIAM, 5 Byron, North Byron.
BOYNTON WILLIAM, 34 Cascade, Alaska.
BRADFORD MOSES, 29 Grand Rapids, Grand Rapids.
BRADFORD MOSES, 11 Sparta, Sparta Center.
Bradford Perry, 11 Sparta, Sparta Cen.
Bradford Robert N., Lowell.
Bradfield Edward, 34 Ada, Ada.
Bradfield Henry H., 34 Ada, Ada.
BRADFIELD JOHN R., 34 Ada, Ada.
Rradfield Sidney C., Lowell.
Bradfield Washington, 13 Algoma, Edgerton.
Bradish Joshua, 10 Grand Rapids.
Bradish Benjamin, Lisbon.
Bradley Hyacinth M., 11 Courtland, Courtland Center.
Bradley Lansel, 7 Algoma, Sparta Cen.
BRADIN JOHN, 15 Grattan, Grattan Center.
Brady Charles, 21 Lowell, Lowell.
Brady Hugh, 21 Lowell, Lowell.
Bradshaw Edward, 23 Spencer, Spencer Mills.
Bradshaw Jared, 28 Spencer, Spencer Mills.
Braford Mrs., 33 Ada, Ada.
Braford Joseph J., 19 Cannon, Austerlitz.
Braford Jesse, 30 Cannon, Austerlitz.

Braam Adrian, 29 Grand Rapids.
Brabb George, Rockford.
Brabb George, Rockford.
BRACE AVERY, 3 Walker, Indian Creek.
Brace Hiram L., Cedar Springs.
Brace Emmett, 3 Walker, Indian Creek.
Brace George W., 3 Sparta, Sparta Center.
BRACKETT ALBERT, Sparta Center.
Brackone John, 11 Paris Grand Rapids
Bradbury William, Lisbon.
Bradford Abner S., 30 Cannon, Austerlitz.
BRADFORD CHARLES H., 21 Walker, Grand Rapids.
Bradford Durfee T., 21 Walker, Grand Rapids.
Bradford Mrs. Eunice, 16 Sparta, Sparta Center.
Bradford Ephraim A., 10 Sparta, Sparta Center.
Bradford Edmund, 31 Cannon, Austerlitz.
BRADFORD EDWARD, Sparta Cen.
BRADFORD JASON S., Sparta Cen.
Bragg Alexander, 13 Gaines, Hammond.
BRAGG ELMER M., 13 Gaines, Hammond.
BRAGG GEO. N., 13 Gaines, Hammond.
Brainard Alfred, 18 Gaines, Gainesville.
Brainard Dudley, 33 Wyoming, Grandville.
Brainard Hugh, 33 Wyoming, Grandville.
Brakey Thomas, 17 Lowell, Lowell.
Braman H. O., 20 Lowell, Lowell.
Branagan John, 18 Vergennes, Vergennes.
Brandon Adam, Alaska Village.
Brandt Adelbert. 28 Alpine, G. Rapids.
Brannan Isaac, 32 Lowell, Alto.
Brannan John, 32 Lowell, Alto.
BRANNAN JAMES, 32 Lowell, Alto.
BRANT JOHN, 31 Plainfield, Mill Creek.
Brantner George, 2 Plainfield, Rockford.
Brantner John, Rockford.
Brasted Silas, 6 Lowell, Lowell.
Brasted Silas, Jr., 6 Lowell, Lowell.

Brownell George, 11 Plainfield, Austerlitz.
Bray Benj. C., 12 Gaines, Hammond.
BRAYMAN JAMES H., 7 Nelson, Cedar Springs.
Brearley Amos, 35 Gaines, Cody's Mills.
BREARLEY EMORY, 35 Gaines, Caledonia Station.
BREAK ABRAHAM B., 20 Caledonia, Caledonia Station.
Brechting William, 23 Alpine, Grand Rapids.
Breese John, Village Cedar Springs.
Bremer Francis, 15 Walker, G. Rapids.
Bremer Henry, Rockford.
BRENNER ANDREW, Burch's Mills.
Brenner Isaac, Burch's Mills.
Brenenstuhl George, 15 Grattan, Grattan Center.
Bresee Jared N., 34 Ada, Ada.
Bresnahan Ellen, 18 Grattan, Grattan Center.
Bresnahan John, 18 Grattan, Grattan Center.
Bresnahan Patrick, 20 Grattan, Grattan Center.
BREWER AARON, 9 Gaines, Grand Rapids.
Brewer Alonzo, 9 Alpine, Grand Rapids
BRIGGS ROBERT, 6 Grand Rapids, Grand Rapids.
Briggs Richard, 18 Nelson, Cedar Springs.
Briggs Spencer B., 23 Solon, Cedar Springs.
Briggs S. M., 25 Algoma, Rockford.
Briggs Simeon L., 23 Byron, Byron Center.
Briggs Volney, 13 Algoma, Edgerton.
Brigham Fitch M., 10 Walker, Grand Rapids.
Brigham George, 32 Oakfield, Grattan Center.
Brigham John, 32 Oakfield, Oakfield.
Brigham Timothy, 10 Walker, Grand Rapids.
Brink John, 25 Grand Rapids.
BRINK LOREN, Village Cannonsburg.
Brinkman Herbert, 35 Solon, Cedar Springs.
Bristol Bethel, 34 Ada, Ada.
Britton Dewitt C., Grandville.
Broad Charles, Lowell.
Broad William, Lowell.
Broadbent Thomas, 7 Bowne, Alaska.
BROCK JAMES, 31 Caledonia, Alaska.
Bromman Charles, 5 Sparta, Lisbon.
Bromman Franklin, 5 Sparta, Lisbon.

Brewer Francis, 9 Alpine, G. Rapids.
BREWER FREEMAN, 9 Gaines, G. Rapids.
Brewer Nelson, 16 Gaines, G. Rapids.
Bresee Charles W., 22 Walker, Grand Rapids.
Bride Francis W., 17 Plainfield, Austerlitz.
Brigham Albert, 35 Algoma, Rockford.
Briggs B. B., 13 Algoma, Edgerton.
Briggs Barnett W., 36 Algoma, Rockford.
Briggs Barber, 7 Grand Rapids.
Briggs Charles, 13 Algoma, Edgerton.
Briggs Charles, 13 Solon, Cedar Springs
Briggs E. L., 7 Grand Rapids.
Briggs Mrs. E. A., Cedar Springs.
BRIGGS GEO. A., 14 Algoma, Edgerton.
BRIGGS HORACE J., 3 Solon, Cedar Springs.
Briggs Hiram, 25 Algoma, Rockford.
Briggs Isaac, 18 Nelson, Cedar Springs.
Britton Josiah, 21 Algoma, Rockford.
Briggs Joshua, 25 Algoma, Rockford.
Briggs Jason, 18 Nelson, Cedar Springs
Briggs Richard, Rockford.
Bromman John, 5 Sparta, Lisbon.
Bromman Jones, 5 Sparta, Lisbon.
Bromman Peter, 5 Sparta, Lisbon.
BRONSON FRANK, 35 Bowne, Fillmore, Barry County.
Bronson H. S., 16 Tyrone, Casnovia.
Broomhall John, 3 Cascade, Ada.
Brooks Elias, 30 Courtland, Rockford.
Brooks Elisha, 33 Oakfield, Grattan Center.
Brooks Hollis L., 4 Grattan, Grattan Center.
BROOKS JOSEPH A., Grandville.
Brooks Joseph, Lisbon.
BROOKS JOHN, Lisbon.
Brooks James, 23 Plainfield, Austerlitz.
Brooks Lucius, 4 Grattan, Grattan Cen.
Brooks Willis, 11 Nelson, Nelson.
Brooks Lemuel, 33 Oakfield, Grattan Center.
Brot Washington, 33 Tyrone, Sparta Center.
Brothwell George E., 6 Cannon, Rockford.
Brott Washington, 33 Tyrone, Sparta Center.

Dr. E. WOODRUFF,

Botanic Physician.

OFFICE AT HIS

Root, Bark and Herb Store,

87 CANAL STREET, GRAND RAPIDS, MICH.,

Where, for 10 years, every Description of

Acute, Chronic and Private Diseases has been
Successfully Treated,

STRICTLY ON BOTANIC PRINCIPLES. NO POISON USED.

P. O. Drawer, 2391. *Counsel at Office Free.*

L. J. RINDGE & CO.,

MANUFACTURERS AND DEALERS IN

Boots and Shoes,

14 Canal Street,

GRAND RAPIDS, - - MICHIGAN,

SMITH, MOSELY & CO.,

Manufacturers of the

CELEBRATED

And Jobbers in

BOOTS, SHOES AND RUBBERS,

17 Canal Street, up stairs,

C. F. SMITH,
TOM. C. MOSELY,

A. WOOD,
M. H. WALKER.

GRAND RAPIDS, MICH.

Broughan Dennis, 31 Cascade, Grand Rapids.
BROUGHAN JOHN, 31 Cascade, Grand Rapids.
Broughan William, 31 Cascade, Grand Rapids.
Brownell Philo, 3 Plainfield, Rockford.
Brownell Wm. 21 Vergennes, Lowell.
Brownell Charles, 10 Walker, Grand Rapids.
Brower Abraham C., 24 Gaines, Caledonia Station.
Brower Daniel C., 22 Gaines, Grand Rapids.
BROWER HENRY C., 22 Gaines, Caledonia Station.
BROWER ISAAC C., 22 Gaines, Grand Rapids.
BROWER JOHN C., 24 Gaines, Caledonia Station.
BROWER JOSEPH, 19 Caledonia, Caledonia Station.
Brower Moses C., 25 Gaines, Caledonia Station.
Brower Sylvester, Lowell.
Brower Wm., 22 Gaines, Grand Rapids.
Brown Azetus, 31 Tyrone, Casnovia.
BROWN ALLEN, 23 Cannon, Cannonsburg.
Brown Ezra, 9 Alpine, Grand Rapids.
Brown Edward, 1 Byron, Gainesville.
Brown F. Z., 29 Sparta, Lisbon.
Brown George E., 15 Caledonia, Alaska.
Brown Henry, 34 Walker, G. Rapids.
Brown Hosea, 11 Alpine, Englishville.
Brown Hiram, 33 Sparta, Englishville.
Brown H. F., 22 Algoma, Edgerton.
Brown Hugh B., 30 Cascade, Cascade.
Brown I. E., Rockford.
BROWN JOHN R., 16 Walker, Grand Rapids.
Brown James, 36 Paris, Grand Rapids.
Brown John, 13 Algoma, Edgerton.
Brown Jarvis, 18 Alpine, Pleasant.
BROWN JAMES M., 4 Byron, North Byron.
Brown John A., Sparta Center.
BROWN JOHN, 34 Sparta, Englishville.
Brown John, Sparta Center.
BROWN JOSEPH, 19 Ada, Ada.
Brown Joseph, 6 Gaines, Gainesville.
Brown Kearney, 2 Alpine, Englishville.
Brown Mrs. Lavinia, Lowell.
Brown Lorenzo, 17 Alpine, G. Rapids.
Brown Lorenzo D., Rockford.
Brown Martin, 30 Gaines, Cody's Mills.
BROWN O. L., Rockford.

Brown Albert E., Rockford.
Brown Bester, 27 Paris, Grand Rapids.
Brown Byron, 1 Plainfield, Rockford.
Brown Charles, 32 Gaines, Cody's Mills.
Brown Charles, South 5 Walker, Grand Rapids.
Brown Charles H., 15 Cascade, Cascade.
Brown Charles, 36 Sparta.
Brown Christy, 31 Alpine, Indian Creek.
BROWN CHARLES E., 9 Oakfield, Oakfield.
Brown Charles, 32 Wyoming, Grandville.
Brown Charles H., 19 Caledonia, Caledonia Station.
Brown Charles, 31 Algoma, Englishville.
Brown Clark, 33 Sparta, Englishville.
Brown David T., 15 Oakfield, Oakfield.
BROWN EPHRAIM E., 6 Plainfield, Englishville.
BROWN EUGENE, 25 Byron, Cody's Mills.
BROWN EDGAR, 1 Algoma, Burch's Mills.
BROWN ELISHA T., 29 Alpine, Indian Creek.
BROWN OLIVER, 5 Oakfield, Oakfield.
Brown O. E., 13 Alpine, Alpine.
Brown Peter C., Cedar Springs.
Brown Perry, 33 Sparta, Englishville.
Brown Fletcher, 29 Gaines, Cody's Mills.
Brown Robert J., 5 Courtland, Courtland Center.
Brown Robert J., 26 Grand Rapids.
Brown Roswell, Grandville.
BROWN ROBERT, 20 Grand Rapids.
Brown Stillman, 4 Alpine, Englishville.
Brown Samuel, 1 Courtland, Oakfield.
Brown T. F., Lowell.
Brown Thomas, 18 Gaines, Gainesville.
Brown William, 15 Cannon, Cannonsburg.
Brown William, 31 Plainfield, Mill Creek.
Brown William A. C., Lowell.
Brown William, 29 Grand Rapids, Grand Rapids.
Brown William E., 1 Vergennes, Alton.
BROWN WM. H., 1 Vergennes, Alton.
Brown William, 13 Algoma, Edgerton.
BROWN WILLIAM, 16 Cannon, Cannonsburg.

Brown William, 19 Oakfield, Oakfield.
Brown William, 32 Wyoming, Grandville.
BROWN WM. H., Alaska.
Brudi Charles, 4 Byron, North Byron.
BRUDI JOHN C., 4 Byron, North Byron.
Brudi Jacob, 35 Wyoming, North Byron.
Brunell David, 13 Spencer, Spencer Mills.
Bruner Anthony, Lowell.
Bruton Mrs. Ann, 30 Bowne, Harris Creek.
Bruton Michael, 24 Caledonia, Caledonia.
Bruton Patrick, 24 Caledonia, Caledonia.
Bruton Robert, 24 Caledonia, Caledonia.
Bruner Richard, 12 Cannon, Bostwick Lake.
Brunner Joseph M., 19 Lowell, Lowell.
Brunner W., 29 Grand Rapids.
Bryant Amos, 25 Vergennes, Lowell.
Bryant Caspar W., 8 Courtland, Courtland Center.
Bryant Daniel, 33 Lowell, Lowell.
Buchanan Augustus, 35 Vergennes, Lowell.
Budway Daniel, 34 Nelson, Cedar Springs.
Buel Alfred, 36 Grand Rapids.
BUEL MARCUS, 11 Caledonia, Alaska.
Buel Mrs. Susan, 36 Grand Rapids.
Buell William, 31 Ada, Ada.
Bull J. N., 16 Grand Rapids.
Bullard Edwin M., 8 Walker, Grand Rapids.
BULLARD JOSEPH, 1 Alpine, Englishville.
Bullard Martin, 9 Bowne, Alto.
Bullen Chauncey, 22 Walker, Grand Rapids.
Bullen Mrs. Hannah, 3 Walker, Indian Creek.
BULLEN JOSEPH, 33 Alpine, Indian Creek.
Bulliment Thomas, — Wyoming, Grandville.
Bullis Isaac, 33 Grand Rapids.
Bullis James, 1 Walker, Mill Creek.
BULLOCK JOHN, 24 Algoma, Edgerton.
BULLOCK JOSEPH, Cedar Springs.
Bunce Aaron, 3 Lowell. Lowell.
BUNKER EDWIN A., 16 Bowne, Alto.
Burch Alfred, 11 Vergennes, Lowell.
Burch Noah, 16 Lowell. Lowell,

BUCHANAN JAMES R., 25 Lowell, Lowell.
BUCHANAN JAMES W., 29 Bowne, Harris Creek.
Buchanan Samuel, 36 Sparta, Englishville.
Buck Alonzo, Rockford.
Buck Cary, 4 Alpine, Lisbon.
BUCK CURTIS, Village Cedar Springs.
BUCK ELIJAH, 12 Caledonia, Alaska.
Buck Eli S., 34 Paris, Grand Rapids.
Buck Judson J., 4 Alpine, Lisbon.
Buck Ira J., 12 Lowell, Lowell.
Buck Myron, Village Cedar Springs.
Buck Seeley S., 34 Paris, Grand Rapids.
Buck Seralpha A., 21 Gaines, Grand Rapids.
Buck Seralpha C., 21 Gaines, Grand Rapids.
BUCK THOMAS D., 23 Caledonia, Caledonia.
Buckle William, 7 Oakfield, Oakfield.
Buckley P. B., Rockford.
Buddinger Mrs. Margaret, 19 Byron, Byron Center.
BUDLONG WM. H., 18 Gaines, Gainesville.
Burch Alpheus, 8 Lowell, Lowell.
Burch David, 16 Solon, Cedar Springs.
Burch D. W. C., Rockford.
BURCH HOMER A., 19 Courtland, Courtland Center.
Burch Jefferson, 5 Nelson, Sand Lake.
Burch Mrs. Lucy, 20 Courtland, Courtland Center.
Burch L. R., 14 Tyrone, Sparta Cen.
BURCH TRUMAN H., 16 Plainfield, Belmont.
Burch Truman H., 16 Plainfield, Belmont.
Burchard A. H., 33 Grand Rapids.
Burdick Eli, Lowell.
Burdick Marcus T., 19 Ada, Ada.
Burdick Truman C., 18 Ada, Ada.
Burd Joseph, 20 Walker, G. Rapids.
Burdison Andrew, 12 Oakfield, Greenville.
Burgess Cyrus N., 35 Cannon, Cannonsburg.
Burgess E. J., Rockford.
Burgess John M., Village Cannonsburg.
Burger Stephen S., 34 Ada, Ada.
Burget Isaac, 8 Algoma, Sparta Center.
Burgi Joseph, 35 Byron, Cody's Mills.

Dikeman's Watch Depot,

Established in 1837,

By Aaron Dikeman, Esq.,

Who, by honest and liberal dealing for THIRTY-THREE YEARS, has built up a large business, and, having succeeded him in business, it will be my *chief aim* to retain his good name and business. I have constantly on hand all the

FINEST STYLES

—OF—

LADIES' AND GENT'S

GOLD WATCHES,

All Grades of the

Waltham and Elgin Watches,

A Large Stock of the

FINEST JEWELRY, RINGS AND CHAINS,

All Patterns and Styles of the Seth Thomas Clocks,

FINE BRONZE CLOCKS, STERLING FINE SILVER WARE

And a Large Stock of Silver Plated Ware.

Sole Agent for the H & O PERRETT WATCHES,

Also for the

CELEBRATED DIAMOND SPECTACLES.

All of my stock I shall endeavor to Sell as Cheap as any First-Class Goods can be sold.

Call at 26 Canal St.

ED. B. DIKEMAN.

NOTICE—Remember, after the 1st of May, 1871, I shall remove to No. 38 Canal Street, when, with great expense, I shall have the handsomest store and largest stock in the city, and I can say outside of Detroit.

ED. B. DIKEMAN.

Burke John, 29 Paris, Grand Rapids.
Burke James, 29 Paris, Grand Rapids.
Burkholder David, 28 Paris, Grand Rapids.
Burkholder John, 28 Paris, G. Rapids.
BURLINGAME HENRY D.. 17 Courtland, Courtland Center.
BURLINGAME EDWIN A., 2 Wyoming, Grand Rapids.
Burlingame Eseck, 18 Gaines, Gainesville.
Burlingame James, 5 Oakfield, Oakfield.
BURLESON STEPHEN, 14 Plainfield, Austerlitz.
Burns Dennis, 12 Wyoming, Grand Rapids.
Burns Felix, 23 Walker, G. Rapids.
Burns Francis, 32 Cascade, Alaska.
BURNS LAWRENCE, 34 Ada, Ada.
Burns Michael, 32 Cascade, Alaska.
Burns Patrick, 12 Wyoming, Grand Rapids.
Burns Philip, Burchville (Burch's Mills.)
Burns Thomas, 16 Paris, G. Rapids.
Burns Thomas, 23 Caledonia, Caledonia.
Burt B. E., Lowell.
Burt Beldin H., 27 Sparta, Sparta Cen.
Burt Justus W., 29 Ada, Ada.
Burton E. O., 13 Algoma, Edgerton.
Burton Henry, 16 Plainfield, Belmont.
Burton Henry, Cedar Springs.
Burton George, 32 Gaines, Cody's Mills.
Burt Lucien, 2 Wyoming, G. Rapids.
BURTCH HARMON A., 20 Courtland, Courtland Center.
BURTCH HIRAM, 9 Alpine, Grand Rapids.
BUSH DANIEL. 15 Walker, Grand Rapids.
Bush Daniel, 10 Walker, Indian Creek.
Bush Mrs. Fanny, 18 Plainfield, Alpine.
Bush Horatio N., Village Caunonsburg.
Bush H. T., 10 Walker, Indian Creek.
BUSH ISAAC, 11 Cannon, Bostwick Lake.
BUSH JAMES, 18 Grattan, Grattan Center.
Bush Jacob, Village Cannonsburg.
Bush William, 10 Cannon, Bostwick Lake.
Bush William H., 10 Cannon, Bostwick Lake.
BUTLER CHARLES H., 31 Nelson, Cedar Springs.

BURNS WILLIAM, 36 Oakfield, Ashley.
Burns John, 6 Ada, Plainfield.
Burns Sr. John, 25 Caledonia, Caledonia.
Burns James, 24 Plainfield, Grand Rapids.
Burns Jr. John, 25 Caledonia, Caledonia.
Burns James, 32 Cascade, Alaska.
Burnham Charles, 23 Wyoming, Grand Rapids.
Burnap Tracy, 7 Grand Rapids.
Burnett Wm., 13 Lowell, Lowell.
Burpee George, 16 Walker, Grand Rapids.
Burroughs Mrs. R. E., Lowell.
Burroughs Mrs. E. J., Lowell.
Burroughs Sanford, 9 Caledonia, Alaska.
Burrill Z., 29 Sparta, Lisbon.
Burr Aaron, 4 Cascade, Cascade.
BURR EDMUND, 18 Nelson, Cedar Springs.
Burr Levi, 18 Lowell, Lowell.
Burse Esburn, 17 Courtland, Courtland Center.
Butler Cornelius, 36 Caledonia, Caledonia.
Butler Edwin H., 12 Walker, Grand Rapids.
Butler Helen L., 34 Ada, Ada.
Butler Henry, 12 Plainfield, Austerlitz.
BUTLER WM. H., 7 Nelson, Cedar Springs.
Butler I. G., 2 Alpine, Englishville.
BUTLER JAMES, 25 Caledonia, Caledonia.
Butler Jonah, 36 Sparta, Englishville.
BUTLER MRS. MARGARET, 26 Caledonia, Caledonia.
Butler Henry N., 28 Plainfield, Grand Rapids.
Butler William, 36 Caledonia, Caledonia.
Butrick Charles, South 1, Ada, Lowell.
Butterfield Albert, South 5 Walker, Grand Rapids.
BUTTERFIELD CHESTER, 6 Caledonia, Grand Rapids.
BUTTERFIELD JOHN N., South 5 Walker, Grand Rapids.
Butterfield William, South 5 Walker, Grand Rapids.

BUTTON DARIUS T., 23 Walker, G. Rapids.
Button Ira, 11 Lowell, Lowell.
BUXTON THOMAS H., Grandville.
Byers John, Jr., 20 Algoma, Sparta Center.
Byers Jacob, 32 Courtland, Rockford.
BYRNE JOHN, 28 Grattan, Grattan Center.
Byrne Lawrence, 13 Ada, Ada.
BYRNE THOMAS, 2 Grattan, Grattan Center.
BYRNE MICHAEL, 28 Grattan, Grattan Center.
Byrne William, Jr., 22 Grattan, Grattan Center.
BYRNES THOMAS, 18 Vergennes, Vergennes.
Byrnes Toboise, 32 Grattan, Cannonsburg.
BYRNES JAMES, 18 Vergennes, Vergennes.
CABOT FRANCIS M., 34 Tyrone, Sparta Center.
Cady Elisha, 22 Wyoming, Grand Rapids.
Cahill Edward, 25 Tyrone, Sparta Cen.
Cahill Patrick, 9 Walker, Indian Creek.
Cahoon Geo. H., 15 Lowell, Lowell.
Camp Mrs. Sarah A., 10 Walker, Indian Creek.
Campbell Chas., 12 Lowell, Lowell.
Campbell Edward, 12 Solon, Cedar Springs.
Campbell Finley, Lisbon.
CAMPBELL G. W., 2 Sparta, Sparta Center.
Campbell Hugh, 34 Tyrone, Sparta Center.
Campbell Ira, 13 Oakfield, Greenville.
Campbell Isaac M., 1 Algoma, Burch's Mills.
Campbell John J., 6 Bowne, Alto.
Campbell Lemuel H., 10 Oakfield, Oakfield.
Campbell Lewis, 13 Oakfield, Greenville.
Campbell Mrs. Mary, 25 Plainfield, Austerlitz.
Campbell Peter, 19 Walker, G. Rapids.
Campbell Peter, 10 Nelson, Nelson.
Campbell Mrs. Phila A., 5 Bowne, Alto.
Campbell Sophronia, 18 Grattan, Grattan Center.
Campbell Samuel, 22 Plainfield, Austerlitz.
CAMPBELL STEVEN, 2 Sparta, Sparta Center.

CAINE JAMES E., 16 Algoma, Edgerton.
Cairns Thomas, 26 Tyrone, Sparta Cen.
CALDWELL HENRY O., 33 Ada, Ada
Caldwell Walter, Alaska Village.
CALKINS ALANSON, 30 Lowell, Lowell.
Calkins Addison, 31 Paris, G. Rapids.
Calkins Andrew M., 30 Lowell, Lowell.
CALKINS DANIEL, 26 Spencer, Spencer Mills.
Calkins John, 25 Vergennes, Lowell.
Calkins Milo, 25 Vergennes, Lowell.
CALLEN JOHN, 3 Grand Rapids.
Callen Peter, 3 Grand Rapids.
Callard Robert, 9 Walker, G. Rapids.
Callard Samuel. Sr., 9 Walker, Grand Rapids.
Callard Samuel. Jr., 9 Walker, Grand Rapids.
Callard Thomas. 7 Walker, G. Rapids.
Camp Charles, 27 Algoma, Rockford.
Camp Edward P., 4 Walker, Indian Creek.
CAMP JOHN, 33 Ada, Ada.
CAMP P. SPENCER, 4 Walker, Indian Creek.
Campbell Wilton, Cedar Springs.
Campbell Wm. T., 9 Wyoming, Grandville.
CAMPAU EDWARD, 11 Caledonia, Alaska.
Campfield Frank, 27 Ada, Ada.
Camfield Bradford, 33 Lowell, Alto.
Candle James, South 5 Walker, Grand Rapids.
Canfield Alfred N., 16 Ada, Ada.
Canfield J. H., 5 Ada, Ada.
CANFIELD MOULTON H., 12 Grattan, Grattan Center.
Canfield William, 12 Grattan, Grattan Center.
CANEN CARLTON, 29 Tyrone, Casnovia.
Canen Michael, 29 Tyrone, Casnovia.
Cane William, Burchville (Burch's Mills.)
Canton Michael, 10 Grand Rapids.
Caples Michael, 22 Sparta, Grand Rapids.
Caples Michael, 29 Walker, Grand Rapids.
Card J. H., 7 Alpine, Pleasant.
Carey William, 30 Ada, Grand Rapids.

Carey John, 3 Ada, Ada.
Carlton Lewis M., 14 Paris, Grand Rapids.
Carlton Norman L., 16 Cascade, Cascade.
Carlton Nicholas, 11 Paris, Grand Rapids.
CARLTON PHIL. P., 15 Cannon, Cannonsburg.
CARLTON ROBERT, Ada Village.
Carlton William, 8 Wyoming, Grandville.
CARLISLE JAMES, 35 Gaines, Middleville, Barry County.
Carlisle William, 4 Cannon, Rockford.
Carlyle Charles H., 21 Courtland, Courtland Center.
Carlyle John, Jr., 28 Courtland, Courtland Center.
Carlyle John, 28 Courtland, Courtland Center.
CARLYLE ROBERT, 32 Courtland, Rockford.
Carll Gideon, 27 Cascade, Alaska.
Carll John, 27 Cascade, Alaska.
Carl Ralph L., Lowell.
Carl William P., 29 Ada, Ada.
Carlan Edward, 34 Walker, Grand Rapids.
CARR ALFRED B., 26 Plainfield, Austerlitz.
Carr Aaron, 17 Sparta, Sparta Center.
Carr Caleb E., 26 Plainfield, Austerlitz.
Carr Edward, Lowell.
Carr Geo. E., 1 Lowell, Lowell.
Carr John, 22 Grand Rapids.
CARR ROBERT, 26 Spencer, Spencer Mills.
Carr William, 17 Sparta, Sparta Center.
Carson Charles, 30 Cascade, Grand Rapids.
CARSON ROBERT, 23 Walker, Grand Rapids.
CARTER CHAS. B., 3 Lowell, Lowell.
Carter Theodore, 36 Vergennes, Lowell.
CARTER ZENA W., 29 Lowell, Lowell.
Cartwright M. H., Burchville (Burch's Mills.)
Carty Maggie, 27 Oakfield, Ashley.
Carver Sarah W., 10 Vergennes, Alton.
Cary Charles, 18 Lowell, Lowell.
Cary Horace, 18 Lowell, Lowell.
Carey Patrick, 1 Courtland, Courtland Center.
Cary Patrick, 33 Cascade, Alaska.
Cary Patrick, 7 Vergennes, Vergennes.
Case David, Lisbon.
Case Horace, 7 Nelson, Cedar Springs.

Carlton Nelson, 11 Paris, Grand Rapids.
Carmer William, 36 Solon, Cedar Springs.
Carner Hiram, 2 Wyoming, Grandville.
Carold Daniel, 31 Grattan, Cannonsburg.
Carpenter Benj. T., 18 Nelson, Cedar Springs.
Carpenter Chasper H., 36 Bowne, Fillmore, Barry County.
Carpenter Darius W., 21 Byron, Byron Center.
CARPENTER H. D., 29 Grand Rapids, Grand Rapids.
Carpenter James, 21 Byron, Byron Cen.
Carpenter Jasper B., 17 Paris, Grand Rapids.
Carpenter Levi, 23 Caledonia, Caledonia.
Carpenter Lorenzo, 13 Plainfield, Austerlitz.
Carpenter Oscar P., 32 Gaines, Cody's Mills.
Carpenter Mrs. Melinda, 12 Plainfield, Austerlitz.
Carpenter Peter, 10 Byron, Byron Cen.
Case Justus, 17 Bowne, Alto.
Case William C., Sparta Center
CASEY JAMES, 15 Vergennes, Lowell.
Casner George, 3 Grattan, Grattan Cen.
Casner Jerry, 8 Grattan, Grattan Cen.
Casner Peter, 5 Grattan, Grattan Cen.
Casner William, 3 Grattan, Grattan Center.
Cassada Albert B., Rockford.
Cassady John, 27 Walker, Grand Rapids.
Cassedy James, 25 Sparta, Sparta Cen.
CASSEL ABRAHAM B., 16 Gaines, Grand Rapids.
Caswell Benj. C., 26 Oakfield, Ashley.
Caswell Elisha B., 27 Nelson, Cedar Springs.
CATHEY GEORGE, 9 Oakfield, Oakfield.
Cathey Geo. L., 9 Oakfield, Oakfield.
Caton Thomas, 25 Grattan, Grant.
Caukin Rufin, 31 Oakfield, Oakfield.
CAUKIN VOLNEY W., 10 Sparta, Sparta Center.
Cavener Alexander, Rockford.
CAVNER JAMES, 8 Nelson, Cedar Springs.
Cazier Edward, 18 Alpine, Pleasant.

Empire Organ Company,

Manufacturers of the

EMPIRE

ORGAN

—AND—

Melodeon

Also Dealers in

PIANOS,

Sheet Music, Musical Merchandise,

&c., &c.

FACTORY and SALES ROOMS

No. 65 Monroe Street,

GRAND RAPIDS, - MICHIGAN.

GEO. PIGGOTT. A. F. BURCH.

☞ Those desiring Good Organs will find it to their advantage to purchase of us, or our regularly employed Agents, as in so doing they can save at least one commission on the instruments, thereby getting them cheaper than if purchased of foreign companies.

We invite all interested in the purchase of *Good Instruments*, to call at our Factory and examine our stock.

ALL GOODS ARE FULLY WARRANTED.

Cazier Samuel, 19 Alpine, Pleasant.
Ceah Christian, 1 Byron, North Byron.
Cisco Warren, 3 Gaines, Hammond.
CHAFFEE E. M., 23 Algoma, Rockford.
Chaffee Edwin N., 33 Ada, Ada.
Chaffee Rodolphus G., 35 Ada, Ada.
Chaffee W. T., 24 Algoma, Rockford.
Chalmers Andrew, 28 Algoma, Rockford.
Chalmers John, 32 Algoma, Rockford.
Chambers Geo. W., 16 Alpine, Grand Rapids.
Chambers George, 16 Alpine, Alpine.
Chambers Joseph, 10 Ada, Ada.
CHAMBERS HIRAM J., 16 Alpine, Grand Rapids.
Chambers Mrs. Lydia, 16 Alpine, Grand Rapids.
Chamberlin Charles L., Village Cannonsburg.
Chamberlain Frank, 16 Alpine, Grand Rapids.
Chamberlain John H., Rockford.
Champion David, Jr., 5 Walker, Indian Creek.
Champion J. D., 19 Tyrone, Casnovia.
Champlin Jeffery C., 20 Walker, Grand Rapids.
CHAPEL JESSE B., 17 Bowne, Harris Creek.
Chapel Jerod, Sparta Center.
CHAPEL LEMON B., 27 Ada, Ada.
CHAPEL M. D. L., 5 Ada, Ada.
CHAPMAN BENJ., 26 Solon, Cedar Springs.
Chapman Milton, 11 Lowell, Lowell.
Chase Amos G., 34 Ada, Ada.
Chase Abel, 16 Alpine, Grand Rapids.
Chase Homer, 20 Alpine, Indian Creek.
Chase James S., Village Cannonsburg.
Chase Lafayette, 34 Ada, Ada.
Chase S., Village Cannonsburg.
CHASE SEYMOUR, Village Cannonsburg.
Chase William, 16 Alpine, Grand Rapids.
Charles Joel, 12 Wyoming, Grand Rapids.
Charles James, 8 Paris, Grand Rapids.
CHATERDON GEO. W., 31 Lowell, Alaska.
CHATERDON JOHN, 32 Lowell, Alto.
Chaterdon Mrs. Minerva, 31 Lowell, Alto.
Chaterdon William, 31 Lowell, Alto.
Chester Brayton, 19 Sparta, Lisbon.
CHESTER ELISHA H., Cedar Springs.

Champlin J. C., 20 Grand Rapids.
Chapman Anthony, 26 Sparta, Sparta Center.
Chapman Charles M., 16 Sparta, Sparta Center.
Chapman D., 6 Grand Rapids, Grand Rapids.
Chapman E. A., Lowell.
Chapman Jared, 7 Grand Rapids.
Chapman John C., 35 Cannon, Cannonsburg.
CHAPMAN JOSEPH B., South 5 Walker, Grand Rapids.
Chapman Lorenzo, 36 Tyrone, Sparta Center.
CHAPMAN LE GRAND C., 35 Cannon, Cannonsburg.
Chapman William, 30 Sparta, Lisbon.
CHAPIN E. E., Rockford.
Chapin Flavel, 13 Grattan, Grant.
Chapin Gilbert A., 9 Grand Rapids.
Chapin Joseph, 9 Grand Rapids.
CHAPIN J. ELY, Lowell.
CHAPPELL DAN N., 7 Walker, Berlin.
Chappell George S., 7 Walker, Berlin.
Chapel Gurden, 27 Ada, Ada.
Chester Elisha, 19 Sparta, Lisbon.
Chester Elijah, 19 Sparta, Lisbon.
CHESEBRO ALLEN D., 8 Paris, Grand Rapids.
Chesebro Mrs. Isabella, 5 Paris, Grand Rapids.
CHEESEBROUGH JOB, 31 Caledonia, Caledonia Station.
Cheeseman James, Lowell.
Cheney Amherst B., Sparta Center.
Cheney Elliott, 27 Paris, Grand Rapids.
Cheney Nehemiah N., 22 Sparta, Sparta Center.
Chick Charles, 24 Vergennes, Fallassburg.
CHILD E. K, Burchville (Burch's Mills.)
Child George, 1 Vergennes, Alton.
Childs James W., 35 Sparta, Englishville.
Childs Nicholas, 22 Courtland, Courtland Center.
CHILDS WM. H., 2 Plainfield, Rockford.
Child Stephen, 1 Vergennes, Alton.
Chilson Alonzo, 19 Cannon, Austerlitz.
Chilson William, 30 Cannon, Austerlitz.

Chipman John B., 2 Algoma, Burchville (Burch's Mills.)
CHIPMAN WALTER, 2 Algoma, Burchville (Burch's Mills.)
Chirgwin Martin, 28 Cannon, Cannonsburg.
Chirgwin Thomas H., 26 Cannon, Cannonsburg.
Chirgwin Richard, 28 Cannon, Cannonsburg.
CHITTENDEN F., 17 Grand Rapids.
Chittenden James, 3 Grand Rapids.
Christy John, 26 Lowell, Lowell.
Christy Lafayette, 8 Algoma, Rockford.
Christenson John, 12 Oakfield, Greenville.
Christenson Nelson, 12 Oakfield, Greenville.
Christenson Samuel, 13 Algoma, Edgerton.
Chubbuck Horace G., 8 Tyrone, Casnovia.
CHUBB GEO. S., Lisbon.
Chubb Lorenzo, Lisbon.
CHUBB LEWIS L., Burchville (Burch's Mills.)
CHUBB MILES, Lisbon.
CHUBB URIAH, 30 Tyrone, Casnovia.
CHURCH ALBERT, 10 Bowne, Alto.
Clark Alex., 30 Paris, Grand Rapids.
Clark Alvin, 6 Paris, Grand Rapids.
Clark Almond, 5 Paris, Grand Rapids.
Clark Arba, 1 Plainfield, Rockford.
CLARK ARUNA S., 15 Grand Rapids.
CLARK ASA, 36 Tyrone, Sparta Center.
Clark Mrs. Bridget, 16 Wyoming, Grandville.
Clark Benjamin, 12 Paris, Grand Rapids.
Clark Charles H., 8 Alpine, Grand Rapids.
Clark Charles, 11 Paris, Grand Rapids.
Clark Chas. 28 Lowell, Lowell.
Clark David, 19 Tyrone, Casnovia.
Clark David H., 23 Cascade, Cascade.
Clark Eli, 2 Cascade, Ada.
Clark Edward, 20 Lowell, Lowell.
Clark Frederick, 29 Paris, Grand Rapids.
Clark Goodhand, 2 Plainfield, Rockford.
Clark George H., 3 Cascade, Ada.
Clark H. F., Lowell.
Clark Henry A., 11 Lowell, Lowell.
Clark Henry, 34 Walker, Grand Rapids.

Church Cephas, 19 Spencer, Nelson.
Church Chauncey, 26 Tyrone, Sparta Center.
CHURCH COLBIN E., 2 Alpine, Englishville.
Church Calvin, 7 Gaines, Gainesville.
CHURCH CHESTER, 3 Vergennes, Alton.
Church David C., 19 Spencer, Nelson.
Church Eustes E., 36 Lowell, Lowell.
Church George W., 19 Spencer, Nelson.
Church John, 13 Solon, Cedar Springs.
Church Henry, Lowell.
Church Henry S., 2 Alpine, Englishville.
Church Lewis H., 2 Alpine, Englishville.
CHURCH LEONARD W., 34 Ada, Ada.
Church Silas, 5 Bowne, Alto.
Church Wilson, 12 Vergennes, Alton.
Church William, 13 Solon, Cedar Springs.
Clackner J. F., 24 Sparta, Sparta Cen.
Clackner J. H., 24 Sparta, Sparta Center.
Clapp William, 9 Byron, North Byron.
Clark Henry, 34 Walker, Grand Rapids.
Clark, N. M., Lowell.
Clark Henry, 11 Tyrone, Sparta Center.
CLARK HARMON, 36 Cascade, Alaska.
Clark Henry, 3 Cascade, Ada.
CLARK ISAAC M., village of Cedar Springs.
Clark Jay, 3 Cascade, Ada.
Clark James D., 17 Solon, Cedar Springs.
Clark John, 20 Paris, Grand Rapids.
Clark, John H., 31 Plainfield, Mill Creek.
Clark John R., 13 Wyoming, Grand Rapids.
Clark John H., 36 Alpine, Mill Creek.
CLARK JOSEPH M., 5 Nelson, Cedar Springs.
Clark Lyman, 19 Tyrone, Casnovia.
Clark Oresta E., Rockford.
Clark Lewis P., 23 Grand Rapids.
CLARK LEWIS S., 25 Cascade, Lowell.
Clark M. J., Cedar Springs.
Clark Peter S., 12 Plainfield, Rockford.
Clark Perry, 15 Bowne, Alto.

BANK.

D. L. LATOURETTE, - BANKER.

Business paper discounted.
Business accounts solicited.
Deposits Received. Daily accounts and special deposits,
Collections made on all points.
Interest paid on Deposits.
Foreign Exchange on all points for sale.
Specie, U. S. Bonds, &c., bought and sold.
Savings deposits received. Interest allowed.
Exchange on New York, and all points bought and sold.
Revenue Stamps for sale.
Office hours, 8 to 5 daily. Saturday, 8 A. M. to 8 P. M.

D. L. LATOURETTE, Banker.
Grand Rapids, opposite Postoffice.

References:—National Park Bank, New York; Central National Bank, New York; Second National Bank, Detroit; Manufacturers' National Bank, Chicago; Banks and Bankers throughout the State.

R. BUTTON, DENTIST,

Has permanently Located in

GRAND RAPIDS,

And has neatly fitted up the Rooms formerly occupied by the City Council. He feels confident, after an experience of 18 years, of giving satisfaction to all wishing the services of his profession.

PRICES VERY MODERATE.

REMEMBER THE NUMBER,

34 CANAL STREET,

Two Doors South of the Star Clothing House, up stairs. Call and see Specimens.

C. J. KRUGER & Co.

Manufacturers and Dealers in

Saddles, Harness, Trunks, and all kinds of Horse Clothing,

Buffalo Robes, Whips, &c.,

ALSO SOLE MANUFACTURERS OF THE

Common Sense Neck Pad!

For Horse Collars,

The Only Pad Known to Prevent Galling the Neck or Cutting the Mane.

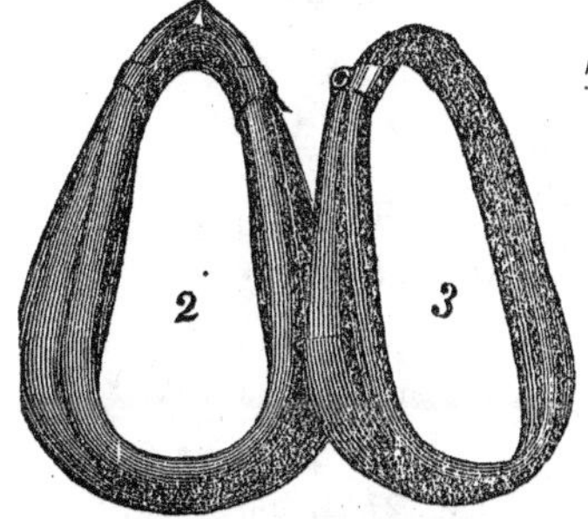

Ladies' Saratoga & Sole Leather Trunks,

Of our own manufacture, always on hand.

72 Monroe Street,

Grand Rapids, - - - Michigan.

THE OLDEST AND LARGEST ESTABLISHMENT IN THE STATE.

CLARK PHEBE J., 13 Vergennes, Fallassburg.
Clark Robert, 3 Alpine, Englishville.
Clark Timothy C., Grandville.
Clark Thomas, 22 Plainfield, Austerlitz.
Clark Warren, 1 Sparta, Sparta Center.
Clark William M., 15 Grand Rapids.
Clark William S., 16 Sparta, Sparta Center.
Clark William, 3 Courtland, Courtland Center.
Clark William H., 5 Nelson, Cedar Springs.
Clark Walter, 13 Vergennes, Fallassburg.
Clark William, 36 Cascade, Alaska.
Clausen Martin, 29 Grand Rapids.
Claun Charles, Bowne, Alto.
CLEMENS AMOS M., 17 Gaines, Grand Rapids.
Clemens Abraham C., 17 Gaines, Grand Rapids.
Clemens Christian, 34 Gaines, Grand Rapids.
Clemens Henry W, 36 Bowne, Fillmore, Barry County.
CLEMONS ALONZO, 34 Oakfield, Grattan Center.
Close Edward R., 32 Courtland, Rockford.
Close Samuel A., 33 Courtland, Rockford.
Close William W., 4 Cannon, Rockford.
Clousterhouse Claus, 21 Grand Rapids.
Clousterhouse Ralph, 21 Grand Rapids.
CLUTE DARWIN B., 28 Tyrone, Casnovia.
CLUTE ORLANDO H., 30 Tyrone, Casnovia.
Clyne Elias, Alaska Village.
CLYNE PETER, 9 Caledonia, Alaska.
Coats Mrs. A., Lowell.
Coats Freeman, 16 Wyoming, Grandville.
Coats Leman J., 16 Wyoming, Grandville.
Coats Marvin, 16 Wyoming, Grandville.
Coats Oliver, Lowell.
Cochlan Patrick, 20 Walker, Grand Rapids.
Cochlan Michael, 34 Walker, Grand Rapids.
Cobb Ezekiel H., 8 Cascade, Cascade.
COBB JAMES, JR., 8 Bowne, Alto.
Cobb James, 8 Bowne, Alto.
Cobb Thomas M., 34 Walker, Grand Rapids.

Clemons Henry, 3 Grattan, Grattan Center.
Clements John L., 34 Ada, Ada.
Clements Jacob, 21 Plainfield, Belmont.
Clepper Henry, 20 Courtland, Rockford.
Clerk Henry F., Lowell.
CLEVELAND ELEAZER B, 36 Spencer, Spencer Mill.
CLEVELAND W. H., 23 Sparta, Sparta Center.
Clifford Frederick, 17 Sparta, Lisbon.
Clifford James, 23 Oakfield, Ashley.
CLINGER HENRY J., Village Cannonsburg.
CLINTON CHAS. E., 7 Courtland, Cedar Springs.
Clinton Frederick, 1 Grand Rapids.
Clock Henry W., Village of Cedar Springs.
Cloffenstein John, 26 Gaines, Cody's Mill.
CLOSE CONVERSE, 11 Grattan, Grattan Center.
Close Elnathan D., 4 Cannon, Rockford.
CLOSE EVAN, 4 Cannon, Rockford.
Coburn Andrew J., 9 Byron, North Byron.
Coe George F., 12 Byron, Gainesville.
Coe William, 29 Grand Rapids.
COFFEE JOHN, 19 Alpine, Pleasant.
COFFIN MARION E., 18 Plainfield, Mill Creek.
Coffin Monroe, 20 Plainfield, Austerlitz.
Coger Charles, 8 Cascade, Cascade.
COGER JABEZ D., 8 Cascade, Cascade.
Cogshall Henry, 24 Bowne, Bowne.
Cogswell Harvey D., 11 Walker, Grand Rapids.
COGSWELL LUMAN W., 13 Lowell, Lowell.
Cogswell Martin, Lowell.
Coil John, 16 Ada, Ada.
Coker Albert, 2 Plainfield, Rockford.
COLBY HORACE, 33 Courtland, Rockford.
Colby Isaac C., 18 Bowne, Alto.
Colby James, 33 Courtland, Rockford.
Colby Truman, Rockford.
Colby Truman W., Rockford.
Colby Spencer, 27 Tyrone, Sparta Cen.
COLBURN ANDREW K., 19 Tyrone, Casnovia.

Colburn Benj. Q., 33 Gaines, Cody's Mills.
Colburn David, 6 Grand Rapids, Grand Rapids.
Colburn R. H., 19 Tyrone, Casnovia.
Colburn Sylvester, 13 Caledonia, Alaska.
COLBORN AMOS, Caledonia Station.
Colborn John, Caledonia Station.
Cole Albert, 8 Sparta, Sparta Center.
COLE ABRAM, 33 Ada, Ada.
COLE ANDREW, 30 Vergennes, Vergennes.
Cole Bradley, 9 Sparta, Sparta Center.
Cole Charles, 33 Ada, Ada.
Cole Franklin, 33 Ada, Ada.
COLE GARRETT, 15 Wyoming, Grandville.
COLE G. FILLMORE, 15 Walker, Grand Rapids.
Cole Henry, 15 Wyoming, Grandville.
Cole Harlan, 28 Bowne, Harris Creek.
Cole Hiram, 19 Alpine, Pleasant.
Cole John D., 33 Ada, Ada.
Cole James, 26 Gaines, Hammond.
Cole James, 19 Grattan, Grattan Cen.
Cole Lemuel, 24 Spencer, Spencer Mills.
Cole Luther, 33 Ada, Ada.
Cole Peter, 18 Paris, Grand Rapids.
Cole Peter B., 12 Gaines, Hammond.
Colley Watson, 15 Byron, Byron Center.
Collagan John, 19 Ada, Ada.
COLSON SHERMAN T., Alaska.
Colton Benton, 19 Plainfield, Austerlitz.
Colton Gideon, 13 Alpine, Alpine.
Colvin Eli, 3 Caledonia, Alaska.
Colvin James, 13 Vergennes, Fallassburg.
Colvin George, 29 Lowell, Alaska.
Colvin Samuel, 3 Caledonia, Alaska.
Colwell Hulbert, 28 Byron, Byron Center.
Colwell Josiah, 19 Wyoming, Grandville.
Colwell Weaver B., 19 Wyoming, Grandville.
Colyer Henry J., 30 Nelson, Cedar Springs.
Colyer N. J., 33 Sparta, Lisbon.
Combs Charles, 13 Bowne, Bowne.
Combes Thomas, 18 Walker, Grand Rapids.
Compton A. T., 28 Algoma, Rockford.
Compton Franklin W., 31 Plainfield, Mill Creek.
Compton James R., 31 Plainfield, Mill Creek.

Cole Reiley, 18 Paris, Grand Rapids.
Cole William, 29 Sparta, Lisbon.
Coleman Albert, 7 Alpine, Pleasant.
Collar Abraham, Lowell.
Collar Charles D., 25 Ada, Lowell.
Collar E. R., Lowell.
COLLAR NELSON, 29 Vergennes, Vergennes.
COLLAR SILAS, 31 Vergennes, Lowell.
Collar Sylvester W., 15 Ada, Ada.
Collins Charles, 25 Byron, Cody's Mills.
Collins Cornelius, 31 Spencer, Oakfield.
Collins Dennis, 1 Nelson, Nelson.
COLLINS JAMES, 5 Nelson, Sand Lake.
Collins Julian, 29 Tyrone, Casnovia.
Collins James, Rockford.
Collins Jabez, 29 Tyrone, Casnovia.
Collins James, 1 Grand Rapids.
Collins Michael, 24 Grand Rapids.
Collins Simon, 24 Grand Rapids.
Collins Thomas W., 1 Alpine, Englishville.
Collins Timothy B., 5 Nelson, Sand Lake.
Collum Samuel, 11 Lowell, Lowell.
Compton Oscar, Lisbon.
Comstock Charles, 28 Tyrone, Casnovia.
Comstock Joseph, 28 Tyrone, Casnovia.
Comstock Nathan, 21 Tyrone, Casnovia.
Conant Chester, 9 Courtland, Courtland Center.
Conant Horace, 28 Cascade, Alaska.
Conant Plimpton, 22 Solon, Cedar Springs.
Concidine John, 16 Byron, Byron Center.
Condon H. W., 31 Algoma, Englishville.
Condon John, 17 Walker, Grand Rapids.
CONDON SAMUEL, 12 Vergennes, Lowell.
Condon Thomas, 12 Vergennes, Lowell.
Cone Ira, Village of Cedar Springs.
Congdon William C., Burchville, (Burch's Mills.)
Congdon George R., Burchville, (Burch's Mills.)
Conklin Alfred, 19 Oakfield, Oakfield.

Conklin Charles C., 14 Wyoming, Grand Rapids.
Conklin Du Bois, 21 Alpine, Grand Rapids.
CONKLIN GEORGE M., 17 Courtland, Rockford.
Connelly Edward, 2 Grand Rapids.
Connelly James, 2 Grand Rapids.
Connelly Patrick, 2 Grand Rapids.
Conolly John, 15 Grand Rapids.
Conner T. W., 18 Wyoming, Grandville.
Conrad Edmund L., Lisbon.
Conula Peter, 29 Grand Rapids.
Converse James, 27 Vergennes, Lowell.
Conway Nicholas, 34 Wyoming, North Byron.
Cook Ariston J., 23 Byron, Cody's Mills.
Cook Abraham, 24 Paris, Grand Rapids.
COOK CLEVELAND C., 35 Byron, Cody's Mills.
Cook Emery, 16 Algoma, Rockford.
COOK EZRA, 26 Nelson, Cedar Springs.
Cook G. W., 15 Byron, Byron Center.
COOK GEORGE, 17 Gaines, Gainesville.
COOK HENRY, 23 Walker, Grand Rapids.
Cook Henry V., 8 Gaines, Grand Rapids.
Cool Benj. J., Cedar Springs.
Cool Eli J., 32 Nelson, Cedar Springs.
COOL URI, 32 Nelson, Cedar Springs.
Cooley Geo. N., 14 Caledonia, Alaska.
Cooley Geo. B., Lowell.
Cooley George W., 21 Solon, Cedar Springs.
Cooley John, Lowell.
COOLEY SEYMOUR E., 21 Solon, Cedar Springs.
COONS A. LEWIS, 23 Bowne, Bowne.
Coons Jacob J., 23 Bowne, Bowne.
Coon Dennis, 9 Walker, Grand Rapids.
COON CHARLES L., 23 Sparta, Sparta Center.
Coon Geo. T., 5 Walker, Berlin.
COON GEORGE, 22 Algoma, Edgerton.
Coon George, 30 Gaines, Cody's Mills.
Coon Hally B., 5 Walker, Berlin.
COON JACKSON, 13 Algoma, Edgerton.
Coon Phillip, 9 Walker, Grand Rapids.
COON REUBEN, 4 Byron, North Byron.
Cooper Adelbert, 23 Lowell, Lowell.
Cooper Calvin C., 17 Spencer, Spencer Mills.
Cooney F., 32 Grand Rapids.

Cook Ira, 17 Gaines, Gainesville.
Cook Jackson, 7 Cascade, Cascade.
COOK JOEL P., 1 Grattan, Ashley.
Cook John F., 28 Cascade, Alaska.
Cook Jehial, 6 Cannon, Rockford.
Cook Jesse, 24 Paris, Grand Rapids.
Cook Joseph, 25 Alpine, Alpine.
COOK SYLVESTER R., 28 Cascade, Alaska.
COOK LEWIS, 7 Cascade, Cascade.
COOK LUTHER B., 12 Grattan, Otisco, Ionia County.
Cook Martin, 19 Gaines, Cody's Mills.
Cook Madison W., 24 Paris, Grand Rapids.
Cook Oliver, 27 Wyoming, Grandville.
Cook Orson, 17 Gaines, Gainesville.
Cook Reuben W., 28 Tyrone, Casnovia.
COOK TRUMAN F., 12 Grattan, Otisco, Ionia County.
COOK THOMAS, 7 Cascade, Cascade.
Cook William, 9 Spencer, Spencer Mills.
Cook William, 36 Byron, Cody's Mills.
Cook Wm. G., 17 Nelson, Cedar Springs.
Cook Wm. F., 28 Cascade, Alaska.
Cool Benj. H., Cedar Springs.
Cooper Franklin H., 36 Spencer, Spencer Mills.
Cooper Edwin, 7 Oakfield, Oakfield.
Cooper George W., 36 Grattan, Alton.
Cooper Horatio N., 22 Byron, Byron Center.
Cooper John D., 20 Spencer, Spencer Mills.
Cooper Justus, 11 Algoma, Burchville (Burch's Mills.)
Cooper James, 2 Paris, Grand Rapids.
Cooper J. C., Burchville (Burch's Mills.)
Cooper John, 13 Alpine, Alpine.
Cooper Lewis C., 28 Byron, Byron Cen.
Cooper Nelson F., 27 Byron, Byron Center.
Cooper Owen, 17 Spencer, Spencer Mills.
Cooper Rogers C., 36 Spencer, Spencer Mills.
Cooper Samuel, 22 Plainfield, Austerlitz.
Cooper Samuel, 22 Plainfield, Austerlitz.
Cooper William, 7 Bowne, Alaska.

Cooper Warren, 16 Spencer, Spencer Mills.
Cooper William, 1 Courtland, Courtland Center.
Cope Albert A., Rockford.
Cope George, 6 Ada, Austerlitz.
Cope Robert, 31 Cannon, Austerlitz.
Cope Robert, 31 Cannon, Cannonsburg.
Copeland Joseph B., Grandville.
COPPENS CHARLES, 26 Bowne, Bowne.
Coppens Francis, 9 Bowne, Alto.
Coppens Peter T., Lowell.
Coppernoll Peter, 2 Gaines, Hammond.
Corbett Reuel, 24 Alpine, Alpine.
Corbin Charles G., 7 Byron, Grandville.
CORCORAN JAMES, 28 Ada, Ada.
Corcoran Thomas, 29 Paris, Grand Rapids.
CORDES CASPAR, 27 Alpine, Grand Rapids.
Cordes Eberhard, 26 Alpine, Grand Rapids.
Cordes William, 26 Alpine, Grand Rapids.
Corey Daniel, 18 Gaines, Gainesville.
Corey F. G., 29 Byron, Byron Center.
Cornell Perry, 32 Bowne, Harris Creek.
CORNELL ROBERT B., 36 Courtland, Bostwick Lake.
Cornell William M., 22 Oakfield, Oakfield.
Cornwell Charles M., 28 Nelson, Cedar Springs.
Cornwell John A., 2 Vergennes, Alton.
Cornwell John K., 12 Vergennes, Alton.
Cornue P. D., 20 Lowell, Lowell.
Cornula Martin, 29 Grand Rapids.
Corporon Samuel, 16 Walker, Grand Rapids.
CORRIGAN PETER, 10 Vergennes, Alton.
Corrigan Patrick, 27 Ada, Ada.
Corser George W. N., 28 Walker, G. Rapids.
Cortright Cornelius, 16 Ada, Ada.
Cortright Samuel, 29 Wyoming, Grandville.
Cory Mary, 20 Byron, Byron Centre.
Cory Philip, Lowell.
CORYELL CHARLES E., 7 Courtland, Edgerton.
Cotney Mrs. Ann, 16 Walker, Grand Rapids.
Cotney Henry, 18 Walker, G. Rapids.
Cotney James, 16 Walker, G. Rapids.

Corey Harvey T., 27 Sparta, Sparta Center.
Corey Joseph J., 29 Byron, Byron Center.
Corey Lyman H., 35 Wyoming, North Byron.
Corey Rufus B., 18 Gaines, Gainesville.
Corey Silas W., 27 Sparta, Sparta Center.
Corkins Geo. W., 10 Wyoming, Grand Rapids.
CORKINS ORSAMUS, 10 Wyoming, Grand Rapids.
CORKINS RUFUS, 3 Wyoming, Grand Rapids.
Corkins Wariner, 10 Wyoming, Grand Rapids.
Corlis Cornelius, Lowell.
Corlis John S., 34 Walker, Grand Rapids.
Corman Isaac, 34 Lowell, Lowell.
Cornall James, 13 Algoma, Edgerton.
Corn N. B., 3 Alpine, Englishville.
Cornell David, 10 Walker, Grand Rapids.
Cornell John, 17 Courtland, Courtland Center.
Cotney Thomas W., 8 Walker, Grand Rapids.
Court Marcus D., 16 Lowell, Lowell.
Court John H., 16 Lowell, Lowell.
Courson Hampton, 8 Wyoming, Grandville.
Courtwright Aaron, 31 Sparta, Lisbon.
COURTNEY BERNARD, 34 Walker, Grand Rapids.
Covell Charles, 13 Algoma, Edgerton.
Covell Daniel, 34 Algoma, Rockford.
Covell Gideon R., 14 Cascade, Cascade.
Covell George, 29 Ada, Ada.
Covell Joseph W., 13 Algoma, Edgerton.
Covell James, 13 Algoma, Edgerton.
COVELL P. F., 22 Walker, G. Rapids.
Covell Martin, 1 Plainfield, Rockford.
COVEY E. H., 4 Walker, Indian Creek.
Covey John W., 2 Algoma, Burch's Mills.
COVEY L. R., 35 Tyrone, Sparta Cen.
Covert Dyer, 2 Vergennes, Lowell.
COVERT JOHN L., 2 Vergennes, Lowell.
Corey Silas W., 27 Sparta, Sparta Cen.
Cowan Austin, 32 Courtland, Rockford.

Cowan Alonzo P., 18 Grattan, Bostwick Lake.
Cowan Alexander, 32 Courtland, Rockford.
COWAN ALEXANDER, 2nd, 6 Grattan, Bostwick Lake.
Cowan Alexander T., 32 Courtland, Rockford.
Cowan David, 14 Plainfield, Austerlitz.
Cowan Mrs. Eunice, 19 Courtland, Rockford.
COWAN JOHN C., 6 Grattan, Bostwick Lake.
Cowan Peter, 18 Grattan, Bostwick Lake.
COWAN THOMAS M., 32 Courtland, Rockford.
Cowan Thomas, 1 Cannon, Bostwick Lake.
Cowan Wm. S., 18 Grattan, Bostwick Lake.
COWELL ISAAC, 34 Bowne, Fillmore, Barry County.
COWLEY JOHN, 22 Vergennes, Lowell.
Cowley Robert, Lowell.
COWLES SHEPARD B., 29 Spencer, Nelson.
Cox John, 9 Courtland, Courtland Cen.
Crane Samuel M., 24 Vergennes, Fallassburg.
Crane William, Lowell.
Cranston Gardner, 15 Plainfield, Belmont.
CRANSTON THOMAS, 15 Plainfield, Belmont.
Crannell Wm. W., 16 Grattan, Grattan Center.
CRANMER CHARLES, 11 Plainfield, Rockford.
Cranmer Eugene, Lisbon.
Cranmer Israel, 9 Alpine, Grand Rapids.
Cranmer James M., 12 Plainfield, Rockford.
CRANMER JOHN, 9 Alpine, Grand Rapids.
Crandall Alonzo H., 16 Plainfield, Belmont.
Crandle Joseph, 14 Paris, Grand Rapids.
Crandall Myron, 30 Courtland, Rockford.
Crandall Nathan, 17 Courtland, Courtland Center.
Crandall Ormond F., 36 Wyoming, Kelloggsville.

Cox James, 8 Paris, Grand Rapids.
Cox Nicholas, 29 Plainfield, Grand Rapids.
Coy Daniel, 1 Caledonia, Alaska.
Crabtree Wm. B., 20 Byron, Byron Cen.
Crager Cornelius, 18 Paris, Grand Rapids.
CRAHAN JAMES, 24 Grand Rapids.
Crahan Martin, 24 Grand Rapids.
Crahen John, 25 Grand Rapids.
Craig Wm. T., 27 Grand Rapids.
CRAKES FRANCIS, 25 Ada, Ada.
Crakes George, 28 Vergennes, Lowell.
Crakes John J., 31 Vergennes, Lowell.
Crakes Theodore W., 35 Vergennes, Lowell.
Cramer Adelbert, 29 Vergennes, Vergennes.
Cramer George, 20 Paris, Grand Rapids.
CRAMER JEROME, 20 Paris, Grand Rapids.
Cramer John G., 20 Paris, Grand Rapids.
CRAMTON ALANSON, 21 Ada, Ada.
Cramton Charles, 27 Ada, Ada.
Crans W. J., 10 Walker, Indian Creek.
Crandall Stuart, 17 Gaines, Gainesville.
CRAW EDWIN R., Lowell.
Crawford David, 25 Oakfield, Ashley.
Crawford Green B., 11 Grattan, Grattan Center.
Crawford George, 8 Oakfield, Oakfield.
Crawford James, 26 Plainfield, Austerlitz.
Crawford John, Lowell.
Crawford James, Lowell.
CRAWFORD JOHN W., 11 Grand Rapids.
Crawford Samuel, 36 Oakfield, Ashley.
Creamer Thomas, Sparta Center.
Creager John, 30 Caledonia, Caledonia Station.
Creager William, 30 Caledonia, Caledonia Station.
Creit Averd, 29 Grand Rapids.
CREVLING BENJAMIN, 7 Plainfield, Alpine.
Crill Mark, 13 Alpine, Alpine.
Crinion Michael, 10 Courtland, Courtland Center.
Crinion Thomas, 15 Courtland, Courtland Center.

Crinnian Thomas, 34 Walker, Grand Rapids.
Crippen Alfred A., 36 Wyoming, Kelloggsville.
CRIPPEN W. S., 36 Wyoming, Kelloggsville.
CRISHER JOHN L., 24 Alpine.
Crissey, J. W., 13 Algoma, Edgerton.
CRISSEY WILLIAM S., 13 Algoma, Edgerton.
CRISSMAN JOHN, 29 Grand Rapids, Grand Rapids.
Crissman William, 7 Cannon, Rockford.
Crissman Henry, 21 Plainfield, Austerlitz.
Crissman Henry K., 13 Plainfield, Rockford.
Crits George, 32 Paris, Grand Rapids.
Critchett Geo. W., 19 Ada, Ada.
Crocker Alanson, 14 Byron, Byron Center.
Crocker Alvan, 30 Gaines, Cody's Mills.
Crocker Lewis N., 11 Byron, Byron Center.
Crocker Samuel J., 30 Gaines, Cody's Mills.
Cromwell Alexander, 24 Vergennes, Fallassburg.
Crowley Patrick, 28 Sparta, Sparta Cen.
Crowley William, 28 Sparta, Sparta Center.
CROW GEORGE, 21 Ada, Ada.
Crumback Mrs. Charity M., 35 Gaines, Cody's Mills.
Crumback George, 26 Bowne, Bowne.
CRUMBACK GERHARD W., 34 Gaines, Cody's Mills.
Crumback James T., 26 Gaines, Hammond.
CRUMBACK SAMUEL W., 25 Gaines, Caledonia Station.
CRUMBACK SAMUEL, 26 Bowne, Bowne.
Crusen John, 11 Lowell, Lowell.
Crysler Henry, 30 Paris, Grand Rapids.
Cubitt William, 33 Ada, Ada.
Cudahie M., 23 Grand Rapids.
Cuddeback Solomon, 26 Walker, Grand Rapids.
Cuddihie James, 14 Grand Rapids.
Cuddihie Michael, 14 Grand Rapids.
Cudeihy Thomas, 11 Bowne, Alto.
Cudington Peter, 17 Courtland, Courtland Center.
Culp Hiram, 9 Algoma, Sparta Center.
Culver Mrs. Azuba, 35 Sparta, Englishville.

Cromwell B. C., 16 Grand Rapids.
Cromwell Geo. W., 2 Plainfield, Rockford.
Cronan Timothy, 20 Grand Rapids.
CRONINGER DANIEL, 35 Cascade, Alaska.
Croninger Jacob, 35 Cascade, Alaska.
Croninger Joseph, 23 Caledonia, Caledonia.
CRONINGER MICHAEL, 23 Caledonia, Caledonia.
Croninger Talcott R., 35 Cascade, Alaska.
CRONINGER WM. B., 2 Caledonia, Alaska.
Crook Wm. A., 11 Lowell, Lowell.
CROOK JOHN R., 11 Lowell, Lowell.
Crosby Geo. W., 29 Vergennes, Lowell.
CROSBY WM., 13 Courtland, Courtland Center.
Cross Charles H., Rockford.
Cross Elry E., 35 Paris, Grand Rapids.
CROSS SHUBEL, 29 Grand Rapids.
Crossman Jacob, 29 Algoma, Sparta Center.
Crowley Jerry, 28 Sparta, Sparta Cen.
Culver Lewis M., 24 Caledonia, Alaska.
Culver Orris, 35 Sparta, Englishville.
Culver Robert G., 35 Caledonia, Caledonia.
CUMINGS ALLEN, 26 Tyrone, Sparta Center.
Cummings Mrs. Bridget, 30 Walker, Grand Rapids.
Cumings Edwin, 3 Alpine, Englishville.
Cumings Fred. M., 13 Sparta, Sparta Center.
CUMINGS JOSEPH M., 13 Sparta, Sparta Center.
Cummings John, 24 Plainfield, Austerlitz.
Cummings John, 30 Walker, Grand Rapids.
Cumings Marcus, 18 Algoma, Sparta Center.
CUMINGS MARCENE, 13 Sparta, Sparta Center.
CUMINGS NORMAN, 34 Sparta, Englishville.
Cumings Nelson, 3 Alpine, Englishville.
CUMMER JACOB, Cedar Springs.

Cummer Wellington W., Cedar Springs.
Cunningham Allen, 29 Wyoming, Gradville.
CUNNANE PETER, 3 Ada, Ada.
CUPPLES ROBERT, 17 Sparta, Lisbon.
Curley James, 20 Grattan, Grattan Cen.
Curley John, 20 Grattan, Grattan Cen.
Curley James, 32 Grattan, Vergennes.
Curley Patrick, 19 Bowne, Bowne.
CURRAN JOHN, 33 Walker, Grand Rapids.
CURREN EZRA, 1 Courtland, Courtland Center.
CURREN LEVI, 1 Courtland, Cedar Springs.
CURREN WELLEN, 1 Courtland, Courtland Center.
Currin Charles W., 25 Solon, Cedar Springs.
Curren Jerome M., 25 Oakfield, Greenville.
Curtiss Charles, 16 Plainfield, Belmont.
Curtis Chas. F., 27 Vergennes, Lowell.
Curtis Charles, 16 Plainfield, Belmont.
Curtiss Charles H., 16 Plainfield, Belmont.
Curtiss Chauncey, 22 Plainfield, Austerlitz.
Curtis Elliott, 13 Alpine, Alpine.
Curtiss George, 11 Plainfield, Rockford.
Curtiss John L., 26 Ada, Ada.
Cure Andrew J., 12 Byron, Gainesville.
Curtiss S. P., 29 Lowell, Lowell.
CUSACK MARTIN, 28 Paris, Grand Rapids.
Cushman Alphonzo, 26 Tyrone, Sparta Center.
Cushman J. B., Lowell.
Cushelman Michael, 10 Alpine, Englishville.
Cushway Paul, 16 Grand Rapids.
Cusser Isaac, 11 Vergennes, Alton.
Cutler Charles J., 6 Gaines, Gainesville.
Cutler John I., 6 Gaines, Cody's Mills.
CUTLER JOHN, 6 Gaines, Kelloggsville.
Cuttenbacker John, 1 Walker, Mill Creek.
Cutts George, 21 Courtland, Courtland Center.
CUYKENDALL JASPER, 23 Bowne, Bowne.
Cuykendall Solomon, 23 Bowne, Bowne.

D

Dager John, 11 Lowell, Lowell.
Daggett Marshall, 36 Sparta, Englishville.
Daggett William, 38 Tyrone, Casnovia.
Daily Henry, Grandville.
Daily John, 20 Grand Rapids.
Dalberg Charles, 28 Sparta, Lisbon.
Daily Dennis, 11 Wyoming, Grand Rapids.
Daley James, 2 Plainfield, Rockford.
Danforth Albert, 2 Plainfield, Rockford.
DANFORTH MORTIMER W., 9 Cascade, Cascade.
DANFORTH WILLIAM A., Rockford.
DANIELS AARON F., 31 Vergennes, Lowell.
DANIELS CHAS. H., 7 Lowell, Lowell.
Daniels John S., 33 Vergennes, Lowell.
Daniels Howard, Rockford.
Daniels Napoleon, 32 Cascade, Alaska.
DANIELS THOMPSON I., 33 Vergennes, Lowell.
Daniels William, 36 Grattan, Smyrna, Ionia County.
Danielson Andrew, 19 Sparta, Lisbon.
Darling Edward, 8 Alpine, Pleasant.
Darling Elias, 18 Sparta, Lisbon.
Darling George, 22 Alpine, Alpine.
Darling Hiram H., 10 Paris, Grand Rapids.
DARLING MARTIN, 21 Lowell, Lowelll.
Darling Silas, 16 Paris, Grand Rapids.
DARLING SAMUEL, 25 Grand Rapids.
Darrow Alexander L., 31 Courtland, Rockford.
Darrow John, 31 Courtland, Rockford.
Darrin Byron, 5 Nelson, Sand Lake.
DART FREEMAN, 3 Vergennes, Alton.
Darwin Erastus, 27 Spencer, Spencer Mills.
Daugherty John, 1 Wyoming, Grand Rapids.

Davenport Aaron, 30 Plainfield, Mill Creek.
Davenport George, 9 Oakfield, Oakfield.
Davenport George, 16 Cannon Cannonsburg.
Davenport Ithamer, 30 Plainfield, Mill Creek.
Davenport Jonathan, 19 Plainfield, Mill Creek.
Davenport Mrs. Miriam, 30 Plainfield, Mill Creek.
DAVIS ALBERT W. 12 Cannon, Bostwick Lake.
Davis Alonzo, 13 Paris, Cascade.
Davis Alanson, 23 Algoma, Edgerton.
Davis Abraham, 26 Paris, Grand Rapids.
Davis Alexander D., 27 Solon, Cedar Springs.
Davis Asa B., 27 Paris, Grand Rapids.
Davis Chyler, B., 29 Oakfield, Oakfield.
Davis Daniel, 14 Courtland, Courtland Center.
Davis Dennis G., 15 Courtland, Courtland Center.
Davis Daniel S., 15 Courtland, Courtland Center.
Davis John, jun., 23 Algoma, Edgerton.
Davis John H., Rockford.
Davis James M., 25 Sparta, Englishville.
Davis Jerome. 9 Wyoming, Grandville.
DAVIS JAMES P., 19 Oakfield, Oakfield.
Davis Jordan, 16 Grattan, Grattan Center.
Davis Joseph, 29 Courtland, Rockford
Davis John, 23 Algoma, Edgerton.
Davis John, 20 Grand Rapids.
DAVIS ISAAC D., 29 Paris, Grand Rapids.
DAVIS KING S., 16 Plainfield, Belmont.
Davis L. H., 14 Wyoming, G. Rapids.
DAVIS LUTHER B., 25 Grand Rapids.
Davis Martin, 17 Nelson, Cedar Springs.
DAVIS MARTIN, Rockford.
Davis Nancy N., 12 Cannon, Bostwick Lake.
Davis Perry M., 23 Algoma, Edgerton.
DAVIS PETER, 3 Wyoming, Grand Rapids.

Davis Elisha, Rocktord.
Davis Ezekiel W., 20 Grand Rapids.
DAVIE EDWARD, 7 Cannon, Rockford.
DAVIS EBENEZER, 9 Wyoming, Grandville.
Davis Emmet B., 20 Sparta, Lisbon.
Davis Franklin M., 18 Cascade, Cascade.
Davis Frank, 14 Wyoming, Grand Rapids.
Davis George, Lowell.
DAVIS GEORGE C., 27 Solon, Cedar Springs.
DAVIS GEORGE W., 36 Bowne, Fillmore, Barry County.
DAVIS HIRAM R., 10 Courtland, Courtland Center.
Davis Henry, 24 Grattan, Smyrna, Ionia County.
DAVIS H. B., 20 Grand Rapids, Grand Rapids.
DAVIS HORACE W., Grandville.
DAVIS HENRY S., 7 Cannon, Rockford.
DAVIS JOHN S., 34 Grand Rapids.
Davis Reuben, 1 Cannon, Bostwick Lake.
Davis Reuben E., 9 Wyoming, Grandville.
Davis Stephen B., 26 Paris, Grand Rapids.
Davis Solomon, 20 Sparta, Lisbon.
Davis Wm. H. H., 29 Oakfield, Oakfield.
DAVIS WM. R., 19 Oakfield, Oakfield.
Davis, Wm. W., 34 Ada, Ada.
Davison William, 17 Byron, Byron Center.
Davidson Walter, 8 Ada, G. Rapids.
DAVIDSON WILLIAM C., South 7 Walker, Grand Rapids.
Dawley Charles K., Rockford.
Dawson David, Lowell.
Dawson Elias, Lowell.
Dawson Heman F., Lowell.
Dawson James H., Lowell.
Dawson Richard L., 35 Vergennes, Lowell.
Day Elexis, 20 Lowell, Lowell.
DAY LEVI, Grandville.
DEACON ELIJAH E., Cedar Springs.
Deacon Jonathan, 17 Paris, G. Rapids.

Deal, Joshua, 25 Oakfield, Ashley.
Deal Jasper, 35 Oakfield, Ashley.
DEAL SOLOMON, 35 Oakfield, Ashley.
DEAN ALEXANDER, 21 Courtland, Courtland Center.
Dean, A. J., Lowell.
Dean Bethuel P., 31 Nelson, Cedar Springs.
DEAN D. J., 20 Grand Rapids.
Dean Elisha, 32 Nelson, Cedar Springs.
Dean John F., Lowell.
Dean Mortimer B., 16 Courtland, Courtland Center.
Dean Russell J., 3 Caledonia, Alaska.
DEAN WM. A., 33 Nelson, Cedar Springs.
De Boer Brown, 10 Wyoming, Grand Rapids.
De Bout Leonard, 18 Paris, Grand Rapids.
DEARLING JAMES, Lowell.
De Camp E. W., 25 Byron, Cody's Mills.
DECK WILLIAM, 3 Cannon, Cannonsburg.
Decker George, 31 Caledonia, Caledonia.
Decker Mrs. Maria, 20 Paris, Grand Rapids.
DECKER MICHAEL S., Lisbon

Delavan John, 3 Nelson, Sand Lake.
Demings Phillier, 30 Wyoming, Grandville
Deming Aaron S., 23 Bowne, Bowne.
Deming Charles, 23 Bowne, Bowne.
Demor Lander, 8 Paris, Grand Rapids.
Dempsey Simpson, 2 Plainfield, Rockford.
Demund Edward, 3 Gaines, Hammond.
Demund George R., 3 Gaines, Hammond.
Denise William, 11 Lowell, Lowell.
Denise David H., 11 Lowell, Lowell.
DENISON CALVIN W., Cedar Springs.
Denison Henry A., 28 Alpine, Indian Creek.
Denison William, 17 Alpine, Grand Rapids.
DENNIS AARON, 19 Vergennes, Vergennes.
Dennis Byron, 19 Vergennes, Vergennes.
Dennis James, 24 Wyoming, Grand Rapids.
Dennis John, 19 Vergennes, Vergennes.
Dennis Leonard L., 11 Oakfield, Greenville.
Dennis Mahlon, 32 Ada, Ada.

Decker William, 17 Courtland, Courtland Center.
DE COU GEO. W., 23 Nelson, Nelson.
DE COU BENJ. F., 24 Nelson, Cedar Springs.
Deen John J., Cedar Springs.
Deer George, 2 Plainfield, Rockford.
De Forrest Sylvester, 14 Solon, Cedar Springs.
Defreze John, 32 Grand Rapids.
Defries W., 29 Grand Rapids.
Deger James, 22 Walker, Grand Rapids.
De Glopper Cornelius, 3 Wyoming, Grand Rapids.
De Groot Dirk, 19 Wyoming, Grandville.
De Graw Augustus M., 2 Oakfield, Greenville.
De Graw John, 3 Oakfield, Greenville.
De Graw Joseph, 32 Spencer, Oakfield.
De Graw Nelson, 31 Spencer, Oakfield.
DEISHER CHARLES, 34 Ada, Ada.
De Jonge Ingle, 4 Paris, Grand Rapids.
DELANEY JOHN, 4 Vergennes, Alton.
DELANEY KER, 35 Wyoming, Grand Rapids.
Delaney William, 4 Vergennes, Alton.

DENNIS WM. H., 16 Oakfield, Oakfield.
Dennis Mrs. Eleanor, 15 Ada, Ada.
Dennis James A., 15 Ada, Ada.
Dennison Lorenzo N., 17 Alpine, Grand Rapids.
Dennison Morris W., 3 Cascade, Ada.
DENNISON DANIEL P., 34 Ada, Ada.
Denison Henry C., 11 Cascade, Cascade.
DENNEY MAXIM, 24 Vergennes, Fallassburg.
Dennison Asahel J., 14 Paris, Grand Rapids.
Dennison Barnard M., 14 Paris, Grand Rapids.
Denison Charles M., 8 Cascade, Cascade.
Denmau John, 1 Oakfield, Greenville.
Denmau Joseph, 1 Oakfield, Greenville.
Denny Jesse F., 33 Ada, Ada.
Denny Joseph, Lowell.
Denny Joseph, 1 Lowell, Lowell.
Densmore Luther, 34 Ada, Ada.
Dent Samuel, Burchville (Burch's Mills.)
Denton Alexander, 36 Vergennes, Lowell.

Denton George, 36 Vergennes, Lowell.
Denton George, 11 Lowell, Lowell.
Denton Joseph, 2 Walker,. Grand Rapids.
De Pew John, 33 Algoma, Rockford.
De Pew Ralph, 36 Algoma, Rockford.
DERMITT THOMAS, 31 Paris, Grand Rapids.
De Ruiter Henry R., Grandville.
Detray Albert C., 26 Gaines, Cody's Mills.
Detray Henry M., 32 Gaines, Cody's Mills.
DETRAY JACKSON B., 26 Gaines, Cody's Mills.
Detwilder Abraham W., 7 Caledonia, Hammond.
Detwilder Isaac, 29 Caledonia, Caledonia Station.
Detwilder Joseph, 28 Caledonia, Caledonia Station.
Deuel Joseph, 35 Courtland, Rockford.
De Vall Elizabeth, 12 Cascade, Cascade.
DEVENDORF CLARK M., Lowell.
DEVENDORF C. V., 29 Grand Rapids, Grand Rapids.
Devendorf David, 17 Wyoming, Grandville.
DEVENDORF J. J., Lowell.
De Young Gurt, 29 Grand Rapids.
Dias David, 19 Gaines, Gainesville.
Dias John, Sr., 19 Gaines, Gainesville.
DIAS JOHN, Jr., 19 Gaines, Gainesville.
Dias James, 19 Gaines, Gainesville.
Dias William, 19 Gaines, Gainesville.
Dibri Peter, 19 Byron, Byron Center.
Dice Stephen, 35 Alpine, Alpine.
Dickson Daniel, 18 Vergennes, Vergennes.
Dickson Edward, 18 Vergennes, Vergennes.
Dickerson Gilbert, 15 Plainfield, Belmont.
Dickerson Isaiah, 16 Plainfield, Belmont
Dickerson James H., 16 Plainfield, Belmont.
DICKERSON SILAS M., 9 Oakfield, Oakfield.
DICKINSON G. W., 22 Grand Rapids.
Dicks John, 11 Lowell, Lowell.
DIETRICH C. J., 29 Grand Rapids.
DIEFENBACKER JACOB, Alaska.
Dieffenbacker Jacob, 9 Caledonia, Alaska.
Diefenbacker Philip, Alaska.
Dikemaster John, 20 Gaines, Grand Rapids.

DEVINE EDWARD, 8 Vergennes, Vergennes.
Devine John, 4 Grattan, Grattan Cen.
Devine Mary A., 3 Vergennes, Alton.
Devine William, 8 Vergennes, Vergennes.
Devore Ransom, 1 Alpine, Englishville.
Devore William, 7 Plainfield, Englishville.
De Vriend Charles, 7 Ada, Grand Rapids.
Dewey Egbert, 21 Wyoming, Grandville.
Dewitt Issacher, 2 Wyoming, Grand Rapids.
Dewey Lafayette, 25 Oakfield, Greenville.
De Wolf John, 29 Plainfield, Grand Rapids.
DEYARMOND ALEX. F., 10 Vergennes, Alton.
DE YOUNG ADRIAN D., 26 Grand Rapids.
De Young Cornelius, 29 Grand Rapids.
De Young James, 26 Grand Rapids.
DE YOUNG JOHANNES, 29 Grand Rapids.
Dikestraw Garam, 32 Grand Rapids.
Dikestraw John, 29 Grand Rapids.
Dikestraw William, 29 Grand Rapids.
Dikestraw John, 32 Grand Rapids.
Dikeman Reynard, 5 Cascade, Cascade.
DILLENBACK BYRON A., 14 Wyoming, Grand Rapids.
DILLENBACK CHRISTIAN, 14 Wyoming, Grand Rapids.
DILLENBACK GEO. W., 35 Wyoming, Grand Rapids.
Dildine Harmon, 4 Algoma, Rockford.
Dilley Calvin F., 30 Algoma, Sparta Center.
DILLINGER JOHN M., 29 Bowne, Harris Creek.
Dillingham James C., 18 Cannon, Rockford.
Dimick Leander B., 11 Grattan, Grattan Center.
Dines Joseph, 28 Solon, Cedar Springs.
Dines Philip, 21 Solon, Cedar Springs.
Dines Wm., 21 Solon, Cedar Springs.
Dinger Joseph, 13 Walker, Grand Rapids.
Ditmus J., 7 Sparta, Lisbon.
Divine Wm. H., 17 Oakfield, Oakfield.

DIVINE LEANDER G., 19 Oakfield, Oakfield.
DIVINE WILLIAM, 24 Caledonia, Caledonia.
Dixon Mrs. Isabel, 13 Ada, Vergennes.
Dixon Roger, 34 Walker, Grand Rapids.
Dobson John, 4 Walker, Grand Rapids.
Dobson John, jr., 4 Walker, Grand Rapids.
Dockeray Clarence H., 6 Cannon, Rockford.
Dockeray Clarence, 25 Algoma, Edgerton.
DOCKERAY JOSEPH, 6 Cannon, Rockford.
Dockeray Joseph A., 5 Cannon, Rockford.
DOCKERAY JAMES, 5 Cannon, Rockford.
DOCKERAY R. L., Rockford.
Dockeray Robert, 6 Cannon, Rockford.
Dockeray R. Lewis, 5 Cannon, Rockford.
Dodge Henry A., 17 Tyrone, Casnovia.
Dodge Isaac, Lowell.
Dodge Isaac F., Lowell.
Dodge Joshua, 10 Lowell, Lowell.
Dooley Patrick, 33 Bowne, Harris Creek.
Doolittle Franklin, 27 Nelson, Cedar Springs.
Dorand John, Grandville.
Dory William, 8 Byron, North Byron.
Doster Peter, Rockford.
DOTY ELWOOD F., Lowell.
DOTY JOHN S., 23 Algoma, Edgerton.
Dougherty John, 27 Tyrone, Sparta Center.
DOUGHERTY JERRY, 3 Plainfield, Rockford.
Douglas Edward, 5 Walker, Indian Creek.
Douglas James, 11 Caledonia, Alaska.
DOUGLASS ORLIN, 24 Vergennes, Fallassburg.
DOUGLASS ROBERT, 16 Grattan, Grattan Center.
Douglas T., 18 Grand Rapids, Grand Rapids.
DOUGHAN JOHN, 28 Walker, Grand Rapids.
Dowling John, 3 Walker, Grand Rapids.
DOWLING MELVIN, 3 Walker, Grand Rapids.
DOWLING WM. C., 14 Alpine, Alpine.

DODGE OWEN, 20 Gaines, Gainesville.
Dodson David, 35 Paris, Grand Rapids.
Dole Charles, 16 Alpine, Grand Rapids.
DOLE JAMES E., Burch's Mills.
Dole Martin P., 33 Alpine, Indian Creek.
Doller Jacob, 32 Byron, Byron Center.
DONALDSON DWIGHT, 20 Grattan, Grattan Center.
Donaldson James, 24 Plainfield, Austerlitz.
Donaldson James, 26 Plainfield, Austerlitz.
Donahoe Gerald, 21 Cascade, Cascade.
Donahue Charles, 6 Oakfield, Oakfield.
DONNELL J. O., 34 Grattan, Alton.
Donovon Daniel, 2 Wyoming, Grand Rapids.
Donovan Fulmoth, 24 Grattan, Grant.
Donovon John, 2 Wyoming, Grand Rapids.
Donovan William, 24 Grattan, Grant.
Doody Patrick, 33 Cannon, Cannonsburg.
DOWNER AVERY, 15 Alpine, Alpine.
Downer Chas., Cedar Springs.
DOWNER SILAS B., Burch's Mills.
Downs Michael, 12 Ada, Ada.
Downing Abraham, 28 Sparta, Lisbon.
Downing Erastus, 14 Sparta, Sparta Center.
Downing William, 3 Tyrone, Casnovia.
Doyle Barney, 4 Paris, Grand Rapids.
Doyle John, 8 Grand Rapids.
Doyle John, 5 Vergennes, Alton.
Doyle Michael, 20 Grand Rapids.
Doyle Martin, 20 Grattan, Grattan Cen.
Doyle Michael, 1 Ada, Cannonsburg.
Doyle Owen, 30 Grattan, Grattan Cen.
Doyle Thomas, 5 Vergennes, Cannonsburg.
Doyle Thomas, 1 Ada, Cannonsburg.
Doyle William, 29 Tyrone, Casnovia.
Draper Jacob S., 3 Bowne, Alto.
Drake Dwight S., 34 Paris, Grand Rapids.
Drake Gilbert, 34 Sparta, Englishville.
Drakey Frank, 16 Gaines, Hammond.
Dresser A. L., Lowell.
Dresser William, 15 Sparta, Sparta Cen.
DREW DELOS, 28 Grand Rapids.

DREW GEO. H., 20 Grand Rapids.
Drew Patrick, 28 Grattan, Grattan.
Drinkall John, 20 Byron, Byron Center.
Drinkall William, 17 Byron, Byron Cen.
DRINDLE A., Lowell.
Driscoll Daniel, 8 Vergennes, Alton.
Driscoll Dennis, 8 Vergennes, Vergennes.
Driscoll Daniel, Lowell.
Driscoll Dennis, 32 Grattan, Alton.
Driscoll D., 34 Walker, Grand Rapids.
Driscoll John, 32 Bowne, Harris Creek.
Driscoll James, 30 Walker, G. Rapids.
Driscoll Michael, 30 Walker, G. Rapids
Driscoll Mrs. Margaret, 30 Walker, Grand Rapids.
Driscoll Patrick, 5 Vergennes, Vergennes.
Druce Charles, 23 Cascade, Cascade.
DRUCE MARK, 27 Bowne, Fillmore, Barry County.
Dry Peter, 32 Grand Rapids.
Dudbridge John, 24 Vergennes, Fallassburg.
DUFF PATRICK, 34 Ada, Ada.
Duffey Charles, 18 Paris, Grand Rapids.
DUFFEY JEROME, 1 Plainfield, Rockford.
Dunham James H., 17 Lowell, Lowell.
Dunham Johnson A., Cedar Springs.
Dunham Linnaeus, 31 Bowne, Harris Creek.
Dunlap James H., 15 Walker, Grand Rapids.
DUNDAP RILEY R., 15 Walker, Grand Rapids.
DUNLAP SAMUEL M., 14 Walker, Grand Rapids.
Dunn Dennis, 20 Lowell, Lowell.
Dunn Joseph, 20 Lowell, Lowell.
Dunn Lewis, 8 Sparta, Lisbon.
Dunn Robert, 30 Algoma, Sparta Center.
Dunn Wm., 8 Lowell, Lowell.
Dunnett Wm., 16 Walker, G. Rapids.
Dunton R. M., 14 Solon, Cedar Springs.
Dunwoody William, Burch's Mills.
Dupee David C., 24 Lowell, Lowell.
DUPEE FRANK, 24 Lowell, Lowell.
Durend Milo, 12 Byron, Gainesville.
Durfee Milton J., 14 Nelson, Nelson.
Durfey Nathan, 26 Ada, Ada.
Duster Peter, Rockford.
Dutcher Charles, 32 Ada, Ada.

Duffey James, 15 Vergennes, Lowell.
Duffey Robert, 1 Plainfield, Rockford.
Duffie William, 6 Oakfield, Oakfield.
Duffy Cairn, 34 Walker, Grand Rapids.
Duffy John, 9 Vergennes, Alton.
Duffy Patrick, 34 Walker, G. Rapids.
DUGA JEROME A., 27 Grattan, Lowell.
Duga Alexander, 27 Grattan, Lowell.
DULEY JAMES, 17 Algoma, Rockford.
Dumas Peter, 23 Nelson, Nelson.
Dumphy Adam, Rockford.
Dunphey Addison, Rockford.
Duncan Ebenezer, 22 Cascade, Cascade.
Dundas A. A., 20 Grand Rapids.
DUNHAM ABNER, 32 Grand Rapids.
DUNHAM ANDREW J. Grandville.
Dunham Charles B., 16 Caledonia, Alaska.
Dunham Eden S., Grandville.
Dunham John F., Grandville.
Dutcher Charles W., 32 Ada, Ada.
Dutcher David, 14 Caledonia, Alaska.
Dutmers John, 19 Plainfield, Alpine.
Dutmers Martin, 1 Wyoming, Grand Rapids.
Dutt Philip, Grandville.
DUTTON ALFRED, 24 Alpine, Alpine.
Dutton Ira, 24 Alpine, Alpine.
Dutton Edwin, 24 Alpine, Alpine.
Dutton Ralph, 24 Alpine, Alpine.
DWYER JAMES, 26 Caledonia, Caledonia.
Dwyer William, 26 Caledonia, Caledonia.
Dwyer Walter, 26 Caledonia, Caledonia.
Dwyer Edward, 31 Plainfield, Mill Creek.
Dyer John, Sparta Center.
Dygert Thomas, 13 Caledonia, Alaska.
Dyke Jacob L., 8 Wyoming, Grandville.

E

Eagan Mrs. Catherine, 5 Caledonia, Alaska.
Eagan Keeran, 4 Caledonia, Alaska.
Earhardt John, 28 Ada, Ada.
Earhardt William, 28 Ada, Ada.
Eardley James W., 21 Cascade, Cascade.
Eardly John, 19 Cascade, Cascade.
Eardly James, 20 Cascade, Cascade.
Eardley Patrick, 32 Cascade, Cascade.
EARDLY WILLIAM, 20 Cascade, Cascade.
EARDLY THOMAS, 19 Cascade, Cascade.
Earle Adelbert, 13 Plainfield, Rockford.
Earl Catharine, 4 Courtland, Courtland Centre.
EARLL NATHAN, 13 Walker, Grand Rapids.
Easterby James, 27 Lowell, Lowell.
Easterbrook Henry, 16 Lowell, Lowell.
Eastman Alexander, 20 Tyrone, Casnovia.
Easton E. A., 17 Grand Rapids.
Eastwood Charles, 11 Sparta, Sparta Center.
Eaton E. L., 12 Lowell, Lowell.
Edgerton Zeno, 18 Algoma, Sparta Cen.
Edie D. W., Lowell.
Edie James, Lowell.
Edie S. N., 36 Alpine, Grand Rapids.
Edie William, Lowell.
Edison Albert R., 27 Walker, Grand Rapids.
Edison Enos, 2 Walker, Grand Rapids.
Edison George M., 21 Walker, Grand Rapids.
Edison George, 2 Walker, G. Rapids.
Edison Haines, 2 Walker, Grand Rapids.
Edison Isaac, 9 Walker, Grand Rapids.
EDISON JOHN, 27 Walker, Grand Rapids.
EDISON JAMES R., 21 Walker, Grand Rapids.
EDISON JOHN H., 2 Alpine, Englishville.
Edison Milo H., 2 Walker, G. Rapids.
Edison Mrs. O. M., 28 Walker, Grand Rapids.
Edmunds Samuel F., 5 Lowell, Lowell.
Edwards Charles B., 10 Walker, Grand Rapids.

Eber Aaron, 20 Paris, Grand Rapids.
Ebrass Henry, 11 Alpine, Alpine.
Ecker Wm. S., 5 Paris, Grand Rapids.
Ecker Wm. J., Lowell.
Ecklestaffer Ernest, 21 Plainfield, Belmont.
ECKLESTAFFER LEONARD, 21 Plainfield, Belmont.
Eddy Charles, 16 Grattan, Grattan Cen.
Eddy Charles C., Lisbon.
Eddy Mrs. E. M., 16 Alpine, Alpine.
Eddy James, 33 Plainfield, Grand Rapids.
EDDY MRS. MALINDA, Lisbon.
EDDY MRS. MARION A., Cedar Springs.
Eddy Malcom, 16 Grattan, Grattan Center.
Eddy Wallace, 15 Grattan, Grattan Center.
EDDY WM. H., Lowell.
Ede Edwin E. H., 11 Walker, Grand Rapids.
Edgerton Albert, 2 Plainfield, Rockford.
Edgerton Curtis, 32 Solon, Cedar Springs.
Edwards Ephraim, 7 Vergennes, Vergennes.
Edwards H. B., 10 Wyoming, Grandville.
Edwards Henry E., 10 Wyoming, Grandville.
EDWARDS JAMES, 15 Oakfield, Oakfield.
Edwards P. S., Rockford.
Eggleston Harvey, 35 Algoma, Rockford.
EGGLESTON HARRISON, 8 Cannon, Rockford.
Eggleston James, 35 Algoma, Rockford.
Eldridge Daniel, 8 Caledonia, Alaska.
Eldridge Edward, 8 Caledonia, Alaska.
ELDRIDGE EDGAR M., 24 Grattan, Grattan Center.
Eldridge Harry W., 24 Grattan, Grant.
Eldridge Ira, 10 Courtland, Courtland Center.
Eldridge Ira, Jr., 10 Courtland, Courtland Center.
Eldridge Charles J., 7 Caledonia, Alaska.
Eldridge Charles, 10 Courtland, Courtland Center.

Eldridge Chas. J., 7 Caledonia, Alaska.
Eldridge Reuben N., 24 Grattan, Grattan Center.
Eldridge William, 10 Courtland, Courtland Center.
Eldridge Wm. J., 16 Byron, Byron Cen.
ELDRED A. J., 15 Walker, Grand Rapids.
Eldred Amos, 12 Plainfield, Rockford.
ELDRED BENEDICT, 8 Plainfield, Belmont.
Eldred Clarisa, 8 Cannon, Rockford.
ELDRED JOHN, 17 Cannon, Austerlitz.
ELDRED SAMUEL T., 5 Plainfield, Belmont.
ELKINS AUGUSTUS W., 35 Courtland, Rockford.
Elkins Squire F., 30 Courtland, Rockford.
ELKINS WM. J., 6 Grattan, Bostwick Lake.
ELMONDORPH JAMES L., 18 Walker, Grand Rapids.
Elmer Charles, Burchville (Burch's Mills.)
Ellerton Thomas, 20 Grattan, Grattan Center.
ELLSWORTH ZARA W., 5 Nelsen, Sand Lake.
Elsby Daniel B., 33 Plainfield, Grand Rapids.
Elsbey James, 31 Oakfield, Oakfield.
Elsbey John E., 31 Oakfield, Oakfield.
Ellwell Chauncey, 12 Byron, Gainesville.
Ely John J., Rockford.
Emerson George, 33 Walker, G. Rapids.
Emery Hiram, 33 Nelson, Cedar Springs.
Emery Horace F., 9 Walker, Grand Rapids.
Emmert Isaac, 21 Wyoming, Grandville.
Emmons Andrew K., 14 Byron, Byron Centre.
Emmons Christopher, 18 Algoma, Sparta Centre.
Emmons Charles E., 29 Caledonia, Caledonia Station.
EMMONS CHARLES, 11 Grattan, Grattan Centre.
EMMONS DAVID V., 15 Oakfield, Oakfield.
Emmons Ervin J., Sparta Centre.
Emmons Hiram, 13 Grattan, Otisco, Ionia Co.
EMMONS JOHN T., 34 Wyoming, North Byron.

ELLIS ALFRED, 10 Sparta, Sparta Center.
ELLIS ARTHUR, 7 Bowne, Alaska.
Ellis Albert G., Village Cannonsburg.
Ellis Benjamin, 12 Caledonia, Alaska.
Ellis Hiram, — Sparta, Sparta Center.
Ellis Hiram, 27 Sparta, Sparta Cen.
Elis Ira, Village Cannonsburg.
Ellis John, Lowell.
Ellis John J., 13 Alpine, Alpine.
ELLIS JOHN, Grandville.
Ellis Mrs. Maria, 7 Bowne, Alaska.
Ellis Williard, 13 Alpine, Alpine.
Elliott Dolly, 22 Oakfield, Oakfield.
Elliott George M., 22 Oakfield, Oakfield.
Elliott Henry, 31 Algoma, Englishville.
Elliott Hiram, 23 Plainfield, Austerlitz
Elliott John H., 22 Oakfield, Oakfield.
Elliott Nelson T., 22 Oakfield, Oakfield.
Elliott William J., 4 Sparta, Sparta Centre.
ELLMAKER CHARLES V., 34 Ada, Ada.
Ellson F. W. C., Lowell.
ELSWORTH A. M., Lowell.
ELSWORTH HENRY, Rockford.
Emmons John, 6 Grattan, Grattan Cen.
Emmons Nicholas, 18 Algoma, Sparta Centre.
Emmons Nicoll D., 34 Wyoming, North Byron.
Emmons Simon, 9 Algoma, Sparta Cen.
EMMONS WM. K., 34 Wyoming, North Byron.
Emmons Uriah, 6 Grattan, Grattan Cen.
Emmons Uriah, 11 Grattan, Grattan Centre.
Endres Fritz, 29 Byron, Byron Center.
Eness Geo. L., 28 Ada, Ada.
Engel Louis, 25 Wyoming, Grand Rapids.
Engles John, 4 Lowell, Lowell.
Engel Louis, 35 Wyoming, Grand Rapids.
English Edward S., 36 Sparta, Englishville.
English Joseph S., 36 Sparta, Englishville.
English Joseph S. jun., 35 Sparta, Englishville.
English Richard S., 36 Sparta, Englishville.

English William S., 35 Sparta, Englishville.
Ennig Goddfried, 31 Byron, New Salem.
ENOS RUSSELL J., Lowell.
Enrich John, 20 Spencer, Spencer Mills.
Enrich Leonard, 19 Spencer, Nelson.
Entricon George, 28 Sparta, Lisbon.
Entwistle Alfred, Lowell.
Erb Moses, 24 Lowell, Lowell.
ERB D. C., 13 Lowell, Lowell.
Erwin Jared, 28 Byron, Byron Center.
Erler Titus, 24 Gaines, Caledonia Station.
Ernst Frank, 10 Lowell, Lowell.
Ernst Joseph, 10 Lowell, Lowell.
ESCOTT GEORGE S., 15 Walker Grand Rapids.
ESCOTT JOSEPH, 15 Walker, Grand Rapids.
Esterlee Peter, 15 Vergennes, Lowell.
Esterlee Peter, jr., 15 Vergennes, Lowell.
Eulrich Philip, 33 Spencer, Spencer Mills.
Evans Amos, 22 Plainfield, Austerlitz.
Evans Alfred, 35 Bowne, Bowne.
Evans Edward, 30 Vergennes, Lowell.
Evans Ira, 10 Wyoming, G. Rapids.
EVANS JAMES A., 29 Gaines, Cody's Mills.
EVANS NATHANIEL, Lowell.
EVANS THOMAS, 11 Bowne, Bowne.
Evans Thomas J., 23 Plainfield, Austerlitz.
Evans William, Sen., 12 Ada, Ada.
Evans William, Jr., 12 Ada, Ada.
Evans William I., 23 Byron, Byron Center.
Evans Wm., 26 Lowell, Lowell.
Evarts S. H., 29 Grand Rapids.
EVERETT BENJAMIN F., 22 Sparta, Sparta Center.
Everet Tonas B., 26 Sparta, Sparta Center.
Everts H. P., 25 Byron, Cody's Mills.
Everts N. K., 25 Byron, Cody's Mills.
Ewing Alexander, 10 Byron, Byron Center.
Ewing George W., 26 Byron, Cody's Mills.
EWING WEBSTER B., 6 Gaines, G. Rapids.
EWING JAMES, 22 Grand Rapids, Grand Rapids.

Evans Judson, 26 Sparta, Sparta Center.
Evans Charles, 36 Sparta, Englishville.
Evans Charles, 23 Sparta, Sparta Center.
EYER MICHAEL, 14 Gaines, Hammond.
Eyester Matthias, 6 Oakfield, Oakfield.

F

Fahay Patrick, 20 Grand Rapids.
Fain Michael, 7 Paris, Grand Rapids.
FAIRCHILD A. B., 14 Solon, Cedar Springs.
Fairchild Benjamin, 17 Vergennes, Vergennes.
Fairchild Benj., 29 Lowell, Lowell.
Fairchild Mrs. Betsey, 15 Solon, Cedar Springs.
FAIRCHILD BENJ., Cedar Springs.
FAIRCHILD WM. F., 17 Vergennes, Vergennes.
Fairchild Eliezer, 35 Grand Rapids.
Fairchild Horace R., 1 Caledonia, Alaska.
Fairchild Joseph E., Lowell.
Fairchild John, 1 Caledonia, Alaska.
Fairchild L. L., 29 Lowell, Lowell.
Fairchild Mrs. N. A., Lowell.
FALEN MICHAEL, South 5 Walker, Grand Rapids.
FALLASS HENRY B., 24 Vergennes, Fallassburg.
Fallasston James, 18 Cannon, Austerlitz.
Fallass J. Wesley, 24 Vergennes, Fallassburg.
FALLASS SILAS S., 23 Vergennes, Fallassburg.
Fallass Silas S., jun., 23 Vergennes, Fallassburg.
FALLASS WILLIAM A., Lowell.
Fancher Andrew, 33 Grand Rapids.
Fancett Charles, 19 Ada, Ada.
Fannagan Lewis, 21 Cascade, Cascade.
Fanning Peter, Lowell.
Fanniburg Edward, 18 Paris, Grand Rapids.

Farmer Giles A., 23 Wyoming, Grand Rapids.
Farmer David O., 30 Lowell, Lowell.
Farnam Reuben, 4 Nelson, Cedar Springs.
Farnham Benjamin, 7 Caledonia, Hammond.
Farbam Caroline E., 10 Cascade, Ada.
Farnham Darwin, 18 Nelson, Cedar Springs.
FARNHAM WM. D., 7 Caledonia, Alaska.
Farnsworth B. C., 27 Walker, Grand Rapids.
FARR CHARLES, 5 Courtland, Courtland Center.
FARR ELI A., 13 Solon, Cedar Springs.
FARR HENRY F., 14 Cannon, Cannonsburg.
FARR JEHU, 32 Nelson, Cedar Springs.
Farr Thomas, 5 Courtland, Cedar Springs.
Farril John, 28 Cascade, Cascade.
Farrall Garrett, 14 Ada, Ada.
Farrall Michael, 11 Ada, Ada.
Farrall William, 11 Ada, Ada.
Fasel Matthias, 31 Byron, Byron Center
FAUNCE CHESTER R., 34 Ada, Ada.
Faulkner Arnold T., 11 Lowell, Lowell.
Ferrand L., 34 Walker, Grand Rapids.
Ferrand Louis G., 15 Wyoming, Grandville.
Fero Charles G., Lowell.
Ferc James D., 13 Ada, Ada.
FERO, MUNSON B., 18 Vergennes, Vergennes.
Ferris Josiah B., 31 Ada, Ada.
FERRY A. P., 18 Cannon, Rockford.
Ferry George, 24 Cannon, Cannonsburg.
Ferry John, 18 Cannon, Rockford.
FERNER STEPHEN, 25 Nelson, Nelson.
FESSEL G. M., Cedar Springs.
Fessendon Henry, 13 Wyoming, Grand Rapids.
Fewlass John R., 11 Gaines, Hammond.
Fiance Andrew, 24 Plainfield, Austerlitz.
Fiance Cornelius, 24 Plainfield, Austerlitz.
Field B. F., 15 Walker, Grand Rapids.
Field Charles S., 26 Sparta, Sparta Cen.
Field Chauncey B., 2 Alpine, Englishville.
Field Gaylor, 35 Sparta, Englishville.
Field Jesse B., 5 Alpine, Pleasant.
Field John W., 28 Sparta, Lisbon.

Faulkner Frances E., 11 Lowell, Lowell
Faurot David, 7 Tyrone, Casnovia.
Faurot James, 8 Tyrone, Casnovia.
FAUST JOHN, 29 Grand Rapids.
Faxon Samuel, Ada Village, Postmaster.
Fekin Edward, 1 Wyoming, Grand Rapids.
Felo C. B., Lowell.
Fenton Ambrose W., 14 Sparta, Sparta Center.
Fenning Peter, 20 Lowell, Lowell.
Fenn Edwin T., 34 Algoma, Rockford.
Fenton Joseph, 18 Algoma, Sparta Cen.
Fenton Lewis, 35 Sparta, Sparta Cen.
Fenton Thomas, 2 Plainfield, Rockford.
Ferguson Andrew, 7 Byron, Grandville
Ferguson B. C., 35 Solon, Cedar Springs
Ferguson George, 2 Byron, North Byron.
Ferguson James, 7 Gaines, Gainesville.
Ferguson Matthew, 19 Paris, Grand Rapids.
Ferguson Stephen, 29 Gaines, Grand Rapids.
Ferrand Charles, 34 Walker, Grand Rapids.
Field Lyman, 6 Alpine, Pleasant.
FIELD SYLVESTER H., 35 Sparta, Englishville.
Fifield Jehial, 24 Vergennes, Fallassburg.
Fifield Jebiel, 4 Grattan, Grattan Cen.
Fifield Philbert E., 12 Courtland, Courtland Center.
Filkins Alphonso, Lowell.
Filkins Elijah, 15 Plainfield, Belmont.
Filkins Hiram, Lowell.
Filkins Isaac, 6 Lowell, Lowell.
Filkins John, Lowell.
Filkins William, 2 Courtland, Courtland Center.
FINCH ASA, 32 Grand Rapids.
Finch Alfred, 33 Sparta, Lisbon.
Finch Albert, 33 Sparta, Lisbon.
Finch Franklin, 33 Sparta, Lisbon.
Finch Henry, 27 Walker, G. Rapids.
FINCH JAMES N., 8 Plainfield, Belmont.
FINCH JAMES, 13 Grand Rapids.
Finch Nathan, 8 Plainfield, Belmont.
Finch Noah, 13 Grand Rapids.
Finch William E., 8 Plainfield, Belmont.

Findlay Alexander, 9 Ada, Ada.
Findlay John, 9 Ada, Ada.
Findlay William, 9 Ada, Ada.
Fingleton Dan'l, 35 Cannon, Cannonsburg.
FINGLETON PATRICK, 2 Ada, Cannonsburg.
Fingleton William, 34 Cannon, Cannonsburg.
Finn James, 8 Vergennes, Vergennes.
Finn James, 1 Ada, Ada.
Finn John, 1 Wyoming, Grand Rapids.
Finney J. G., Lowell.
Finney James A., 10 Paris, G. Rapids.
FINTON CHAS. H., 20 Gaines, Cody's Mills.
Finton James W., 20 Gaines, Cody's Mills.
Fisher Albert, 17 Paris, Grand Rapids.
Fisher Albert, 29 Grand Rapids.
Fisher Daniel, 33 Wyoming, North Byron.
FISHER ELIAS T., 1 Plainfield, Rockford.
FISHER JAMES, 29 Grand Rapids,
Fisher Leonard, 30 Lowell, Lowell.
FISHER LEVI W., Alaska.
Fisher Michael, 24 Alpine, Alpine.
Fisher William H., 34 Paris, G. Rapids.
Fitzgerald Isaac, 33 Walker, G. Rapids.
Fitzgeralds Joel, 18 Alpine, Pleasant.
Fitzgerald Michael, 28 Walker, Grand Rapids.
Fitzgerald Michael, 6 Oakfield, Oakfield.
Fitzgerald Patrick, 12 Lowell, Lowell.
Fitzgerald Thomas, 34 Ada, Ada.
Fitzgerald William, 10 Vergennes, Alton.
FITRGERALDS WM., 7 Alpine, Pleasant.
Fitzpatrick James, 1 Wyoming, Grand Rapids.
Fitzpatrick Michael, 26 Walker, Grand Rapids.
FITZPATRICK PATRICK, Rockford.
Flanagin Isaac D., 3 Walker, Indian Creek.
Flanagan John, 26 Grattan, Grant.
Flanigan Terry, 24 Cannon, Cannonsburg.
Flanigan Michael, 24 Oakfield, Ashley.
Flannery Adeline, 24 Byron, Gainesville.
Flanner Rodolphus J., 31 Plainfield, Grand Rapids.
FLEMING MARTIN J., 30 Paris, Grand Rapids.

Fish Charles D., 10 Walker, G. Rapids.
Fish Emory W., 1 Paris, Grand Rapids.
Fish John, 7 Cascade, Cascade.
Fish Sanford G., 6 Cascade, Cascade.
Fisk John W., 28 Grand Rapids.
Fisk Nathaniel, 27 Walker, G. Rapids.
Fisk William H., Sparta Center.
Fitch Amasa, 31 Sparta, Lisbon.
Fitch Benjamin, 30 Algoma, Sparta Center.
Fitch Charles A., 14 Cannon, Bostwick Lake.
Fitch Calvin, 14 Cannon, Bostwick Lake.
Fitch George, 13 Algoma, Edgerton.
Fitch Joseph, 30 Algoma, Sparta Center.
Fitch Norton, 5 Alpine, Lisbon.
FITCH NELSON H., 31 Walker, G. Rapids.
FITCH WELLINGTON, 32 Sparta, Lisbon.
FITCHET MERRITT, 3 Vergennes, Alton.
Fitzmorris James, 8 Walker, G. Rapids.
FITZGERALD DENNIS, 34 Ada, Ada.
Fitzgeralds George, 7 Alpine, Pleasant.
Fleming Watson B., 30 Paris, Grand Rapids.
Flemming John, Cedar Springs.
Fletcher David, 32 Cannon, Austerlitz.
FLETCHER DANIEL C., 30 Cannon, Austerlitz.
Fletcher George, 1 Vergennes, Alton.
Fletcher Jerome, 24 Lowell, Lowell.
FLETCHER JESSE, 13 Lowell, Lowell.
Fletcher James, 27 Plainfield, Grand Rapids.
Fletcher John, 13 Lowell, Lowell.
Fletcher James, 1 Vergennes, Alton.
Fletcher John R., 30 Cannon, Austerlitz.
Fletcher Levi, 13 Lowell, Lowell.
Flood Dennis, 27 Grand Rapids.
Flood Thomas, 27 Grand Rapids.
FLUENT ANDREW J., 22 Solon Cedar Springs.
FLYNN BERNARD, 33 Bowne, Harris Creek.
Flynn Edward M., Jr., 28 Grattan, Grattan Center.
Flynn Edward, 28 Grattan, Grattan Center.

FLYNN FRANK, 28 Bowne, Harris Creek.
Flynn John, 34 Walker, Grand Rapids.
Flynn James, 34 Walker, Grand Rapids.
FLYNN PETER, 25 Caledonia, Caledonia.
Flynn William, 23 Courtland, Courtland Center.
FOGARTY MRS. MARGARET, 31 Walker, Grand Rapids.
Fogle Jacob, 11 Alpine, Alpine.
Foley James, 27 Plainfield, G. Rapids.
Foley John, 27 Plainfield, G. Rapids.
Foley Martin, 11 Grand Rapids.
Foley Thomas, 27 Plainfield, Austerlitz.
Foley Thomas, 3 Ada, Ada.
Follett Harmon L., 1 Wyoming, Grand Rapids.
Folsom George, Sparta Center.
Folsom Benj. G., 34 Ada, Ada.
Fonger James, 24 Wyoming, Grand Rapids.
Fonger Levi, 24 Wyoming, G. Rapids.
Foote James, 32 Wyoming, Grandville.
Foote Merritt, 6 Oakfield, Cedar Springs
Foote Lavias H., 11 Byron, Byron Cen.
FOOTE OBED H., 8 Grand Rapids.
FOOTE PETER S., 29 Grand Rapids, Grand Rapids.
Ford Orren, 35 Grattan, Alton.
FORD WARREN, 34 Grattan, Alton.
Forman Edwin, Lowell.
Forney Eli, 25 Paris, Grand Rapids.
Forrest James E., 20 Solon, Cedar Springs.
FORT EDWIN M., Lowell.
Fort John, 20 Lowell, Lowell.
Fort John P., 20 Lowell, Lowell.
Foster Abraham, 20 Lowell, Lowell.
Foster Charles M., 13 Bowne, Bowne.
Foster Emery, 14 Vergennes, Lowell.
Foster Gilbert, 31 Bowne, Harris Creek.
Foster John, 32 Ada, Ada.
FOSTER NORMAN, 13 Bowne, Bowne.
Foster Oscar, 21 Wyoming, Grandville.
FOSTER RUFUS, JR., 35 Grattan, Alton.
Foster Thomas H., 5 Paris, G. Rapids.
Foster Wm. H., 14 Vergennes, Lowell.
Fountain Benjamin, 35 Cascade, Alaska
Fountain Cornelius, 29 Grand Rapids.
FOWLER E. D., 20 Algoma, Sparta Center.
Fox Ammond, 4 Algoma, Cedar Springs
Fox Amos, 34 Bowne, Fillmore, Barry County.
Fox Ambrose L., 6 Byron, Grandville.
FOX BENTON D., Lowell.

Foote Wm. R., 2 Cannon, Bostwick Lake.
Forbes John W., 2 Paris, Grand Rapids
Forbes William, 3 Lowell, Lowell.
Forbes William, 21 Tyrone, Casnovia.
FORCE BRITTON, 5 Cannon, Rockford.
Fordham Theodore, 4 Sparta, Sparta Center.
Ford Abel, 2 Vergennes, Alton.
FORD ANNA M., 2 Vergennes, Alton.
FORD ALFRED T., 2 Vergennes, Alton.
Ford Abel, 21 Bowne, Bowne.
Ford Amos, 11 Grattan, Grattan Center
Ford Alfred T., 11 Lowell, Lowell.
Ford Andrew C., Cedar Springs.
FORD CHESTER S., Cedar Springs.
Ford Hiram, 11 Lowell, Lowell.
Ford Horace B., 25 Grattan, Smyrna, Ionia County.
Ford Ira, 10 Vergennes, Alton.
Ford Joseph T., 2 Vergennes, Alton.
Ford John H., 2 Paris, Grand Rapids.
FORD JACOB A., 16 Spencer, Spencer Mills.
FORD LEVI, 24 Bowne, Bowne.
Fox Charles, 13 Algoma, Edgerton.
Fox Charles M., Lowell.
FOX DANIEL R., 8 Caledonia, Alaska.
Fox Erastus J., 22 Alpine, Indian Creek
FOX GEORGE, Alaska Village.
Fox Gilbert, 13 Algoma, Edgerton.
Fox Henry, 6 Byron, Grandville.
Fox John M., Lowell.
Fox Jacob, 27 Vergennes, Lowell.
FOX JAMES S., 33 Vergennes, Lowell.
Fox Jacob, 29 Vergennes, Lowell.
Fox Josiah, 29 Wyoming, Grandville.
FOX JORDAN, 34 Bowne, Fillmore.
Fox Wesley, 11 Lowell, Lowell.
Fox William, 11 Lowell, Lowell.
Fox Philip W., 27 Vergennes, Lowell.
FOX RICHARD, 32 Vergennes, Lowell.
Fox Theron J., 22 Alpine, Indian Creek.
Fox William H., 27 Vergennes, Lowell.
FRANCISCO CHAS., 26 Grattan, Alton.
Francisco Chas. E., 34 Grattan, Alton.
Francisco Henry D., 31 Bowne, Harris Creek.
Francisco Jeremiah, 21 Algoma, Rockford.

FRANCISCO LEVI J., 27 Grattan, Alton.
FRANCE W. W., 29 Grand Rapids.
Frank George, 32 Spencer, Cedar Springs.
Frantz John, 11 Byron, Byron Center.
Fraser John H., 35 Cascade, Alaska.
Fraser John C., 35 Cascade, Alaska.
Fravel George, 5 Nelson, Sand Lake.
Frawley James 24, Grand Rapids.
Frawley Patrick, 19 Ada, G. Rapids.
Frawley Simon, 24 Grand Rapids.
Frawley Thomas, 24 Grand Rapids.
Frayer Abram, 24 Cascade, Lowell.
Frayer Martin J., 24 Cascade, Lowell.
Frayer Robert, 24 Cascade, Lowell.
Frazier Alex., Cedar Springs.
Frazier Charles, 35 Ada, Ada.
Frazier Darius N., 15 Grattan, Grattan Center.
FRAZIER GEORGE, 31 Vergennes, Lowell.
Frazier Ira, 35 Ada, Ada.
Frazier Nelson, 31 Vergennes, Lowell.
Fredenberg Elijah, 32 Tyrone, Casnovia.
Freddelfeilt Henry, 13 Walker, Grand Rapids.
Free Daniel, 24 Byron, Cody's Mills.
FREYERMUTH JOHN, 30 Lowell, Lowell.
FREY ADAM, 30 Cannon, Austerlitz.
Frick William, 30 Sparta, Lisbon.
FRIEND CHRISTIAN P., 24 Paris, Grand Rapids.
FBOST ALEXANDER B., Lisbon.
Frost Charles J., 23 Plainfield, Austerlitz.
FROST CHARLES H., 26 Cascade, Cascade.
Frost Sylvanus H., 31 Plainfield, Grand Rapids.
FROST SAMUEL, 32 Plainfield, Grand Rapids.
Frost Sylvanus, 34 Plainfield, Grand Rapids.
Frost William, 9 Gaines, Hammond.
Frost William, 25 Wyoming, Grand Rapids.
Fry Allen S., 19 Oakfield, Oakfield.
Fry Samuel M., 21 Walker, G. Rapids.
Fry Wm. J., 9 Lowell, Lowell.
Fulbert Peter, 13 Walker, G. Rapids.
FULKERSON BURNETT, 19 Tyrone, Casnovia.
FULKERSON LOT, 30 Tyrone, Casnovia.

Free Mrs. Huldah, 25 Byron, Cody's Mills.
Free Patrick O., 19 Grattan, Grattan Center.
Free William, 25 Byron, Cody's Mills.
FREEMAN CYRUS, 31 Wyoming, Grandville.
FREEMAN ERASTUS, Cedar Springs.
Freeman George, 24 Vergennes, Fallassburg.
Freeman Seymour, 28 Nelson, Cedar Springs.
FREEMAN MORRIS, 16 Gaines, Grand Rapids.
Freeman Otis, 32 Wyoming, Grandville.
Friedenthaler Christian, 20 Tyrone, Casnovia.
French Arod, 18 Lowell, Lowell.
French, Mrs. Deborah, 12 Lowell, Lowell.
French George, Rockford.
French Hiram W., 9 Cascade, Cascade.
French Steven, 30 Algoma, Sparta Center.
French Wyman, 12 Solon, Cedar Springs.
Fuller Charles, 6 Grattan, Grattan Center.
Fuller Elisha W., 10 Alpine, Alpine.
Fuller Elijah, Lowell.
FULLER EDWARD S., 13 Courtland, Courtland Center.
Fuller Hiram, Rockford.
Fuller Horatio, 6 Grattan, Grattan Center.
Fuller Henry A., 6 Grattan, Grattan Center.
Fuller James, 6 Walker, Berlin.
FULLER MORRIS, 27 Courtland, Courtland Center.
Fuller O. B., Lowell.
Fuller Olney B., Lowell.
Fuller Suel, 6 Walker, Berlin.
Fuller Sanford, 25 Ada, Ada.
Fuller William, 24 Cascade, Cascade.
FULLER WINDFIELD S., 11 Grattan Grattan Center.
Fullerton S. S., Lowell.
FULLINGTON GEORGE W., 10 Vergennes, Alton.
Fullington Norman, 21 Vergennes, Lowell.

FULLINGTON ORMUS, 21 Vergennes, Lowell.
Furlong Geo. W., 27 Cannon, Cannonsburg.
Furman James W., Grandville.
FURTNEY AMOS, 8 Gaines, Gainesville.
FURTNEY SAMUEL C., 36 Gaines, Cody's Mills.
Furtney Samuel F., 36 Gaines, Cody's Mills.

G

Gains Frank, 24 Grattan, Grant.
Gaines Frank, 10 Lowell, Lowell.
Gaines J., 10 Lowell, Lowell.
GAIN WILLIAM, 7 Sparta, Lisbon.
Gaiter Nicholas, 26 Alpine, Indian Creek.
Gale Benj. F., 15 Cascade, Cascade.
Gallaway Andrew, Jr., Grandville.
Gallaway Andrew S., Grandville.
Gallaway Washington L., Grandville.
Gallaway Wm. H., Grandville.
Gallup Ira, 11 Lowell, Lowell.
Gannon Chauncey S., 33 Gaines, Cody's Mills.
Gano Julius C., 20 Alpine, G. Rapids.
Ganson John, 29 Grand Rapids, Grand Rapids.
Garber Henry, 16 Gaines, Gainesville.
Gasper Joseph S., 25 Vergennes, Lowell
Gaulthier Lewis, 1 Walker, G. Rapids.
GAVIN JOHN, South 5 Walker, Grand Rapids.
Gavin Thomas, 34 Walker, G. Rapids.
Gaylord Orson, 23 Vergennes, Fallassburg.
Gean James, 25 Cannon, Cannonsburg.
Gee Charles, 31 Alpine, Indian Creek.
Gee Orrin, 31 Alpine, Indian Creek.
Gee Walter S., Rockford.
Geges Henry, 1 Solon, Sand Lake.
Geib George, 6 Caledonia, Alaska.
GEIB NICHOLAS, 22 Gaines, Grand Rapids.
Geiger George, 35 Bowne, Fillmore, Barry County.
Geill Frank A., 27 Vergennes, Lowell.

GARDNER DANIEL C., 9 Sparta, Sparta Center.
Gardiner Earls, 34 Ada, Ada.
Gardner Frank N., 10 Sparta, Sparta Center.
Gardner Ira, 34 Walker, Grand Rapids.
GARDNER IRA, 9 Bowne, Alto.
Gardner Ira, 25 Grattan, Smyrna, Ionia County.
GARDENER JULIUS, Sparta Center.
Gardner Jonathan, 28 Nelson, Cedar Springs.
Gardner Robert H., 15 Cascade, Cascade.
GARDNER W. B., Lowell.
GARFIELD SAMUEL M, 7 Paris, G. Rapids.
Garity John, 16 Courtland, Courtland Center.
Garity James, 16 Courtland, Courtland Center.
Garlick Robert, 15 Plainfield, Belmont.
Garlick William, 15 Plainfield, Belmont.
Garrity Patrick, 10 Courtland, Courtland Center.
Gasper Freeman S., Lowell.
Geill F. E., Lowell.
Gelfoyle John, 33 Spencer, Spencer Mills.
Gerald Fitz, 34 Grattan, Grattan.
Gettings Louis, 8 Oakfield, Oakfield.
Getman Warner F., 19 Spencer, Nelson.
Gibby Abraham, 19 Paris, G. Rapids.
Gibbs Alfred O., 23 Ada, Ada.
Gibbs Mrs. Anna, 4 Ada, Ada.
Gibbs Charles N., 23 Ada, Ada.
Gibbs Calvin, 17 Byron, Byron Center.
Gibbs Edmund L., 23 Ada, Ada.
Gibbs James W., 23 Ada, Ada.
Gibbs Job, 23 Ada, Ada.
Gibbs Josiah H., 4 Grattan, Grattan Center.
Gibbs Thomas W., 19 Alpine, Pleasant.
Gibbs Wm. H., 4 Ada, Ada.
Gibbon John, Grandville.
Gibson Archibald K., 25 Ada, Ada.
GIBSON CHARLES K., Ada Village.
Gibson Henry, 21 Algoma, Rockford.
GIBSON JOHN A., 2 Bowne, Alto.
GIBSON WILLIAM, 14 Bowne, Bowne.
Gibson William, 20 Lowell, Lowell.
Giffin Johnson M., 13 Grattan, Otisco, Ionia County.

Gilbert Charles, 23 Byron, Cody's Mills.
Gilbert David J., 19 Oakfield, Oakfield.
Gilbert Egbert, 20 Lowell, Lowell.
GILBERT JOHN W., 19 Oakfield, Oakfield.
Gilbert John W., 30 Tyrone, Casnovia.
Gilbert Truman, 3 Byron, North Byron.
Gilbert Thomas M., 12 Solon, Cedar Springs.
Gilbert Norton, 23 Byron, Cody's Mills.
Gilden Robert, 24 Paris, Grand Rapids.
Giles Alpha, 9 Byron, North Byron.
GILES CHARLES L., 13 Solon, Cedar Springs.
Giles Elijah, 25 Sparta, Sparta Center.
Giles Edward W., 13 Solon, Cedar Springs.
Giles Edwin, 13 Solon, Cedar Springs.
GILES JOHN, Lowell.
Giles Richard, 32 Grattan, Cannonsburg.
Giles Richard, jr, 32 Grattan, Cannonsburg.
Gilfelling Joseph, 1 Algoma, Cedar Springs.
Gilfoyle Michael, 28 Spencer, Spencer Spencer Mills.
Gilfoyle William, 32 Spencer, Spencer Mills.
Gillmore Henry, 19 Tyrone, Casnovia.
Gillmore James C., 19 Tyrone Casnovia.
Gilner Frederick, 2 Wyoming, Grand Rapids.
Gilson Asa J., 32 Sparta, Lisbon.
Gimble William, 17 Caledonia, Caledonia Station.
Girdler Benjamin C., 7 Walker, Berlin.
Girdler William P., 7 Walker, Berlin.
Gitchell Lafayette, 22 Plainfield, Austerlitz.
Glacier Seneca, 17 Caledonia, Alaska.
Glass Cyrus, 16 Plainfield, Belmont.
Glass Peter, 16 Plainfield, Belmont.
GOBLE JACOB, 11 Vergennes, Alton.
Godfrey George F., 5 Byron, North Byron.
GODFREY GEO. H., 11 Vergennes, Alton.
Godfrey Joseph G., 22 Bowne, Bowne.
Godfrey Newcomb, 2 Vergennes, Alton.
Godfrey Smith, 2 Vergennes, Alton.
Godfrey Zerah, 22 Bowne, Bowne.
Godwin Augustine, 13 Wyoming, Grand Rapids.
Goff Charles, 17 Grand Rapids.
Goff W. H., 31 Algoma, Englishville.

Gillett Alex., 31 Paris, Grand Rapids.
Gillet Dan'l A., 2 Alpine, Englishville.
GILLETT GEO. H., 30 Paris, Grand Rapids.
Gillett Lewis E., 30 Paris, G. Rapids.
Gillett Wilkes, 30 Paris, Grand Rapids.
Gill Buell, 4 Caledonia, Alaska.
GILL CHARLES N., 16 Gaines, Hammond.
Gill Isaac, 16 Gaines, Hammond.
Gill Jay J., 6 Walker, Berlin.
Gill Mrs. Joanna, 4 Caledonia, Alaska.
GILL PATRICK, 15 Grand Rapids.
Gill Simon, 15 Gaines, Hammond.
GILL GODFREY, 28 Alpine, Indian Creek.
GILLAM BENJAMIN, 22 Sparta, Sparta Center.
Gillam John, 27 Sparta, Sparta Center.
Gilleland James O., Rockford.
GILMAN GEORGE, 26 Sparta, Sparta Center.
Gilman Jacob M., 17 Cannon, Cannonsburg.
Gilman Steven, 27 Sparta, Sparta Center.
Gillmore Darwin, 31 Tyrone, Casnovia.
Goggins Barney, 34 Bowne, Harris Creek.
Goggins Patrick, 29 Bowne, Harris Creek.
Goggin Thomas, 12 Wyoming, Grand Rapids.
Goler John, 25 Alpine, Mill Creek.
GOLDS GEORGE, 14 Ada, Ada.
Golden Charles, 10 Tyrone, Casnovia.
Goldner John, 13 Alpine, Alpine.
Goldsmith Vincent J., 30 Nelson, Cedar Springs.
Gooch Benjamin, 1 Alpine, Englishville.
Gooch Nathan W., 18 Plainfield, Alpine
Goodell Duwane, 9 Paris, Grand Rapids
Goodell John, 9 Paris, Grand Rapids.
Goodell Warren, 9 Paris, Grand Rapids
Goodenough Fred., 25 Ada, Lowell.
Goodfruit Chas. G., 29 Ada, Ada.
Goodfellow James, 22 Sparta, Sparta Center
Gooding C. C., 7 Alpine, Pleasant.
Gooding Richmond, 19 Alpine, Pleasant.
Gooding Seymour, 20 Alpine, Grand Rapids.
Goodin Philip, 26 Vergennes, Lowell.

Goodsell D. M., Lowell.
GOODSELL JOHN O., 24 Vergennes, Fallassburg.
Goozen Peter, 15 Solon, Cedar Springs.
GORDON GEO. W., 33 Cascade, Alaska
Gordon Charles, 31 Lowell, Lowell.
Gordon Harvey, Alaska.
GORDON ISAAC H., 7 Cannon, Rockford.
Gore John, 20 Grand Rapids.
Gore John, Jr., 20 Grand Rapids.
Gorham George W., 16 Cascade, Cascade.
GORHAM MARVIN, 4 Caledonia, Alaska.
GORMAN PATRICK, 10 G. Rapids.
Gormin Patrick, 27 Ada, Ada.
GOSCH ALBERT, 29 Bowne, Harris Creek.
Gosch Henry, 29 Bowne, Harris Creek.
Gosch Zerubabel, 29 Bowne, Harris Creek.
Goss Benson O., 12 Cannon, Bostwick Lake.
Goss Darius, 12 Cannon, Bostwick Lake.
Goss Keyes H., 19 Nelson, Cedar Springs.
Graham James, 32 Cascade, Cascade.
Graham John F., 26 Courtland, Courtland Center.
Graham Joseph, 27 Lowell, Lowell.
Graham John G., Cedar Springs.
Graham Jason, 27 Spencer, Spencer Mills.
GRAHAM NELSON, 26 Courtland, Courtland Center.
Graham Philip, 35 Wyoming, Grand Rapids.
Graham Wm. K., 22 Lowell, Lowell.
GRAHAM WM. B., 27 Lowell, Lowell.
Gramberg Chas. A., Lisbon.
Grant Alfred, 32 Algoma, Rockford.
Grant George, 32 Algoma, Rockford.
GRANT GEORGE, Cedar Springs.
Grant James, 13 Lowell, Lowell.
Grant James, 8 Ada, Ada.
Grant John, 32 Algoma, Rockford.
GRANT JOHN, 15 Ada, Ada.
Grant William, 5 Ada, Ada.
Graves George G., 6 Gaines, Gainesville.
Graves Jeremiah A., 24 Cascade, Lowell.
Graves John W., 9 Ada, Ada.
Graves N. B., 6 Ada, Ada.
Graves William, 6 Ada, Ada.

Goss Orin L., 11 Cannon, Bostwick Lake.
Gougerty William, 20 Bowne, Harris Creek.
Gould Charles, 8 Nelson, Cedar Springs.
GOULD H. L., 10 Lowell, Lowell.
Gould Joseph W., 27 Plainfield, Grand Rapids.
Gould J. B., Sparta Center.
GOULD NATHAN H., 35 Oakfield, Oakfield.
Gould Platt, 2 Oakfield, Greenville.
Gould Simeon, 8 Nelson, Cedar Springs.
Gould Wm. W., 5 Paris, Grand Rapids.
Gouldsborough Robert J., 30 Nelson, Cedar Springs.
GOVE EDMUND D., 15 Cascade, Cascade.
Grachtrup Joseph, 35 Alpine, Grand Rapids.
GRAHAM ARCHIBALD, 15 Grand Rapids.
Graham Charles, 22 Lowell, Lowell.
Graham Elwood, 27 Walker, G. Rapids.
Graham James, 25 Cannon, Cannonsburg.
GRAVES LIVEUS, 6 Gaines, Grand Rapids.
GRAVES Mrs. M. B., 30 Walker, Grand Rapids.
Grawn Augustus, 16 Sparta, Sparta Center.
Grawn Andrew, 8 Sparta, Lisbon.
Gray Darius, 3 Oakfield, Spencer Mills.
Gray James, 8 Wyoming, Grandville.
GRAY JAMES, 8 Caledonia, Alaska.
Gray John, 33 Sparta, Englishville.
Gray Lyman C., 29 Alpine, Indian Creek.
Gray Ogden, 19 Cannon, Austerlitz.
Gray Thomas, 13 Spencer, Spencer Mills.
GRAY WM. H., 36 Grattan, Grant.
GREEN ANSEL D., 14 Grattan, Grattan Centre.
Green Birdsley, 19 Tyrone, Casnovia.
Greene Benjamin, Lowell.
GREEN EDMUND, 8 Courtland, Courtland Centre.
Green Henry, 12 Grattan, Grattan Cen.
GREEN H. W., 26 Grand Rapids.
Green Henry, 13 Grattan, Otisco, Ionia Co.

Green Isaac D., 15 Bowne, Bowne.
Green Obidiah S., 32 Lowell Lowell.
GREEN SAMUEL J., 35 Spencer, Spencer Mills.
Green Thomas, 16 Grand Rapids.
Green Wm., 11 Lowell, Lowell.
GREEN WILLIAM W. G., 16 Bowne, Alto.
GREEN WARREN, 8 Grand Rapids.
Green William, 26 Grand Rapids.
GREENLY HARLAN A., 20 Alpine, Grand Rapids.
GREENMAN BRYAN, 18 Gaines, Gainesville.
Greenwood Joseph, 6 Algoma, Sparta Centre.
Gregory Abraham, 13 Algoma, Edgerton.
Gregory Giles, 27 Wyoming, G. Rapids.
Gregory Lorenzo, 24 Cascade, Cascade.
Greiner Julius, Lisbon.
Gridley Charles, Grandville.
Gridley George W., South 7 Walker, Grand Rapids.
GRIDLEY WILLIAM C., South 6 Walker, Grand Rapids.
GRIFFIN CHARLES, 15 Plainfield, Belmont.
Groner Jacob, 28 Cannon, Cannonsburg.
Groner Theodore, 33 Cannon, Cannonsburg.
Groner Valentine, 33 Cannon, Cannonsburg.
Groom Matthew, 16 Byron, Byron Center.
Gross Alexander, 34 Algoma, Rockford.
Grose Charles, 32 Solon, Cedar Springs.
Grose Frank, 34 Algoma, Rockford.
Grose Reuben, 34 Algoma, Rockford.
GROSE WILLIAM, 20 Algoma, Rockford.
Gross Henry, 34 Algoma, Rockford.
Gross J. P., Lowell.
GROSS MICHAEL, 14 Paris, Grand Rapids.
Gross Samuel, 2 Plainfield, Rockford.
Grossman Christian, 30 Cannon, Austerlitz.
Grouw Jacob, 14 Grand Rapids.
GROSVENOR EDWARD, 14 Solon, Cedar Springs.
GRUNWELL WILLIAM, 3 Sparta, Sparta Center.
Grutsch Peter, 17 Caledonia, Caledonia Station.

Griffin James, 5 Vergennes, Cannonsburg.
Griffin John, 21 Wyoming, Grandville.
Griffith Rha P., 5 Ada, Ada.
Griffith Grffiith E., 32 Oakfield, Oakfield.
Griggs George W., 6 Paris, G. Rapids.
Griggs Joseph E., Lowell.
GRIGGS LEVERETT S., Lowell.
Grindle Mrs., Lowell.
Griswold Jabez W., 32 Spencer, Cedar Springs.
Griswold Scott, 32 Spencer, Cedar Springs.
GROAT NICHOLAS, Rockford.
Groff Henry, 32 Caledonia, Caledonia Station.
Grommet James, 2 Plainfield, Rockford.
Grutter Garrat, Grandville.
Grutter Jacob, Grandville.
Guild Albert H., 8 Paris, G. Rapids.
Guild Edward, 4 Paris, Grand Rapids.
Guild Horace H., 4 Paris, G. Rapids.
Guilmer Thomas, 2 Plainfield, Rockford.
Gulliford James, Lowell.
Gunn Hector W., 21 Walker, Grand Rapids.
Gunning Stephen, 9 Vergennes, Alton.
Gurnee Caleb, 15 Solon, Cedar Springs.
GURNEE SAMUEL B., 14 Solon, Cedar Springs.
Gwinnell Daniel, 11 Algoma, Burch's Mills.
Gwinn Mrs. M. A., 1 Byron, G. Rapids.

H

Haas Christopher, 25 Wyoming, Grand Rapids.
Hachmuth Christy C., 36 Alpine, G. Rapids.
Hachmuth Henry, 1 Walker, Grand Rapids.
Hackett James, 26 Caledonia, Caledonia.
HACKING HENRY, 27 Walker, G. Rapids.
Hadden Horace, 13 Walker, G. Rapids.
Hadden Thomas, 28 Bowne, Harris Creek.
Hadley Martin, 11 Alpine, Alpine.
Haede Koop, 28 Walker, G. Rapids.
Haffer George, 24 Byron, Gainesville.
HAFFY THOMAS, 33 Courtland, Courtland Center.
Hagerty Timothy, 32 Walker, Grand Rapids.
Hagadone Peter, 7 Sparta, Lisbon.
Hagadone William H., 7 Sparta, Lisbon.
Hagget John, 26 Walker, G. Rapids.
Haines Harvey, 18 Cannon, Austerlitz.
Haines Henry, 34 Walker, G. Rapids.
Hall Elihu, 27 Plainfield, Austerlitz.
HALL E. D., 12 Algoma, Edgerton.
Hall Edward, 12 Solon, Cedar Springs
Hall E. M., Rockford.
HALL ELIAS, 28 Plainfield, Grand Rapids.
HALL GEO. W., 26 Byron, Cody's Mills.
Hall Frederick, 16 Byron, Byron Cen.
Hall Henry, 26 Solon, Cedar Springs.
Hall Harrison, 18 Nelson, Cedar Springs
Hall Henry S., 9 Gaines, Grand Rapids
Hall Jonathan B., 1 Grattan, Ashley.
Hall J. F., 20 Algoma, Sparta Center.
Hall James I., 28 Walker, G. Rapids.
HALL JOSEPH, Lowell.
Hall John B., 23 Lowell, Lowell.
Hall Levi, 2 Cascade, Ada.
Hall M. E., Rockford.
HALL SETH T., 11 Grand Rapids.
Hall Samuel C., 11 Gaines, Hammond.
Hall Thomas, 11 Solon, Cedar Springs.
Hall Wm. H., Lowell.
Halpen James, 24 Ada, Ada.
Halpen John, 14 Ada, Ada.
Halpen Mrs. Mary, 14 Ada, Ada.

Haines Moses D., 5 Cannon, Rockford.
Haines William, 34 Paris, G. Rapids.
Haines Virgil, 21 Cannon, Cannonsburg.
Haight George, 19 Caledonia, Caledonia Station.
Haight Mrs. Lowell.
Hait John, 32 Vergennes, Lowell.
Haket Cyprus, 19 Ada, Ada.
Halcro James, 17 Alpine, Pleasant.
Halders Tees, 32 Grand Rapids.
HALDANE MRS. EMELINE T., South 4 Walker, Grand Rapids.
Haldane Arthur W., 4 Walker, Grand Rapids.
HALE DAVID P., 22 Caledonia, Alaska.
Hale Elisha G., 31 Wyoming, Grandville.
Hale Henry W., 32 Nelson, Cedar Springs.
HALE WARREN S., Alaska.
Hall A. G., 1 Alpine, Englishville.
Hall Alfred A., 14 Lowell, Lowell.
Hall Charles, 21 Wyoming, Grandville.
Hall Dwight E., 1 Grattan, Ashley.
Hall Daniel, 19 Wyoming, Grandville.
Halsted David, 29 Tyrone, Casnovia.
Hamburg Peter, 11 Lowell, Lowell.
Hamer John D., 12 Paris, G. Rapids.
Hamer John D., Jr., 12 Paris, Grand Rapids.
HAMILTON AMOS H., 29 Byron, Byron Center.
Hamilton David, 2 Bowne, Alto.
HAMILTON HARMON, 19 Tyrone, Casnovia.
Hamlinton Henry F., 16 Courtland, Courtland Center.
Hamilton Isaiah B., 8 Wyoming, Grandville.
Hamilton James W., Cedar Springs.
Hamilton Robert, 20 Lowell, Lowell.
HAMILTON SILAS L., 21 Byron, Byron Center.
Hamlin John R., Grandville.
Hamlin Loomis, 18 Algoma, Sparta Center.
Hammersmith Frank, 22 Alpine, Grand Rapids.
Hammond Mrs. Anna, 11 Gaines, Hammond.
Hammond Charles, 17 Walker, Grand Rapids.

HAMMOND ESASMUS L., 14 Gaines, Hammond.
Hammond Eli E., 11 Gaines, Hammond.
Hammond Horace C., 8 Gaines, Hammond.
Hammond Horton G., 14 Gaines, Hammond.
Hammond Ira H., 6 Caledonia, Alaska.
Hammond James, 11 Gaines, Hammond.
Hammond John O., 13 Gaines, Hammond.
Hammond Randall S., 11 Gaines, Hammond.
Hammond Stephen A., 11 Gaines, Hammond.
Hammond William, 2 Walker, Grand Rapids.
Hanchett Edward E., Lowell.
Hancock George, 28 Solon, Cedar Springs.
Hancock Lewis S., 28 Solon, Cedar Springs.
Hand Caleb M., 29 Grand Rapids.
Hand Thomas, 31 Wyoming, Grandville.
Handlin Thomas, 30 Bowne, Harris Creek.
Haner Alfred, Lowell.
HANSON DANIEL N., 29 Tyrone, Casnovia.
Hanson John, 33 Oakfield, Ashley.
Hanson S. H., Lowell.
Hanson William, 14 Solon, Cedar Springs.
Hapeman John G., 35 Grattan, Alton.
HARD W. P., South 6 Walker, Grand Rapids.
Hardy George W., 9 Paris, G. Rapids.
Hardy John, 19 Nelson, Cedar Springs.
Hardy Eugene, 9 Gaines, Grand Rapids
HARDY WM. J., 9 Gaines, G. Rapids.
Hardy John, 26 Solon, Cedar Springs.
Hardy William, 20 Byron, Byron Cen.
Hardwick James, 34 Bowne, Fillmore, Barry County.
Harger Harvey, 13 Caledonia, Alaska.
Harger Leonidas, 13 Caledonia, Alaska.
HARLAN JOSEPH, 5 Cascade, Cascade.
Harmon Anthony, 25 Cannon, Cannonsburg.
Harmon Delos, 4 Bowne, Alto.
Harmon James, 25 Paris, Grand Rapids
Harmon John, 31 Caledonia, Caledonia Station.
Harmon Michael, 6 Caledonia, Alaska.
Harmcn William, 24 Byron, Gainesville

Hanes John, 2 Byron, North Byron.
Haner Conrad, 35 Vergennes, Lowell.
Haner Charles, Rockford.
Hanei John, 27 Plainfield, G. Rapids.
Hanes Reuben F., 2 Byron, North Byron.
HANNA JOHN M., 26 Gaines, Hammond.
HANNA JOHN, 2 Gaines, Hammond.
HANNA KENNEDY, 30 Gaines, Cody's Mills.
Hanna Kennedy, 28 Grand Rapids.
HANNA SAMUEL, 26 Gaines, Cody's Mills.
Hanna Wesley, Lisbon.
Hanna William, 26 Gaines, Hammond.
Hanrahan John, 33 Spencer, Spencer Mills.
Hanrahan Thomas, 33 Spencer, Spencer Mills.
Hanrahan William, 33 Spencer, Spencer Mills.
Hanscom Abner L., 13 Nelson, Nelson.
Hanscom Zebulon J., 13 Nelson, Nelson
HANSES ANTHONY, 13 Walker, Grand Rapids.
Hansen Casper, 35 Alpine, G. Rapids.
HARNISH FINDLEY, South 7 Walker, Grand Rapids.
Harnish Jacob, South 7 Walker, Grand Rapids.
Harper John, 15 Caledonia, Caledonia.
Harrigan Michael, 1 Wyoming, Grand Rapids.
Harrington John, 2 Walker, G. Rapids.
Harrington Jasper, 1 Plainfield, Rockford.
Harrington Levi M., Burchville (Burch's Mills.)
Harrington Vernon, 2 Walker, Grand Rapids.
Harrison Luther C., 15 Paris, Grand Rapids.
Harris George W., 30 Nelson, Cedar Springs.
Harris George W., 36 Spencer, Spencer Mills.
Harris Richard, 11 Cascade, Cascade.
Harris Robert, 34 Ada, Ada.
Harris William, 15 Cascade, Cascade.
Harroun Henry E., Lowell.
Harsey Lawton, 19 Spencer, Nelson.
HART LUTHFR, 6 Oakfield, Oakfield.
Hart Sarah, 8 Oakfield, Oakfield.

Hart Thomas, 1 Solon, Sand Lake.
HART WILLARD M., 8 Oakfield, Oakfield.
Hartt John, 12 Lowell, Lowell.
Hartt George W., 12 Lowell, Lowell.
Hartley John, 32 Lowell, Alto.
Hartman David, 17 Byron, Byron Cen.
Hartwell John W., 34 Cannon, Cannonsburg.
Hartwell John, 34 Cannon, Cannonsburg.
Hartwell Mrs. M. J., 35 Cannon, Cannonsburg.
Hartwell Wm. Chas., Village Cannonsburg.
HARTWELL WILLIAM, 27 Cannon, Cannonsburg.
Hartz John, 13 Walker, Grand Rapids.
Hartzy Antoine, 15 Byron, Grandville.
Hartzy Henry, 5 Byron, Grandville.
Hartzy Peter, 5 Byron, Grandville.
Hasha Barnhart, 18 Lowell, Cascade.
Hashbarger Abraham, 36 Paris, Grand Rapids.
Hashbarger Tobias, 36 Paris, Grand Rapids.
Haskin Clark, 8 Ada, Ada.
Haskin Mrs. M., 8 Ada, Ada.
Haskins Asa, Lowell.
HAVENS CHAS. R., 31 Nelson, Cedar Springs.
HAVEN JOHN V. D., Grandville.
Havens John W., 15 Paris, Grand Rapids.
Havens Nathaniel, 15 Oakfield, Oakfield.
Haviland Daniel L., Alaska Village.
HAVILAND DANIEL S., Alaska.
Hawkins Abraham, 14 Caledonia, Alaska.
Hawkins Charles, 16 Sparta, Sparta Cen.
Hawkins Hiram, 14 Caledonia, Alaska.
Hawkins G. C., Rockford.
Hawkins Richard, Lisbon.
Hawkinson John, 7 Sparta, Lisbon.
Hawk Edward, 22 Cannon, Cannonsburg.
Hawley James, 32 Alpine, Indian Creek.
Hawley Salma B., 3 Alpine, Englishville.
Hawthorn Thomas, 25 Plainfield, Austerlitz.
HAYDOCK WILLIAM, 35 Nelson, Courtland Center.
Hayes Daniel, 20 Plainfield, Mill Creek.

Haskins Jesse, 34 Spencer, Spencer Mills.
HASLEM JOHN, 28 Walker, Grand Rapids.
Hastie Archie, 28 Lowell, Lowell.
Hastie James, 22 Lowell, Lowell.
Hastings George H., 23 Sparta, Sparta Center.
HASTINGS W. H., 3 Lowell, Lowell.
Hastings Thomas B., 4 Lowell, Lowell.
Hastings W. G., 3 Sparta, Sparta Cen.
Hatchew Mrs. Lena, Lowell.
Hatch Alphens, Lowell.
Hatch B. G., 29 Grand Rapids, Grand Rapids.
Hatch Charles W., Lowell.
Hatch Ephriam, Lowell.
HATCH JOHN F., 24 Lowell, Lowell.
HATCH JOHN, 29 Grand Rapids, Grand Rapids.
HATCH MATTHEW B., 17 Spencer, Spencer Mills.
HATCH WM. W., Lowell.
Hathaway H. M., 22 Byron, Byron Cen.
Hattan Charles, 20 Lowell, Lowell.
HATTON GILES, 21 Bowne, Bowne.
Hatton Leslie, 21 Bowne, Bowne.
HAYES EDWIN P., 30 Nelson, Cedar Springs.
HAYES HORACE N., Burch's Mills.
Hayes Ira A., 22 Courtland, Courtland Center.
HAYES JOSEPH F., 22 Courtland, Courtland Center.
HAYES PATRICK, 20 Plainfield, Mill Creek.
Hayes Roday, 19 Plainfield, Alpine.
Haymaker Mrs. Mary A., 25 Byron, Cody's Mills.
Haynes David, 27 Courtland, Courtland Center.
Haynes George, 21 Alpine, G. Rapids.
HAYNES ISAAC, 21 Alpine, Indian Creek.
HAYNES HIRAM B., 34 Paris, Grand Rapids.
Haynes Oscar, 2 Courtland, Courtland Center.
HAYNES ROBERT, 34 Paris, Grand Rapids.
HAYNES FRANCIS, 21 Alpine, Grand Rapids.
Hays Virgil, 30 Nelson, Cedar Springs.
Hayward Edward, 30 Tyrone, Casnovia.

HAYWARD J. W., Sparta Center.
Hazelton John, 12 Sparta, Sparta Center.
Hazen Isaac D., 7 Paris, Grand Rapids.
Head Albert A., 22 Plainfield, Austerlitz.
Headley Artemus S., Rockford.
Headley George, Ada Village.
Headley Hiram, Ada Village.
Headley John, Ada Village.
Headley Orville, 2 Plainfield, Rockford.
HEADWORTH CHARLES, 21 Bowne, Bowne.
HEADWORTH WILLIAM, 27 Plainfield, Austerlitz.
Healy Henry J., 29 Walker, Grand Rapids.
Healy John, 34 Walker, G. Rapids.
HEALY THOMAS, 29 Walker, Grand Rapids.
Heaton Abraham, 31 Ada, Ada.
Heaton Mrs. Eunice, 29 Ada, Ada.
Heath Caleb, 19 Plainfield, Mill Creek.
Heath Daniel, 19 Plainfield, Mill Creek.
Heath George L., 20 Sparta, Lisbon.
Heath Guy, 32 Sparta, Lisbon.
Heath George, 20 Sparta, Lisbon.
Heath Jesse B., 26 Sparta, Lisbon.
Heintzleman Andrew J., 36 Paris, Grand Rapids.
Heintzleman Joseph, 30 Cascade, G. Rapids.
Heintzleman Nathan, 25 Paris, Grand Rapids.
Heintzleman Peter, 36 Paris, Grand Rapids.
Heintzelman Reuben, 30 Cascade, Grand Rapids.
Heintz Henry, 27 Gaines, Cody's Mills.
HEINTZ JOHN, 34 Gaines, Cody's Mills.
Heinrich William, 26 Bowne, Bowne.
Hellehen James, 30 Nelson, Cedar Springs.
Helmer Henry, Lowell.
Helmlka Henry, 15 Walker, G. Rapids.
Helmka Henry S., 16 Walker, Grand Rapids.
Helpin Peter, 32 Vergennes, Lowell.
Helsel Henry, 21 Algoma, Rockford.
Helsel Joseph, 8 Caledonia, Alaska.
HELSAL JOHN, 7 Caledonia, Alaska.
Helsal Joseph, 7 Caledonia, Alaska.
Helsel Lester, 16 Algoma, Rockford.
Helsel Noah, 22 Algoma, Rockford.
Helsel Noah F., 21 Algoma, Rockford.
Helsel Philip, Burchville, (Burch's Mills)

Heath Jonathan, 19 Plainfield, Mill Creek.
HEATH OSCAR L., 30 Alpine, Indian Creek.
Heath Mrs. Susan D., 19 Plainfield, Mill Creek.
HEATH WASHINGTON, Lisbon.
Hebard Ezra A., 16 Walker, G. Rapids.
Hecox Don, 24 Vergennes, Fallassburg.
Hecox Francis M., 23 Vergennes, Lowell.
Heffron Daniel, 36 Cannon, Cannonsburg.
Heffron Edward, 35 Cannon, Cannonsburg.
HEFFRON GEORGE, 25 Cannon, Cannonsburg.
HEFFLON HIRAM, 6 Lowell, Lowell.
HEFFRON JAMES, 25 Cannon, Cannonsburg.
Heffron Michael, 20 Grand Rapids.
Heffron William, 31 Grattan, Cannonsburg.
Heidchuh Philip, jun., 11 Bowne, Alto.
Heidchuh Philip, 11 Bowne, Alto.
HEIMLER JOHN B., 20 Caledonia, Caledonia Station.
Helsel P. F., 33 Algoma, Rockford.
HEMBLING ABRAHAM D., Alaska Village.
Hemmingway Gabriel, 27 Oakfield, Oakfield.
Hemmingway Moses, 22 Oakfield, Oakfield.
HEMMINGWAY LAWSON, 27 Oakfield, Oakfield.
Hemphrey George, 23 Cascade, Cascade.
Hemsley William, 31 Tyrone, Casnovia.
Hemsworth James, 26 Walker, Grand Rapids.
HEMSLEY GEORGE, 31 Tyrone, Casnovia.
Hendrick D. Millard, 2 Vergennes, Lowell.
HENDRICH ERWIN, 5 Gaines, G. Rapids.
Hendrick Gideon A., 2 Vergennes, Lowell.
Hendrick Harlan, 6 Gaines, Grand Rapids.
Hendrick Henry M., 5 Gaines, Grand Rapids.
Hendrick Wm., 5 Gaines, G. Rapids.

Henderson Isaac, 31 Vergennes, Lowell.
Henderson Philo P., 12 Oakfield, Greenville.
Henderson Samuel, 7 Walker, Berlin.
Hene Philip, 17 Walker, G. Rapids.
Hennessey John, 31 Cascade, Grand Rapids.
Hennessey William, 21 Cascade, Cascade.
Hennagin George, 31 Courtland, Rockford.
Henry Charles, 5 Grattan, Grattan Center.
Henry David, 11 Plainfield, Austerlitz.
Henry Dewitt C., 34 Sparta, Sparta Center.
Henry Deloss G., 25 Ada, Ada.
Henry Mrs. Haley, 5 Grattan, Grattan Center.
Henry James, 17 Cascade, Cascade.
Henry Thomas M., 5 Grattan, Grattan Center.
Hensel, Michael, 31 Byron, New Salem.
Henshaw Albert T., 4 Byron, North Byron.
Henshaw Charles J., 16 Cascade, Cascade.
Henshaw Horace, 16 Cascade, Cascade.
Henteg George, 33 Grand Rapids.
Heyford Charles, 24 Spencer, Spencer Mills.
Hibbard Charles H., Grandville.
Hibel Adam, 18 Byron, Byron Center.
Hibel John, 18 Byron, Byron Center.
Hice, Adam, 32 Walker, Grand Rapids.
HICE JOSEPH, 32 Walker, G. Rapids.
Hice Jerome, 32 Walker, G. Rapids,
HICKEY SYLVESTER K., Alaska.
HICKS ALBERT R., 27 Spencer, Spencer Mills.
HICKS, BENJAMIN H., 28 Lowell, Lowell.
Hicks Daniel, 22 Solon, Cedar Springs.
Hicks, Daniel C., 28 Lowell, Lowell.
Hicks Frederick, 1 Solon, Cedar Springs.
Hicks Martin, 25 Solon, Cedar Springs.
HICKS ROBBINS, 1 Solon, Cedar Springs.
Hicks, Stephen, 6 Cannon, Rockford.
Hicks Seely, 32 Spencer, Cedar Springs.
HICKS WILLIAM, Rockford.
HICKOCK BENJAMIN F., 5 Nelson, Sand Lake.
HICKOX LUCIUS L., 22 Byron, Byron Center.
Hickox William C., 15 Byron, Byron, Center.

Henteg Frank M., 33 Grand Rapids.
Hergrove James, 26 Grattan, Grant.
Hergrove William, 24 Grattan, Grant.
Herman Ira S., 35 Vergennes, Lowell.
HERRICK DAVID, 21 Alpine, Grand Rapids.
Herrick Martin C., 13 Gaines, Hammond.
Herrick Wm., 31 Gaines, Cody's Mills.
HERRIMAN IRA S., Lowell.
Herron James O., 19 Bowne, Caledonia.
Hershey Isaac, 22 Courtland, Courtland Center.
Hertley Martin, 11 Alpine, Englishville.
Hesler Gottlieb, 32 Courtland, Rockford.
HESS E. W., 1 Wyoming, G. Rapids.
Hessler Charles, 3 Byron, North Byron.
Hettis William, 15 Courtland, Courtland Center.
Hevers Michael, 32 Walker, G. Rapids.
Hewes Joseph, 20 Lowell, Lowell.
HEWITT, J. B., Rockford.
Hewitt, Rosannah, 21 Courtland, Courtland Center.
Hewitt William W., 22 Spencer, Spencer Mills.
HIDE URIAH R., Village of Cannonsburg.
Hidesgetter John, 15 Alpine, Alpine.
Hier John, 24 Gaines, Caledonia Station.
Higby Stephen, 14 Byron, Byron Cen.
Higgins Henry, 29 Grand Rapids.
Hike Case, 2 Wyoming, Grand Rapids.
Hildebrandt Wm., 14 Alpine, Alpine.
HILDRETH A. S., Lisbon.
Hildreth Cyrus, 30 Wyoming, Grandville.
Hildreth John A., Lisbon.
Hildreth Lester C., Lowell.
Hiler Milo, Lowell.
Hiler Mrs. M., Lowell.
HILER WALTER, 28 Vergennes, Vergennes.
HILLS AARON H., 23 Alpine, Alpine.
Hill Andrew, 33 Algoma, Rockford.
Hill Albert, 1 Walker, Grand Rapids.
Hills Mrs. Adelia, 13 Alpine, Alpine.
Hill Albert C., 16 Bowne, Alto.
HILL ALPHEUS G., 15 Caledonia, Alaska.
Hill Bryant, 25 Solon, Cedar Springs.
Hill Chas. O., 11 Lowell, Lowell.
Hills David E., Rockford.

HILL ELDIN G., 32 Cannon, Ada.
Hills H. R., 13 Alpine, Alpine.
Hill Horatio, 11 Lowell, Lowell.
Hill Hughes S., 15 Caledonia, Alaska.
HILL JAMES, 17 Alpine, G. Rapids.
Hill John, 32 Algoma, Rockford.
Hill James, 32 Cannon, Ada.
Hill Lone, 22 Tyrone, Casnovia.
HILL NICHOLAS R., 31 Nelson, Cedar Springs.
HILL PRENTICE, 11 Walker, Grand Rapids.
HILL OTIS, 19 Ada, Ada.
Hill Orton, 11 Lowell, Lowell.
Hill Ole, 5 Plainfield, Belmont.
HILL ORPHEUS B., Village Cedar Springs.
Hills Jefferson, 35 Grand Rapids.
HILLS PERRY, 25 Grand Rapids.
Hill Thompson, 31 Gaines, Cody's Mills.
Hilliker Wm. H., 23 Paris, G. Rapids.
Hillman Samuel B., 24 Nelson, Nelson.
Hillock Joseph, Caledonia Station.
Hilty David, 24 Gaines, Caledonia Station.
HILTON ALANSON V., 21 Sparta, Sparta Centre.

Hitchcock Hugh, Sparta Center.
Hittle John, 36 Algoma, Rockford.
Hitzert William, 2 Byron, North Byron.
HINE (M. D.,) DEMAS, 30 Cannon, Austerlitz.
HINE JAS. W., Lowell.
HINE M. B., 30 Cannon, Austerlitz.
Hine Martin N., Lowell.
Hines John, 21 Wyoming, Grandville.
Hines Stephen, 16 Wyoming, Grandville.
Hinkson James, 16 Sparta, Sparta Center.
HINMAN ALFRED S., 4 Sparta, Sparta Center.
Hinman C. C., 32 Sparta, Lisbon.
Hinman Charles, Sparta Center.
Hinman Enoch, Cedar Springs.
Hinman John, Sparta Center.
Hinman J. T., Sparta Center.
Hinman Norman, Sparta Center.
Hinman Newell, Sparta Center.
Hinman N. D, 33 Sparta, Lisbon.
HINMAN, Z. M., 9 Sparta, Sparta Center.
Hinyan Oliver P., 33 Lowell, Alto.
HIXSON JOHN, Lowell.
HOAG ALBERT, 26 Tyrone, Sparta Center.

Hilton Artemas, 28 Alpine, Indian Creek.
HILTON DAVID, 35 Alpine, Indian Creek.
HILTON DAVID W., 6 Walker, Indian Creek.
HILTON GEORGE W., 7 Cannon, Rockford.
HILTON MRS. JANE, 8 Grand Rapids.
Hilton J. K., 26 Byron, Cody's Mills.
HILTON LEONARD R., 3 Walker, Indian Creek.
Hilton Newell, Burch's Mills.
Hilton W. W., 34 Alpine, Indian Creek.
Hilze Matthias, 32 Byron, Byron Center.
Himes Amasa, 5 Alpine, Lisbon.
HIMBECK JOSEPH, 12 Alpine, Alpine.
Hirst George, 21 Byron, Byron Center.
Hirst Thomas, 21 Byron, Byron Center.
HINE CHAS. R., Lowell.
Hinckley George, 14 Gaines, Hammond.
Hipler Joseph, 34 Alpine, G. Rapids.
Himbeck Frederick, 12 Alpine, Alpine.

HOAG ARTEMUS R., 30 Vergennes, Vergennes.
Hoag Catherine, 31 Courtland, Rockford.
Hoag Earl, 2 Grand Rapids.
Hoag John E., 23 Cannon, Cannonsburg.
HOAG LYMAN V., 26 Tyrone, Sparta Center.
HOAG LORENZO D., 23 Cannon, Cannonsburg.
Hoag Myron B., 23 Cannon, Cannonsburg.
HOAG SIDNEY E., 34 Vergennes, Lowell.
Hoag Warren, 26 Tyrone, Sparta Cen.
Hoagesteeger, Adrian, 33 Grand Rapids
Hobourt H. A., Burchville (Burch's Mills.)
HOBBS WILLIAM, 17 Bowne, Alto.
Hodley Norton, 16 Algoma, Rockford.
Hodley John, 23 Algoma, Rockford.
HODGES AMOS, 32 Vergennes, Lowell
Hodges Chester D., 22 Lowell, Lowell.
Hodges James, 21 Lowell, Lowell.
Hodges Levi, 16 Sparta, Sparta Center.

HODGES OREN S., 33 Vergennes, Lowell.
Hodges Russell, 4 Alpine, Englishville.
Hodges Sylvester, 33 Vergennes, Lowell
Hodgers John, 6 Plainfield, Belmont.
Hoffman Adam, Lisbon.
Hoffman Hugh, 1 Bowne, Lowell.
Hogan Heman E., 1 Lowell, Lowell.
Hogan Michael, 1 Wyoming, G. Rapids.
Hogan Patrick, 27 Grattan, Grant.
Hogan S. G., 4 Lowell, Lowell.
Hogadone Edwin D., 28 Walker, Grand Rapids.
HOGADONE HENRY C., 19 Walker, Grand Rapids.
HOGADONE JOHN B., 28 Walker, Grand Rapids.
HOGLE GEO. W., 30 Nelson, Cedar Springs.
Holben Beniamin, 20 Tyrone, Casnovia.
Holbs James, 36 Spencer, Spencer Mills.
Holben Jacob, 20 Tyrone, Casnovia.
Holcomb Edwin R., 5 Nelson, Sand Lake.
Holcomb Horace, 31 Vergennes, Lowell
HOLCOMB MARTIN A., 26 Bowne, Harris Creek.
Holcomb Phineas W., 3 Algoma, Cedar Springs.

Holmdon William, 24 Oakfield, Greenville.
HOLMES ALBERT N., 31 Tyrone, Casnovia.
Holmes Edgar C., 17 Grattan, Grattan Center.
Holmes George, 10 Byron, North Byron.
Holmes John, 10 Alpine, Englishville.
Holmes Mrs. Martha, 1 Wyoming, G. Rapids.
HOLMES NELSON, 17 Grattan, Grattan Center.
Holmes Robert, 34 Ada, Ada.
Holoway Samuel, 11 Alpine, Englishville.
Holst John, 20 Lowell, Lowell.
Holt. H. Gaylord, 3 Cascade, Cascade.
HOLT HENRY, 3 Cascade, Cascade.
Holt Simeon D., 35 Ada, Ada.
Holy Christian, 16 Gaines, Hammond.
Homrich John, 30 Byron, Byron Cen.
Homrich Peter, 31 Byron, Byron Cen.
Homrich Sebastian, 29 Byron, Byron Center.
Honeyman George, 26 Walker, Grand Rapids.
HOOD ANDREW, 26 Grand Rapids.
Hookstraw B., 32 Grand Rapids.

HOLCOMB W. F., 27 Cannon, Cannonsburg.
Holden Chapin B., 18 Courtland, Rockford.
Holden Charles M., 18 Courtland, Rockford.
Holden Horatio S., 18 Courtland, Rockford.
HOLDEN WM. W., 27 Wyoming, Grand Rapids.
Holiday George W., 29 Algoma, Rockford.
Holiday Henry, 17 Algoma, Rockford.
Holldridder Franklin, Lowell.
Holiday John A., 36 Sparta, Englishville.
Holland John, 10 Courtland, Courtland Center.
Holland Theodore, 32 Sparta, Lisbon.
HOLLISTER WILLIAM, Sparta Cen.
Hollis A., 31 Wyoming, Grandville.
Holly James, 1 Gaines, Hammond.
Holly Milo B., 18 Caledonia, Hammond.
HOLLY ORLANDO H., 1 Gaines, Hammond.
Holm John P., 33 Caledonia, Caledonia Station.

Hookstraw Martin, 32 Grand Rapids.
Hookstraw Nater, 32 Grand Rapids.
HOOKER CYPRIAN S., 11 Lowell, Lowell.
HOOKER EDWARD C., 18 Gaines, Gainesville.
Hooker George W., 25 Plainfield, Austerlitz.
Hooker J. S., Lowell.
HOOK MARK, 14 Wyoming, Grand Rapids.
Hooper Clement, Grandville.
Hooper David, 30 Wyoming, Grandville.
Hooper Elam, Village Cedar Springs.
Hooper Edward, 30 Wyoming, Grandville.
Hooper Joseph, 30 Wyoming, Grandville.
Hooper Henry, 30 Wyoming, Grandville.
HOOSE MADISON, 1 Alpine, Englishville.
HOOVER ABRAHAM, 36 Gaines, Caledonia Station.
HOOVER BARNEY, 33 Gaines, Cody's Mills.

Hoover John, 24 Gaines, Hammond.
Hoover John, 33 Gaines, Cody's Mills.
HOPE HENRY, 3 Sparta, Sparta Cen.
HOPE JOSEPH, 23 Sparta, Sparta Center.
HOPE JAMES M., 23 Sparta, Sparta Center.
HOPKINS ANSEL, 4 Grand Rapids.
Hopkins Truman H., 10 Lowell, Lowell.
HOPKINS GIRDIN, 29 Alpine, Indian Creek.
HOPKINS HIRAM, 5 Grand Rapids, Grand Rapids.
HOPKINS JOHN L., Alaska Village.
Hopkins John T., Lowell.
Hopkins Lewis, 32 Alpine, Indian Creek.
Hopkins Nelson R., 30 Alpine, Indian Creek.
Hopkins Mrs. Noel, 32 Alpine, Indian Creek.
HOPKINS SIMON P., 29 Courtland, Rockford.
Hoppe William, 35 Wyoming, Grand Rapids.
Horagan Martin, 34 Walker, Grand Rapids.
Hornbrook Peter, 24 Lowell, Lowell.
HOUGH FAYETTE, 29 Spencer, Spencer Mills.
Houghtaling E. F., 16 Grand Rapids.
Houghtaling Henry, 1 Paris, Grand Rapids.
Houghtaling Ransom, 23 Plainfield, Austerlitz.
HOUGHTALING W. O., 16 G. Rapids.
Hough Theodore G., 23 Gaines, Hammond.
Houlihan Patrick, 3 Vergennes, Alton.
Hounsom John H., Sparta Center.
HOUSE ABRAHAM P., 30 Nelson, Cedar Springs.
HOUSE ANDREW, 13 Algoma, Edgerton.
House Abraham, Rockford.
House Alonzo, 1 Alpine, Englishville.
House Conrad, 5 Plainfield, Belmont.
House James W., 23 Algoma, Edgerton
House Oscar, 24 Algoma, Edgerton.
House Robert, Rockford.
Housman Charles F., Cedar Springs.
Houseman Jacob, 11 Lowell, Lowell.
Housell James, 11 Plainfield, Rockford.
Houser Frederick, 9 Vergennes, Alton.
Houser Gustavus, 9 Vergennes, Alton.
HOVER MRS. CATHARINE, 23 Bowne, Bowne.

Horton I. W., 17 Wyoming, Grandville.
Horton Isaac, 17 Wyoming, Grandville.
Horton Jesse M., Grandville.
Horton John. 17 Wyoming, Grandville.
Horton, James B., 9 Wyoming, Grand Rapids.
Horton John, 8 Byron, North Byron.
Horton Peter, 8 Byron, Grandville.
HORTON SILAS P., 7 Oakfield, Oakfield.
HORTON Mrs. S. M., Cannonsburg.
HORTON WILLIAM, 17 Wyoming, Grandville.
Hosford Fred. H., Lowell.
Hosford Frank H., Lowell.
Hoskins Henry, 33 Ada, Ada.
HOSKINS JAMES R., 26 Solon, Cedar Springs.
Hosley Jabez J., 34 Byron, Cody's Mills.
Host Anthony, 30 Alpine, Indian Creek.
Host John, 30 Alpine, Indian Creek.
HOUCK FAYETTE, 23 Bowne, Bowne.
Hovey G. E., Rockford.
Howarth Edmond, 17 Cannon, Cannonsburg.
Howard Andrew, 16 Grattan, Grattan Center.
Howard Christopher, 6 Plainfield, Englishville.
Howard Crispan, 6 Plainfield, Englishville.
Howard Daniel, 5 Vergennes, Vergennes.
HOWARD JOHN, Lowell.
Howard James, 22 Cannon, Cannonsburg.
Howard John, 8 Vergennes, Vergennes.
Howard Mary, 8 Vergennes, Vergennes.
Howard Orville, 1 Algoma, Burchville (Burch's Mills.)
Howard Owen, 8 Vergennes, Vergennes.
Howard Robert, 4 Grattan, Grattan Center.
Howard William, Jr., 4 Grattan, Grattan Center.
Howe C. E., Lowell.
Howe Elisha B., 22 Walker, G. Rapids.
HOWE GARDNER, 5 Nelson, Sand Lake.

Howe H. A., Lowell.
Howe Jesse B., 36 Plainfield, Grand Rapids
Howe Zadok, Lowell.
HOWELL HEZAKIAH, 31 Ada, Grand Rapids.
Howell Joshua, 10 Grattan, Grattan Center.
Howell John, 10 Grattan, Grattan Cen.
Howell Rebecca, 10 Grattan, Grattan Center.
Howell Theodore I., 31 Ada, G. Rapids.
Howell William, 31 Ada, Ada.
Howk Andrew J;, Lowell.
Howk Jacob, Lowell.
Howlett Thomas, 29 Wyoming, Grandville.
Howlett William, 29 Wyoming, Grandville.
Howman John, 30 Paris, Grand Rapids.
Hoxie Collins, 5 Grand Rapids, Grand Rapids.
HOXIE WM. H., 5 Grand Rapids, Grand Rapids.
HOYLE GEORGE, 35 Solon, Cedar Springs.
Hoyle Henry, 20 Nelson, Cedar Springs.
Hoyt Albert, Rockford.
Hoyt Edwin, 7 Paris, Grand Rapids.
Hughes Mrs. Lydia, Rockford.
Hughes Monroe, 2 Sparta, Sparta Cen.
Hughes W. Scott, 24 Wyoming, Grand Rapids.
Hughes William, 11 Sparta, Sparta Cen.
Hughey Nathaniel, 34 Nelson, Cedar Springs.
Hughson T. E., Lowell.
Huggins George, Lowell.
Huggins John, Lowell.
Huggins Wm. R., Lowell.
Huggard Francis, 12 Nelson, Nelson.
Huggard John, 1 Nelson, Nelson.
Hulbert Charles E., Lowell.
HULBERT JOHN W., 22 Cascade, Cascade.
Hulburt Thomas J., 10 Cascade, Cascade.
Hulburt William, 22 Cascade, Cascade.
Hull Amasa, 2 Oakfield, Greenville.
HULL CYRUS, Alaska.
Hull E. F., Alaska.
HULL GEO. F., Alaska.
HULL JOHN, 8 Algoma, Rockford.
Hull John, 24 Vergennes, Fallassburg.
HULL SYLVANUS E., 7 Bowne, Alto.
Hull William H., 8 Algoma, Rockford.
Hull Zachary, 1 Oakfield, Greenville.

Hoyt Nathan, Lowell.
Hoyt Wilbur, Rockford.
HUBBARD AUGUSTUS, Lisbon.
Hubbard Charles, Lisbon.
Hubbard Joel M., 9 Paris, Grand Rapids
Hubbard John, 25 Solon, Cedar Springs
Hubbell Elmon S., 31 Oakfield, Grattan Center.
Hubble Eurotus G., 25 Grattan, Grant.
Hubbel Elmon S., 1 Cannon, Grattan Center.
Hubbell John, 31 Oakfield, Grattan Center.
Hubbel John, 1 Cannon, Grattan Cen.
Hudson Alexander, 11 Lowell, Lowell.
Hudson Joseph, 22 Algoma, Edgerton.
Hudson Samuel S., 11 Lowell, Lowell.
Huff Andrew, 22 Gaines, Hammond.
Huff Adam, 22 Gaines, Hammond.
Huff Frederick, 22 Gaines, Hammond.
Huff Hermon, 13 Byron, Gainesville.
Huff Isaac, 21 Sparta, Lisbon.
Huff James F., 32 Tyrone, Casnovia.
Hughes James, 10 Grattan, Grattan Center.
Hughes John, 24 Wyoming, Grand Rapids.
Hulliberger Lee, 2 Courtland, Courtland Center.
Hull Jabez H., 36 Ada, Ada.
Humes Cornelius, 9 Courtland, Courtland Center.
Hummer George, Grandville.
Hummer Jacob, Grandville.
Hunt Leonard H., Lowell.
Hunt Simeon, Lowell.
HUNT WILLARD, Cedar Springs.
Hunt Zenas, 1 Plainfield, Rockford.
Hunter Arvine P., Lowell.
Hunter Adelmer, 1 Solon, Sand Lake.
HUNTER C. P., Lowell.
HUNTER E. B., Lowell.
Hunter Edwin, Lowell.
HUNTER JAMES I., Lowell.
Hunter John, 30 Spencer, Nelson.
Hunter Mathew, 20 Lowell, Lowell.
Hunter, Robert, jun., Lowell.
Hunter Robert C., 20 Lowell, Lowell.
HUNTER ROBERT, sen., Lowell.
Hunter William, sen., 16 Spencer, Spencer Mills.
Hunting Edward B., 28 Courtland, Courtland Center.

HUNTING GEORGE S., 28 Courtland, Courtland Center.
HUNTING ISAAC M., 24 Courtland, Courtland Center.
Huntington Thomas, 28 Bowne, Bowne.
Huntington William, 23 Bowne, Bowne.
HUNTLEY ADELBERT C., 11 Grattan, Grattan Center.
Huntley Erwin, 11 Grattan, Grattan Center.
Huntley Mrs. Francis, 36 G. Rapids.
Huntley James, 20 Lowell, Lowell.
HUNTLEY ORIN P., 27 Ada, Ada.
HUNTLEY THOMAS, 35 Paris, Hammond.
HURD A. D., 13 Alpine, Alpine.
Hurd Charles W., 3 Paris, G. Rapids.
Hurd Everett, 10 Paris, Grand Rapids.
Hurd John, 26 Wyoming, G. Rapids.
Hurley Christopher, 5 Vergennes, Vergennes.
Hurley William, 6 Vergennes, Vergennes.
Hurlburt Charles, 32 Grand Rapids.
Hurlburt P. S., 32 Grand Rapids.
Huse Carr, 36 Sparta, Englishville.
Husted Elijah, 16 Lowell, Lowell.
Husted James D., 20 Lowell, Lowell.
HUSTED NOAH P., 20 Lowell, Lowell.
HUSTED SYLVESTER, 8 Lowell, Lowell.
Hutchinson Bradley, 17 Paris, Grand Rapids.
Hutchins Charles, Cedar Springs.
Huttle Henry, 5 Vergennes, Vergennes.
HUWER ANDREW, 26 Alpine, Alpine.
Huwer Mrs. Barbara, 26 Alpine, Alpine.
Huxley Edward, Lowell.
HYDE C. G., Rockford.
Hyde Charles N., Rockford.
Hyde Charles N., 1 Plainfield, Rockford.
HYDE OSCAR F., Rockford.
Hyde Oscar, 1 Plainfield, Rockford.
HYDORN HENRY C., 23 Ada, Ada.
Hyland Peter, 30 Tyrone, Casnovia.
Hyler Wm., 6 Alpine, Lisbon.
HYSER WILLIAM, 23 Plainfield, Austerlitz.
HYSTE THOMAS, Grandville.
Hyste James, Grandville.

I

Ide Edwin, 20 Byron, Byron Center.
Ide Eleazear R., 20 Byron, Byron Cen.
Ide Frank, 10 Lowell, Lowell.
Ide Orville, 28 Byron, Byron Center.
Ingersoll Berlin, 31 Algoma, Rockford.
Ingersoll Theodore P., 17 Lowell, Lowell.
Ingraham Aaron, 16 Spencer, Spencer Mills.
Ingraham Frank E., 35 Spencer, Spencer Mills.
INGRAHAM ISAAC M., 18 Paris, G. Rapids.
Inwood James, 19 Cannon, Austerlitz.
Ipe Jacob, 5 Algoma, Sparta Centre.
IPE MRS. ELIZA, 5 Algoma, Sparta Centre.
IPE FREDERICK, 8 Algoma, Sparta Centre.
Ipe Jackson, 28 Solon, Cedar Springs.
Ipe Solomon, 23 Solon, Cedar Springs.
Ireland Wm. H., 9 Walker, G. Rapids.
Irish E. L., Lowell.
Irish Heman, Lisbon.
IRISH H. B., Lisbon.
Irons Andrew, 6 Caledonia, Alaska.
IRONS JOSIAH, Alaska.
Irwin David, 17 Byron, Byron Cen.
Irwin Nelson, 17 Byron, Byron Cen.
ISHAM MRS. LOVINA, 14 Alpine, Englishville.
Isham Robert A., 14 Alpine, Alpine.
Isham Charles, 14 Alpine, Alpine.
Isham James, 14 Alpine, Alpine.
Ives Benager, 19 Plainfield, Mill Creek.
Ives Chas. W., 5 Cannon, Rockford.
IVES FLOYD H., 19 Plainfield, Mill Creek.
Ivinson Thomas, 2 Cannon, Rockford.

J

JACKSON DUDLEY, 33 Oakfield, Grattan Centre.
JACKSON HARLOW, 30 Tyrone, Casnovia.
Jackson Henry, 2 Caledonia, Alaska.
JACKSON JOEL G., 2 Caledonia, Alaska.
JACKSON ROBERT S., Alaska.
Jackson Robert, 16 Byron, Byron Cen.
Jackson William, 14 Caledonia, Alaska.
JACOBS FRANK E., 20 Sparta, Lisbon.
Jacobs John H., 20 Algoma, Rockford.
JACOBS REUBEN, Village Cedar Springs.
JACOBS WM. S., 30 Nelson, Cedar Springs.
Jacox Allen B., 10 Gaines, Hammond.
Jacox David, 24 Byron, Gainesville.
Jakeway Asa, 23 Grattan, Grant.
Jakeway Ami, 26 Grattan, Grant.
Jakeway John H., 23 Grattan, Grant.
JAKEWAY JAMES, 23 Grattan, Grant.
JAMISON EUGENE, 13 Caledonia, Alaska.
Jennings Daniel, 29 Algoma, Rockford.
Jennings David, 24 Cascade, Cascade.
Jennings Howard, 8 Paris, G. Rapids.
Jennings Miss, Lowell.
JENNINGS THOMAS, 20 Plainfield, Mill Creek.
JEWELL CHAS. A, 5 Nelson, Sand Lake.
Jewell Edward, Village Cedar Springs.
Jewell George, 2 Plainfield, Rockford.
Jewell Harmon, 33 Wyoming, Grandville.
Jewe l James, 8 Wyoming, Grandville.
Jewell Loomis, 33 Algoma, Rockford.
Jewell Rodolphus D., 26 Algoma, Rockford.
JEWELL SILAS E., 5 Nelson, Sand Lake.
Jipson Almond, 15 Grand Rapids.
Johnston Robert, 25 Courtland, Courtland Center.
JOINER PAULINA, 16 Grattan, Grattan Center.
Johnson Abram H., 26 Courtland, Courtland Center.

JAMISON HUGH, 13 Caledonia, Alaska.
Jameson James, Cedar Springs.
Jaqua Charles D., 31 Courtland, Rockford.
JAQUA CHARLES J., 31 Courtland, Rockford.
Jaques Lewis, 11 Lowell, Lowell.
JAQUA NELSON, 5 Nelson, Sand Lake.
JARMAN JOHN C., Alaska.
Jarman Henry J., Alaska.
Jarvis Morris, 11 Walker, G. Rapids.
Jastopher Michael, — Cannon, Cannonsburg.
Jean Jerry, 35 Conrtland, Rockford.
JENKS C. W., 35 Alpine, Indian Creek.
Jenkins Jabez, 25 Byron, Cody's Mills.
Jenkins John, 21 Wyoming, Grandville.
JENNE LANSING K., 7 Grand Rapids, Grand Rapids.
Jenne Newton E., 16 Courtland, Courtland Centre.
Jenness Mrs. John, Grandville.
Jennings Daniel, 6 Grand Rapids, G. Rapids.
Johnson Alfred C., 28 Grattan, Grattan Center.
JOHNSTON BARTON, 22 Courtland, Courtland Center.
Johnson Benjamin, 22 Courtland, Courtland Center.
Johnson Calvin D., 24 Caledonia, Alaska.
Johnson Charles, Lowell.
Johnson Charles, Sparta Center.
Johnson Cord, 2 Plainfield, Rockford.
Johnson Chandler, Lowell.
Johnson Carl, Grandville.
Johnson Chas. W., Cedar Springs.
Johnson Charles P., 36 Spencer, Spencer Mills.
Johnson Charles, 36 Gaines, Caledonia Station.
JOHNSTON CHAS. L., 25 Byron, Cody's Mills.
Johnson Charles W., 24 Byron, Gainesville.
Johnson Charles, 30 Alpine, Indian Creek.
JOHNSON CHAS. B., Sparta Center.
JOHNSON CHARLES, 17 Sparta, Lisbon.

JOHNSON DAVID R., 35 Solon, Cedar Springs.
Johnson Daniel, Sparta Center.
Johnson Enos, 21 Gaines, Gainesville.
Johnson Erastus W., 10 Walker, Indian Creek.
JOHNSON EDGAR R., 17 Cascade, Cascade.
JOHNSON EZRA D., 16 Cascade, Cascade.
Johnson Mrs. E. M., Lowell.
Johnson Edwin O., Lowell.
Johnson Eli D., 23 Caledonia, Caledonia.
Johnson Frederick, 29 Lowell, Lowell.
JOHNSON GEORGE, 7 Grattan, Grattan Center.
Johnson Gilbert E., 13 Courtland, Courtland Center.
Johnson George W., 10 Courtland, Courtland Center.
Johnson George, Lowell.
Johnson Gust, 8 Sparta, Lisbon.
Johnson Harley M., 16 Cascade, Cascade.
Johnson Heber W., 15 Oakfield, Oakfield.
Johnson Henry, 20 Grand Rapids.
Johnson Henry E., Lowell.
JOHNSON LUKE, 3 Gaines, Hammond.
Johnson Lewis, 28 Alpine, Indian Creek.
JOHNSON LUTHER H, 33 Alpine, Indian Creek.
Johnson Michael B., 29 Caledonia, Caledonia Station.
Johnson Morris, Lowell.
JOHNSON MINER T., 30 Tyrone, Casnovia.
Johnson Martin W., Rockford.
Johnson Marquis L., 2 Cannon, Bostwick Lake.
Johnson Nathaniel, Lowell.
Johnson Nathaniel C., 22 Bowne, Bowne.
JOHNSON NELSON M., 1 Cannon, Bostwick Lake.
JOHNSON ORRIN L., 15 Bowne, Bowne.
Johnson Pyrrhus E., 18 Grattan, Grattan Center.
Johnson Mrs. Phebe, Rockford.
JOHNSON PERLEY W., 4 Walker, Indian Creek.
Johnson Peter, 18 Sparta, Lisbon.
Johnson Sabin, 1 Plainfield, Rockford.

JOHNSON ISAAC W., 34 Ada, Ada.
Johnson John, 6 Nelson, Sand Lake.
JOHNSON JAMES C., 16 Bowne, Bowne.
JOHNSON JEFFERSON, 15 Cascade, Cascade.
JOHNSON JONATHAN R., 17 Cascade, Cascade.
JOHNSON JAMES, 8 Grand Rapids.
Johnson Joseph, 28 Grattan, Grattan Center.
Johnson John, 34 Walker, G. Rapids.
Johnson John, 4 Walker, Indian Creek.
Johnson Joseph, 22 Courtland, Courtland Center.
Johnson John, 23 Algoma, Edgerton.
Johnson Joseph, 29 Tyrone, Casnovia.
Johnson Jasper, 22 Bowne, Bowne.
Johnson John, 17 Sparta, Lisbon.
Johnson John C., 22 Bowne, Bowne.
JOHNSON JAMES E., 10 Alpine, Englishville.
Johnson James, 13 Algoma, Edgerton.
JOHNSON JOSEPH B., Rockford.
JOHNSON JAMES, 21 Cannon, Cannonsburg.
Johnson Salem, 36 Courtland, Rockford.
JOHNSON STEPHEN, 22 Bowne, Bowne.
Johnson Samuel W., Lowell.
Johnson Thomas C., 23 Courtland, Courtland Centre.
Johnson Thomas, 26 Grattan, Grant.
Johnson William A., 22 Courtland, Courtland Centre.
JOHNSON W. W., 32 Grand Rapids, G. Rapids.
JOHNSON WILLIAM B., Rockford.
JOHNSON WILLIAM C., 21 Courtland, Courtland Centre.
Johnson Wesley, 30 Lowell, Lowell.
JOHNSON W. W. JR., 30 Lowell, Lowell.
Johnson William, 4 Sparta, Sparta Center.
Johnson Wm. S., 23 Solon, Cedar Springs.
Johns Richard, 20 Grand Rapids.
Joles Albert A., 9 Caledonia, Alaska.
Joles Alfred A., 9 Caledonia, Alaska.
Joles James, 9 Caledonia, Alaska.
Jones Alvah, 12 Lowell, Lowell.

Jones Abram, 2 Byron, North Byron.
Jones Mrs. Amelia, 22 Plainfield, Austerlitz.
Jones Almon, 11 Walker, G. Rapids.
JONES A. B., 6 Grand Rapids, Grand Rapids.
JONES CHARLES, 27 Wyoming, Grand Rapids.
Jones Cyrus, 13 Wyoming, G. Rapids.
JONES MRS. ELIZABETH, 13 Caledonia, Alaska.
Jones Edward, 21 Oakfield, Oakfield.
JONES E. E., 13 Algoma, Edgerton.
Jones Frederick, Lowell.
Jones George, 16 Courtland, Courtland Center.
JONES GAYLORD, 11 Walker, Grand Rapids.
Jones George G., 11 Vergennes, Alton.
JONES ISAAC, 19 Tyrone, Casnovia.
Jones Ira B., 16 Lowell, Lowell.
JONES JOHN S., 33 Nelson, Cedar Springs.
JONES JOHN, 8 Plainfield, Belmont.
Jones James M. W., 3 Byron, North Byron.
Jones John, 2 Byron, North Byron.
Jones James, 3 Ada, Cannonsburg.
Jones Loven, 21 Oakfield, Oakfield.
Jones Orrin E., 16 Grattan, Grattan Center.
Jones Philip, 11 Vergennes, Alton.
Jones Philip A., 13 Caledonia, Alaska.
JONES PHILETUS P., Village of Cannonsburg.
Jones Ross, 14 Caledonia, Caledonia.
Jones Riley A., 24 Grattan, Grant.
JONES ROBERT R., 17 Gaines, Gainesville.
Jones Samuel, 29 Tyrone, Casnovia.
JONES THOMAS J., 33 Nelson, Cedar Springs.
Jones Thomas, 21 Oakfield, Oakfield.
Jones Wm., 13 Lowell, Lowell.
Jones William, 21 Grattan, Grattan Center.
Jones Wesley, 10 Vergennes, Alton.
Jones Wm. H., 11 Walker, G. Rapids.
JONES WILLIAM R., 12 Oakfield, Greenville.
JORDAN HENRY C., jr., 20 Paris, Grand Rapids.
Jordan Henry C., 20 Paris, G. Rapids.
Joslin Blynn D., Alaska.
JOSLIN BENJAMIN, 34 Nelson, Cedar Springs.
Joslin William W., 33 Nelson, Cedar Springs.

Jones Leonard S., 23 Cannon, Cannonsbnrg.
Jones Michael, 21 Grattan, Grattan Center.
Jones Owen, 22 Grattan, Grattan Cen.
Judd A. H., 20 Lowell, Lowell.
Judd Martin, 35 Wyoming, G. Rapids.
JUDSON ELLA, 8 Byron, Byron Cen.
Judson H. T., 9 Wyoming, Grandville.
JUNE GEORGE, 23 Paris, G. Rapids.
June Hanford, 1 Plainfield, Rockford.
June Henry, 23 Paris, Grand Rapids.

K

Kane Thomas, Rockford.
Kannedy Alonzo, 11 Vergennes, Alton.
Karcher Adam, 26 Bowne, Bowne.
KARCHER GEORGE, 26 Bowne, Bowne.
Karmsen Charles, 11 Lowell, Lowell.
KARMSEN WILLIAM, Lowell.
KARSCHNER JOHN, 34 Vergennes, Lowell.
Kating Patrick, 4 Grattan, Grattan Center.
Kauffman Jonas, 13 Bowne, Lowell.
Kavenaugh Thomas, 6 Vergennes, Cannonsburg.
Kealiher Sewell, 22 Sparta, Sparta Cen.
Keamerling Servaas, 26 G. Rapids.
Kearney N., 34 Walker, G. Rapids.
Kearney Patrick, 27 Wyoming, Grand Rapids.
Kearns James, 16 Grattan, Grattan Center.
Keary John, 23 Paris, G. Rapids.
Keary James, 25 Paris, Grand Rapids.
Keech Andrew, 6 Walker, Berlin.
Keech Alexander, 36 Algoma, Rockford.
Keech David H., 13 Cannon, Bostwick Lake.
KEECH HENRY, 14 Grattan, Grant.
Keech Joseph, 13 Cannon, Bostwick Lake.
Keech Peter, 23 Grattan, Grant.

Keech William, 6 Walker, Berlin.
Keefer Charles S., 15 Gaines, Hammond.
Keefer Joel C., 15 Gaines, Hammond.
KEEFER CHARLES B., 15 Gaines, Hamnond.
Keeler George W., 25 Oakfield, Ashley.
Keeler Timothy D., 25 Oakfield, Ashley.
Keena John, 10 Ada, Ada.
KEENEY FRANKLIN, 25 Grattan, Grant.
Keeney Francis, 10 Bowne, Alto.
KEENEY JOHN M., 10 Bowne, Alto.
Kegal Fred., Alaska.
Kehoe Patrick, 1 Ada, Cannonsburg.
Keifer Andrew J., Grandville.
Keifer Furman, Grandville.
Keifer Samuel, 16 Wyoming, Grandville.
Kelder Peter, 16 Wyoming, Grandville.
KELLER CHRISTIAN, jun., 24 Bowne, Bowne.
Keller Christian, 24 Bowne, Bowne.
Kellier John, 28 Tyrone, Casnovia.
KELLEY AUGUSTUS, 31 Paris, Gainesville.
Kelly Dennis, 29 Cascade, G. Rapids.
KELLEY DAN'L B., 33 Lowell, Lowell.
Hellogg H. H., Cedar Springs.
Kellogg Isaac, Lowell.
Kellogg Jason, 31 Plainfield, Mill Creek
Kellogg Lafayette, 3 Byron, North Byron.
KELLOGG LEWIS B., 3 Byron, North Byron.
KELLOGG ORSON, 29 Grand Rapids, Grand Rapids.
Kellogg Orrin, South 1 Ada, Lowell.
Kellogg Titus, 17 Vergennes, Vergennes.
Kellogg Wm. H., 3 Byron, North Byron
Kelsey Samuel, 17 Cascade, Cascade.
Kelsey Theron A., 17 Cascade, Cascade.
KEMP JOHN, 34 Ada, Ada.
Kemp Nicholas, 2 Wyoming, Grand Rapids.
KENNEDY ALEXANDER, Sparta Center.
Kennedy James, 14 Gaines, Hammond.
Kennedy James, 30 Grattan, Cannonsburg.
Kennedy James, 34 Walker, G. Rapids.
KENNEDY MRS. JANE, 17 G. Rapids.
Kennedy Joseph, 17 Grand Rapids.
Kennedy John N., 8 Walker, G. Rapids.
Kennedy Michael, 19 Grattan, Cannonsburg.

Kelley Charles W., 21 Gaines, Grand Rapids.
KELLEY CHARLES, 4 Gaines, Grand Rapids.
Kelley Foster, 4 Gaines, G. Rapids.
KELLEY HENRY, 17 Gaines, Grand Rapids.
Kelley Lee, 4 Gaines, Grand Rapids.
Kelley Nelson, 4 Gaines, Grand Rapids.
Kelley James, 27 Ada, Ada.
Kelley James, 2 Paris, Grand Rapids.
Kelley Norman, 12 Grattan, Otisco, Ionia County.
Kelly Patrick, 24 Grand Rapids.
Kelly Patrick, 8 Walker, Grand Rapids
Kelley Patrick, 25 Nelson, Nelson.
Kelley Patrick, Cedar Springs.
Kelley Patrick, 34 Walker, G. Rapids.
Kelley Randolph, 33 Courtland, Rockford.
Kelley Timothy, 34 Walker, G. Rapids.
Kelley William, 20 Gaines, G. Rapids.
Kellogg Charles, 2 Paris, Grand Rapids
KELLOGG FRANKLIN B., 30 Nelson, Cedar Springs.
Kellogg Francis N., Cedar Springs.
Kellogg Harmon, 3 Byron, North Byron
Kennedy Michael, 30 Grattan, Cannonsburg.
Kennedy Michael, 19 Grattan, Cannonsburg.
Kennedy Patrick, 19 Paris, G. Rapids.
KENNEDY SIMON, 30 Grattan, Cannonsburg.
Kennedy Sherman, 11 Vergennes, Alton
Kennedy Wm. W., 17 Grand Rapids.
Kenney Edward, 34 Ada, Ada.
Kenney Elijah, 13 Vergennes, Fallassburg.
Kenney James, 2 Plainfield, Rockford.
KENNY JOHN, 8 Walker, G. Rapids.
Kenny Mrs. Mary, 8 Walker, G. Rapids
Kenny Patrick, 8 Walker, G. Rapids.
KENNEL ENOCH J., 5 Nelson, Sand Lake.
Kennon Marshall, 34 Walker, G. Rapids
Kenny Thomas, 33 Walker, G. Rapids.
Kent Cyrus, Rockford.
KENT MARCUS A., 11 Caledonia, Alaska.
Kent Marvin, 9 Grand Rapids.
Kent Simeon, 11 Caledonia, Alaska.
KENT WILLIAM, 1 Solon, Sand Lake.

KENYON CRANDALL A., 4 Plainfield, Rockford.
Kenyon George W., 1 Wyoming, Grand Rapids.
Kenyon E. G., 19 Byron, Byron Center.
Kepkey Frederick, 22 Caledonia, Alaska
Kerickes M. Bela, 1 Lowell, Lowell.
Kerr Ed., 31 Algoma, Englishville.
Kerr James L. B., 22 Vergennes, Vergennes.
KERR JAMES N., 22 Vergennes, Vergennes.
Kerrer John, 20 Caledonia, Caledonia Station.
Kerrer Michael, 19 Caledonia, Caledonia Station.
Kerrer Michael, 20 Caledonia, Caledonia Station.
Ketchum Edward, 9 Lowell, Lowell.
KETCHUM LORIN E., 21 Solon, Cedar Springs.
Keyes Henry D., 18 Paris, Grand Rapids
Keyes James, 33 Paris, Grand Rapids.
KEYES JAMES A., 33 Paris, Grand Rapids.
Kilts Nicholas, 17 Nelson, Cedar Springs.
Kimball Charles W., 12 Nelson, Nelson.
Kinche Danforth, Lowell.
King George, 13 Lowell, Lowell.
KING JOHN L., 26 Cascade, Alaska.
King John J., 26 Cascade, Alaska.
King Thomas, 33 Ada, Ada.
King Michael G., 24 Vergennes, Fallassburg.
KING MYRON J., 34 Vergennes, Lowell.
King Melvin A., 34 Grattan, Alton.
King Myron A., 26 Cascade, Cascade.
KINGIN HARRY H., 19 Courtland, Edgerton.
KINGIN JAMES, 20 Courtland, Rockford.
Kingin Oliver T., 20 Courtland, Rockford.
Kinne Edwin, 5 Grand Rapids, Grand Rapids.
Kinne Lyman, 5 Grand Rapids, Grand Rapids.
KINNEY DANIEL G., 34 Ada, Ada.
Kinney Daniel, 8 Ada, Ada.
Kinney Daniel, Lowell.
Kinney George, 14 Paris, Grand Rapids
Kinsley Abisha, Lowell.
Kinsey David, Caledonia Station.
Kinsey Isaac, 30 Caledonia, Caledonia Station.

Kindry Wm. S., 27 Tyrone, Sparta Cen.
King Alvin B., 27 Cascade, Alaska.
King Augustus, 13 Cascade, Cascade.
Kies Othniel, 2 Wyoming, G. Rapids.
Kibble Richard, 33 Bowne, Harris Creek.
Kibboom Jacob, 8 Paris, Grand Rapids.
KIDDER M. C., 11 Algoma, Edgerton.
Kiefer Samuel E., 19 Walker, Grand Rapids.
Kiel Simon, 19 Lowell, Lowell.
Kies William, 13 Lowell, Lowell.
Kies Joseph, 19 Tyrone, Casnovia.
KILBURN JOSIAH R., 34 Wyoming, Grand Rapids.
Kilgus Frederick, 1 Bowne, Alto.
Killmartin Jerry, 5 Caledonia, Alaska.
KILMER VAN RENSSELAER, 20 Cascade, Cascade.
Kilmer Simon, 9 Caledonia, Alaska.
King Arza H., 34 Grattan, Alton.
King Charles B., 13 Alpine, Alpine.
King David H., 34 Vergennes, Lowell.
King Darius, 18 Walker, Grand Rapids
King Edmund, 10 Vergennes, Alton.
King Erastus, 20 Ada, Ada.
KING FRANK W., 1 Grattan, Ashley.
Kinsey Jacob, 30 Caledonia, Caledonia Station.
KINSEY JOHN, 4 Gaines, Hammond.
Kinsman A. C., Lowell.
KINSMAN JOHN H., 11 Lowell, Lowell.
Kinyon Joseph, 23 Lowell, Lowell.
Kinyon Jas. W., 16 Lowell, Lowell.
KINYON WM. W., 16 Lowell, Lowell.
KIPP JESSE, 21 Walker, G. Rapids.
KIPP MOSES J., 4 Cannon, Rockford.
Kirby Peter, 3 Wyoming, G. Rapids.
Kirchner Fred, Lisbon.
KIRKLAND JACOB C., Burchville, (Burch's Mills.)
Kistler Washington, 8 Gaines, Gainesville.
Kistler Manelious S., 8 Gaines, Gainesville.
Kitchen Henry, 3 Paris, G. Rapids.
KITCHEN Z. E., 12 Walker, Grand Rapids.
Klaus Peter, 36 Alpine, G. Rapids.
Kleinlogel Charles, 1 Solon, Sand Lake.
Klenk G., 30 Sparta, Lisbon.
Klenk John F., 19 Alpine, Pleasant.

Kline Julia A., 24 Vergennes, Fallassburg.
KLINE JOHN W., 1 Bowne, Alto.
Kline Philip, Rockford.
Kline William, Burchville, (Burch's Mills.)
KLINGMAN DAVID, 23 Gaines, Hammond.
Klingman Jacob, 23 Gaines, Hammond.
Klingman John K., 25 Gaines, Grand Rapids.
Kloot Joost, 29 Grand Rapids.
Klumpp August E., Lowell.
Klumpp William E., Lowell.
Knapp Amasa, 27 Vergennes, Lowell.
Knapp Albert B., 21 Wyoming, Grandville.
Knapp Abner, Lowell.
KNAPP E. U., 17 Grand Rapids.
Knapp Franklin C., 27 Vergennes, Lowell.
KNAPP HARRY, Lowell.
KNAPP STEVEN B., Lowell.
Knee Wesley H., 35 Grattan, Alton.
KNIFFIN HIRAM, Alaska.
Knickerbocker Charles, 16 Caledonia, Alaska.
Kodderetsch August W., 26 Paris, Grand Rapids.
Konkle Abraham, 28 Solon, Cedar Springs.
Konkle Elijah, 21 Plainfield, Belmont.
KONKLE HOLLIS, 28 Plainfield, Belmont.
Konkle Phineas, 31 Plainfield, Mill Creek.
KONKLE TIMOTHY, 28 Solon, Cedar Springs.
Kooistra John, 17 Wyoming, Grandville.
KOON CHARLES E., Lisbon.
KOON WM. L., 19 Tyrone, Casnovia.
KOON SHERMAN J., Lisbon.
Koopman Cornelius, 29 Grand Rapids.
Kopf Goodrich, Lowell.
KOPF JOHN, Lowell.
Koster Henry, Grandville.
Koyack Anthony, 6 Plainfield, Englishville.
KRAFT GEORGE B., Caledonia, Alaska.
KRAFT VALENTINE, Lowell.
Kramer Nicholas, 13 Walker, Grand Rapids.
Kramer Peter, 33 Alpine, Indian Creek.

Knickerbocker Cyrenius, 16 Caledonia, Alaska.
Knickerbocker Porter, 16 Caledonia, Alaska.
Knickerbocker Walter, 12 Oakfield, Greenville.
Knickerbocker Sylvanus, 16 Caledonia, Alaska.
Knight George W., 3 Byron, North Byron.
Knight Homer, 13 Algoma, Edgerton.
KNIFFIN ADGATE C., 20 Lowell, Lowell.
Kniffin Colossian, Lowell.
Kniffin Charles, 20 Lowell, Lowell.
KNIFFIN HIRAM, Alaska.
Knowles James A., Grandville.
Kocher Albert, Sparta Center.
KOCHER CHRISTOPHER, 3 Sparta, Sparta Center.
Kocher Elmon A., 3 Sparta, Sparta Center.
Krance Christian, 12 Walker, G. Rapids.
Kreke Conrad, 35 Wyoming, North Byron.
Kritcher Conrad, Lisbon.
Kromer Augustus, Cannonsburg.
KROMER ABRAHAM, Village Cannonsburg.
KROMER RUSSELL, 30 Nelson, Cedar Springs.
KRUM ADELBERT, 31 Vergennes, Lowell.
Krum Abram, 32 Vergennes, Lowell.
KRUM CORNELIUS, 31 Vergennes, Lowell.
Krum Edwin B., 32 Vergennes, Lowell.
KRUM WILLIAM, 31 Vergennes, Lowell.
Krupp Daniel, 12 Alpine, Alpine.
KULP JARED, Alaska.
Kusterer Christian, 20 Walker, Grand Rapids.
Kusterer Jacob, 9 Cascade, Cascade.
KUTZ S. B., Rockford.

L

Laawenman Gaart, 32 Grand Rapids.
LaBarge Benjamin, 16 Caledonia, Alaska.
LaBarge Francis, 16 Caledonia, Alaska.
LABARGE GEORGE, 35 G. Rapids.
LaBarge Stephen H., 32 Ada, Ada.
LaBarge William, 29 Ada, Ada.
LaBarr Joseph H., 30 Sparta, Lisbon.
LaBarres James, Rockford.
Laberdy James, 1 Lowell, Lowell.
LACEY HEZEKIAH, Cedar Springs.
Lacey John R., Village Cannonsburg.
Laddbury Lewellyn, 12 Gaines, Hammond.
Ladner Herbert, 36 Cannon, Cannonsburg.
Ladner Francis, 36 Cannon, Cannonsburg.
Ladner Henry, 26 Cannon, Cannonsburg.
Ladner James, 36 Cannon, Cannonsburg.
LADNER JAMES, 26 Cannon, Cannonsburg.
Lafayette Isaac, 18 Spencer, Nelson.
Lamphier Lorenzo, 29 Grand Rapids.
Lamoreaux Andrew W., 13 Plainfield, Mill Creek.
Lamoreaux Andrew W., 31 Plainfield, Mill Creek.
Lamoreaux Andrew J., 1 Walker, Mill Creek.
Lamoreaux Andrew, 1 Walker, Mill Creek.
LAMOREAUX AMBROSE, 8 Ada, Ada.
Lamoreaux David, 31 Plainfield, Mill Creek.
Lamoreaux Florence, 1 Walker, Mill Creek.
LAMOREAUX, GEORGE W., 13 Plainfield, Austerlitz.
Lamoreaux Lester H., 1 Walker, Mill Creek.
Lamoreaux Peter, 26 Plainfield, Austerlitz.
Lamoreaux Wm. M., 29 Cannon, Austerlitz.
Lamont Alexander, 34 Walker, Grand Rapids.

Laison Jacob, 1 Wyoming, G. Rapid.
Laison John, 1 Wyoming, G. Rapids.
Lake John T., 21 Bowne, Bowne.
Lallor Joseph, 17 Walker, G. Rapids.
Lally Martin, 11 Bowne, Bowne.
LALLY PATRICK H., 27 Grattan, Grant.
Lally Thomas S., 11 Bowne, Bowne.
Lally Thomas, 27 Grattan, Grant.
Lamb Thomas B., Lowell.
LAMBERTON DANIEL C., 5 Grand Rapids, Grand Rapids.
Lamberton, Daniel C., Jr., 5 Grand Rapids, Grand Rapids.
Lamberton Charles, 17 Spencer, Spencer Mills.
LAMBERTON JACOB, 17 Spencer, Spencer Mills.
Lamberton Theron, 17 Spencer, Spencer Mills.
Lampman Henry, 25 Lowell, Lowell.
Lampman James, 25 Lowell, Lowell.
Lampee Henry, 19 Alpine, Pleasant.
Lamphier Albert, 17 Grand Rapids.
Lamphere Calvin, 17 Wyoming, Grandville.
Lamphere Lester S., 31 Ada, G. Rapids.
Lamont John, 34 Walker, G. Rapids.
Lamont Silas H., 16 Vergennes, Lowell.
Landon Adonijah, 1 Ada, Cannonsburg.
Landon David F., Lisbon.
LANDON D. F., Lisbon.
LANDON IRA, Cannonsburg.
Landis Eli, 7 Byron, Grandville.
Landis John, 18 Byron, Grandville.
Landis Samuel, 18 Byron, Grandville.
Lane C. C., 14 Lowell, Lowell.
Lane Mrs. F. A., Lowell.
Lane Geo., 13 Lowell, Lowell.
Lane George F., 22 Vergennes, Lowell.
Lane James M., 25 Byron, Cody's Mills.
Lane John, 24 Grattan, Grant.
Lane Jonas H., Lowell.
Lane Palmer, 25 Vergennes, Lowell.
Lane Wm. E., 13 Lowell, Lowell.
Langley George, Lowell.
Langley Warren, Lowell.
Langs Alonzo, 11 Lowell, Lowell.
Langs Jacob, 11 Vergennes, Alton.
Langs James M., 11 Vergennes, Alton.
Langs, Mrs. Mary, 11 Lowell, Lowell.
Langs Wallace W., 11 Lowell, Lowell.

LANNING EDWARD, 12 Courtland, Oakfield.
Lapham Darius A., Rockford.
Lapham Embre B., Rockford.
LAPHAM SMITH, Rockford.
Lappin Michael, 31 Grattan, Cannonsburg.
Laraway Alvin, 17 Paris, G. Rapids.
Laraway Barney J., 8 Paris, G., Rapids.
LARAWAY JAMES R., 4 Cascade, Cascade.
LARAWAY WILLIAM, 28 G. Rapids.
Larimer James, 32 Alpine, Indian Creek.
Larkin Peter, Cedar Springs.
Larson Lars, 9 Grattan, Grattan Cen.
Last William, 26 Grand Rapids.
Latham Leonard, 21 Wyoming, Grandville.
Laughlin John, 7 Vergennes, Vergennes.
Laughlin James, 28 Grattan, Grattan Center.
Laughlin Patrick, 8 Vergennes, Vergennes.
Laughlin William, 36 Cannon, Cannonsburg.
Lavendar John, 10 Vergennes, Lowell.
LAWYER JOHN, 3 Bowne, Alto.
LAWYER MRS. LYDIA, 35 Grand Rapids.
Lawyer Wm. R., 35 Grand Rapids.
Lazier James, 33 Alpine, Indian Creek.
Leach Cerril, 12 Plainfield, Rockford.
Leach Collins, Rockford.
LEATHERS DEWITT, 22 Cascade, Cascade.
LEATHERS D. J., Rockford.
Leathers Samuel, 36 Algoma, Rockford.
Leatherman John, 16 Gaines, G. Rapids
Leavitt Henry A., 16 Oakfield, Oakfield.
LEAVENWORTH ALONZO D., 24 Algoma, Edgerton.
Leavenworth Fred. M., 24 Algoma, Edgerton.
Le Baron William, 4 Alpine, G. Rapids
Leclear Baptist, 36 Cascade, Alaska.
Leclear Daniel, 35 Cascade, Alaska.
LECLEAR FRANCIS, 36 Cascade, Alaska.
Leclear James, 35 Cascade, Alaska.
LECLEAR LEVI, 27 Cascade, Cascade.
LE CLEAR GEORGE R., 15 Caledonia, Alaska.
LE CLEAR THOMAS, 15 Caledonia, Alaska.

Lavender Mrs. Lucretia, 7 Walker, Grand Rapids.
Lavender Marvin B., 7 Walker, Grand Rapids.
Laverty Henry, 14 Grattan, Grattan Center.
LAVERTY HARVEY E., 14 Grattan, Grattan Center.
Lawless James, 5 Vergennes, Vergennes.
LAWRASON ROBERT, 25 Cascade, Alaska.
Lawrence C. D., 15 Grand Rapids.
Lawrence George, 21 Plainfield, Belmont.
LAWRENCE LYMAN, 11 Walker, Grand Rapids.
Lawrence Thomas, 13 Walker, Grand Rapids.
Lawrence Wm. Cedar Springs.
Lowry Ephraim, 2 Bowne, Alto.
Lowry Leonard B., 17 Cascade, Cascade.
LOWRY MOSES, 2 Bowne, Alto.
Lawson Lewis G., 13 Walker, Grand Rapids.
Lawyer Fred., 21 Lowell, Lowell.
Ledger James, 15 Byron, Byron Center
Ledward John, 29 Grand Rapids.
Ledyard Wm. B., South 6 Walker, Grand Rapids.
Lee Benj. J., 28 Bowne, Bowne.
Lee Charles H., 36 Paris, Grand Rapids
LEE EDMUND Jr., Lowell.
Lee J. Edwin, Lowell.
Lee Leverett J., 34 Vergennes, Lowell.
LEE PETER, Lowell.
LEE SOLOMON, 34 Vergennes, Lowell.
Lee William, 20 Oakfield, Oakfield.
LEE WILLIAM, 27 Bowne, Bowne.
Leece Ferdinand, 11 Bowne, Alto.
Leece John, 1 Bowne, South Boston.
LEEMAN WALTER, 16 Oakfield, Oakfield.
Leeuw Abram, 32 Paris, Grand Rapids.
LEFFINGWELL C. W., 22 G. Rapids.
Leffler David, 28 Alpine, Indian Creek.
Leffingwell Henry H., 12 G. Rapids.
LEFEVER, FRANCIS M., 35 Paris, Hammond.
LeFever Stark, 35 Paris, Hammond.
Legg Elijah, Rockford.

Lowe Hiram. 28 Bowne, Harris Creek.
Lown Joseph, 12 Sparta, Sparta Cen.
Lowry Ephraim, 2 Bowne, Alto.
Lowry Leonard B., 17 Cascade, Cascade.
LOWRY HENRY NEWELL, 17 Cascade, Cascade.
LOWRY MOSES, 2 Bowne, Alto.
Loyd Patrick, 18 Paris, Grand Rapids.
Loyer Christian, 33 Lowell, Lowell.
Loyer Jacob, 34 Lowell, Lowell.
Lucas Henry, 32 Paris, Grand Rapids.
LUCAS HOWARD J., 32 Paris, Grand Rapids.
LUCE E. M., Lisbon.
Luce Hiram C., 24 Cascade, Cascade.
Ludington Wm. D., 1 Byron, Kelloggsville.
Ludwig Endres, 30 Byron, Byron Cen.
LULL LUCIAN B., Lowell.
Lull Lyman, 21 Vergennes, Lowell.
Lundun Charles, 9 Sparta, Lisbon.
Lundeen Gustavus, 5 Sparta, Lisbon.
Luneke Luis, 25 Byron, Cody's Mills.
Lusher John. 28 Algoma, Rockford.
Lusk Eliza P., 14 Lowell, Lowell.
Lusk Jeremiah, 36 Lowell, Lowell.
Lybarker George, 24 Caledonia, Alaska.
LYBARKER LAFAYETTE, 23 Caledonia, Caledonia Station.
LYNCH JEREMIAH, 31 Walker, G. Rapids.
Lynch Jeremiah, 1 Wyoming, Grand Rapids.
Lynch Mrs. J., 1 Wyoming, G. Rapids.
Lynch Timothy, 1 Wyoming, Grand Rapids.
Lyndyck Peter, 13 Wyoming, Grand Rapids.
Lynch Patrick, 31 Walker, G. Rapids.
Lynn Nathan, 15 Gaines, Hammond.
Lyon Henry M., 8 Bowne, Alto.
Lyon Morgan L., Lowell.
Lyon Morgan, 20 Vergennes, Vergennes.
Lyon Nelson T., 8 Lowell, Lowell.
Lyon R. B., 7 Lowell, Lowell.
Lyon Sanford W., 28 Grand Rapids.
Lyon Wm. B., 8 Lowell, Lowell.
Lyons John, 31 Vergennes, Lowell.
Lyons Orsamus, 16 Spencer, Spencer Mills.

M

Maas Joseph, 13 Alpine, Alpine.
Maben Charles, 13 Paris, Cascade.
Mabie Amos C., 28 Solon, Cedar Springs.
MABIE ELIAS, 11 Solon, Cedar Springs.
Mabie Nelson, 21 Solon, Cadar Springs.
MABIE JOHN F., 13 Solon, Cedar Springs.
Macomber Horatio B., 11 Cannon, Bostwick Lake.
Mack Nathaniel, 12 Oakfield, Greenville.
Maddern Edwin, 26 Cannon, Cannonsburg.
Maddern Frank, Village of Cannonsburg.
Maddocks Alphonso, 14 Sparta, Sparta Center.
Madan Owen, 19 Paris, Grand Rapids.
Madigan James, 20 Cascade, Cascade.
Madison Cass B., 16 Grattan, Grattan Center.
Madison Charles, 36 Tyrone, Sparta Center.
MADISON GRANVILLE, 13 Cannon Bostwick Lake.
MADISON LUTHER K., 16 Grattan Grattan Center.
Madron David, 7 Vergennes, Vergennes.
Maera William, 20 Ada, Ada.
Magaron John, 26 Plainfield, Austelitz.
Magaron John, 24 Plainfield, Austerlitz.
MAGEE FRANS, 4 Grand Rapids.
Magoon Henry, 17 Algoma, Sparta Center.
Magoon Thomas, 17 Algoma, Sparta Centre.
Mahane John, 19 Grattan, Cannonsburg.
Mahoney J., 34 Walker, G. Rapids.
MAIER JACOB, 24 Gaines, Caledonia Station.

MAIN GEORGE, 1 Oakfield, Greenville.
Main John, 34 Algoma, Rockford.
Main Samuel, 26 Tyrone, Sparta Cen.
Main William, 1 Oakfield, Greenville.
Makkas Garrat, 18 Wyoming, Grandville.
Makkas Klaas, 18 Wyoming, Grandville.
MALCOLM ISAAC B., Alaska.
Malcolm Joshua T., 15 Walker, Grand Rapids.
Malcolm John, 20 Walker, G. Rapids.
Malcolm James W., 20 Walker, Grand Rapids.
MALCOLM JAMES, Alaska.
Malin William, 8 Byron, Grandville.
MALIN PATRICK, 8 Byron, Grandville.
Mallory M., Burchville, (Burch's Mills.)
MALLORY RUSSEL, 20 Courtland, Courtland Center.
Malone John, 28 Grattan, Grattan Cen.
Malone John, 29 Grattan, Grattan Center.
Malone Michael, 22 Grattan, Grattan Center.
Malone Patrick, 3 Ada, Cannonsburg.
Manning Martin, 36 Grand Rapids.
Manwaring Wm. H., 8 Wyoming, Grandville.
MANWARING WILLIAM, 8 Wyoming, Grandville.
Mapes Andrew, 27 Sparta, Sparta Cen.
Mapes Barnabas, 27 Sparta, Sparta Cen.
Mapes Fernando C., 21 Lowell, Lowell.
Mapes Joseph, 6 Plainfield, Englishville
Mapes Jesse, 8 Plainfield, Belmont.
Mapes Nehemiah, 28 Sparta, Sparta Center.
Mapons Wm. H., 10 Byron, North Byron.
March Wilbur S., 29 Bowne, Harris Creek.
Morgan Charles, 7 Lowell, Lowell.
MARIS PAUL, 29 Grand Rapids.
MARKEN THOMAS, 2 Grand Rapids.
Markham Bradley, 21 Alpine, Berlin.
Markham Chauncey, 18 Alpine, Pleasant.
Marks John, Alaska.
Marritt James, 15 Byron, Byron Center
MARSH CHAS C., 5 Cascade, Cascade
Marsh Henry B., Alaska.
MARSH PHILETUS L., 11 Gaines, Hammond.
MARSH THOMAS, 8 Cascade, Cascade

Malone Patrick, 36 Cannon, Cannonsburg.
Malone Sidney, 33 Gaines, Cody's Mills.
Malony Michael, 30 Caledonia, Caledonia Station.
Maloy P., 29 Grand Rapids, Grand Rapids.
Malpass Daniel, Lowell.
MANCHESTER JOHN, 7 Sparta, Lisbon.
MANCHESTER MARTIN, 18 Bowne, Alaska.
Mangletz E., Grandville.
Manktalow Charles J., 16 G. Rapids.
MANLY EDMUND, 4 Walker, Indian Creek.
Manly Edwin, 6 Alpine, Pleasant.
Manly John, 4 Walker, Indian Creek.
MANLY MRS. J., 32 Sparta, Lisbon.
Manly Sherebiah H., Lisbon.
MANN CHARLES, 33 Courtland, Rockford.
Mann Christian, 18 Sparta, Lisbon.
MANN JACOB F., Lisbon.
Mann Peter, 16 Vergennes, Lowell.
Manning John, 36 Grand Rapids.
Marshall George, 2 Byron, North Byron
Marshall Isaiah, 10 Byron, North Byron
Marshall Joseph, 3 Byron, North Byron
Marshall Robert, Lowell.
MARSHALL SAMUEL, 2 Byron, North Byron.
Marshall Scott, 16 Courtland, Courtland Center.
Marshall Wm. D., 33 Lowell, Alto.
Martin Conrad, 27 Alpine, G. Rapids.
MARTIN DANIEL W., 18 Caledonia, Caledonia Station.
Martin David, 13 Algoma, Edgerton.
Martin Ensley, Rockford.
Martin Frederick, 13 Algoma, Edgerton.
Martin Gandliff, 13 Algoma, Edgerton.
Martin George, 1 Solon, Sand Lake.
MARTIN JOSIAH, 18 Oakfield, Oakfield.
MARTIN JOSEPH, 6 Gaines, Grand Rapids.
MARTIN JAMES H., 36 G. Rapids.
Martin Joseph A., 32 Walker, Grand Rapids.
Martin John, Alaska Village.

DAVID S. HOPKINS,

ARCHITECT.

Designs for City and Country furnished upon Short Notice.

Office, 26 Canal St., (up stairs,)

Grand Rapids, Mich.

West Side Drug Store,

Martin's Block, Bridge St., (West.)

GEO. M. STUART,

DEALER IN

DRUGS, MEDICINES AND CHEMICALS,

Oils, Paints, Varnishes and Brushes.

The Choicest Brands of Cigars, Smoking & Chewing Tobaccos.

A Carefully Selected Assortment of

STATIONERY & SCHOOL BOOKS

Has been added to the above stock.

GRAND RAPIDS, MICH.

Manufacturer of

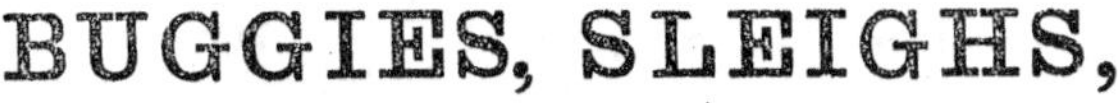

LIGHT AND HEAVY LUMBER WAGONS,

BLACKSMITHING AND ALL KINDS OF REPAIRING.

Nos. 12 and 14, Cor. Bronson and Kent Sts.,

Grand Rapids, - - - Michigan.

Martin N. M., 5 Grand Rapids, Grand Rapids.
MARTIN RUFUS W., 6 Cascade, Cascade.
MARTIN SIMON P., 9 Caledonia, Alaska.
Martin Thomas, 30 Vergennes, Vergennes.
MARTIN THOMAS W., 16 Paris, Grand Rapids.
MARTIN THOMAS, 6 Paris, Grand Rapids.
MARTIN THOMAS S., 26 Paris, Grand Rapids.
Martindale Benjamin F., 27 Walker, Grand Rapids.
MARTINDALE CHARLES J., 11 Sparta, Sparta Center.
Martindale David B., Sparta Center.
MARTINDALE THEODORE F., 34 Alpine, Indian Creek.
MARVIN ORVILLE G., 5 Nelson, Sand Lake.
Mason Mrs. A. H., Lowell.
Mason Benjamin, 16 Grattan, Grattan Center.
MASON ELLIOTT, 25 Grattan, Grant.
Mason Frank, Lowell.
Mason James, 3 Ada, Cannonsburg.
Maxfield Allen D., 34 Spencer, Spencer Mills.
Maxfield Matthew M., 27 Spencer, Spencer Mills.
Maxfield W. W., 24 Grand Rapids.
Maxim Mrs. Mary, 13 Algoma, Edgerton.
MAXWELL HUGH T., 4 Sparta, Sparta Center.
May Gustavus, 34 Alpine, Indian Creek
May James, 20 Cascade, Cascade.
Maybee William, 1 Alpine, Englishville
Mayer Jacob, 30 Plainfield, Mill Creek.
MAYNARD JOHN, 12 Lowell, Lowell.
MAYNARD THOMAS R., 28 Walker, Grand Rapids.
Mayne Andrew, 33 Spencer, Spencer Mills.
MAZE JAMES H., Cedar Springs.
McALISTER HUGH B., Alaska.
McAlon Swindle, 33 Plainfield, Grand Rapids.
McArthur Frank, 32 Oakfield, Grattan Center.
McARTHUR GILES, 32 Oakfield, Grattan Center.
McARTHUR HARRY, 33 Oakfield, Grattan Center.

Mason Martin, 24 Grattan, Grattan Center.
MASON SAILSBURY, 2 Wyoming, Grand Rapids.
Mason Theodore W., Lowell.
Mason William, 34 Plainfield, Grand Rapids.
MASON WM. R., 26 Grattan, Grant.
MASTENBROECK HENRY, 23 Vergennes, Fallassburg.
Masterbrooks John, 30 Paris, Grand Rapids.
Matthewson Jno. E. W., 24 Gaines, Hammond.
MATHEWSON J. M., Lowell.
Mathewson Neil, 32 Oakfield, Oakfield.
Matthews John, 18 Alpine, Pleasant.
Matthews James E., 18 Alpine, Pleasant.
Matthews John, 1 Lowell, Lowell.
Matthews Michael, 16 Cascade, Cascade.
Matthews Philip F., 18 Alpine, Pleasant.
Maurer Mrs. Anna M., 6 Paris, Grand Rapids.
McArthur Orange, 33 Oakfield, Grattan Center.
McArthur Robert, 20 Bowne, Harris Creek.
McArthur Solomon, 30 Oakfield, Oakfield.
McArthur Truman, 26 Byron, Cody's Mills.
McBRIDE ALEX., 13 Lowell, Lowell.
McBRIDE WM. T., 13 Lowell, Lowell.
McCabe Andrew, 36 Cannon, Cannonsburg.
McCabe Chester, Lowell.
McCabe Henry, Lowell.
McCaine Simon, 13 Lowell, Lowell.
McCall Mrs. Catharine, 4 Bowne, Alto.
McCALLUM DUNCAN, 29 Bowne, Harris Creek.
McCarthy Charles, 29 Walker, Grand Rapids.
McCARTHY CHARLES, 30 Grattan, Cannonsburg.
McCarthy Dennis, 30 Grattan, Cannonsburg.
McCarthy Dennis, 34 Walker, Grand Rapids.

McCarthy Jeremiah, 29 Walker, Grand Rapids.
McCarthy John, 30 Grattan, Grattan Center.
McCarthy John, 7 Vergennes, Vergennes.
McCarthy William, 30 Grattan, Cannonsburg.
McCarty Charles, Lowell.
McCarty Charles, 33 Bowne, Harris Creek.
McCarty Daniel, 34 Walker, G. Rapids.
McCarty John, 1 Wyoming, G. Rapids.
McCarty Moses A., 31 Gaines, Cody's Mills.
McCARTY MICHAEL, 31 Gaines, Cody's Mills.
McCarty N. L., Lowell.
McCARTY PERRY, 35 Bowne, Fillmore, Barry County.
McCaul Benj. R., 26 Ada, Ada.
McCaul Charles S., 26 Ada, Ada.
McCaul, Wm. H., 26 Ada, Ada.
McCauley Barney, 32 Grattan, Cannonsburg.
McCauley James, 28 Grattan, Grattan Center.
McCauley Patrick, 33 Oakfield, Grattan Center.
McConnell William, 28 Byron, Byron Center.
McConnell Wm. A., Lowell.
McConnell William, 3 Caledonia, Alaska
McConnon Patrick, 23 Paris, Grand Rapids.
McCord Patrick, 20 Grand Rapids.
McCORMICK EDWARD, 2 Ada, Cannonsburg.
McCormick H. F., 23 Grand Rapids.
McCormick James, 2 Ada, Cannonsburg.
McCormick Michael, 35 Cannon, Cannonsburg.
McCOY MARK H., Grandville.
McCoy Sheldon, Lowell.
McCrath Charles, 21 Grand Rapids.
McCRATH JAMES, 21 Grand Rapids.
McCrath Lewis, 9 Paris, Grand Rapids.
McCrory E. S., Rockford.
McCULLY THOMAS, 20 Bowne, Harris Creek.
McDaniel Daniel, Lowell.
McDannell O. C., Lowell.
McDIARMID ANGUS, 15 Bowne, Bowne.
McDIARMID CHAUNCEY, 27 Bowne, Bowne.
McDiarmid Duncan, 15 Bowne, Bowne.

McCauley Peter, 33 Oakfield, Grattan Center.
McCauley Wm. H., 26 Plainfield, Austerlitz.
McCHESNEY JOHN M., Village Cedar Springs.
McClelan James L., 33 Ada, Ada.
McClelan Wm. H., 33 Ada, Ada.
McClure Jay, 11 Algoma, Edgerton.
McClure Oliver P., 27 Spencer, Spencer Mills.
McCombs Hiram, 20 Walker, Grand Rapids.
McConnell Gilbert C., Rockford.
McConnell Geo. W., 5 Sparta, Sparta Center.
McConnell Guian, 3 Caledonia, Alaska.
McConnell Jemima, Village Cedar Springs.
McConnell John, 23 Bowne, Bowne.
McCONNELL JOHN S., 22 Caledonia, Alaska.
McConnell Lafayette, Rockford.
McConnell Luther, 29 Lowell, Lowell.
McCONNELL MARCUS, 4 Caledonia, Alaska.
McConnell Milo, 3 Caledonia, Alaska.
McDiarmid James D., 22 Bowne, Bowne.
McDIARMID JAMES, 22 Bowne, Bowne.
McDIARMID JOHN D., 29 Bowne, Harris Creek.
McDONALD ALEXANDER, 18 Bowne, Alaska.
McDONALD ALEXANDER, 5 Nelson, Cedar Springs.
McDonald Angus, 2 Alpine, Englishville.
McDONALD ANDREW JR., 5 Vergennes, Alton.
McDonald Andrew, 5 Vergennes, Alton.
McDonald Barney, 17 Wyoming, Grandville.
McDonald Charles 17, Wyoming, Grandville.
McDonald Duncan, 13 Sparta, Sparta Center.
McDonald Edward, 23 Walker, Grand Rapids.
McDonald Finley, 34 Ada, Ada.
McDONALD JOHN, 32 Bowne, Harris Creek.

McDONALD JAMES, 32 Bowne, Harris Creek.
McDonald John, 4 Sparta, Sparta Cen.
McDonald John, 12 Alpine, Grand Rapids.
McDonald James, 34 Walker, Grand Rapids.
McDonald Patrick, 8 Walker, Grand Rapids.
McDonald Peter, 5 Vergennes, Alton.
McDonald Thomas, 30 Wyoming, Grandville.
McDONALD WASHINGTON, 35 Algoma, Rockford.
McDonald William, 2 Alpine, Englishville.
McDorman Geo. W., 14 Solon, Cedar Springs.
McDougal James, 36 Tyrone, Sparta Center.
McDowell Jas. A., 36 Byron, Cody's Mills.
McEwen Charles, 3 Wyoming, Grand Rapids.
McEwing Daniel, 8 Bowne, Alto.
McEwen Patrick, 20 Grand Rapids.
McEwen Mrs. Sarah, 3 Wyoming, Grand Rapids.
McGlin Timothy, 7 Vergennes, Vergennes.
McGlynn Patrick, 34 Walker, Grand Rapids.
McGovern Michael, 10 Grattan, Grattan Center.
McGovern Patrick, 11 Nelson, Nelson.
McGovern Thomas, 11 Nelson, Nelson.
McGoveran Hugh, 34 Walker, Grand Rapids.
McGuire James, 34 Walker, G. Rapids.
McGuire James, 16 Lowell, Lowell.
McGurk James, 36 Oakfield, Ashley.
McGrain Daniel, 35 Wyoming, Grand Rapids.
McGRATH THOMAS, 30 Alpine, Berlin.
McGregor A. H., Lowell.
McGREGOR AMOS H., 13 Lowell, Lowell.
McGregor Asa, 10 Walker, Indian Creek.
McHugh John, 11 Ada, Cannonsburg.
McIntire James, 8 Lowell, Lowell.
McIntosh James, 20 Lowell, Lowell.
McIntyre Fayette E., 4 Caledonia, Alaska.
McInroy, Alexander, Grandville.
McInroy William, Grandville.

McEwen William, 3 Wyoming, Grand Rapids.
McFadden James, Burchville, (Burch's Mills.)
McFall Jonathan, 20 Algoma, Rockford.
McFarland John, 26 Lowell, Lowell.
McGann Michael, 3 Ada, Ada.
McGARRY JAMES, 25 Caledonia, Caledonia.
McGaven John, 34 Plainfield, Austerlitz.
McGEE BERNARD, 10 Vergennes, Alton.
McGee Cormick, 33 Grattan, Grattan Center.
McGee James, 21 Grattan, Grattan Cen.
McGEE JOHN, 28 Grattan, Grattan Center.
McGee James, 10 Vergennes, Alton.
McGee Owen, 34 Grattan, Grattan Cen.
McGILLIVRAY DUNCAN D., Station Agent at Ada Village.
McGinnis John, 18 Bowne, Harris Creek.
McGinnis Kerns, 3 Ada, Cannonsburg.
McKee William, 10 Cascade, Ada.
McKenzie Alexander, 27 Walker, G. Rapids.
McKenzie Mrs. Marion E., 13 Walker, Grand Rapids.
McKenna James, 34 Walker, Grand Rapids.
McKenney James K., 20 Byron, Byron Center.
McKENNEY SAMUEL, 17 Byron, Byron Center.
McKnight James, 29 Cascade, Cascade.
McKnight Thomas, 29 Cascade, Cascade.
McKinzie Kinneth, 8 Walker, Grand Rapids.
McKinster Charles, Cedar Springs.
McKinney John, 3 Cannon, Rockford.
McKinney William, 3 Cannon, Rockford.
McKoy Wm. M., 7 Grand Rapids.
McLain Abner, 30 Cannon, Austerlitz.
McLain George, 34 Ada, Ada.
McLain Mrs. James, 6 Alpine, Lisbon.
McLAIN JOHN, 34 Ada, Ada.
McLane Curtis, 8 Alpine, Pleasant.
McLane David, 8 Alpine, Pleasant.

McLaughlin Michael, 9 Vergennes, Alton.
McLAUGHLIN THOMAS, 5 Vergennes, Alton.
McLEAN ALEXANDER, 19 Vergennes, Vergennes.
McLean Neil, 19 Vergennes, Vergennes.
McLean Peter, 13 Ada, Ada.
McLenethan Charles, 36 Gaines, Caledonia Station.
McLOUTH PETER H., Village of Cedar Springs.
McMahon Owen, 2 Ada, Cannonsburg.
McMann John, 11 Grand Rapids.
McMANN THOMAS, 11 Grand Rapids.
McMann William, 22 Plainfield, Austerlitz.
McMannus J. P., 31 Grattan, Grattan Center.
McMillan Archibald, Jr., 5 Ada, Ada.
McMILLAN ARCHIBALD, 32 Cannon, Ada.
McMillan Cornelius, 32 Cannon, Ada.
McMILLAN JOHN, 4 Ada, Ada.
McMillen John, 34 Walker, G. Rapids.
McMinnis B. F., 12 Solon, Cedar Springs.
McMullen Isaac, 12 Lowell, Lowell.
McMurray Mrs. Hannah, 34 Ada, Ada.
McNitt William, 4 Walker, Indian Creek.
McNorton William, 13 Lowell, Lowell.
McPherson John, 32 Cannon, Ada.
McPherson Peter W., 18 Vergennes, Vergennes.
McPHERSON WILLIAM, 18 Vergennes, Vergennes.
McPoland Terry, 34 Walker, G. Rapids.
McQUARRIE JOHN, 23 Caledonia, Caledonia.
McQUEEN JOHN, 35 Cascade, Alaska.
McQueen J. G., 29 Sparta, Lisbon.
McTammany John, 23 Tyrone, Sparta Center.
McVEAN DAVID E., 10 Bowne, Alto.
McVean Hobert, 3 Bowne, Alto.
McVEAN MRS. LUCY, 10 Bowne, Alto.
McVicker Mrs. M., Lowell.
McWHINNEY WILLIAM, 26 Bowne, Bowne.
Meach Asa W., 15 Paris, Grand Rapids.
Meach Charles, 15 Paris, G. Rapids.
Meach David, 11 Paris, Grand Rapids.
Meach George, 15 Paris, Grand Rapids.
Meach Volney, 11 Paris, Grand Rapids.
Mead Clark, 12 Alpine, Alpine.
Mead Ebenezer, 5 Bowne, Alto.

McNamara John, 20 Grand Rapids.
McNamara Michael, 16 Wyoming, Grandville.
McNamara Michael, 34 Walker, Grand Rapids.
McNamara Martin, 23 Grand Rapids.
McNamara Michael, 1 Paris, G. Rapids
McNamara Simon, 34 Walker, Grand Rapids.
McNana, Patrick, 12 Grand Rapids.
McNaughton Archibald, 30 Bowne, Harris Creek.
McNaughton Alexander, 18 Ada, Ada.
McNAUGHTON DOUGALD, 33 Cannon Cannonsburg.
McNaughton Dougald, 18 Ada, Ada.
McNaughton John, 33 Cannon, Cannonsburg.
McNAUGHTON JOHN D., 9 Ada, Ada
McNaughton Mrs. M., 4 Ada, Cannonsburg.
McNAUGHTON RICHARD D., 31 Bowne, Harris Creek.
McNeal Abram H., 11 Caledonia, Alaska
McNee James, 29 Bowne, Harris Creek.
McNitt Frank, Lisbon.
McNITT SAMUEL, Lisbon.
Mead Enos, 12 Alpine, Englishville.
MEAD LAFAYETTE, 34 G. Rapids.
Mead Wm., 12 Alpine, Alpine.
Meaks Charles, 16 Plainfield, Belmont.
Mears A. T., Lowell.
Medler Charles, 4 Courtland, Courtland Center.
Medler Samuel F., 34 Nelson, Cedar Springs.
Medler W. J., Lowell.
MEDLER WM. H., 34 Nelson, Cedar Springs.
Meech Lawrence, 7 Cascade, Cascade.
MEEHAN MICHAEL T., 24 Gaines, Hammond.
Meeker Allen, 29 Sparta, Lisbon.
Meggison William, 13 Algoma, Edgerton.
MEKEEL WILLIAM H., 30 Ada, Ada.
Melervy John, 34 Walker, G. Rapids.
MELONING EMMETT, Village of Cedar Springs.
Melville John, 29 Grand Rapids.
Meredith Joseph, 8 Paris, G. Rapids.
Merley August, Alaska Village.
Merren John, 9 Nelson, Cedar Springs.

Merren Patrick, 19 Nelson, Cedar Springs.
MERRILL CHARLES, 30 Tyrone, Casnovia.
Merrill Orsemus, 26 Paris, G. Rapids.
Merrill Roswell, 26 Paris, G. Rapids.
Merritt Emmett, Lowell.
MERRIMAN WILLIS L., 30 Vergennes, Lowell.
MERVAU ANDREW, 15 Gaines, Hammond.
MESLER WILLIAM C., 14 Paris, Grand Rapids.
MESNARD CYRUS, 29 Gaines, Gainesville.
Mesnard Enoch, 25 Gaines, Gainesville.
MESNARD GEORGE E., 25 Gaines, Gainesville.
MESNARD NOAH W., 16 Gaines, Gainesville.
Messmore E. M., Rockford.
Metcalf Joseph, Rockford.
Meyers Andrew, 24 Sparta, Sparta Cen.
Meyers Andrew P., 24 Sparta, Sparta Center.
Meyers Andrew, 18 Algoma, Sparta Center.
Meyers George, 4 Algoma, Rockford.
MILLER DAVID H., 35 Bowne, Fillmore, Barry County.
Miller David, 4 Alpine, Pleasant.
Miller, David M., 29 Vargennes, Lowell.
Miller Ezra, 17 Oakfield, Oakfield.
Miller Edward, south 6 Walker, Grand Rapids.
MILLER ELI J. 32 Gaines, Cody's Mills.
MILLER EZRA C., 12 Paris, Grand Rapids.
Miller Gariat, Grandville.
Miller G. W., 17 Alpine, Indian Creek.
Miller George, 23 Plainfield, Austerlitz.
Miller George, 17 Plainfield, Austerlitz.
Miller Henry B., 18 Oakfield, Oakfield.
Miller Henry S., Rockford.
MILLER HENRY M., 19 Cannon, Austerlitz.
Miller Homer, 19 Cannon, Austerlitz.
Miller Hugh, 14 Paris, Grand Rapids.
Miller Henry D., 11 Grattan, Grattan Center.
MILLER H. B., 34 Grand Rapids.
MILLER JARED, 5 Bowne, Alto.
Miller John, 11 Sparta, Sparta Center.
Miller John S., 9 Walker, Indian Creek.

MEYERS HIRAM H., 24 Sparta, Sparta Center.
Meyers James M., 32 Caledonia, Caledonia Station.
MEYERS PETER, 24 Sparta, Sparta Center.
MICHAEL ANTHONY, 19 Walker, Grand Rapids.
Midendorf Martin, 3 Wyoming, Grand Rapids.
Milan Mrs. Margaret, 34 Walker, Grand Rapids.
Miles Reuben, 23 Solon, Cedar Springs
Milford Thomas, 24 Nelson, Nelson.
Miller Abram, 23 Vergennes, Fallassburg.
Miller Alfred, 23 Plainfield, Austerlitz.
Miller Anthony, 33 Cascade, Alaska.
Miller Alfred P., 35 Oakfield, Ashley.
Miller Benjamin, 27 Cascade, Alaska.
Miller Charles W., 17 Oakfield, Oakfield.
Miller Charles, 27 Plainfield, Austerlitz.
Miller Charles D., 24 Cannon, Cannonsburg.
Miller Charles, 1 Courtland, Courtland Center.
Miller James S., 36 Tyrone, Sparta Center.
Miller John, 6 Lowell, Lowell.
Miller John, 15 Grand Rapids.
Miller James, 10 Byron, Byron Center.
Miller John D., Rockford.
Miller James B., 23 Vergennes, Lowell.
Miller John H., 1 Alpine, Englishville.
Miller Joseph, Lisbon.
Miller John, 36 Algoma, Rockford.
MILLER JOHN, 35 Bowne, Fillmore, Barry County.
Miller John T., 34 Grand Rapids.
Miller J. H., 9 Walker, Grand Rapids.
Miller John, 20 Sparta, Lisbon.
Miller Levi, 24 Cannon, Cannonsburg.
Miller Levi, 25 Gaines, Caledonia Station.
Miller Lyman, 12 Walker, G. Rapids.
Miller Mrs. Mary, Grandville.
Miller Major, 34 Ada, Ada.
Miller Manson, 34 Ada, Ada.
Miller Moses, 28 Cascade, Alaska.
Miller Michael, 15 Grand Rapids.
Miller Martin, 15 Grand Rapids.
Miller Oliver, 2 Alpine, Englishville.
Miller Peter, 24 Bowne, Bowne.

MILLER REV. C. C., 1 Grattan, Ashley
Miller Wm. H., 24 Cannon, Cannonsburg.
Miller Wm. R., 15 Lowell, Lowell.
MILLER WM. E., 1 Alpine, Englishville.
MILLER WM. H., 23 Plainfield, Austerlitz.
Mills Aaron, Rockford.
Mills Benj. P., 15 Grand Rapids.
Mills Daniel, Grandville.
Mills Daniel W., Rockford.
MILLS ELNATHAN, 12 Paris, Grand Rapids.
Mills Ephraim F., 24 Cannon, Cannonsburg.
Mills Hezakiah, 16 Grand Rapids.
Mills John, 32 Wyoming, Grandville.
Mims Henry, Lowell.
Minderhout Cornelius, Grandville.
Minderhout Martin, 27 Wyoming, North Byron.
MINER EDWARD, 4 Walker, Indian Creek.
Miner Hubbard, 7 Byron, Grandville.
Mines Matthew, 12 Alpine, Alpine.
Minisee John, 18 Byron, Grandville.
Minisee William, 2 Gaines, Hammond.
Minzey Franklin, 15 Walker, G. Rapids
MITCHELL HENRY, Lowell.
Mitchell Isaac, Lowell.
Mix Mrs. Sarah, Sparta Center.
Mizner Abner, Rockford.
Mizner Henry, 24 Nelson, Nelson.
MIZNER HIRAM W., 1 Alpine, Englishville.
Moe Irving W., 16 Grattan Center Cen.
Moe Robert, Lowell.
MOFFIT EDMUND G., 4 Caledonia, Alaska.
Moffit Jasper, 4 Caledonia, Alaska.
Moffit Lester C., Alaska.
Moffit Mrs. Nancy J., 4 Caledonia, Alaska.
MOFFIT NEWTON, 4 Caledonia, Alaska.
Moffitt William S., 32 Cannon, Austerlitz.
Moffitt William B., 32 Cannon, Austerlitz.
Molesta Henry, 16 Paris, Grand Rapids.
Moll Abram, 13 Wyoming, G. Rapids.
Monger Edwin, 17 Walker, G. Rapids.
Mongersall Samuel, 21 Sparta, Sparta Center.
Monks Philip A., Lowell.
Mountstephens John, 13 Walker, Grand Rapids.

Minzey James, 15 Walker, Grand Rapids
MISNER ANDREW, 33 Vergennes, Lowell.
MISNER CHRISTOPHER, 33 Vergennes, Lowell.
Misner Charles C., 33 Vergennes, Lowell
MISNER DANIEL, Lowell.
Misner George, 7 Algoma, Sparta Cen.
MISNER HIRAM, 30 Tyrone, Casnovia.
MISNER JAMES, 26 Cannon, Cannonsburg.
Misner John, 7 Algoma, Sparta Center.
Misner John, 4 Algoma, Cedar Springs.
Misner John, 14 Cannon, Cannonsburg.
Misner John, 12 Cannon, Bostwick Lake.
Misner Peter, 26 Cannon, Cannonsburg.
Misner Peter, 24 Plainfield, Austerlitz.
Misner Wm. H., 14 Cannon, Cannonsburg.
MISNER WILLIAM H., Lowell.
Mitchell Charles, 14 Solon, Cedar Springs.
MITCHELL CHESTER C., 7 Gaines, Gainesville.
Mitchell Charles, 31 Ada, Ada.
MONROE C. W., 32 Alpine, Indian Creek.
MONROE DAVID, 6 Walker, Indian Creek.
Montross David, 24 Vergennes, Fallassburg.
MONROE EDWIN, Alaska.
Monroe Henry D., Village of Cedar Springs.
Monroe Harvey B., 5 Walker, Indian Creek.
Monroe James, 5 Paris, Grand Rapids.
MONROE ORVILLE B., 5 Walker, Indian Creek.
Monroe Stephen, 5 Walker, Indian Creek.
MONSEAU EDWARD, 10 Gaines, Hammond.
MONSEAU EDWARD, 10 Gaines, Hammond.
Montgomery Henry, 7 Algoma, Sparta Center.
Montgomery James, 20 Algoma, Rockford.
Montgomery Thomas, 7 Algoma, Sparta Center.

Montgomery William, 7 Algoma, Sparta Center.
Moody C. W., 32 Grand Rapids.
Moody Charles L., Grandville.
MOODY LEWIS, Grandville.
MOODY WATSON, 6 Alpine, Pleasant.
MOON CHARLES B., 34 Nelson, Cedar Springs.
Moon Cassius, 14 Solon, Cedar Springs.
Moon Henry B., 4 Vergennes, Alton.
Mooney Ann, 4 Grattan, Grattan Cen.
Mooney Henry, 5 Vergennes, Grand Rapids.
Mooney Jacob, 35 Spencer, Spencer Mills.
Mooney John, 5 Vergennes, Alton.
Mooney Peter, 5 Vergennes, G. Rapids
Moore Albert, 8 Grattan, Grattan Cen.
Moore Albert, 22 Plainfield, Austerlitz.
Moore Benjamin, 8 Grattan, Grattan Center.
Moore Charles, Burchville (Burch's Mills.)
MOORE CURTISS T., Lowell.
MOORE CHARLES H., 6 Gaines, Gainesville.
Moore Daniel, 25 Spencer, Spencer Mills.
Moore John, Lowell.
MOORE JOHN D., 15 Oakfield, Oakfield.
Moore James M., 6 Oakfield, Oakfield.
MOORE NELSON H., 18 Oakfield, Oakfield.
MOORE RICHARD, 19 Wyoming, Grandville.
Moore Wm. L., 8 Oakfield, Oakfield.
MOORE WM. R., 31 Paris, G. Rapids.
Moore William, 23 Algoma, Edgerton.
Moorman William, 7 Byron, Grandville.
Moorman Wm. T., 7 Byron, Grandville.
Moran John, 28 Spencer, Spencer Mills.
Moran James, 28 Spencer, Spencer Mills.
Moran John, 5 Oakfield, Oakfield.
Moran Thomas, 28 Spencer, Spencer Mills.
Morduff James, 10 Gaines, Hammond.
Morduff Proctor, 10 Gaines, Hammond.
MORE MRS. ANN M., 23 Caledonia, Caledonia.
Morehouse Emery, 1 Algoma, Burchville (Burch's Mills.)
Morehouse Mrs. Euceline, 22 Solon, Cedar Springs.
MOREHOUSE EDMUND, 23 Bowne, Bowne.

MOORE DANIEL S., 22 Courtland, Courtland Center.
Moore David S., 6 Oakfield, Oakfield.
Moore Edward, 25 Byron, Cody's Mills.
MOORE FREDERICK, 23 Algoma, Edgerton.
Moore Geo. I., Jr., 21 Walker, Grand Rapids.
MOORE GEO. I., 21 Walker, Grand Rapids.
Moore Henry, 22 Plainfield, Austerlitz.
Moore Hiram, 7 Oakfield, Oakfield.
Moore John, 30 Tyrone, Casnovia.
Moore John D., 35 Alpine, Indian Creek.
Moore John, 22 Algoma, Rockford.
MOORE JAMES W., 25 Spencer, Spencer Mills.
Moore James, 8 Grattan, Grattan Cen.
Moore John, Lowell.
MOORE JOSEPH, 22 Cannon, Cannonsburg.
Moore James, 22 Cannon, Cannonsburg.
Moore James, 36 Wyoming, Kelloggsville.
Moore John R., 34 Wyoming, Grand Rapids.
Morehouse George, 22 Solon, Cedar Springs.
Morey John C., 32 Nelson, Cedar Springs.
Morgan Isaac W., 16 Grattan, Grattan Center.
Morgan J. G., 5 Grand Rapids, Grand Rapids.
Norman George, 18 Byron, Byron Cen.
Morman Ransaler, 19 Byron, Byron Center.
Morningstar Henry, 17 Algoma, Rockford.
Morningstar Henry, Jr., 17 Algoma, Rockford.
Morningstar John, 16 Algoma, Rockford.
Morningstar Wm. H., 16 Algoma, Rockford.
Morrell Alfred, 22 Plainfield, Belmont.
Morrell George, 16 Plainfield, Belmont.
Morris Edwin A., 15 Plainfield, Belmont.
Morris George, 11 Courtland, Courtland Center.
Morris Isaac D., Lowell.

Morris James K., 15 Plainfield, Belmont.
Morris John, 28 Bowne, Harris Creek.
MORRIS LEANDER E., Cedar Springs.
MORRIS NELSON, 1 Caledonia, Alaska.
Morris Robert, 17 Byron, Byron Cen.
MORRIS WAYNE E., Lowell.
MORRIS WEBSTER, Lowell.
Morrison David, 23 Algoma, Edgerton.
Morrison Daniel, Alaska Village.
Morrison Lewis, 15 Grand Rapids.
Morrissy Martin, 1 Grand Rapids.
Morrissey Thomas, 34 Ada, Ada.
Morrill Andrew J., 35 Wyoming, Grand Rapids.
Morrill James M., 35 Wyoming, North Byron.
Morse Benj., 32 Lowell, Lowell.
Morse Carrolton, 6 Bowne, Alto.
MORSE CHARLES, Lowell.
Morse Edgar S., Lowell.
Morse Freeman, 24 Wyoming, Grand Rapids.
MORSE FRANK, 20 Walker, Grand Rapids.
MORSE HENRY, 10 Solon, Cedar Springs.
Mount Nisbet, Sparta Center.
Mount Nathan, Sparta Center.
Mowat John, 12 Ada, Ada.
Mower Jacob, 11 Lowell, Lowell.
MOXON J. S., 5 Grand Rapids, Grand Rapids.
Moye Samuel, 25 Vergennes, Lowell.
MOYER GIDEON M., 15 Gaines, Hammond.
MOYER JONATHAN E., 28 Gaines, Grand Rapids.
Moyer Nathan, 15 Gaines, Hammond.
Muchler Lorenzo E., 2 Cascade, Ada.
MUELLER THEODORE, Lowell.
Muir Alexander, 27 Grand Rapids.
Muir Hugh, 3 Paris, Grand Rapids.
Muir John, 16 Plainfield, Belmont.
Muir Thomas, 3 Paris, Grand Rapids.
MULFORD MILES, 26 Sparta, Sparta Center.
Mulford Thomas, 24 Nelson, Nelson.
MULHOLLAND JACKSON, 7 Byron, North Byron.
Mullin Michael, 17 Walker, G. Rapids.
MULL DANIEL J., Grandville.
Mulligan Michael, 16 Ada, Ada.
Mulligan Patrick, 3 Ada, Ada.
Multer R. P., 14 Solon, Cedar Springs.

Morse Joel, 6 Lowell, Lowell.
Morse James, 11 Lowell, Lowell.
MORSE LAURA A., 16 Grattan, Grattan Center.
Morse Nathan, 22 Lowell, Lowell.
Morse Peter, 31 Lowell, Alto.
Morse Peter, 20 Lowell, Lowell.
Morse Wm., Lowell.
Morey Wm. C., 9 Alpine, G. Rapids.
Mosher Mrs. Almini, 33 Algoma, Rockford.
Mosher Electa, 11 Vergennes, Lowell.
Mosher Edwin, 24 Vergennes, Fallassburg.
Mosher Eseck J., 11 Vergennes, Lowell.
Mosher H. P., 7 Algoma, Sparta Cen.
Mosher James, 33 Algoma, Rockford.
MOSHER WILLIAM, 11 Vergennes, Lowell.
Mosier Alrenzo, 4 Walker, Indian Creek.
Mosier Wm., 11 Lowell, Lowell.
Moss Martin, Lowell.
Motley William, 9 Cascade, Cascade.
Moulsta Frank, 7 Paris, G. Rapids.
Moulsta John, 18 Paris, Grand Rapids.
Moulton Marcus C., 8 Ada, Ada.
Mulohill Larence, 1 Wyoming, Grand Rapids.
Mulyneeney John, 19 Vergennes, Vergennes.
Munger D. C., 16 Grand Rapids.
Munn Jonathan S., 11 Sparta, Sparta Center.
MUNRO DAVID, 13 Algoma, Edgerton.
Munson C W., Lowell.
Munson Truman, 15 Plainfield, Belmont.
Munson Wm., 20 Lowell, Lowell.
Munshaw Lambert, 21 Paris, Grand Rapids.
MURPHY ARCHIBALD, 34 Ada, Ada.
Murphy Andrew, 31 Courtland, Rockford.
Murphy Daniel, jr., 18 Grattan, Grattan Center.
Murphy Daniel, 18 Grattan, Grattan Center.
Murphy Daniel, 14 Cannon, Bostwick Lake.
Murphy Edward, 3 Gaines, Hammond.

MURPHY FRANK, 22 Grattan, Grattan Center.
Murphy George, 2 Plainfield, Rockford,
MURPHY GEORGE, 35 Solon, Cedar Springs.
MURPHY HENRY E., 14 Cannon, Bostwick Lake.
Murphy James, 10 Ada, Ada.
Murphy John, 10 Ada, Ada.
Murphy James, 14 Cannon, Bostwick Lake.
Murphy John, 10 Vergennes, Alton.
Murphy John, 21 Grattan, Grattan Cen
Murphy Michael, 26 Cannon, Cannonsburg.
Murphy Margaret, 22 Grattan, Grattan Center.
MURPHY PETER, 10 Ada, Ada.
Murphy Patrick, 5 Vergennes, Vergennes.
Murphy Patrick, 29 Grand Rapids.
Murphy Patrick, 2 Paris, Grand Rapids
Murphy Patrick, 21 Cascade, Cascade.
MURPHY THOMAS, 21 Grattan, Grattan Center.
MURPHY THOMAS G., 1 Solon, Sand Lake.
Murphy Richard, 23 Lowell, Lowell.
Murphy William, 26 Lowell, Lowell.
MURRAY MICHAEL, 29 Walker, Grand Rapids.
MURRAY NATHAN C., 4 Courtland, Courtland Center.
Murray Patrick, 12 Ada, Ada.
Murray Patrick, 29 Walker, Grand Rapids.
Murray William, 28 Bowne, Harris Creek.
Murray Wm. H., 32 Bowne, Harris Creek.
Murthy John, 33 Bowne, Harris Creek.
Muste John, 29 Grand Rapids.
Muste Leonard, 29 Grand Rapids.
Mussen Richard, 26 Plainfield, Austerlitz.
Mutching Martin, 13 Alpine, Alpine.
Myers Charles K., 11 Sparta, Sparta Center.
MYERS DURANCE, 19 Plainfield, Mill Creek.
MYERS HENRY, 9 Bowne, Alto.
Myers Henry, 24 Sparta, Sparta Center.
MYERS JOHN D., 11 Grattan, Grattan Center.
Myers John, 9 Bowne, Alto.
Myer Jacob, 15 Alpine, Alpine.
MYERS JOHN P., 3 Bowne, Alto.

Murray Daniel, 33 Grattan, Grattan Center.
Murray George, 13 Grand Rapids.
Murray John, 24 Caledonia, Caledonia.
MURRAY JAMES N., 3 Vergennes, Alton.
MURRAY LYMAN, 5 Alpine, Lisbon.
Murray Lucius B., 6 Tyrone, Casnovia.
Murray Michael, 12 Alpine, Alpine.
Murray Mrs. Margaret, 29 Walker, Grand Rapids.
Myers Martin, 12 Ada, Ada.
Myers Merritt, 23 Plainfield, Austerlitz
Myers Mrs. R., 24 Sparta, Sparta Center
Myers Spencer J., 10 Grattan, Grattan Center.
Myers Mrs. Sarah, 23 Plainfield, Austerlitz.
MYERS THOMAS H., 24 Sparta, Sparta Center.
Myers Wm. H., 28 Courtland, Courtland Center.

N

Naftzger Josiah, 24 Vergennes, Fallassburg.
Nairracon Henry C., 34 Ada, Ada.
Naramor John, 35 Oakfield, Ashley.
NARDIN GEORGE, 33 Walker, Grand Rapids.
NARDIN JOHN P., 33 Walker, Grand Rapids.
Nardin John James, 33 Walker, Grand Rapids.
Narregang Owen, 8 Wyoming, Grandville.
Nash Mrs., Lowell.
Nash David, 36 Caledonia, Middleville, Barry County.
Nash Harmon, Lowell.
Nash Ira, Lowell.
NASH JONATHAN E., Sparta Center.
NASH JAMES M., 23 Bowne, Bowne.
Nash Levi, 6 Lowell, Lowell.
Nash M. B., Sparta Center.
Nason Charles F., 32 Plainfield, Grand Rapids.

Nason Wm. A., 34 Plainfield, Grand Rapids.
NAYSMITH JOHN, 9 Ada, Ada.
NAYSMITH JAMES, 10 Grand Rapids.
NEAL D. B., 16 Grand Rapids.
Neal James R., 25 Plainfield, Austerlitz
Neal Jesse, 20 Grand Rapids.
Neal Lewis, 29 Grand Rapids, Grand Rapids.
Near Abram, 2 Byron, North Byron.
Needham Bela C., 33 Lowell, Lowell.
Needham Geo. G., 23 Lowell, Lowell.
Neinhens Venedert, 2 Wyoming, G. Rapids.
Nelist William P., 14 Paris, Grand Rapids.
Nellins Henry, 6 Bowne, Alto.
Nellist John D., 13 Paris, G. Rapids.
Nelles John J., 2 Walker, Indian Creek.
NELSON CHARLES, 3 Vergennes, Alton.
Nelson F. W., Lowell.
Nelson Geo., Lowell.
Nelson John, Cedar Springs.
Nelson Michael, 25 Algoma, Rockford.
Nelson N., 13 Algoma, Edgerton.
Nelson Peter, 12 Oakfield, Greenville.

Newland James, 22 Spencer, Spencer Mills.
NEWLAND STEPHEN S., 13 Sparta, Sparta Center.
NEWMAN JOHN W., 26 Caledonia, Caledonia.
Newman Lewis, 24 Nelson, Nelson.
Newson Mrs. Emily M., Alaska.
NEWSON HORACE S., Alaska.
Newton Clark, Lowell.
Newton Dewitt, Burchville, (Burch's Mills.
NEWTON DUDLEY, 17 Grattan, Grattan Center.
Newton Daniel, Grandville.
Newton Gifford, Burchville (Burch's Mills.)
Newton Henry, 17 Grattan, Grattan Center.
Newton John, Burchville (Burch's Mills.)
NEYGUS ISAAC, Cedar Springs.
Nicely Elias, 19 Tyrone, Casnovia.
Nicholson A. H., Burchville (Burch's Mills.)
Nichols F. R., Rockford.
Nichols A. L., 31 Cannon, Austerlitz.
Nicholson Geo. W., 26 Courtland, Courtland Center.

NELSON SHEAR, 15 Oakfield, Oakfield.
NELSON THEODORE, Lowell.
Nelson Theodore, jun., Lowell.
Nesbitt James, Cannonsburg.
Nesler Christian, 33 Courtland, Courtland Center.
NESTLE HARVEY, 35 Tyrone, Sparta Center.
Nestle Peter, 25 Tyrone, Sparta Center.
Nestle William H., 25 Tyrone, Sparta Center.
Nevius John S., 1 Wyoming, Grand Rapids.
Nevius William S., 32 Grand Rapids.
NEWBERRY HENRY B., 33 Cannon, Cannonsburg.
Newcomb Alfred J., South 5 Walker, Grand Rapids.
NEWHALL EUGENE J., Alaska.
Newhall John W., 15 Wyoming, Grandville.
Newins Thomas, 31 Caledonia, Caledonia Station.
Newkirk Aaron B., 6 Paris, Grand Rapids.

Nichols I. C., Rockford.
NICHOLS HENRY C., 14 Oakfield, Oakfield Center.
Nichols Henry, 4 Walker, Indian Creek
Nichols Jonathan, 15 Vergennes, Alton.
NICHOLS JAMES, 17 Grand Rapids.
Nichols Josiah, 31 Paris, G. Rapids.
NICHOLSON JOHN W., 23 Grattan Grattan Center.
Nichols Levi, 23 Cascade, Cascade.
Nichols Mary A., 31 Cannon, Austerlitz.
Nichoson Matilda, 23 Grattan, Grattan Center.
NICHOLS MRS. MARIA L., 27 Caledonia, Alaska.
Nichols Uriah, M., Rockford.
NICHOLSON WM. D., 8 Nelson, Cedar Springs.
NICKOLS ABRAM, 12 Lowell, Lowell.
Nickols Benj. F., 11 Lowell, Lowell.
Niehaus Henry, 23 Alpine, G. Rapids.
Nightlinger John, 36 Vergennes, Lowell
Niles Edgar, 28 Ada, Ada.
Nippress Gilbert, 20 Lowell, Lowell.
Nippress Thomas, 14 Ada, Ada.
Nippress William, 20 Lowell, Lowell.

Nixon Martin, 7 Plainfield, Englishville
Nobbs Matthew, 11 Paris, Grand Rapids
Noble B. R., Lowell.
Noble Benj. C., 16 Oakfield, Oakfield.
NOBLES ERASTUS, 17 Sparta, Lisbon.
Noble Joseph, 20 Cannon, Austerlitz.
NOBLE JOHN, 5 Nelson, Sand Lake.
Noel John, 17 Wyoming, Grandville.
NOEL PETER R., 20 Wyoming, Grandville.
Nolen Henry, 6 Sparta, Lisbon.
Nolon John, 7 Walker, Grand Rapids.
Noonan John, 31 Plainfield, Grand Rapids.
Noonan John, 3 Grand Rapids.
Noonan Peter, 3 Grand Rapids.
Noonan Thomas, 25 Cannon, Cannonsburg.
Noonan William, 3 Grand Rapids.
Noonan William, 25 Cannon, Cannonsburg.
Norcutt Daniel, 4 Lowell, Lowell.
Norman Edward, 24 Byron, Cody's Mills.
Norman Samuel, Lowell.
Normen John, 3 Cannon, Bostwick Lake.
North Abram, 22 Plainfield, Austerlitz.
North Giles, 22 Plainfield, Austerlitz.
NORTON ANSON N., 4 Wyoming, Grand Rapids.
NORTON AARON, 7 Spencer, Spencer Mill.
Norton C. C., 13 Walker, G. Rapids.
NORTON ERASTUS W., 3 Sparta Sparta Center.
Norton Fred A., Lowell.
NORTON JAMES W., Lowell.
NORTON JOHN, 24 Alpine, Alpine.
Norton James, 27 Oakfield, Ashley.
Norton John, 27 Oakfield, Ashley.
Norton John, 22 Oakfield, Ashley.
Norton John, 34 Courtland, Rockford.
Norton M., 8 Grand Rapids, G. Rapids.
Norton Mary, 35 Oakfield, Ashley.
NORTON NELSON A., 23 Alpine, Alpine.
Norton Patrick, 22 Oakfield, Ashley.
Notting Albert, Grandville.
Noy Thomas, 21 Cannon, Cannonsburg.
Nugent Daniel, 24 Cannon, Cannonsburg.
Nugent Emanuel, 6 Grattan, Grattan Center.
Nugent Hugh, 24 Cannon, Cannonsburg.
Nugent James, 24 Cannon, Cannonsburg.

North Mrs. Helen, 6 Bowne, Alaska.
North James, 20 Lowell, Lowell.
North Robert, Rockford.
North Robert, 22 Plainfield, Austerlitz.
Northrup Needham, 13 Algoma, Edgerton.
Northrup Olivier L., 21 Cannon, Rockford.
Nugent John, 24 Cannon, Cannonsburg
Nugent Russell, 16 Byron, Byron Cen.
Nulty James, 31 Cascade, Alaska.
Numa Henry, Cedar Springs.
NUTLER JOHN M., 3 Cannon, Rockford.
NYE LEONARD J., 25 Gaines, Hammond.

O

Obely Caleb, 25 Vergennes, Lowell.
O'Brien Daniel, 11 Wyoming, Grand Rapids.
O'Brien Dennis, 25 Alpine, Mill Creek.
O'Brien James, 25 Alpine, Mill Creek.
O'Brien Michael, 30 Walker, G. Rapids.
O'Brien Michael, 26 Oakfield, Ashley.
O'Brien Mary, 26 Oakfield, Ashley.
O'Brien Patrick, 29 Walker, G. Rapids.
O'BRIEN STEPHEN, 32 Walker, Grand Rapids.
O'Brien Scalley, 26 Grattan, Grant.
O'Brien Timothy, 3 Lowell, Lowell.
O'Brien William, 30 Bowne, Harris Creek.
O'Brien William, 34 Walker, G. Rapids
O'Brien William, 30 Walker, G. Rapids
O'Brien William, 26 Oakfield, Ashley.
O'Conner John, 20 Paris, Grand Rapids
O'Conner John, 34 Caledonia, Caledonia Station.
ODELL ADELBERT, 20 Vergennes, Vergennes.
Odell Charles, Lowell.
Odell Orson, 9 Courtland, Courtland Center.

Odell Mrs. Silence W., 20 Vergennes, Vergennes.
Odell Simeon J., Lowell.
O'Donald James, 26 Plainfield, Austerlitz.
O'Donald John, 24 Plainfield, Austerlitz.
O'DONNELL MICHAEL, 16 Ada, Ada.
O'Farrell Garret, 16 Wyoming, Grandville.
Offen George, 4 Nelson, Sand Lake.
Offen Justus, 10 Nelson, Nelson.
Ogden William L., 23 Cascade, Ada.
Ogg Andrew, 10 Nelson, Sand Lake.
Ogg John, 3 Nelson, Sand Lake.
OGILVIE ALEXANDER, 6 Grattan, Grattan Center.
Ogilvie John, 6 Grattan, Grattan Cen.
O'Haire Michael, 1 Wyoming, Grand Rapids.
O'Hara H., 23 Lowell, Lowell.
O'Heran Timothy, 34 Walker, Grand Rapids.
Ohler Adam, Grandville.
Ohler Jacob, 24 Sparta, Sparta Center.
Ohler Peter, 32 Walker, Grand Rapids.
O'Keefe James, 34 Walker, Gr. Rapids.
OMANS LEVI, 33 Cannon, Cannonsburg.
Onan Alex. J., 17 Lowell, Lowell.
Onan Gabriel, 13 Vergennes, Lowell.
ONAN SAMUEL, 17 Lowell, Lowell.
O'Neil Cornelius, 19 Paris, Gr. Rapids.
O'Neil Dennis, 19 Paris, Grand Rapids.
O'Neill Daniel, 8 Walker, Gr. Rapids.
ORCOTT SAMUEL G., 33 Tyrone, Sparta Center.
ORCUTT Mrs. J. S., 32 Solon, Cedar Springs.
Orcutt Matthew, 20 Plainfield, Austerlitz.
Orcutt Samuel, 32 Solon, Cedar Springs.
Orlop John, 28 Ada, Ada.
Orlop Jacob, 28 Ada, Ada.
Orman Patrick, 31 Walker, G. Rapids.
Ormiston James B., Lowell.
Orr Peter A., Rockford.
Orrin Albert N., 1 Wyoming, Grand Rapids.
Orser Henry, 25 Sparta, Sparta Center.
ORTH BERNARD, 20 Grand Rapids.
Orth Peter, 20 Grand Rapids.
Osborn Dan'l, 19 Lowell, Cascade.
Osborn David, 33 Ada, Ada.
OSBORN GEORGE W., 21 Wyoming, Grand Rapids.

Olbske Joseph, 8 Walker, Indian Creek.
Olcott Mrs. Elizabeth H., 11 Lowell, Lowell.
Olcott Philander W., 11 Lowell, Lowell.
OLDFIELD CHAS., Cedar Springs.
OLDS ALBERT, 22 Wyoming, Grandville.
Olds Mathew, 16 Grattan, Grattan Cen.
O'Leary Mrs. Margaret, Cedar Springs.
Oleson John, 8 Grand Rapids.
Olin John C., 32 Solon, Cedar Springs.
Olin Osmond, 2 Alpine, Englishville.
Olin Henry, 15 Lowell, Lowell.
Olish Hubert, 35 Alpine, G. Rapids.
Olish Joseph, 35 Alpine, G. Rapids.
Olish Matthias, 24 Alpine, Alpine.
Oliver John, Grandville.
Oliver William, 36 Grand Rapids.
Olmsted Gideon, 25 Solon, Cedar Springs.
Olmsted Isaac, 25 Solon, Cedar Springs.
Olmsted Joseph, Sparta Center.
OLMSTED ROBERT, 19 Oakfield, Oakfield.
OLMSTED W. C., Sparta Center.
Olmstead W. I., Sparta Center.
OSBORN HIRAM, Alaska Village.
Osburn Albert, 11 Tyrone, Sparta Cen
Osburn Eli, 10 Tyrone, Sparta Center.
Osgood Harry, 10 Oakfield, Oakfield.
O'SHIRTZ HENRY, 21 Wyoming, Grandville.
Osmar Henry, 35 Cannon, Cannonsburg.
OSTERHAND P., Cedar Springs.
Osterwick Matthew, 18 Wyoming, Grandville.
Osterhouse Jacob, 14 Paris, Grand Rapids.
Osterhouse Nicholas, 22 Paris, Grand Rapids.
Osterhuis George, 18 Wyoming, Grandville.
Osterhuis Henry, Grandville.
Osterhuis Nicholas, Grandville.
OSTROM JACOB L., 32 Paris, Grand Rapids.
O'Sullivan Timothy, 30 Walker, Grand Rapids.
Otis John, 16 Paris, Grand Rapids.
Otterbach Christian, 28 Spencer, Spencer Mills.

Otterbach Gottlib, 28 Spencer, Spencer Mills.
Otterbach John, 20 Spencer, Nelson.
Otterbach Jacob, 19 Spencer, Nelson.
Otterbien Ambrose, 18 Walker, Grand Rapids.
Outhouse Geo. H , 11 Plainfield, Rockford.
Overholt Abraham, 10 Gaines, Hammond.
Overholt Amos, 10 Gaines, Hammond.
Overholt John, 10 Gaines, Hammond.
Overholt William, 10 Gaines, Hammond.
Overbeck Francis, 29 Grand Rapids.
Overlay Martin, 11 Nelson, Nelson.
Overlay Thomas, 5 Nelson, Sand Lake.
Ovenshire John F., 18 Lowell, Lowell.
Ovenshire Richard G., 18 Lowell, Lowell.
OWEN HIRAM G., 3 Oakfield, Greenville.
Owen James H., Lowell.
OWEN TALBOT L., 6 Ada, Ada.

P

Packard John, 25 Byron, Cody's Mills.
Page George, 29 Lowell, Lowell.
Page Wright, 35 Byron, Cody's Mills.
Paine Ephraim, 4 Walker, Indian Creek
Paine Hiram H., 34 Wyoming, Grand Rapids.
Paine Lawson A., 3 Alpine, Englishville.
Paine Marvin H., Cedar Springs.
Paine R. N.. 34 Sparta, Englishville.
PAKE KRYNNES, 29 Grand Rapids, Grand Rapids.
Pangborn Luther W., Burchville (Burch's Mills.)
Pangborn Samuel, Cedar Springs.
PANGBORN SALMON H., Burchville (Burch's Mills.)
Pannell John, 11 Walker, Grand Rapids
Pardee Eli, 14 Bowne, Bowne.
Pardee James W., 24 Bowne, Bowne.
Pardee Ozi, 14 Bowne, Bowne.
PARDEE WAYNE, 13 Bowne, Bowne.
Parish Leonard, 5 Algoma, Cedar Springs.

Palmatier Daniel. 27 Walker, Grand Rapids.
Palmer Amos, 8 Caledonia, Alaska.
Palmer Alonzo J., 4 Byron, North Byron.
Palmer Amos W., 15 Caledonia, Alaska
Palmer Alexander, 32 Byron, Byron Center.
Palmer Benjamin, 32 Solon, Cedar Springs.
PALMER CHARLES, 32 Solon, Cedar Springs.
Palmer Carlos H., 25 Paris, Alaska.
Palmer Davis, 33 Spencer, Spencer Mills.
Palmer Geo. F., 14 Paris, Grand Rapids
Palmer Hiram, 17 Caledonia, Alaska.
PALMER LOYAL, 29 Byron, Byron Center.
PALMER L. E., 9 Grand Rapids.
Palmer Oliver, 22 Solon, Cedar Springs
PALMERLEE HEMAN, 2 Walker, Grand Rapids.
Palmiter Edson, 13 Lowell, Lowell.
PANGBORN ALBERT, Cedar Springs
Pangborn Joel S., Cedar Springs.
Parker Charles, 10 Oakfield, Oakfield.
PARKER ELIAS D., 4 Lowell, Lowell.
Parker Elisha D., 3 Caledonia, Alaska.
Parker George, 4 Lowell, Lowell.
Parker G. W., Lowell.
PARKER GEORGE J., 7 Walker, Grand Rapids.
Parker Henry W., 27 Oakfield, Ashley.
Parker James, Cedar Springs.
Parker Jane, 7 Vergennes, Vergennes.
Parker John, 5 Nelson, Sand Lake.
Parker Leonard F., 7 Walker, Grand Rapids.
Parker Thomas, 18 Bowne, Alto.
Parker Robert, 7 Vergennes, Vergennes.
PARKER SHELDON, 21 Vergennes, Lowell.
PARKER THOS., Jr., 4 Nelson, Sand Lake.
Parker Thos., Senr., 4 Nelson, Sand Lake.
Parker Wm. H., 31 Vergennes, Lowell.
Parker Wm. H., Jr., 31 Vergennes, Lowell.
Parker Wilson J., 4 Bowne, Alto.
PARKHURST ISABELLA, 19 Plainfield, Alpine.

PARKINSON HENRY, 8 Courtland, Courtland Center.
Parkinson Robert, 8 Courtland, Courtland Center.
Parks Beriah G., 19 Spencer, Nelson.
PARKS C. C., Lowell.
Parks Leonard C., Alaska.
Parks Mortimer, Lowell.
Parks Oliver, 7 Bowne, Alaska.
Parks Wm. R., 6 Lowell, Lowell.
Parmer Abram H., 12 Courtland, Courtland Center.
PARMER LEWIS, 3 Oakfield, Greenville.
Parmlee John, 22 Walker, G. Rapids.
Parr John H, 6 Byron, Grandville.
Parr Stephen S., 6 Byron, Grandville.
Parrish C. B., Lowell.
Parrish Eugene, Lowell.
Parrott Clement, 33 Lowell, Lowell.
Parrott Chas. M. F., 28 Lowell, Lowell.
Parrott George, 32 Lowell, Lowell.
Parrott Jacob, 28 Lowell, Lowell.
Parshall Terry, 32 Spencer, Spencer Mills.
PARSHALL WILLIAM T., 32 Spencer, Spencer Mills.
Parsons William S., 5 Paris, Grand Rapids.
PATTERSON MINER, 13 Paris, Grand Rapids.
Patterson Perry W., 21 Paris, Grand Rapids.
Paterson Perry W., 21 Paris, Grand Rapids.
Paterson Peter, 19 Tyrone, Casnovia.
Patterson Robert, 12 Paris, Cascade.
Patterson Mrs. Rose A., 13 Paris, Grand Rapids.
Patterson Wm. P., 28 Plainfield, Grand Rapids.
Patterson Warren A , 13 Paris, Grand Rapids.
Patterson William, 12 Paris, Cascade.
PATTEN C. H., 20 Grand Rapids, Grand Rapids.
PATTEN MRS. S. L., 35 Alpine, Indian Creek.
PATTISON JOHN, 11 Caledonia, Alaska.
Pattison John, Jr., 11 Caledonia, Alaska.
Paul Anthony, 3 Paris, Grand Rapids.
Paul John, 34 Grand Rapids.
Payne Alonzo, 16 Algoma, Rockford.
Payne Daniel B., 11 Oakfield, Greenville.
Payne Lorenzo, 16 Algoma, Rockford.

Parter John, 31 Paris, Grand Rapids.
PASKIL GEO., 11 Lowell, Lowell.
Patchin William E., 11 Alpine, Alpine.
PATRICK M. A., 26 Cannon, Cannonsburg.
Pattee Asa D., 4 Alpine. Indian Creek.
PATTEE AMOS, 3 Walker, Indian Creek.
PATTEE E. D., Burchville, (Burch's Mills.)
Pattee Gustavus, 21 Sparta, Sparta Center.
PATTERSON ALEXANDER, 29 G. Rapids, Grand Rapids.
Paterson Adam, 19 Tyrone, Casnovia.
Patterson Chauncey, 19 Cascade, Cascade.
Patterson Franklin, 16 Cascade, Cascade.
PATTERSON GEO. W., 29 Bowne, Harris Creek.
Paterson James, 19 Tyrone, Casnovia.
Patterson John M., 19 Cascade, Cascade.
Patterson John, 24 Paris, G. Rapids.
PATTERSON JAMES, 12 Paris, Cascade.
Payne William, 16 Algoma, Rockford.
Peake Lemuel, Rockford.
Pearsall William, Lowell.
PEARSOLL SHERMAN M., 28 Alpine, Grand Rapids.
Peasley Albert, 23 Spencer, Spencer Mills.
Pease Charles D., Lowell.
Pease David P., 33 Sparta, Englishville
PEASE HERMON B., 1 Ada, Ada.
Pease Jerome C., Lowell.
Pease Lester, 24 Courtland, Courtland Center.
PEASLEY CHARLES, 26 Spencer, Spencer Mills.
Peasly Mrs. Marion, 23 Spencer, Spencer Mills.
Peasley Timothy, 35 Spencer, Spencer Mills.
Peat Charles, 6 Bowne, Alto.
PECK ARVINE, Lowell.
Peck C. W., 11 Lowell, Lowell.
Peck Charles, 13 Oakfield, Greenville.
Peck Horatio N., 16 Grand Rapids.
Peck H. B., Lowell.
Peck Horton B., 36 Vergennes, Lowell.
Peck E. R., 11 Lowell, Lowell.

Peck Horace, 13 Oakfield, Greenville.
Peck Manser W., 35 Paris, Hammond.
Peckham Hiram, 6 Plainfield, Belmont.
PECK FREELING W., 35 Paris, Grand Rapids.
Peel George, 34 Plainfield, Grand Rapids.
Peel Thomas, 34 Plainfield, G. Rapids.
Peet Enan, 2 Caledonia, Alaska.
Peet Edgar M., 27 Caledonia, Caledonia.
Peet Kosciusko, 31 Lowell, Alaska.
Peet Oscar D., 22 Caledonia, Alaska.
PEET ROLLA A., 1 Caledonia, Alaska.
Peice Edward, 22 Solon, Cedar Springs.
Peirce L. W., 11 Lowell, Lowell.
Peirce Walter J., 19 Vergennes, Vergennes.
Peirce Warren L., 35 Paris, G. Rapids.
Peiscth John, 31 Byron, Byron Center.
Pellet William H., 4 Courtland, Cedar Springs.
Pellet William, 27 Nelson, Cedar Springs.
Pelton Andrew J., 18 Gaines, Gainesville.
Pelton Alfred, 26 Byron, Cody's Mills.
Pelton Ephraim, 22 Walker, G. Rapids.
PERRIN WILLIAM P., 28 Vergennes, Lowell.
Perry Abijah S., 23 Byron, Cody's Mills.
Perry Albert A., 23 Byron, Cody's Mills.
PERRY ARTHUR E., 17 Plainfield, Belmont.
Perry Mrs. C. R., Lowell.
Perry Edmund, 17 Plainfield, Belmont.
Perry James S., 20 Algoma, Sparta Center.
Perry John D. D., 32 Vergennes, Lowell.
Perry M. M., Lowell.
Perry P. R., 23 Algoma, Rockford.
Perry Wm. H., 24 Ada, Vergennes.
PERRY WILLIAM, 3 Oakfield, Spencer Mills.
Perry Wm. R., Lowell.
Peters Charles, 13 Paris, Grand Rapids
Peters Isaac, 8 Cascade, Cascade.
Peters William, 9 Byron, Byron Center
Peters William, 13 Paris, Grand Rapids
Peterson Alonzo, 22 Courtland, Courtland Center.
Peterson Charles F., 32 Tyrone, Casnovia.

PELTON CHAUNCEY, Village of Cedar Springs.
PELTON J. M., 18 Gaines, Gainesville.
Pelton Samuel, 13 Byron, Gainesville.
Pember John W., 26 Plainfield, Austerlitz.
Penfield Edwin H., 25 Algoma, Rockford.
Pennel John W., 18 Paris, Gr. Rapids.
Pennington James, 34 Courtland, Rockford.
Penny Ross, Lowell.
Perean Richard, Burchville, (Burch's Mill.)
PERKINS CHARLES, Burchville, (Burch's Mill.)
Perkins C. J., 16 Grand Rapids.
Perkins C. S., 16 Grand Rapids.
Perkins Daniel, 9 Cascade, Cascade.
Perkins Erastus, 16 Bowne, Bowne.
Perkins James B., 8 Alpine, Pleasant.
Perkins Mrs. Lucy, 33 Ada, Ada.
Perkins William, 16 Bowne, Bowne.
PerLee Abraham F., 36 Alpine, Mill Creek.
Perrin Theodore, 28 Vergennes, Lowell.
Peterson Frank, 22 Cannon, Cannonsburg.
Peterson G., 32 Tyrone, Casnovia.
Peterson John, 24 Courtland, Courtland Center.
Peterson John, 1 Plainfield, Austerlitz.
Peterson Moses, 35 Oakfield, Ashley.
Peterson William, 20 Oakfield, Oakfield
Peterson Samuel, 20 Oakfield, Oakfield.
Peterson Simon P., 24 Courtland, Courtland Center.
PETERMAN JOHN, 29 Bowne, Harris Creek.
Petit Simon, 11 Lowell, Lowell.
PETTINGILL B. N., 26 Algoma, Rockford.
Pettingill Benjamin, 26 Algoma, Rockford.
Petrie Isaac, 13 Grattan, Otisco, Ionia County.
PETTED BERNARD, 5 Caledonia, Alaska.
PETTED DAVID, 20 Cascade, Cascade.
PETTIS EDWARD, 28 Ada, Ada.
Pfyffer Henry J., 34 Wyoming, North Byron.

Phelps Arthur, 17 Alpine, Grand Rapids
Phelps Asa G., 6 Paris, Grand Rapids.
PHELPS COUNT P., 32 Nelson, Cedar Springs.
Phelps Edgar, 31 Nelson, Cedar Springs
Phelps Eli M., 1 Courtland, Courtland Center.
Phelps G. W., Cedar Springs.
Phelps George, 4 Walker, Indian Creek
Phelps Henry, 9 Courtland, Courtland Center.
Phelps Horace, 10 Courtland, Courtland Center.
Phelps Isaac, 6 Grand Rapids, Grand Rapids.
Phelps Jeremiah, 10 Sparta, Sparta Center.
Phelps Lester, 8 Plainfield, Belmont.
Phelps Lester, 10 Courtland, Courtland Center.
Phelps Lester, 11 Courtland, Courtland Center.
Phelps Mrs. M. J., Lowell.
Phelps Sylvanus, 2 Courtland, Courtland Center.
PHELPS THEODORE, Cedar Springs.
Phelps Wellington, 10 Courtland, Courtland Center.
Phillips Luther E., 14 Plainfield, Austerlitz.
Phillips Levi, 24 Vergennes, Fallassburg.
Phillips Newton, 27 Sparta, Sparta Center.
Phillips Peter, 14 Paris, Grand Rapids.
PHILIPS JOHN, Grandville.
Phillips Spary E., 28 Bowne, Harris Creek.
PHILLIPS WILLIAM H., Burchville, (Burch's Mills.)
Phillips William, 27 Sparta, Sparta Center.
Phœnix Samuel W., 20 Paris, Grand Rapids.
Picard Joseph, Lowell.
Pickerd Adam, 14 Algoma, Edgerton.
PICKERD JOHN, 14 Algoma, Edgerton.
PICKET A. L., Rockford.
Picket Richard, 29 Grand Rapids.
PICKETT WM. B., 33 Gaines, Grand Rapids.
Pikaard John, 29 Grand Rapids.
PIERCE BARTON T., N. E. corner Walker, Mill Creek.
PIERCE CHARLES B., 10 Walker, Grand Rapids.

Phelps Zimri, 32 Nelson, Cedar Springs.
Philpott Abram, 12 Lowell, Lowell.
Phillips Calvin, 7 Cannon, Rockford.
Phillips Conrad, 17 Walker, Grand Rapids.
Phillips David, 3 Nelson, Sand Lake.
Phillips Daniel C., 27 Plainfield, Grand Rapids.
PHILLIPS EDWARD, Burchville, (Burch's Mills.)
Phillips Ensign, 1 Lowell, Lowell.
Phillips Eli C., 1 Lowell, Lowell.
PHILLIPS GEO. W., 7 Cannon, Rockford.
Philips Jerome E., 19 Paris, Grand Rapids.
PHILLIPS JOHN W., 21 Walker, G. Rapids.
Phillips James W., 24 Vergennes, Fallassburg.
Phillips Lewis, 3 Nelson, Sand Lake.
Phillips Levi L., 33 Plainfield, Grand Rapids.
Phillips Lewis, 27 Bowne, Fillmore, Barry County.
Pierce Lewis, 22 Paris, Grand Rapids.
Pierce Solomon, 10 Walker, Grand Rapids.
Pierce Stephen, 27 Grand Rapids.
Pierce Walter, 27 Grand Rapids.
Pierce Warren E., 21 Grand Rapids.
Pierson William, 29 Courtland, Rockford.
PIERCE WARREN H., 14 Gaines, Hammond.
PIERCE WM. W., 2 Gaines, Hammond
Pierson Mrs. C. M., 36 Algoma, Rockford.
Pierson George, 34 Algoma, Rockford.
Pifer Charles W., 7 Gaines, Gainesville.
Pillen Adolphus, 11 Lowell, Lowell.
PINKNEY WM. B., 16 Plainfield, Belmont.
Pinkerton Andrew, 26 Tyrone, Sparta Center.
PINTLER CURTIS, Lisbon.
Pintler Harmon, 14 Bowne, Bowne.
Pintler Mrs. Mary, Lisbon.
Pintler William, 7 Tyrone, Casnovia.
Pisot Henry, 7 Walker, Grand Rapids.
Pitcher Benjamin, 22 Oakfield, Oakfield
Pitcher Harrison, Village Cannonsburg

Pitch Martin, 22 Alpine, Alpine.
Pitts Ransom, 30 Wyoming, Grandville
Pitts William, 7 Courtland, Edgerton.
Pixley Lewis R., 15 Grattan, Grattan Center.
Place Arthur, 5 Alpine, Lisbon.
Plaice Charles, 13 Lowell, Lowell.
PLANK JAMES, 26 Plainfield, Austerlitz.
PLANK JAMES, 8 Cannon, Rockford.
Plass John, 27 Algoma, Rockford.
Platchley John, Cedar Springs.
Platte John, 35 Alpine, Grand Rapids.
Pletcher Daniel E., 10 Lowell, Lowell.
PLEUNE ADRIAN, 15 Grand Rapids.
Pleune Peter, 15 Grand Rapids.
Plowman James, 31 Alpine, Berlin.
PLUMB ELI, 31 Plainfield, Mill Creek.
Plumpton George, 25 Algoma, Rockford.
Plumb Hiram, 18 Spencer, Nelson.
Plumb Henry D., 31 Plainfield, Mill Creek.
Plumb John, 24 Nelson, Nelson.
Poats Ira J., 12 Sparta, Sparta Center.
Poats Schuyler, 19 Algoma, Sparta Center.
Pollock John, 23 Plainfield, Austerlitz.
Poole A. J., 35 Solon, Cedar Springs.
PORTER PETER B., 24 Alpine, Alpine
Porter Ralph, 13 Nelson, Nelson.
Porter Sybean, Alaska.
PORTER SETH, 13 Algoma, Edgerton
Porter Sabine, 16 Caledonia, Alaska.
Porritt John, 28 Bowne, Harris Creek.
Porritt William, 27 Bowne, Bowne.
Post Asher, 7 Tyrone, Casnovia.
Post Alanson, 8 Plainfield, Belmont.
Post Aaron, 10 Courtland, Courtland Center.
Post Christopher, 8 Plainfield, Belmont.
POST GEO. C., 14 Lowell, Lowell.
Post Henry, 28 Algoma, Rockford.
POST J. CARTER, 14 Lowell, Lowell.
Post John, 8 Plainfield, Belmont.
POST JACOB, 8 Plainfield, Belmont.
Post Jacob, jr., 8 Plainfield, Belmont.
Poss John, 30 Plainfield, Mill Creek.
Post Jacob, 10 Walker, Grand Rapids.
Post John, 32 Grand Rapids.
Post Leander J., 14 Lowell, Lowell.
Post McKenzie, 18 Vergennes, Vergennes.
POST PHILIP, 16 Plainfield, Belmont.
Post Robert, 7 Tyrone, Casnovia.
POST SAMUEL, 8 Plainfield, Belmont.
Post William, 23 Plainfield, Austerlitz.

POOLE CLEWREY, 14 Bowne, Bowne
Poole Henry, 14 Bowne, Bowne.
Poole N. C., 35 Solon, Cedar Springs.
Pool Samuel J., 19 Ada, Ada.
Poole S. J., 35 Solon, Cedar Springs.
Pool Wm. A., 21 Paris, Grand Rapids.
Pope George, 4 Plainfield, Belmont.
Pope Mrs. S., 9 Algoma, Rockford.
Pond Cyrus, 35 Oakfield, Ashley.
Pond Edron H., 35 Oakfield, Ashley.
POND HARVEY D., 34 Oakfield, Ashley.
Pond Trafton, 19 Courtland, Rockford.
Ponting Benjamin, 18 Vergennes, Vergennes.
Porter Curtis, 21 Alpine, Grand Rapids
Porter Henry, 20 Alpine, Indian Creek.
Porter Dennis, 17 Courtland, Edgerton
Porter David C., 21 Alpine, G. Rapids.
PORTER GEORGE, 29 Alpine, Indian Creek.
Porter John, 10 Wyoming, G. Rapids.
PORTER LORENZO, 1 Gaines, Hammond.
Porter Martilus, 13 Nelson, Nelson.
Porter Sorens L., 2 Plainfield, Rockford.
Potratz Albert, 20 Lowell, Lowell.
Potter Benjamin, 21 Oakfield, Oakfield.
Potter John, 19 Paris, Grand Rapids.
Potter Joshua, 21 Oakfield, Oakfield.
Potter John, 21 Oakfield, Oakfield.
Potter Joel, 4 Nelson, Sand Lake.
Potter Myron, 12 Oakfield, Greenville.
Potter Mrs. Lois, Sparta Center.
Potter Wm. A., 4 Nelson, Sand Lake.
Pottraz John, 26 Ada, Ada.
Powers A. L., 29 Grand Rapids, Grand Rapids.
POWERS A., 29 Grand Rapids, Grand Rapids.
Powers George W., 19 Algoma, Sparta Center.
Powers Henry, 11 Sparta, Sparta Cen.
POWERS JOHN, 31 Walker, Grand Rapids.
Powers Jonathan, 4 Paris, Gr. Rapids.
Powers John, 28 Ada, Ada.
POWERS J. C., Burchville, (Burch's Mills.)
Powers Mrs. Mary, 20 Walker, Grand Rapids.
Powers Wm., south 5 Walker, Grand Rapids.

Powell Chauncey, Grandville.
Powell Edward, 30 Ada, Ada.
Powell George S., Rockford.
Powell George, Burchville, (Burch's Mills.)
Powell Oscar F., Grandville.
Powell Silas, Grandville.
Powell William, Rockford.
Powell William B., 27 Spencer, Spencer Mills.
Powlison Cornelius, Lowell.
Pratt Asa, 20 Grand Rapids.
Pratt Charles, 27 Vergennes, Lowell.
Pratt Charles, Rockford.
Pratt Charles K., Rockford.
Pratt David C., 9 Cannon, Cannonsburg.
Pratt Elijah V. E., 22 Caledonia, Alaska.
Pratt J. Edwin, 26 Vergennes, Lowell.
PRATT LUTHER C., 10 Solon, Cedar Springs.
Pratt Marshall T., 5 Byron, North Byron.
Pratt Polycarpus S., 26 Vergennes, Lowell.
PRATT URIAH, south 7 Walker, Grand Rapids.
Prentiss Mrs., Lowell.
Proctor Benjamin, Alaska Village.
Proctor Henry H., Alaska.
Proctor Henry, 27 Lowell, Lowell.
Proctor John T., 34 Cascade, Alaska.
Proctor John, 8 Courtland, Courtland Center.
PROCTOR J. B., 35 Caledonia, Caledonia.
Proctor John, 27 Lowell, Lowell.
PROCTOR OLIVER, 26 Cascade, Alaska.
Proctor Wm., Jr., 27 Lowell, Lowell.
Proctor William, 27 Lowell, Lowell.
Proper John, 18 Nelson, Cedar Springs.
PROPER WILLIAM, 14 Solon, Cedar Springs.
PROVIN ANDREW J., 9 Cannon, Cannonsburg.
PROVIN CHAS. A., 16 Cannon, Cannonsburg.
Provin James, 16 Cannon, Cannonsburg.
Provin Tyler W., 17 Cannon, Cannonsburg.
Puddefoot Alfred, Sparta Center.
Pugh A. J., 8 Alpine, Pleasant.
Pugh James, 8 Alpine, Pleasant.
Pullen William, Lowell.

Prentice Byron, Cedar Springs.
PRENTICE ISAAC, 36 Solon, Cedar Springs.
Prentice Richard, 1 Caledonia, Alaska.
PRESCOTT BENJAMIN, 36 Grand Rapids.
Prescott Geo. W., 1 Paris, Gr. Rapids.
Prescott Price H., Rockford.
Prescott William H., Rockford.
Pressey Ransom R., 36 Sparta, Englishville.
Pressey Thomas, 28 Tyrone, Casnovia.
Prestage Henry, 18 Nelson, Cedar Springs.
Preston Sheldon, 27 Walker, Grand Rapids.
Preston John, 17 Alpine, Pleasant.
Price Arthur, 33 Ada, Ada.
PRICE GEORGE, Village of Cannonsburg.
Price Luther G., 29 Vergennes, Vergennes.
PRICE LEWIS N., 30 Nelson, Cedar Springs.
PRINDLE MRS. MARY L., 35 Byron, Cody's Mills.
Prindle Seth, 26 Byron, Cody's Mills.
Pulver Henry N., 26 Sparta, Sparta Center.
Pulte August, 23 Alpine, Grand Rapids
PUNCHES SAMUEL, 20 Nelson, Cedar Springs.
PURDY GEO. W., 25 Grattan, Smyrna, Ionia County.
PURDY HERMAN D., 33 Gaines, Cody's Mills.
Purdy Henry, 14 Grattan, Grant.
Purdy James L., 14 Grattan, Grattan Center.
Purdy John, 25 Grattan, Smyrna, Ionia County.
Purdy Orrin, 16 Grattan, Grattan Cen.
PURDY PERRY, 23 Grattan, Grant.
Purple Daniel, 34 Ada, Ada.
Purple James, 34 Ada, Ada.
Purple Thomas, 34 Ada, Ada.
Purple William, 5 Lowell, Lowell.
PURSEL WM. R., 18 Gaines, Gainesville.
Putnam Alpheus, 6 Cannon, Rockford.
Putnam Chester B., 3 Wyoming, Grand Rapids.
Putnam John, 20 Lowell, Lowell.
Putnam Mrs. Maria, 23 Bowne, Bowne.

Pysher Frederick H., 2 Byron, North Bryon.
Pysher Wm. W., 12 Byron, Gainesville.

Q

Quackenbos Abram, 35 Byron, Cody's Mills.
Quackenbos Wm. P., 35 Byron, Cody's Mills.
QUICK J. H., Lowell.
Quick John, Grandville.
Quick M. S., Lowell.
Quick Reuben S., Lowell.
Quiggle Silas P., 14 Cascade, Cascade.
Quigley Edward R., 30 Tyrone, Casnovia.
Quigley George, 1 Paris, Grand Rapids
Quigley Joseph, 34 Walker, G. Rapids.
Quillin Andrew, 8 Vergennes, Vergennes.
Quillin John, 8 Vergennes, Vergennes.
Quillin Terry, 8 Vergennes, Vergennes.
Quimby Isaac, 10 Nelson, Sand Lake.
Quinsey George, 32 Gaines, Cody's Mills.
Quinsey John, 32 Gaines, Cody's Mills.
Quinsey Mrs. Julia, 32 Gaines, Cody's Mills.
Quinn Daniel, 30 Wyoming, Grandville
Quinn Patrick, 30 Wyoming, Grandville.
Quirk Patrick, 12 Wyoming, G. Rapids
Quirk William, 20 Wyoming, Grandville.

R

Raap Antoine, 1 Wyoming, G. Rapids.
Race Alvin S., 36 Lowell, Lowell.
Race Abraham, 12 Algoma, Burchville (Burch's Mills.)
Race Peter, 6 Paris, Grand Rapids.
Raddigan John, 31 Grattan, Cannonsburg.
Rafferty Mrs. Ann, 8 Walker, Grand Rapids.
Rafferty George, 8 Walker, G. Rapids.
Ragan James, Lowell.
Ramer Samuel, 18 Courtland, Edgerton.
Ramsdill Moses, 15 Alpine, Alpine.
Ramsdill Orrin, 15 Alpine, Alpine.
RAMSDELL JACOB, Lowell.
RAMSDELL SOLOMON, 17 Grattan, Grattan Center.
RANDALL HORATIO, 33 Grand Rapids, Grand Rapids.
RANDALL JOHN L., 16 Grattan, Grattan Center.
RANDALL KINNICUM, 34 Oakfield, Ashley.
Randall Romanzo, 26 Oakfield, Ashley.
Randall Richard F., 20 Sparta, Lisbon.
RANDEL EDMOND S., 10 Cannon, Bostwick Lake.
RANDEL SILAS, 10 Cannon, Bostwick Lake.
Rankin Albert D., 19 Wyoming, Grandville.
RANKIN DWIGHT, 19 Wyoming, Grandville.
Ranney George, 30 Grattan, Cannonsburg.
Ransley John R., 3 Oakfield, Spencer Mills.
Rapelyea John, 17 Plainfield, Austerlitz.
Rarich William, 8 Courtland, Courtland Center.
Rarick Jacob, 12 Sparta, Sparta Cen.
RARICK JOHN D., 13 Sparta, Sparta Center.
Rathbone D. S., 29 Plainfield, Grand Rapids.
Rathbun Seba, 29 Plainfield, Grand Rapids.
RATHBUN G. B., 28 Grand Rapids.
Rathbun Hugo B., 16 Paris, Grand Rapids.
Rathbun James, 26 Caledonia. Caledonia.

RATHBUN LANSING K., 17 Paris, Grand Rapids.
RATHBUN LEVI C., 26 Caledonia, Caledonia.
Rathbun Orsemus, 4 Wyoming, Grandville.
RATHBUN ORSEMUS, 26 Caledonia, Caledonia.
Rathbun Thomas, 35 Caledonia, Caledonia.
Raub Andrew, 27 Spencer, Spencer Mills.
RAUCH JACOB, 6 Byron, Grandville.
Raymer John, 1 Solon, Sand Lake.
Raymond Leander, 15 Sparta, Sparta Center.
Raymond Leander A., 15 Sparta, Sparta Center.
Read Mrs. Loritta, 16 Caledonia, Alaska.
READ THOMAS M., 7 Gaines, Gainesville.
Reagan Dennis, 10 Vergennes, Alton.
Reams Abram, 12 Byron, Gainesville.
Reams John, 10 Courtland, Courtland Center.
Reardon John, 29 Cascade, Cascade.
Rebels Arselas, 26 Lowell, Lowell.
REED NATHANIEL, 27 Bowne, Bowne.
Reed Seymour A., 22 Plainfield, Austerlitz.
Reed Thomas E., 33 Grand Rapids, Grand Rapids.
Reed Theophilus, 11 Paris, Gr. Rapids.
Reed Theophilus, jr., 11 Paris, Grand Rapids.
Reen Timothy, 34 Walker, Gr. Rapids.
REES GUSTAVUS, Lowell.
Rees Theodore, Lowell.
Reese Harmon, 2 Wyoming, Grand Rapids.
REESE OSCAR, Lowell.
REEVES L. F., 28 Cannon, Cannonsburg.
Reid John, 2 Grattan, Grattan Center.
Reid Thomas, 1 Grattan, Ashley.
Reish Peter, 16 Courtland, Courtland Center.
Reiley Edward, 24 Caledonia, Caledonia.
Remington M., jr., 11 Lowell, Lowell.
REMINGTON WAGAR T., 4 Bowne, Alto.
RENHLAN SOLOMON, 23 Walker, Grand Rapids.

Rebroon Edward, 7 Algoma, Sparta Center.
Rockford Rollin, 11 Grand Rapids.
Rector Benjamin, 24 Algoma, Edgerton.
RECTOR EDWARD, 30 Courtland, Rockford.
Rector George, 14 Algoma, Edgerton.
RECTOR HENRY E., 23 Algoma, Rockford.
Rector Jacob, 1 Algoma, Burchville, (Burch's Mill.)
Rector William F., 14 Cascade, Cascade.
Redinger Michael, 35 Lowell, Lowell.
Redinger Gaudloupe, 35 Lowell, Lowell.
Redinger John, 35 Lowell, Lowell.
Redmire John, 17 Walker, G. Rapids.
Redmon John, 11 Courtland, Courtland Center.
REED GIBSON D., 13 Grattan, Otisco, Ionia County.
Reed Horace, 27 Bowne, Bowne.
Reed Henry G., 25 Wyoming, Grand Rapids.
Reed Horace W., 7 Paris, G. Rapids.
REED HARRISON, 32 Grand Rapids.
Renishagen Jacob, 12 Plainfield, Rockford.
Ream Andrew, 1 Wyoming, Grand Rapids.
Rennehen John, 34 Walker, Grand Rapids.
RESH CHARLES, 13 Alpine, Alpine.
Ressequye Harvey, 35 Solon, Cedar Springs.
Retan Andrew E., 33 Wyoming, North Byron.
RETAN JOHN R., 33 Wyoming, North Byron.
RETTINGER WILLIAM, 26 Spencer, Spencer Mills.
Reuletsterz Philip, Lowell.
Rewshaw Francis, South 7 Walker, Grand Rapids.
Rexford William, 24 Vergennes, Fallassburg.
Rexford Alanson, 32 Tyrone, Casnovia.
Rexford Amos, 31 Tyrone, Casnovia.
Rexford David, 31 Tyrone, Casnovia.
Rexford Daniel, 31 Tyrone, Casnovia.
Reynolds Alexander, 11 Nelson, Nelson
Reynolds Benj. F., 10 Cannon, Cannonsburg.

Reynolds Bradley, 1 Plainfield, Rockford.
REYNOLDS D. L., Rockford.
Reynolds Elisha, 19 Lowell, Lowell.
Reynolds George N., 14 Plainfield, Austerlitz.
Reynolds Ira, 14 Plainfield, Austerlitz.
REYNOLD JAMES S., 29 Gaines, Grand Rapids.
Reynolds John M., 14 Plainfield, Austerlitz.
Reynolds Levi, 14 Sparta, Sparta Cen.
Reynolds J. Mason, 20 Plainfield, Austerlitz.
Reynolds Moses, 32 Oakfield, Oakfield.
Reynolds Myron, 25 Nelson, Cedar Springs.
Reynolds Orville, 19 Lowell, Cascade.
REYNOLDS PATRICK, 30 Gaines, Cody's Mills.
Reynolds Stephen, 35 Grattan, Alton.
Reynolds Steven, 27 Sparta, Sparta Cen
RHINES DANIEL, 11 Lowell, Lowell.
RHOADES JOHN H., 20 Spencer, Nelson.
RHODES HIRAM A., 17 Ada, Ada.
Rhodes J. H., 36 Grattan, Grant.
Rhodes John, 36 Grattan, Alton.
Rice Elihu, 27 Sparta, Sparta Center.
Richards Horace, 2 Paris, Gr. Rapids.
RICHARDS HENRY S., 22 Caledonia, Alaska.
Richards J. B., 36 Algoma, Rockford.
RICHARDS J. C., Cedar Springs.
Richards Myron, 10 Paris, Gr. Rapids.
Richards Simeon, Alaska Village.
Richards Truman, 12 Paris, Grand Rapids.
Richards Theodore F., 26 Walker, Grand Rapids.
Richards Warren, 16 Caledonia, Alaska.
Richards Wilson H., 10 Paris, Grand Rapids.
Richardson Andrew, 23 Plainfield, Austerlitz.
Richardson Cornelius, 25 Courtland, Courtland Center.
RICHARDSON CHARLES H., 1 Bowne, South Boston.
Richardson George S., 9 Cascade, Cascade.
Richardson Geo. S., jr., 11 Paris, Gr. Rapids.
RICHARDSON JOSEPH H., 36 Bowne, Fillmore, Barry County.
Richardson Norman, 26 Plainfield, Austerlitz.

Rice Geo. H., 24 Alpine, Alpine.
RICE HUGH, 24 Alpine, Alpine.
Rice H. A., Lowell.
Rice John, 32 Solon, Cedar Springs.
Rice James, 21 Plainfield, Belmont.
Rice Lewis, 30 Nelson, Cedar Springs.
Rice Newell J., 11 Byron, Gainesville.
RICE OREN S., 27 Sparta, Sparta Cen.
Rice Russell, 19 Plainfield, Austerlitz.
Rice Timothy F., 11 Byron, Gainesville
Rice W. F., 24 Alpine, Alpine.
Rice William, 13 Alpine, Alpine.
Richards Alvin, 10 Paris, Grand Rapids
RICHARDS BEZAL E., Alaska Village.
Richards Daniel C., 9 Algoma, Rockford.
Richards Daniel C., 4 Algoma, Rockford.
Richards Edward, 16 Caledonia, Alaska
Richards Erbin, 10 Paris, Grand Rapids
Richards Francis, 8 Paris, Grand Rapids
Richarts Frederick, 35 Wyoming, Grand Rapids.
Richards Fletcher, 9 Algoma, Rockford.
Richards Frank, 17 Paris, Gr. Rapids.
Richards Gilbert, 8 Cascade, Cascade.
Richens Paul H., 15 Wyoming, Grand Rapids.
Rickets Henry, 17 Wyoming, Grandville.
Ricketts William, Lowell.
Richley Jerry, 34 Ada, Ada.
Richmire Augustus, 30 Plainfield, Mill Creek.
RICHMOND BENJAMIN F., 10 Walker, Grand Rapids.
Richmond David, Cedar Springs.
Richmond Mrs. Emma, 11 Gr. Rapids.
Richmond Fred J., 14 Vergennes, Lowell.
Richmond James C., 14 Vergennes, Lowell.
Richmond Olney A., 31 Nelson, Cedar Springs.
Rich Albert P., Lowell.
Rich Frank H., 12 Oakfield, Greenville.
Rich Nelson, 29 Oakfield, Oakfield.
Rider James, 19 Sparta, Lisbon.
Rider Mortise, 26 Alpine, Gr. Rapids.
Ridgeway Levi, 24 Nelson, Nelson.
RIGGS AUGUSTUS H., 24 Ada, Ada.
Riggs E. W., Lowell.

Riggs Orville A., 32 Gaines, Cody's Mills.
Rihbien Earnest, 23 Walker, G. Rapids
RILEY E. E., Cedar Springs.
RILEY EDWARD E., Cedar Springs.
Riley Hugh, 24 Plainfield, Austerlitz.
Riley Isaac, 1 Solon, Sand Lake.
Riley Patrick, 24 Plainfield, Austerlitz.
Riley Thomas, 32 Spencer, Spencer Mills.
Ringuet Henry M., Lowell.
Riordan Michael, 5 Caledonia, Alaska.
Riplow John, 2 Wyoming, Grand Rapids
Rippey Matthew F., 14 Plainfield, Austerlitz.
Risedorph Henry, Lisbon.
Rish Henry, 17 Paris, Grand Rapids.
Rietchow Louis, 35 Wyoming, Grand Rapids.
RITENGER FREDERICK, 2 Bowne, Alto.
ROACH ANTHONY, 8 Lowell, Lowell.
Roach Thomas, 8 Lowell, Lowell.
Roach Thomas, 18 Grand Rapids, Grand Rapids.
Roback Richard, 12 Solon, Rockford.
Robbins Mrs. Elizabeth, 7 Caledonia, Alaska.
Robbins Eber, Cedar Springs.
ROBINSON E. W., 7 Grand Rapids, Grand Rapids.
Robinson G. F., 7 Grand Rapids, Gr. Rapids.
ROBINSON JOHN, 20 Algoma, Sparta Center.
Robinson Jefferson, 35 Vergennes, Lowell.
ROBINSON JESSE H., 35 Tyrone, Sparta Center.
ROBINSON JOHN R., 34 Ada, Ada.
Robinson John T., 21 Lowell, Lowell.
ROBINSON JOHN, jr., 22 Paris, Gr. Rapids.
Robinson Oscar, Lowell.
Robinson James, 27 Paris, Gr. Rapids.
Robinson Jeremiah, 30 Courtland, Rockford.
Robinson Lucas J., 35 Vergennes, Lowell.
Robinson Lucas, 35 Vergennes, Lowell.
ROBINSON MUNSON, 20 Solon, Cedar Springs.
Robinson Mrs. M. H., 13 Algoma, Edgerton.
Robinson Mrs. Mary, Lowell.
Robinson Marion, 13 Algoma, Edgerton.

ROBBINS JOHN C., 7 Caledonia, Alaska.
Robbins John M., 26 Lowell, Lowell.
Robbins Warren, 26 Lowell, Lowell.
Robens Sanford, 16 Paris, Grand Rapids
Roberts Arthur, 5 Paris, Grand Rapids
Roberts Albert, Lowell.
ROBERTS MRS. CATHARINE, 17 Sparta, Lisbon.
Roberts Edson, 8 Sparta, Lisbon.
Roberts Ira, 31 Spencer, Cedar Springs.
Roberts Joseph, 6 Algoma, Sparta Cen.
Roberts Wm. H., Burchville (Burch's Mills.)
Roberts Wm. C., 12 Solon, Cedar Springs.
Roberts Wm. M., 6 Algoma, Sparta Center.
Roberson Wm. W., 24 Wyoming, Grand Rapids.
ROBERTSON DAVID, 33 Grand Rapids, Grand Rapids.
ROBERTSON GEORGE, Cedar Springs
Robinson Allen, 35 Vergennes, Lowell.
ROBINSON ALONZO, 13 Algoma, Edgerton.
ROBINSON MELVIN, 13 Oakfield, Greenville.
Robinson Nelson, 7 Ada, Ada.
Robinson Nathan, 36 Ada, Ada.
Robinson Nathan C., 15 Cannon, Cannonsburg.
Robinson Oscar, Lowell.
Robinson Orville G., Lowell.
Robinson Peter, 16 Caledonia, Caledonia Station.
ROBINSON RODNEY, Lowell.
Robinson Rix, 27 Ada, Ada.
Robinson Rufus, 23 Cascade, Cascade.
Robinson Seth T., 35 Vergennes, Lowell.
Robinson William, 25 Sparta, Sparta Center.
Robinson William J., 22 Paris, Grand Rapids.
Robinson William E., 25 Sparta, Sparta Center.
ROBINSON WILLIAM, 30 Vergennes, Ada.
Robinson William J., Rockford.
Robson Chas. J., 32 Cannon, Austerlitz.

ROBSON JOHN, 31 Cannon, Austerlitz.
ROBY EDWIN A., Sparta Center.
Roe Adam, 5 Nelson, Sand Lake.
Roe James, 29 Grattan, Grattan Center
Roe John, 29 Grand Rapids.
Roe John, 30 Alpine, Pleasant.
ROE MICHAEL, 29 Grattan, Grattan Center.
Roe Patrick, 29 Grattan, Grattan Cen.
ROE PATRICK H., JR., 14 Grattan, Grattan Center.
ROGERS A. JACKSON, 5 Alpine, Pleasant.
ROGERS ALEXANDER, 27 Vergennes, Lowell.
Rogers Mrs. Betsey A., 28 Alpine, Indian Creek.
ROGERS CHARLES J., Grandville.
Rogers Chauncey L., 28 Alpine, Indian Creek.
Rogers Cyrus, 23 Solon, Cedar Springs.
Rogers Erwin M., 14 Wyoming, Grand Rapids.
Rogers Edwin, 21 Solon, Cedar Springs
Rogers Fred., 13 Vergennes, Lowell.
Rogers Geo. W., 5 Alpine, Pleasant.
ROGERS HANSON H., 29 Alpine, Indian Creek.
Rosenkrans Argelos M., 31 Cascade, Grand Rapids.
ROSENKRANS FRANCIS M., 31 Cascade, Grand Rapids.
ROSE ALBERT G., 21 Solon, Cedar Springs.
Rose A. W., Lowell.
Rose Chauncey, 32 Vergennes, Lowell.
ROSE CHARLES H., 15 Walker, Gr. Rapids.
Rose David. 28 Paris, Grand Rapids.
ROSE DAVID, 6 Cannon. Rockford.
ROSE ERASTUS W., 13 Solon, Cedar Springs.
Rose Elmer, 22 Solon, Cedar Springs.
ROSE LYMAN, 15 Bowne, Alto.
ROSENBERGER ABRAHAM, 30 Gaines, Cody's Mills.
ROSENBERGER AMOS, 25 Byron, Cody's Mills.
ROSENBERGER CORNELIUS, 28 Gaines, Cody's Mills.
Rosenberger Daniel, 11 Tyrone, Sparta Center.
Rosenberger Jacob, 30 Gaines, Cody's Mills.
Rosenburg Charles, 13 Lowell, Lowell.
Rosenberger Jacob, sen., 30 Gaines, Cody's Mills.

Rogers Henry L., 20 Alpine, G. Rapids.
Rogers James, 3 Paris, Grand Rapids.
Rogers John, 7 Grattan, Bostwick Lake
ROGERS JUSTUS C., 14 Wyoming, Grand Rapids.
Rogers Joseph, 25 Vergennes, Fallassburg.
Rogers Nelson, 21 Lowell, Lowell.
Rolf Alvah R., 9 Lowell, Lowell.
Rolf Alburn, 7 Lowell, Lowell.
Rolf Ransom, 7 Lowell, Lowell.
Romig John, Lowell.
Ronon Mike, 24 Plainfield, Austerlitz.
Ronan Patrick, 12 Grand Rapids.
Rood Zebulon, 20 Cannon, Austerlitz.
Rooney John, 34 Walker, Grand Rapids
Root Andrew, 29 Paris, Grand Rapids.
Root Elijah, 33 Nelson, Cedar Springs.
Root Gustavus, 12 Alpine, Englishville.
Root J. I., Lowell.
Root Joseph, 12 Alpine, Englishville.
Root Lorin, 29 Paris, Grand Rapids.
Root Samuel V., 9 Walker, Indian Creek.
ROOT WILLIAM, 12 Alpine, Englishville.
ROSENBERG DAVID, 25 Byron, Cody's Mill.
Rosenberg Peter, 13 Lowell, Lowell.
ROSZELLE OBADIAH, 20 Byron, Byron Center.
Rosser Simon P., 32 Tyrone, Casnovia.
Ross Duncan, 19 Bowne, Harris Creek.
Ross Daniel, 26 Byron, Cody's Mills.
ROSS FRANK, 30 Paris, Gr. Rapids.
Ross George, 21 Algoma, Rockford.
Ross Hiram, Lowell.
ROSS HUGH, 18 Plainfield, Alpine.
Ross John S., 17 Tyrone, Casnovia.
Ross James, 34 Algoma, Rockford.
ROSS JOHN, 20 Gaines, Gainesville.
Ross Peter, 20 Gaines, Gainesville.
Ross William, Sparta Center.
Ross William, 22 Sparta, Gr. Rapids.
Ross William, 20 Gaines, Gainesville.
Rounds Ambrose, 1 Algoma, Burchville (Burch's Mills.)
Rounds Eli C., 22 Solon, Cedar Springs
Rounds Geo. W., 30 Courtland, Rockford.
Rounds Henry C., 30 Courtland, Rockford.

Rounds Horton, 30 Courtland, Rockford.
Rounds J. M., 1 Algoma, Cedar Springs
ROUNDS J. M., Jr., Burchville (Burch's Mills.)
ROUNDS LORENZO D., 31 Courtland, Rockford.
Rounds Maudly, 27 Solon, Cedar Springs.
Rounds Nathan, 31 Courtland, Rockford.
Rounds Richard A., 8 Paris, G. Rapids
ROUNDS WM. H., 30 Courtland, Rockford.
Roundtree James, 8 Spencer, Spencer Mills.
ROUNDTREE WM. W., 20 Spencer, Spencer Mills.
Rouse Henry M., 32 Paris, G. Rapids.
ROUSE J., 9 Alpine, Grand Rapids.
ROUSE MRS. NANCY, Sparta Center.
Rouse Simeon, 2 Alpine, Englishville.
Roush John, 36 Bowne, Fillmore, Barry County.
ROUSH JOHN L., 36 Bowne, Fillmore, Barry County.
Roush Michael, 35 Bowne, Fillmore, Barry County.
Roup Jacob, 28 Alpine, Indian Creek.
Roys E. J., Cedar Springs.
Roys Geo., 35 Solon, Cedar Springs.
Roys Holmes, 9 Wyoming, Grandville.
Roys Holmes, 16 Walker, Gr. Rapids.
Roys John E., 35 Solon, Cedar Springs.
ROY JAMES, 4 Walker, Indian Creek.
Roys James, 4 Wyoming, Grandville.
Roys Myron, 9 Wyoming, Grandville.
Rozema Hilbrant, 2 Paris, Gr. Rapids.
RUCKLE DAVID, 36 Bowne, Fillmore, Barry County.
Rudes Aaron, Cedar Springs.
RUDES HENRY M., 31 Nelson, Cedar Springs.
Rugg Samuel, 36 Bowne, Fillmore, Barry County.
Ruhs John, 17 Caledonia, Alaska.
Runion Perry, 23 Plainfield, Austerlitz.
RUTHARDT GEORGE M., 15 Alpine, Alpine.
Ruthardt Phillip, 23 Alpine, Alpine.
Ruthardt William, 15 Alpine, Alpine.
Rusche Anthony, 14 Alpine, Alpine.
Rusche Peter, 14 Alpine, Alpine.
Rusco Isaac C., 33 Tyrone, Casnovia.
Rusco James H., 32 Tyrone, Casnovia.
RUSH A. W., Lowell.
RUSH JOHN, 13 Alpine, Englishville.
Russague Harvey, 8 Grand Rapids.

ROWE DAVID, 35 Tyrone, Sparta Cen
Rowe George, 22 Solon, Cedar Springs
Rowe William, 10 Walker, G. Rapids.
ROWE WALTER, 27 Solon, Cedar Springs.
Rowland Mrs., 31 Tyrone, Casnovia.
Rowland Almond, 20 Lowell, Lowell.
Rowland Franklin, 31 Bowne, Harris Creek.
ROWLAND FRANCIS M., 27 Caledonia, Caledonia.
Rowland Ira B., 8 Grattan, Grattan Center.
Rowland Joseph, 31 Bowne, Harris Creek.
Rowland Luke, 27 Caledonia, Caledonia.
ROWLAND WM. A., 27 Caledonia, Caledonia.
ROWLEY AZARIAH V., 8 Oakfield, Oakfield.
Rowley Henry E., 17 Oakfield, Oakfield
ROWLEY HARVEY A., 15 Oakfield, Oakfield.
ROWLEY JAMES M., 7 Oakfield, Oakfield.
Rowswell T. J., 7 Algoma, Sparta Cen.
Russell Almon, 22 Walker, Gr. Rapids.
RUSSELL EDWIN F., 35 Vergennes, Lowell.
Russell Eliphalet, 3 Caledonia, Alaska.
RUSSELL FILIER, 23 Plainfield, Austerlitz.
RUSSELL HENRY C., Village of Cedar Springs.
Russell Isaac, 14 Caledonia, Caledonia.
Russell Julia A., 11 Grattan, Grattan Center.
Russell Luther, 4 Nelson, Cedar Springs.
Russell Peter L., 36 Courtland, Bostwick Lake.
Russell Warren, 10 Cannon, Cannonsburg.
Russell ——, 8 Paris, Grand Rapids.
Russ Christian, 22 Paris, Grand Rapids
Russ Henry H., 21 Cascade, Cascade.
Russ Nathan H., 21 Cascade, Cascade.
Ryan Mrs. Ann M., 17 Walker, Grand Rapids.
Ryan Joseph L., 17 Walker, Grand Rapids.
Ryan N., 1 Courtland, Courtland Cen.
Ryan Patrick, 3 Ada, Cannonsburg.

Ryan Patrick, 17 Walker, G. Rapids.
Ryan Taylor, 1 Courtland, Courtland Center.
Ryder Benjamin, 35 Vergennes, Lowell.
Ryder Charles C., 1 Algoma, Burchville (Burch's Mills.)
Ryder John, Lowell.
Ryder Rayland, 35 Vergennes, Lowell.
Rykert George W., 25 Ada, Ada.
Rykert George L., 4 Plainfield, Rockford.
Rykert Huldah W., 4 Plainfield, Rockford.
Rykert Sanford, Rockford.
Ryno Ephraim W., 33 Gaines, Cody's Mills.
Ryno Eber, 33 Gaines, Cody's Mills.

S

Sabine H. E., Sparta Center.
Sabin Daniel, 23 Nelson, Nelson.
Sabin James, 23 Nelson, Nelson.
Sach Mrs. Sarah A., 10 Paris, Grand Rapids.
Sackett Wm. H., 33 Sparta, Lisbon.
Sadler Eliphalet, 6 Byron, Grandville.
Sadler Henry, 32 Wyoming, Grandville
Sadler Henry F., 15 Byron, Byron Cen.
Sage Adrian, 30 Wyoming, Grandville.
Sage Amos, 18 Cannon, Rockford.
Sage George A., 1 Plainfield, Rockford
Sage John, 22 Vergennes, Lowell.
Sage Lafayette, 22 Vergennes, Lowell.
SAGE VOLNEY, Rockford.
SANFORD JOHN S., 8 Walker, Grand Rapids.
Sapp Daniel, Lowell.
Sapwell Mrs. Susan, 14 Solon, Cedar Springs.
Sapwell Wm., 14 Solon, Cedar Springs.
Sarel Edwin, Rockford.
Sarel Joseph, 11 Lowell, Lowell.
Saull John, 20 Grattan, Grattan Cen.
Saull Michael, 20 Grattan, Grattan Cen.
Saulsbury William, 6 Oakfield, Oakfield.
SAUNDERS GEORGE T., 16 Courtland, Courtland Center.

Sailor Martin, 22 Alpine, Indian Creek.
Salisbury Nagus. 1 Lowell, Lowell.
SALISBURY RUSSELL W., 5 Nelson, Sand Lake.
Salisbury Wm. M., 18 Nelson, Cedar Springs.
Salkeld Joseph, 25 Courtland, Courtland Center.
SALMON ARCHIBALD, 32 Wyoming, Grandville.
Salmon Vincent J., 29 Wyoming, Grandville.
SALYER DAVID, 18 Oakfield, Oakfield.
Salyer Jacob H., 18 Oakfield, Oakfield.
Samuel Andrew, 21 Sparta, Sparta Cen.
Samuel Alvah, 21 Sparta, Sparta Cen.
Samuel James C., 3 Cascade, Ada.
Samuels Mordecai, 3 Casade, Ada.
Samondinger Leonard, 34 Lowell, Lowell.
SANBORN MRS. CORNELIA, 15 Caledonia, Alaska.
Sanders Joel, Lowell.
Sanders Oliver, Rockford.
SAUNDERS NATHAN D., 15 Courtland, Courtland Center.
Sanders Martin, 15 Courtland, Courtland Center.
Saunders Martin, 22 Plainfield, Austerlitz.
Saur Andrew, 8 Sparta, Lisbon.
Saur Charley, 18 Alpine, Pleasant.
Saur John, 29 Sparta, Lisbon.
Saur Johnson, 8 Alpine, Pleasant.
SAUR PETER, 8 Sparta, Lisbon.
Sawyer Charles, 6 Alpine, Lisbon.
Sawyer Eugene F., 32 Walker, Grand Rapids.
Sawyer James, 32 Walker, Gr. Rapids.
Sawyer Joseph, 5 Byron, Grandville.
SAYLES ALFRED B., 23 Cascade, Cascade.
Sayles Alonzo, 23 Cascade, Cascade.
Sayles Daniel C., 15 Vergennes, Lowell.
SAYLES ELIAS, 36 Vergennes, Lowell.
Sayles Francis, Lowell.
Sayles J. Harris, Lowell.
Sayles Serene, Lowell.
Sayles Thomas, Lowell.

Sayles William G., Lowell.
SAYLES WILLIAM H., 15 Vergennes, Lowell.
Scaddin Charles, 25 Alpine, Mill Creek.
Scally Barnard, 22 Grattan, Grattan Center.
SCALLY JOHN, 27 Grattan, Grant.
Scalley O'Brien, 26 Grattan, Grant.
Scaulz Peter, 23 Paris, Grand Rapids.
Scalley Thomas, 27 Grattan, Grant.
Scally Timothy, 16 Grattan, Grattan Center.
Scarvell Thomas, 13 Algoma, Edgerton.
Scelly Patrick, 34 Walker, Gr. Rapids.
Scelly Thomas, 34 Walker, Gr. Rapids.
SCHAONDORF MICHAEL, 19 Byron, Byron Center.
Schantz Andrew, 6 Caledonia, Alaska.
SCHANTZ HENRY, 6 Caledonia, Alaska.
Schafer John, 28 Cannon, Cannonsburg.
Schaffer Baltas, 27 Alpine, Gr. Rapids.
SCHAFFER JOSEPH, 27 Alpine, Gr. Rapids.
Schaffer Stephen, 27 Alpine, Grand Rapids.
SCHEIDEL HENRY, 32 Caledonia, Caledonia Station.
Schlich Bartholomew, 34 Alpine, Grand Rapids.
Schlief John, 36 Wyoming, G. Rapids.
Schlief Michael, 36 Wyoming, Grand Rapids.
Schmidt John, 13 Walker, G. Rapids.
Schmidt William, 29 Grand Rapids.
Schmidt Waltmer J., 34 Sparta, Sparta Center.
Schmit John, Grandville.
Schnable Henry, Alaska.
Schneider Martin, 19 Lowell, Lowell.
Schneeberger Jacob, 17 Paris, Grand Rapids.
Schnell Augustus, 5 Walker, Indian Creek.
Schnoble H., Alaska.
Schofield John, 1 Solon, Sand Lake.
Schomaker Christian, 25 Byron, Cody's Mills.
Schooley Asa B., 23 Gaines, Hammond.
Schooley John L., 23 Gaines, Hammond.
Schooley Jonas, 16 Caledonia, Alaska.
Schoolmaster Joseph, 17 Paris, Grand Rapids.
Schoonmaker Harrison, 22 Cannon, Cannonsburg.

Scheiffley Frederick, 31 Caledonia, Caledonia Station.
Scheiffley Gideon, Alaska.
SCHENCK JACOB S., 22 Ada, Ada.
Schenck William Y., 36 Ada, Ada.
Schentema K., 32 Grand Rapids.
Scherer Nicholas, 26 Alpine, Alpine.
Schermerhorn Cornelius P., 22 Walker, Grand Rapids.
Schermerhorn Daniel, 22 Walker, Grand Rapids.
Schermerhorn George, 22 Walker, Grand Rapids.
SCHERMERHORN HENRY O., 22 Walker, Grand Rapids.
Schermerhorn Isaac V., 21 Walker, Grand Rapids.
SCHERMERHORN M. R., 28 Cannon, Cannonsburg.
Schindler Edward, 11 Alpine, Englishville.
Schindler Ferdinand, 22 Sparta, Sparta Center.
Schidell Ferdinand, 22 Alpine, Alpine.
Schiedel John, 25 Courtland, Courtland Center.
Schoonmaker James, 21 Cannon, Cannonsburg.
Schoonmaker Walter, Village Cannonsburg.
Schram Abraham, 32 Paris, G. Rapids.
Schrapper Theodore, 2 Courtland, Courtland Center.
Schroeder Mat., 34 Alpine, G. Rapids.
SCHWADERER MRS. FRED., 34 Lowell, Alto.
Schwitzer Nicholas, 35 Alpine, Grand Rapids.
Scott Asa, 31 Algoma, Englishville.
Scott E. L., Lowell.
SCOTT ELIPHALET, 13 Caledonia, Alaska.
Scott Henry, 16 Vergennes, Lowell.
Scott Harley, 16 Alpine, Grand Rapids
Scott Henry, 21 Alpine, Grand Rapids.
Scott James, 14 Cannon, Bostwick Lake
Scott John, 5 Grattan, Grattan Center.
SCOTT JOHN C., Lowell.
Scott Jesse W., 24 Cannon, Cannonsburg.
Scott James, 16 Vergennes, Lowell.
SCOTT JAMES H., 26 Walker, Grand Rapids.

Scott John M., 13 Caledonia, Alaska.
Scott Mrs. Louisa, 31 Tyrone, Casnovia.
Scott Levi, 36 Gaines, Caledonia Station
SCOTT LUTHER W., 18 Grattan, Cannonsburg.
Scott Morgan, 11 Cascade, Ada.
Scott Melvin J., 19 Grattan, Cannonsburg.
Scott Septer, 28 Sparta, Lisbon.
Scott Simon G., 19 Grattan, Cannonsburg.
Scott Thomas, 31 Caledonia, Caledonia Station.
Scott Theodore P., 31 Tyrone, Casnovia.
SCOTT WILLIAM, 14 Plainfield, Austerlitz.
Scott Walter D., 26 Walker, Grand Rapids.
Scoville Cass, 26 Plainfield, Austerlitz.
Scoville Lorenzo, Rockford.
Scoville Marinus, Rockford.
Scranton Leonidas S., 6 Paris, Grand Rapids.
SCRANTON SAMUEL B., 17 Grattan, Grattan Center.
Scudder Cyrus A., 4 Byron, North Byron.
Service Chauncey, Rockford.
Severy Luther, Lowell.
Severy Myron, Lowell.
Sexton Bartley, 27 Walker, Gr. Rapids.
SEXTON BLISS, 26 Sparta, Sparta Center.
Sexton Jonathan W., 4 Cascade, Ada.
Sexton Patrick, 34 Walker, Gr. Rapids.
Sexton William, 4 Cascade, Ada.
SEYMOUR FRANK, 31 Plainfield, Mill Creek.
Seymour Henry, 5 Paris, Gr. Rapids.
Seymour Luther, 18 Tyrone, Casnovia.
SHACKELTON H. H., Rockford.
Shackelton William, 16 Walker, Grand Rapids.
Shadduck Asa, 19 Courtland, Rockford.
Shadduck George W., 19 Courtland, Rockford.
Shaddock Horton, 30 Courtland, Rockford.
Shadle Daniel, 4 Nelson, Sand Lake.
Shafer John, 23 Paris, Grand Rapids.
Shafer John M., 21 Walker, Grand Rapids.
Shafer Lorenzo, G. 10 Walker, Indian Creek.

Scudder Henry W., 4 Byron, North Byron.
SCUDDER SAMUEL, Village Cedar Springs.
Scully James, 1 Grand Rapids.
Seabolt Henry, 15 Cascade, Cascade.
Sears Austin, 2 Caledonia, Alaska.
Sears Charles F., Rockford.
SEARS FRANK O., 2 Caledonia, Alaska.
Sears Horace, 36 Cascade, Alaska.
Sears Luke, 30 Courtland, Rockford.
Sebring John, 14 Paris, Grand Rapids.
Sebring Thomas B., 14 Paris, Grand Rapids.
Sedgwick James, 12 Algoma, Edgerton.
Seely Edward, 20 Byron, Byron Cen.
Seeley William, 1 Sparta, Sparta Cen.
Seitzemer Claus, 1 Wyoming, Grand Rapids.
SELLERS T. M., Cedar Springs.
Senges Charles, Alaska Village.
Sent Frederick, 23 Spencer, Spencer Mills.
Sessions John, 3 Grand Rapids.
SESSIONS RODNEY G., 29 Gaines, Grand Rapids.
SHAFER MASON L., 26 Paris, Grand Rapids.
Shafer Marion A., 26 Paris, Gr. Rapids.
SHAFER OSCAR S., 23 Paris, Grand Rapids.
Shafer Sherman B., 26 Paris, Grand Rapids.
Shaffer Levi, 14 Oakfield, Greenville.
Shaner Sebastian, 20 Courtland, Courtland Center.
Shangles David, 6 Sparta, Casnovia.
Shangles Joseph L., 6 Sparta, Casnovia.
Shangler James, 13 Sparta, Sparta Cen.
SHANK DALLAS M., 29 Courtland, Rockford.
SHANK E. W., 1 Sparta, Sparta Cen.
Shank George, 29 Courtland, Rockford.
Shank Henry, 1 Sparta, Sparta Center.
Shank Jacob, 7 Courtland, Edgerton.
Shantz Jacob, 8 Caledonia, Alaska.
Shapels Peter, 18 Ada, Ada.
Sharp Amos, 9 Paris, Grand Rapids.
Sharp Arthur, 9 Paris, Grand Rapids.
Sharp Augustus C., 18 Gaines, Gainesville.
Sharp James G., 9 Paris, Gr. Rapids.

Sharp John C., 18 Gaines, Gainesville.
SHARP JAMES F., 18 Gaines, Gainesville.
Sharp Lewis, 9 Paris, Grand Rapids.
Shattuck Mrs. Mahala, 17 Sparta, Lisbon.
Shaughlonessy Patrick, 34 Ada, Ada.
Shaver Henry, 17 Byron, Byron Center.
Shaver William, 31 Sparta, Lisbon.
SHAW ALANSON K., 23 Vergennes, Lowell.
Shaw Charles B., 33 Grand Rapids.
Shaw Charles, 36 Sparta, Englishville.
Shaw Edwin P., Lowell.
Shaw Eli, 34 Algoma, Rockford.
SHAW GEORGE N., 30 Courtland, Rockford.
Shaw Henry, 34 Algoma, Rockford.
SHAW JEROME H., Cedar Springs.
Shaw McDole, Lowell.
Shaw Nicholas, 30 Courtland, Rockford.
Shaw Winslow, 25 Algoma, Edgerton.
Shaw Willis C., 33 Lowell, Alto.
Shaw Winslow, Cedar Springs.
Shear Abram G., 21 Paris, Gr. Rapids.
SHEAR ABRAM, 33 Plainfield, Grand Rapids.
Shear Charles, 21 Paris, Grand Rapids.
Shepard Albert E., 13 Ada, Ada.
SHEPARD CHARLES, 34 Bowne, Fillmore, Barry County.
Shepard Casey P., 13 Ada, Ada.
Shepard James, 13 Ada, Ada.
SHEPARD LAWRENCE B., 17 Oakfield, Oakfield.
Shepard Z. W., Lisbon.
Shephard Henry, Lowell.
Shephard Horace, 11 Lowell, Lowell.
Sherck Samuel, Lisbon.
Sheridan Michael, 31 Grattan, Cannonsburg.
SHERINGTON ROBERT, 22 Gaines, Hammond.
SHERK AMOS, 21 Caledonia, Caledonia Station.
SHERK ADAM B., 20 Caledonia, Caledonia Station.
Sherk Aaron G., 17 Caledonia, Caledonia Station.
Sherk Christian, 21 Caledonia, Caledonia Station.
Sherk David, 23 Gaines, Hammond.
SHERK HENRY, 16 Caledonia, Caledonia Station.
Sherk Joseph, 16 Caledonia, Caledonia Station.
SHERK JOHN, 23 Gaines, Hammond.

Shear Charles, 19 Tyrone, Casnovia.
Shear C. L., 12 Grand Rapids.
Shear David E., 4 Lowell, Lowell.
Shear John W., 21 Paris, Gr. Rapids.
SHEAR JOHN B., Lowell.
Shearer Alvin, 23 Alpine, Alpine.
Sheehan Joseph, 10 Vergennes, Alton.
Sheehan John, 32 Cascade, Cascade.
Sheehan Michael, 32 Grattan, Cannonsburg.
Sheehan Patrick, 29 Cascade, Cascade.
Sheehan Patrick, 31 Grattan, Cannonsburg.
Sheffield Harvey H., 8 Paris, Grand Rapids.
SHEICKLER ADOLPH B., 13 Gaines, Alaska.
Sheidel J., Alaska.
Sheldon Geo. W., Village Cedar Springs.
Sheldon Norris B., Village Cedar Springs.
Sheler Calvin, 13 Walker, G. Rapids.
Shelhammer Moses, 27 Algoma, Rockford.
Shelhammer Sylvester, 27 Algoma, Rockford.
Shenaman Lovina, 29 Cascade, Cascade.
SHERK MENNO, 20 Caledonia, Caledonia Station.
Sherk Samuel, 20 Caledonia, Caledonia Station.
SHERMAN & MILLS, Lowell.
Sherman Arthur, Lowell.
Sherman Alfred, 34 Ada, Ada.
Sherman Edward, 2 Courtland, Courtland Center.
Sherman James, 29 Tyrone, Casnovia.
Sherman Oliver, 27 Plainfield, Grand Rapids.
Sherwood Byron D., 30 Paris, Grand Rapids.
Sherwood Charlotte M., 30 Paris, Grand Rapids.
Sherwood Delos, 15 Sparta, Sparta Cen.
SHERWOOD JEROME, Sparta Center.
Shimmel Adam, 2 Plainfield, Rockford.
Shimmel A. N., 21 Tyrone, Casnovia.
Shimmel Henry, 18 Sparta, Lisbon.
Shimmel J. W., 21 Tyrone, Casnovia.
Shine John, 29 Paris, Grand Rapids.
Shimmel John, 33 Sparta, Sparta Cen.
Shipman W., 18 Algoma, Sparta Center
SHOEMAKER CLINTON L., 8 Gaines, Grand Rapids.

SHOEMAKER NICHOLAS, Grandville
Shores William, 7 Bowne, Alaska.
SHOTWELL DAVID S., 35 Courtland, Courtland Center.
Shotwell David S., Jr., 35 Courtland, Courtland Center.
Shotwell Isaac M., 10 Courtland, Courtland Center.
Shoup Austin, 11 Vergennes, Alton.
SHOUP HENRY, 10 Vergennes, Alton.
SHRINER G. HENRY, 21 Sparta, Lisbon.
Shriner Sanford, 21 Sparta, Lisbon.
Shug Henry, 34 Cannon, Cannonsburg.
Shuman Erastus P., 2 Courtland, Courtland Center.
Shumway Leonidas, 4 Nelson, Cedar Springs.
Shupert Eli, 16 Paris, Grand Rapids.
Sibert John, 28 Caledonia, Caledonia Station.
Sibley Abner, Grandville.
Sidon William, 13 Walker, G. Rapids.
Sidon ——, 13 Walker, Grand Rapids.
Silcox Mrs. Adarany, 31 Bowne, Harris Creek.
Sillaway Joseph, 20 Tyrone, Casnovia.
SILVER HORACE, 1 Alpine, Englishville.
SIMPSON JOHN S., 27 Bowne, Bowne
Sinclair Albert G., 24 Cascade, Cascade
Sinclair Barney, 13 Cascade, Cascade.
SINCLAIR DANIEL A., 29 Bowne, Harris Creek.
Sinclair George W., 24 Cascade, Cascade.
Sinclair Hiram, 24 Cascade, Cascade.
Sinclair Hosea B., 13 Cascade, Cascade.
Sinclair John D., 29 Bowne, Harris Creek.
Sinclair Peter J., 29 Bowne, Harris Creek.
Singer Alexander, 10 Caledonia, Alaska
Sipple Christopher, 15 Courtland, Courtland Center.
SIPPLE WILLIAM, 16 Courtland, Courtland Center.
Sissem Albert T., 18 Courtland, Edgerton.
Sissem Benjamin, 12 Algoma, Burchville (Burch's Mills.)
Sissem Charles, 12 Tyrone, Sparta Cen.
Sissem John, 36 Solon, Cedar Springs.
Sisson Reuben B., 26 Plainfield, Austerlitz.
Sisson Samuel B., 7 Nelson, Cedar Springs.
Skellenger Charles B., 34 Ada, Ada.

SIMMONS BORWNELL S., 18 Nelson, Cedar Springs.
Simmons Charles, 11 Wyoming, Grand Rapids.
Simmons Henry, 22 Nelson, Nelson.
SIMMONS HENRY A., 12 Solon, Cedar Springs.
Simmons John, 34 Algoma, Rockford.
Simmons John, 35 Algoma, Rockford.
Simmons Jonas, 13 Solon, Cedar Springs.
SIMMONS JONATHAN B., Village Cedar Springs.
Simmons Oscar A., 35 Algoma, Rockford.
Simmons Sylvester, 13 Solon, Cedar Springs.
SIMMONS WM. W., 18 Nelson, Cedar Springs.
Simonds Joel A., 7 Paris, Grand Rapids
Simonds James, 29 Sparta, Lisbon.
Simonds John A., 20 Sparta, Sparta Center.
Simon Joseph, 19 Byron, Byron Center
SIMPSON FRANK, 1 Bowne, Lowell.
SIMPSON HORACE, 21 Paris, Grand Rapids.
Skellinger Henry, 13 Grattan, Smyrna, Ionia County.
Skellenger James S., Rockford.
Skidmore Mrs. Catharine, 4 Bowne, Alto.
SKIDMORE DAVID M., 4 Bowne, Alto.
Skinner Christopher, Rockford.
Skinner Charles W., 8 Byron, Byron Center.
Skinner David, 8 Byron, Byron Center.
Skinner James, 16 Byron, Byron Center.
SKINNER JOSEPH, 8 Byron, Byron Center.
Skinner John, 1 Plainfield, Rockford.
Skinner Reuben, 1 Plainfield, Rockford.
SKINNER THOMAS W., 23 Paris, Grand Rapids.
Skutt George, 19 Spencer, Nelson.
Skutt Myron, 24 Courtland, Courtland Center.
Slade Merritt, 34 Plainfield, Grand Rapids.
SLAGHT SPENCER, 14 Vergennes, Lowell.
Slate George, 16 Plainfield, Belmont.

Slater George, 15 Paris, G. Rapids.
Slater Isaac, 14 Grand Rapids.
Slater Peter, 22 Vergennes, Vergennes.
Slater Robert, 15 Paris, G. Rapids.
SLAUGHTER ABRAHAM, 10 Oakfield, Oakfield.
Slaughter Daniel, 10 Oakfield, Oakfield
Slaughter Garrett, 22 Plainfield, Austerlitz.
Slawson Leander B., 15 Oakfield, Oakfield.
Slawson Morris, Cedar Springs.
Slawson N. F., Cedar Springs.
SLAYTON ASA W., 22 Grattan, Grant.
SLAYTON CHESTER M., 14 Grattan, Grant.
SLAYTON FRANCIS M., 14 Grattan, Grattan Center.
Slayton Thomas J., Lowell.
SLAYTON WM. C., 24 Grattan, Grant.
Sleeper Americus, 21 Sparta, Sparta Center.
SLEEPER PETER A., Sparta Center.
Sliter Alfred V., Village Cedar Springs.
Sloatmaker Mark, 29 Grand Rapids.
Slover Benjamin, 7 Gaines, Gainesville.
SLUSSAR HARRISON, 9 G. Rapids.

Smith Barlow, 2 Wyoming, Gr. Rapids.
Smith Benjamin, 14 Grand Rapids.
Smith B., 34 Walker, Grand Rapids.
Smith Charles H., 22 Walker, Grand Rapids.
Smith Conrad, 19 Lowell, Lowell.
Smith Charles W., 35 Paris, Grand Rapids..
Smith Cyrenus, 36 Spencer, Spencer Mills.
Smith Charles, 28 Bowne, Harris Creek.
Smith Charles, 24 Ada, Lowell.
Smith Charles R. Burchville.
Smith Mrs. Catharine, 2 Alpine, Englishville.
Smith Charles A. C., 12 Solon, Cedar Springs.
SMITH CHARLES, 10 Alpine, Englishville.
Smith Daniel, 2 Alpine, Englishville.
Smith David G., 35 Algoma, Rockford.
Smith David R., 14 Lowell, Lowell.
Smith Daniel B., 2 Courtland, Courtland Center.
Smith Mrs. D. W., 9 Walker, Grand Rapids.
Smith Edward, 14 Byron, Byron Cen.
Smith Elijah C., South 6 Walker, Gr. Rapids.

Smack William, 13 Algoma, Edgerton.
Smalley John, 5 Grand Rapids, Grand Rapids.
SMILEY MERRILS F., 5 Algoma, Cedar Springs.
Smith A. Oscar, 16 Byron, Byron Cen.
Smith Alfred D., 24 Alpine, Alpine.
Smith Amos J., 14 Byron, Byron Cen.
Smith Anthony D., 12 Sparta, Sparta Center.
Smith Albert, 2 Wyoming, Gr. Rapids.
Smith Abraham, 21 Walker, Grand Rapids.
Smith Asa, south 6 Walker, Grand Rapids.
Smith Albert, 2 Wyoming, Gr. Rapids.
Smith Almon C., 21 Caledonia, Caledonia Station.
Smith Almon K., 16 Caledonia, Caledonia Station.
Smith Abram, 3 Grattan, Grattan Cen.
Smith Aaron, 28 Bowne, Harris Creek.
Smith Alexander, 15 Courtland, Courtland Center.
Smith Alvah, 30 Sparta, Lisbon.
Smith Alonzo, 32 Courtland, Rockford.

Smith Eli, 23 Solon, Cedar Springs.
Smith Edward, 31 Sparta, Lisbon.
Smith Elihu B., 32 Gaines, Cody's Mills.
Smith Evander, 34 Courtland, Courtland Center.
SMITH ELI, 3 Grattan, Grattan Center.
Smith Edward H., 28 Spencer, Spencer Mills.
Smith Elihu, 7 Grand Rapids.
Smith Eugene, 29 Tyrone, Casnovia.
Smith Eli, 22 Solon, Cedar Springs.
SMITH EBENEZER C., 12 Cannon, Bostwick Lake.
Smith Freeman, 3 Grattan, Grattan Center.
Smith Frank, 3 Sparta, Sparta Center.
Smith Franklin DeF., 24 Alpine, Alpine.
Smith George, 36 Lowell, Lowell.
Smith Geo. T., Lowell.
Smith Gilbert, 16 Solon, Cedar Springs.
Smith George, 13 Plainfield, Rockford.
SMITH GEORGE, 22 Walker, Grand Rapids.
Smith George J., 35 Algoma, Rockford.

Smith George, 23 Alpine, Alpine.
Smith Henry K., 31 Ada, Ada.
Smith Henry, 35 Ada, Ada.
Smith Hiram M., 20 Plainfield, Mill Creek.
Smith Heman H., Alaska.
SMITH HARVEY, 7 Courtland, Edgerton.
SMITH HEMAN S., 25 Courtland, Courtland Center.
SMITH HIRAM W., Lisbon.
Smith Israel D., 21 Wyoming, Grandville.
SMITH ISRAEL C., 15 Solon, Cedar Springs.
SMITH ISRAEL, 3 Alpine, Englishville.
Smith John H., Rockford.
Smith John, 10 Solon, Cedar Springs.
Smith Joseph, 15 Bowne, Bowne.
Smith John M., 16 Algoma, Rockford.
Smith James, 34 Walker, G. Rapids.
Smith Jacob A., 35 Sparta, Sparta Center.
Smith John, 2 Oakfield, Greenville.
Smith John, Jr., 12 Oakfield, Greenville
Smith John W., 16 Wyoming, Grandville.
Smith James I., 35 Algoma, Rockford.
Smith Joseph E., Sparta Center.
Smith John H., Rockford.
Smith J. J., Lisbon.
Smith Jacob, 29 Tyrone, Casnovia.
Smith Joseph, 11 Byron, Byron Center
Smith James W., 12 Cannon, Bostwick Lake.
Smith Jack, 7 Cannon, Rockford.
Smith James, 1 Courtland, Courtland Center.
Smith Levi S., 15 Bowne, Bowne.
Smith Leander, 29 Tyrone, Casnovia.
Smith Lyman, 32 Courtland, Rockford.
SMITH LEWIS, 15 Vergennes, Lowell.
Smith Mervin A., 30 Lowell, Lowell.
Smith Michael, 16 Algoma, Rockford.
Smith M. De LaFayette, 2 Courtland, Courtland Center.
Smith Martin C., 2 Grattan, Ashley.
Smith M., 34 Walker, Grand Rapids.
Smith Moses R., 8 Ada, Ada.
SMITH MORTISE, 25 Alpine, Mill Creek.
SMITH NEHEMIAH, 3 Grattan, Grattan Center.
Smith N. J., 11 Walker, Gr. Rapids.
SMITH NEWTON N., 12 Grattan, Otisco, Ionia County.

Smith James W., 23 Wyoming, Grand Rapids.
Smith John W., 29 Spencer, Spencer Mills.
Smith John S., 20 Lowell, Lowell.
Smith John, 18 Nelson, Cedar Springs.
SMITH JOHN W. B., 15 Grattan, Grattan Center.
Smith John C., 2 Grattan, Ashley.
SMITH JOHN, 15 Bowne, Bowne.
Smith Joseph M., 14 Cascade, Cascade.
Smith John S., 23 Cascade, Cascade.
Smith John, 15 Courtland, Courtland Center.
Smith John M., 35 Algoma, Rockford.
Smith John L., 35 Algoma, Rockford.
SMITH JAMES, 24 Algoma, Rockford.
Smith James, 13 Algoma, Edgerton.
Smith James, 26 Algoma, Rockford.
Smith John O., 36 Grand Rapids.
SMITH J. HOWARD, Lowell.
Smith Joseph W., 24 Algoma, Edgerton.
Smith John B., Burchville (Burch's Mills.)
Smith John V., 15 Sparta, Sparta Cen.
SMITH JOSEPH H., 23 Solon, Cedar Springs.
Smith Orlow L., 17 Nelson, Cedar Springs.
Smith Oscar R., 13 Caledonia, Alaska.
SMITH OBADIAH, 11 Solon, Cedar Springs.
Smith Orlow, 17 Nelson, Cedar Springs.
Smith Perry W., Cedar Springs.
Smith Peter K., 30 Ada, Ada.
SMITH PETER, 18 Caledonia, Caledonia Station.
Smith Philo, 33 Spencer, Spencer Mills.
SMITH PHILIP, 1 Courtland, Oakfield.
Smith Peter S., 29 Alpine, Indian Creek.
Smith Phineas P., 6 Cannon, Rockford.
Smith Robert, 4 Lowell, Lowell.
Smith Robert, 33 Paris, Grand Rapids.
Smith Russell, 14 Bowne, Bowne.
SMITH RILEY, 20 Nelson, Cedar Springs.
Smith Robert J., 7 Byron, Grandville.
Smith Seth, 18 Bowne, Alaska.
Smith Samuel B., 28 Spencer, Spencer Mills.
SMITH G. H., 7 Grand Rapids.
Smith Sala, 14 Grand Rapids.
Smith Sydney B., Lowell.

Smith Thomas, 28 Ada, Ada.
Smith Torry, 35 Ada, Ada.
Smith Timothy S., 27 Paris, G. Rapids.
Smith Thomas, 36 Lowell, Lowell.
Smith Thomas, 21 Solon, Cedar Springs.
Smith Thomas, 15 Solon, Cedar Springs.
Smith Valentine, 4 Oakfield, Spencer Mills.
Smith V. R., 33 Cannon, Ada.
Smith William H., 14 Paris, Grand Rapids.
Smith William, 12 Grattan, Otisco, Ionia County.
SMITH WILLIAM H., 21 Spencer, Spencer Mills.
Smith William, 20 Lowell, Lowell.
Smith William H., 1 Cannon, Bostwick Lake.
Smith William O., 18 Tyrone. Casnovia.
SMITH WM. B., 7 Gaines, Gainesville.
Smoake Jacob, 26 Lowell, Lowell.
Snapen Henry, 1 Solon, Sand Lake.
Snell Anson, 2 Wyoming, Gr. Rapids.
Snethen Charles, 10 Solon, Cedar Springs.
Snell Jefferson, 16 Paris, Gr. Rapids.
Snell Joseph C., 12 Lowell, Lowell.
Snyder James, 17 Wyoming, Grandville.
Snyder James, 25 Courtland, Courtland Center.
Snyder John D., Grandville.
Snyder Jacob, 25 Courtland, Courtland Center.
SNYDER JACOB, 22 Ada, Ada.
Snyder Lester E., 18 Oakfield, Courtland Center.
Snyder Lewis C., 30 Courtland, Edgerton.
SNYDER L. C., 13 Algoma, Edgerton.
Snyder Lewis, 29 Oakfield, Oakfield.
Snyder Robert, Grandville.
Snyder Spencer, Grandville.
Snyder William, 27 Walker, G. Rapids
Snyder Wm. T., 27 Tyrone, Casnovia.
Soddard J., 34 Walker, Grand Rapids.
Solomon Mrs. Amanda, 11 Gaines, Hammond.
Solomon Joseph, 21 Plainfield, Austerlitz.
SOLOMON LEWIS A., 4 Gaines, Hammond.
SYMES JOHN, 26 Sparta, Sparta Cen.
Symes James A., 26 Sparta, Sparta Cen.
SYMONDS JOHN P., 35 Grand Rapids
Sones Charles, 20 Grand Rapids.

Snethen John, 11 Solon, Cedar Springs.
Snider Frederick, 19 Vergennes, Vergennes.
Snider Joseph, jr., 15 Alpine, Alpine.
Snider John, 15 Alpine, Alpine.
Snider Jacob, 35 Alpine, Gr. Rapids.
Snider Josiah, 6 Cannon, Rockford.
Snitzler John, Grandville.
Snook Edward, Cedar Springs.
Snow Albert, 36 Spencer, Spencer Mills.
Snow Ansel, 27 Tyrone, Casnovia.
Snow Dewitt, 21 Sparta, Sparta Center.
Snow Horace S., Sparta Center.
Snow Henry, 28 Tyrone, Casnovia.
Snow Uriel, 13 Cascade, Lowell.
Snow William R., 12 Sparta, Sparta Center.
Snow Warren, 13 Cascade, Lowell.
Snowden James A., 17 Alpine, Grand Rapids.
Snyder Albert, 18 Oakfield, Courtland Center.
Snyder Alfred, Grandville.
Snyder George R., south 7 Walker, Grand Rapids.
SOPER DAVID, 3 Paris, Grand Rapids
Soper David, 22 Plainfield, Austerlitz.
Soper Francis B., 3 Paris, Grand Rapids
Soper John W., 5 Paris. Grand Rapids.
Soper James, 3 Paris, Grand Rapids.
Souders John, 6 Courtland, Cedar Springs.
Soule Susan A., 29 Vergennes, Lowell.
Soules B. W., 19 Algoma, Sparta Center
Sours Lawrence, 29 Sparta, Lisbon.
Sours William, 29 Sparta, Lisbon.
Southard Mrs. Margaret, Lowell.
Southwer Fred., Burchville (Burch's Mills.)
Southwick Frank, 32 Alpine, Indian Creek.
Southwick Nelson, 29 Grand Rapids, Grand Rapids.
Soutter Frederick, 30 Caledonia, Caledonia Station.
SOWER ANTHONY, 36 Alpine, Grand Rapids.
Sower Peter, 35 Alpine, Grand Rapids.
SOWERBY EDWARD, 3 Cannon, Rockford.
Sowerby John, 3 Cannon, Rockford.

SOWERBY THOMAS, 4 Cannon, Rockford.
Soy Arthur, 34 Walker, Grand Rapids.
Soy Richard, 34 Walker, Grand Rapids
Spangenberg George, 21 Sparta, Lisbon
Spangenberg Jacob, 21 Sparta, Lisbon.
Spark Ephraim, 8 Plainfield, Belmont.
Sparks Edgar C., 23 Gaines, Hammond
Sparks Geo. W., 23 Gaines, Hammond.
Sparks James, 8 Plainfield, Belmont.
Sparks James, 32 Courtland, Rockford.
Spaulding Charles S., 8 Caledonia, Alaska.
Spaulding Francis, 12 Algoma, Edgerton.
Spaulding Hermon, 21 Nelson, Cedar Springs.
Spaulding Hiram, 33 Cascade, Alaska.
Spaulding Isaiah, 28 Courtland, Courtland Center.
Spaulding J. E., 2 Grand Rapids.
Spaulding John, 36 Plainfield, Grand Rapids.
Spaulding James M., 10 Courtland, Courtland Center.
Spaulding Jefferson, 29 Nelson, Cedar Springs.
Spaulding Jerry, 22 Plainfield, Austerlitz.

SPENCER CHESTER, 17 Bowne, Bowne.
Spencer Enos, Lowell.
Spencer Jacob, 6 Ada, Austerlitz.
Spencer James, 3 Cannon, Rockford.
Spencer John, 17 Ada, Ada.
Spencer Luther D., 17 Bowne, Bowne.
Spencer Reuben, 6 Ada, Austerlitz.
Spence Perry, 17 Ada, Ada.
Spence William, 17 Ada, Ada.
Spence Edward, 17 Ada, Ada.
Spence James, 3 Cascade, Ada.
Spicer Henry L., 5 Algoma, Cedar Springs.
Spicer John, 16 Algoma, Rockford.
Spiker John, 25 Bowne, Lowell.
Spiker Samuel, 24 Bowne, Lowell.
Spiller Daniel, 27 Tyrone, Casnovia.
Spitzer Aaron, 2 Caledonia, Alaska.
Sprague A. S., Cedar Springs.
Sprague Arthur, 13 Oakfield, Greenville
SPRAGUE EDGAR, 5 Sparta, Lisbon.
Sprague John P., 10 Solon, Cedar Springs.
Sprague Joseph W., Lowell.
Sprague J. A., Lowell.
Sprague J. B., Lowell.
SPRAGUE RICHARD, 11 Lowell, Lowell.

SPAULDING LYMAN, 15 Oakfield, Oakfield.
Spaulding Miner, 27 Cascade, Alaska.
SPAULDING MURRAY, 29 Nelson, Springs.
Spaulding Orleans, 12 Paris, Grand Rapids.
Spaulding Ransom L., 12 Paris, Grand Rapids.
Spaulding Samuel, 36 Plainfield, Grand Rapids.
Spaulding Timothy, 25 Sparta, Sparta Center.
Speaker G. D., 10 Lowell, Lowell.
Spears Alexander, 29 Byron, Byron Center.
Speicher Abijah W., 13 Gaines, Hammond.
Speicher Abraham, 13 Gaines, Hammond.
Spencer Almon, 16 Spencer, Spencer Mills.
Spencer Alfred, 6 Ada, Austerlitz.
Spencer Geo. M., 16 Grattan, Grattan Center.
Spencer Charles, 22 Plainfield, Austerlitz.

Sprague Wm. H., 16 Paris, G. Rapids.
Sprague William, 24 Algoma, Edgerton.
Sprague Wesley, 13 Oakfield, Greenville.
Spring Daniel W., 17 Cannon, Cannonsburg.
Spring Jared S., 8 Cannon, Cannonsburg.
Spring Volney, 18 Cannon, Cannonsburg.
Springsted Jacob, 21 Wyoming.
Sponable John, 8 Wyoming, Grandville
Spooner Charles, 19 Wyoming, Grandville.
Spooner Rev. J. G., Alaska.
SPOOR ABRAM, 27 Vergennes, Lowell
Spoor Amaziah, 27 Vergennes, Lowell.
SPORE J. M., Rockford.
Spore Jacob C., Rockford.
Squiers Lewis M., Rockford.
Squiers Robert, 26 Algoma, Rockford.
Squier Mrs. Effie M., 22 Paris, Grand Rapids.
Squires Gideon, 23 Nelson, Nelson.
Squires Gideon, 4 Courtland, Courtland Center.

SQUIRES JASON R., 23 Nelson, Nelson.
SQUIER MILON L., 30 Tyrone, Casnovia.
Squier Manly M., 22 Paris, Grand Rapids
SQUIRES MRS. NATHAN, 24 Courtland, Courtland Center.
Squires Nathan, 24 Courtland, Courtland Center.
Squires Robert, Sr., 35 Courtland, Courtland Center.
Stage George W., 27 Sparta, Sparta Center.
Stage John, 9 Alpine, Englishville.
Stahl Alexander, 12 Bowne, Lowell.
Standish Ira, Lowell.
STANIFORD GEORGE, 28 Sparta, Sparta Center.
Stange John, 32 Caledonia, Caledonia Station.
Stanton C. C., 1 Algoma, Burchville (Burch's Mills.)
STANLEY ISAAC W., 18 Alpine, Pleasant.
Stanton E. W., 7 Grand Rapids.
Stanton Elisha, 15 Grattan, Grattan Center.
Stanton Fletcher L., 1 Algoma, Burchville (Burch's Mills.)
Stauffer Isaac T., 32 Caledonia, Caledonia Station.
Stauffer Isaac, 27 Caledonia, Caledonia Station.
Stauffer William, 33 Caledonia, Caledonia Station.
Stearns James, Lowell.
STEBBINS CHAUNCEY P., 34 Paris, Hammond.
Stebbins Charles D., 26 Sparta, Sparta Center.
Stebbins Gaius P., 26 Sparta, Sparta Center.
Stebbins Joseph P., 33 Paris, Grand Rapids.
Stebbins Orrin, 5 Walker, Gr. Rapids.
STEBBINS WILLIAM G., 1 Sparta, Sparta Center.
Stedman Devillo, 25 Sparta, Englishville.
Stedman Joseph, 25 Sparta, Englishville.
Steed Charles, 36 Sparta, Englishville.
STEEL DANIEL D., 8 Caledonia, Alaska.
STEELE GEORGE, 18 Grattan, Bostwick Lake.
STEELE LUCETTA M., 16 Grattan, Grattan Center.

Stanton F. A., Burchville (Burch's Mills.)
Stanton Harmon, 14 Courtland, Courtland Center.
STANTON LEWIS W., Burchville (Burch's Mills.)
Stanton Lafayette J., 16 Grattan, Grattan Center.
Stanton Zael, 14 Courtland, Courtland Center.
Stang Charles, 35 Spencer, Spencer Mills.
Stapleton Wm. H., 14 Cascade, Cascade
STARK JAMES M., Caledonia Station.
Stark Lewis V., 9 Cascade, Cascade.
Starks Charles H., 11 Alpine, Grand Rapids.
STARKS D. S., 11 Alpine, Englishville
Starks Myron, 16 Bowne, Bowne.
Starr Irving P., 15 Grand Rapids.
STARR JOHN, 15 Grand Rapids.
Staats Jacob, 12 Lowell, Lowell.
Stauffer David, 33 Caledonia, Caledonia Station.
Stauffer Hiram, 20 Caledonia, Caledonia Station.
STEELE NATHANIEL, 13 Cannon, Bostwick Lake.
STEELE SAMUEL H., 13 Cannon, Bostwick Lake.
Steele Samuel, 13 Cannon, Bostwick Lake.
STEKETEE JOHN, 22 Paris, Grand Rapids.
Steketee Peter, 21 Paris, Gr. Rapids.
Stennett Joshua, 4 Sparta, Sparta Cen.
STEPHENSON H. C., Lowell.
Stephenson James R., Lowell.
Sternbergh Sylvester, 15 Wyoming, Grand Rapids.
Sterling Daniel, 21 Lowell, Lowell.
Sterling Marcus, 21 Lowell, Lowell.
Sterling ——, 13 Grand Rapids.
Stetzwick John, 29 Caledonia, Caledonia Station.
Stetzwick Paul, 30 Caledonia, Caledonia Station.
Stetter George, 30 Spencer, Nelson.
Stetter John, 30 Spencer, Nelson.
STEVENS AMOS W., 28 Oakfield, Oakfield.
Stevens B. F., 22 Byron, Byron Cen.

STEVENS CHARLES E., 14 Wyoming, Grand Rapids.
Stevens Gabriel, 17 Oakfield, Oakfield.
Stevens Henry, 23 Alpine, Alpine.
Stevens John S., 21 Cannon, Cannonsburg.
Stevens James D., 2 Plainfield, Rockford.
Stevens John P., 6 Paris, Gr. Rapids.
Stevens John, 22 Oakfield, Oakfield.
Stevens James W., 11 Lowell, Lowell.
Stevens Ransom, 9 Byron, Byron Cen.
Stevens Robert, 13 Caledonia, Alaska.
Stevens Russel, 2 Courtland, Courtland Center.
Stevens Robert, 7 Bowne, Alaska.
Stevens Samuel, 12 Courtland, Oakfield.
Stevens Samuel H., 17 Oakfield, Oakfield.
Stevenson Hiram, 10 Alpine, Englishville.
STEVENSON WM. H., 3 Alpine, Englishville.
Stewart Asa P., Village of Cedar Springs.
Stewart Charles R., 22 Wyoming, Grandville.
STEWART DANIEL, 21 Wyoming, Grandville.
Stilwill Nirum, 33 Courtland, Rockford.
Stilwill Phebe, 28 Courtland, Rockford.
Stingle William H., 35 Ada, Ada.
STINSON H. N., Rockford.
STINTON JOSEPH, 7 Lowell, Lowell.
Stinton Wm., 7 Lowell, Lowell.
STOCKS HENRY, 27 Spencer, Spencer Mills.
Stocks Thomas, 27 Spencer, Spencer Mills.
Stocking Dan'l M., 16 Grattan, Grattan Center.
Stocking Fidius D., Lowell.
Stocking Miller J., 16 Grattan, Grattan Center.
STOCUM D. R., Rockford.
Stoddard Chester S., 27 Solon, Cedar Springs.
Stoddard Eli B., 30 Nelson, Cedar Springs.
Stoddard Geo. M., 30 Nelson, Cedar Springs.
Stoddard Henry W., 30 Cannon, Austerlitz.
Stoddard Mrs. Hannah, 26 Solon, Cedar Springs.
Stoddard Orange W., 30 Cannon, Austerlitz.

Stewart Ezra, 36 Algoma, Rockford.
STEWART HILAN H., 5 Cascade, Ada.
Stewart Henry W., 21 Wyoming, Grandville.
STEWART JOHN, 11 Walker, Grand Rapids.
Stewart Marvin. 36 Algoma, Rockford.
Stewart Mrs. Mary, 20 Grand Rapids.
STEWART OSCAR L., Village of Cedar Springs.
STEWART SIMEON S., 35 Grand Rapids.
STEWART SYLVESTER J., 11 Walker, Grand Rapids.
STEWART WILLIAM H., 5 Bowne, Alto.
Stiles Benjamin, 31 Nelson, Cedar Springs.
STILES CHAS O., Village of Cedar Springs.
Stiles L. W., Cedar Springs.
Stiles Jedediah B., 21 Paris, Grand Rapids.
Stiles Raymond, 9 Plainfield, Belmont.
Stilwell Cyrus, 31 Nelson, Cedar Springs.
Stoddard Richard, Sparta Center.
STOKES WILLIAM H., 20 Plainfield, Austerlitz.
Stolp Leonard, 1 Wyoming, Grand Rapids.
Stoner Alfred, 25 Byron, Cody's Mills.
Stoner Charles, 23 Courtland, Courtland Center.
Stoner Ezra C., 14 Courtland, Courtland Center.
Stoner Jacob J., 23 Courtland, Courtland Center.
STONER JOHN, Rockford.
Stoner Riley, 23 Courtland, Courtland Center.
Stonebraker Albert C., 36 Gr. Rapids.
Stonebreaker Henry, 34 Alpine, Grand Rapids.
Stonehouse John, 25 Alpine, Mill Creek.
Stoneburner John, 16 Wyoming, Grandville.
STONEBURNER LEONARD, 16 Wyoming, Grandville,
Stone A. R., Rockford.
Stone Chester G., Lowell.

Stone David T., Burchville, (Burch's Mills.)
STONE DAVID, Burchville, (Burch's Mills.)
Stone Elias B., 4 Bowne, Alto.
STONE FRANKLIN C., Rockford.
Stone George, 6 Bowne, Alto.
STONE HENRY G., 23 Walker, Gr. Rapids.
STONE ISAAC L., 21 Algoma, Rockford.
Stone John B., Lisbon.
Stone Levi, 6 Bowne, Alto.
Stone Normandus A., Lowell.
Stone O. A., Lisbon.
Stone Oscar, Lowell.
Stone Oliver, 6 Bowne, Alto.
Stone William J., 21 Algoma, Rockford.
STONE WM. H., 6 Bowne, Alto.
Stoops James A., Rockford.
Storm Adam, 27 Alpine, Grand Rapids
Storm Philip, 27 Alpine, Grand Rapids
Stover Fred., 23 Ada, Ada.
Story Benjamin, 4 Grattan, Grattan Center.
Story Benj. A., Jr., 9 Grattan, Grattan Center.
Story Eugene, 13 Lowell, Lowell.
STOWE LOTHROP COOLEY, 18 Cascade, Cascade.
Stow Russell, 24 Paris, Grand Rapids.
STOW THOMAS S., 10 Caledonia, Alaska.
Stow Thomas, 11 Caledonia, Alaska.
Stowe William, 16 Cascade, Cascade.
Stowe Zebulon, 18 Cascade, Cascade.
Stowers Adelbert, 29 Algoma, Rockford.
Stowers Nathan, 29 Algoma, Rockford.
STOWELL NATHANIEL W., 31 Plainfield, Mill Creek.
Straight Royal A., 21 Algoma, Rockford.
Straight Lemuel, 34 Paris, G. Rapids.
Strait Nehemiah, 22 Caledonia, Alaska.
STRAUB E. AUGUST, 30 Nelson, Cedar Springs.
Stroble Benjamin, 30 Grattan, Cannonsburg.
STREETER HARMON D., 28 Nelson, Cedar Springs.
Streeter Mrs. H. M., 2 Cannon, Bostwick Lake.
Streeter Morris N., 2 Cannon, Bostwick Lake.

Story Thomas B., 22 Spencer, Spencer Mills.
STOUT ANDREW, 3 Courtland, Courtland Center.
STOUT ANDREW DE WITT, 19 Plainfield, Austerlitz.
STOUT DAVID B., 34 Nelson, Courtland Center.
Stout Ira, 19 Courtland, Rockford.
STOUT JOSEPH S., 23 Solon, Cedar Springs.
Stout John, 3 Courtland, Courtland Center.
Stout Lafayette, 33 Nelson, Cedar Springs.
Stout Oscar, 5 Nelson, Sand Lake.
Stout Samuel, 19 Courtland, Rockford.
Stout Samuel S., 19 Plainfield, Alpine.
Stout Urias, 36 Spencer, Spencer Mills.
STOUGHTON CHARLES, 35 Lowell, Lowell.
Stow Alfred W., 17 Caledonia, Caledonia Station.
Stow Christopher, 11 Caledonia, Alaska
Stowe Elbridge, 18 Plainfield, Austerlitz.
Stow Joseph, 11 Caledonia, Alaska.
STREETER WARREN, 35 Cascade, Alaska.
Strock Aaron, 32 Cascade, Alaska.
Strock John, 8 Gaines, Gainesville.
Strock Marion, 32 Cascade, Alaska.
Strong Truman, 11 Cascade, Ada.
STRONG GEORGE, 23 Ada, Ada.
STRONG HENRY W., 29 Byron, Byron Center.
STRONG JARED, 11 Cascade, Ada.
Strong Nathan, 11 Cascade, Ada.
STROPE GEORGE W., 25 Spencer, Spencer Mills.
Stroup Edgar, 34 Spencer, Spencer Mills.
STROUP HENRY, Jr., 35 Spencer, Spencer Mills.
STROUP HENRY, 34 Spencer, Spencer Mills.
Stroup Oscar, 34 Spencer, Spencer Mills.
Stuart Charles, 9 Paris, Grand Rapids.
STULTS FRANCIS M., 9 Oakfield, Oakfield.
Stuttard Henry, Sparta Center.
Stuart William, 1 Alpine, Englishville.

SUDDICK JOHN, 14 Wyoming, Grand Rapids.
Sullivan Dennis, 1 Wyoming, Grand Rapids.
SULLIVAN DANIEL, 31 Grattan, Cannonsburg.
Sullivan Florea, 12 Paris, Cascade.
Sullivan John, 31 Walker, Gr. Rapids.
Sullivan John W., 2 Byron, North Byron.
Sullivan James, 34 Walker, Gr. Rapids.
Sullivan John, 31 Grattan, Cannonsburg.
SULLIVAN JOHN, 34 Ada, Ada.
Sullivan Michael, 13 Gaines, Hammond.
Sullivan Michael, 30 Grattan, Cannonsburg.
Sullivan Patrick, 20 Grand Rapids.
Sullivan Patrick, 30 Walker, Grand Rapids.
Sullivan Simon, Grandville.
Sullivan Solomon, 20 Plainfield, Austerlitz.
Sullivan Timothy, Village Cannonsburg.
Sullivan T., 34 Walker, Grand Rapids.
Sunderland Myron W., 10 Paris, Grand Rapids.
SUTTON AVERY J., 26 Spencer, Spencer Mills.
Sutton H. H., Burchville (Burch's Mills.)
Swan Andrew J., 10 Ada, Ada.
Swan Charles, 8 Ada, Ada.
Swan Ebenezer, 9 Ada, Ada.
SWAN EBEN, 8 Ada, Ada.
SWAN JOHN A., Lisbon.
Swan Josiah, 8 Ada, Ada.
Swan Lyman D., 1 Walker, G. Rapids.
Swan Solomon, 8 Ada, Ada.
Swank John, Cedar Springs.
Swank Peter, 21 Paris, Grand Rapids.
Swartout Andrus, 11 Oakfield, Greenville.
Swartout Conrad, 3 Wyoming, Grand Rapids.
SWARTZ AUGUSTUS, Rockford.
SWARTZ EDWIN, 32 Sparta, Lisbon.
Swenson Charles, 5 Sparta, Lisbon.
Swenson Isaac, 5 Sparta, Lisbon.
Sweet Edward O., 5 Algoma, Sparta Center.
Sweet Ebenezer P., 26 Lowell, Lowell.
Sweet John G., 5 Algoma, Sparta Cen.
Sweet Wm. J., 7 Algoma, Sparta Cen.
Sweetland Charles, Lowell.
Sweetland Samuel, Lowell.

Sunderlin Eugene A., Lowell.
Sunderlin E. A., Lowell.
Sutherland Alexander, Lowell.
Sutphen James, 26 Cascade, Alaska.
Swift Morgan L., Lowell.
Swift Silas, 23 Spencer, Spencer Mills.
Sylverthorn Thomas, 24 Vergennes, Fallassburg.
SYMONS JOHN, 2 Sparta, Sparta Cen

T

TABER JAMES, 12 Solon, Rockford.
Taber Justin O., 21 Walker, G. Rapids.
TABER MARCIUS, 5 Walker, Indian Creek.
Taber Nathan, Rockford.
Taft Charles L., 12 Oakfield, Greenville
Taggart Harvey, 27 Sparta, Sparta Cen
Taggart William, 6 Byron, Grandville.
Takens Gaart, 32 Grand Rapids.
Talbot T. F., 5 Grand Rapids, Grand Rapids.
Talbot Dennis, 33 Grattan, Grattan Cen
Talbot Dennis, Jr., 33 Grattan, Vergennes.
TALBOTT JOHN, 33 Grattan, Alton.
TALBOT RICHARD, 33 Grattan, Grattan Center.
Tallman T. W., 18 Sparta, Lisbon.
Tallman John C., Village Cannonsburg.
TALLMAN LEWIS D., Village Cannonsburg.
Talman Edson, Lisbon.
Tanner James H., Alaska Village.
Tanner Levi H., Sparta Center.
TANNER WARREN D., 6 Gaines, Gainesville.
Tate George, 20 Grattan, Grattan Cen.
Tate James, 17 Courtland, Courtland Center.
Taplin Wm. T., 16 Courtland, Courtland Center.
Tapley S., Cedar Springs.
Tate Thomas, Lowell.
TAYLOR A. J., 24 Alpine, Alpine.

Taylor Allen, 18 Algoma, Sparta Center
Taylor Mrs. Catharine, Rockford.
Taylor Corwin, 3 Lowell, Lowell.
Taylor Charles, 31 Vergennes, Lowell.
Taylor Daniel, 18 Algoma, Sparta Cen.
TAYLOR GEO. E., 36 Grand Rapids.
Taylor Geo. P., 16 Lowell, Lowell.
Taylor Henry, Lowell.
TAYLOR HOLLIS R., 36 Grand Rapids
TAYLOR HARMON S., 9 Sparta, Sparta Center.
Taylor John, 20 Lowell, Lowell.
Taylor John, Lowell.
TAYLOR J. BRAINARD, Sparta Cen.
Taylor Kendrick, 12 Bowne, Alto.
Taylor L. L., Lowell.
Taylor Loyal L., 9 Sparta, Sparta Cen.
TAYLOR MRS. MARY, 17 Sparta, Sparta Center.
Taylor Michael, 8 Walker, Indian Creek.
Taylor Martin, Cedar Springs.
Taylor Matthew, 21 Grand Rapids.
Taylor Orlando, 3 Lowell, Lowell.
TAYLOR OLIVER, 26 Cascade, Cascade.
Taylor S. J., Lowell.
Taylor Simeon H., 3 Sparta, Sparta Center.
Templar Gilbert, 32 Spencer, Cedar Springs.
Ten Eyck Joseph, 14 Plainfield, Austerlitz.
Terrill Adelbert S., 10 Byron, Byron Center.
Terrill A. Jackson, 15 Byron, Ryron Center.
Terrill A. Philoman, 10 Byron, Byron Center.
TERRILL EDWARD L., 10 Solon, Cedar Springs.
Terrill Tillitson, 22 Paris, G. Rapids.
Terwilliger Silas W., 25 Solon, Cedar Springs.
Terry Frank, 11 Lowell, Lowell.
Terry Minerva M., Village Cannonsburg
TETLEY WILLIAM, 12 Paris, Grand Rapids.
Thatcher David, 7 Sparta, Lisbon.
Thayer George N., 13 Sparta, Sparta Center.
THAYER LEWIS, 28 Alpine, Indian Creek.
Thede John, 30 Caledonia, Caledonia Station.
Therry Nicholas, Lowell.
Thetge John, Cedar Springs.
Thibos John, 18 Lowell, Lowell.

Taylor Samuel, 18 Algoma, Sparta Center.
Taylor Samuel A., Sparta Center.
Taylor William H., Sparta Center.
Taylor William, 26 Cascade, Alaska.
Teed Lamoreaux, 1 Alpine, Englishville.
Teeple Chas., 8 Lowell, Lowell.
Teeple Elbert B., 33 Cascade, Alaska.
TEEPLE GEORGE W., 18 Cascade, Cascade.
Teeple James, 15 Sparta, Sparta Cen.
Teeple Oscar F., 18 Cascade, Cascade.
TEEPLE PETER, 18 Cascade, Cascade.
TEEPLE PETER, Jr., 20 Cascade, Cascade.
Teeple Seneca, 18 Cascade, Cascade.
Teeple William M., 15 Sparta, Sparta Center.
Teesdale Charles, 27 Algoma, Rockford.
Tefft Amos B., 20 Courtland, Rockford.
Tefft Orrin J., 17 Courtland, Courtland Center.
TELLER P. S., Rockford.
THOMAS ALBERT, 5 Cascade, Ada.
Thomas Abner D., 31 Bowne, Caledonia.
Thomas Ashley, 23 Cascade, Cascade.
Thomas Alexander, 11 Cannon, Bostwick Lake.
Thomas Alfred, 11 Cannon, Bostwick Lake.
Thomas Benjamin, 12 Solon, Cedar Springs.
Thomas Calvin, 27 Wyoming, Grand Rapids.
Thomas Chauncey, 34 Solon, Cedar Springs.
Thomas Charles, 2 Byron, North Byron
THOMAS DEWITT C., 14 Cascade, Ada.
Thomas Edward, 27 Wyoming, Grandville.
THOMAS EDGAR M., 25 Wyoming, Kelloggsville.
THOMAS FRANCIS, 18 Walker, Grand Rapids.
Thomas Hudson B., 16 Plainfield, Belmont.
Thomas Jonathan T., 25 Cascade, Lowell.

THOMAS DR. J. R., 28 Grand Rapids.
Thomas Joseph, Lowell.
Thomas Joshua, 12 Solon, Cedar Springs.
Thomas John H., 30 Tyrone, Casnovia.
THOMAS JAMES, Village Cannonsburg.
Thomas John M., 28 Cannon, Cannonsburg.
Thomas James L., 28 Cannon, Cannonsburg.
Thomas Levi, 34 Spencer, Spencer Mills
Thomas Lewis D., 28 Cannon, Cannonsburg.
THOMAS LORENZO D., 3 Oakfield, Greenville.
THOMAS MARTIN F., 16 Spencer, Spencer Mills.
Thomas Nathan, 29 Grand Rapids, Grand Rapids.
Thomas Peter K., 13 Bowne, Lowell.
Thomas Richard, 16 Plainfield, Belmont.
Thomas Sidney S., 8 Spencer, Spencer Mills.
Thomson Samuel, 11 Lowell, Lowell.
THOMAS WILLIAM, 32 Bowne, Harris Creek.
Thompson Horton, 21 Solon, Cedar Springs.
Thompson John T., 18 Lowell, Lowell.
Thompson John, 25 Courtland, Courtland Center.
THOMPSON JAMES R., 28 Bowne, Bowne.
Thompson John, 32 Tyrone, Casnovia.
Thompson John W., 32 Tyrone, Casnovia.
THOMPSON JAMES, 22 Grand Rapids
Thompson Lorenzo, 23 Cascade, Cascade.
Thompson Leroy, 24 Paris, G. Rapids.
Thompson Michael, 34 Walker, Grand Rapids.
THOMPSON ROBERT, 17 G. Rapids.
Thompson Sylvester A., 21 Spencer, Nelson.
Thompson Sylvanus D., 10 Bowne, Alto
Thompson Thomas, 9 Sparta, Sparta Center.
THOMPSON THOMAS, 36 Wyoming, Kelloggsville.
Thompson William, 28 Grand Rapids.
Thomson Andrew, 31 Ada, G. Rapids.
Thompson Hiram E., 16 Byron, Byron Center.

Thomas William, 18 Walker, Grand Rapids.
Thomas William, Village Cannonsburg.
Thomas Wm. W., 10 Byron, North Byron.
Thomas Mrs. Tabitha, 3 Oakfield, Greenville.
THOMAS WILLIAM, 18 Walker, Grand Rapids.
Thome Michael, 15 Alpine, Alpine.
Thome Peter, 34 Alpine, Indian Creek.
THOMPSON ALMON, 36 Courtland, Courtland Center.
Thompson Adam, 13 Grand Rapids.
THOMPSON ANDREW, 34 Spencer, Spencer Mills.
THOMPSON CALVIN, 25 Courtland, Courtland Center.
Thompson Charles S., 22 Grand Rapids
THOMPSON ELIAS, 18 Sparta, Lisbon
THOMPSON FREDERICK B., 12 Bowne, Bowne.
Thompson Frederick W., 22 G. Rapids.
Thompson George, 25 Sparta, Sparta Center.
THOMPSON HENRY H., 27 Bowne, Harris Creek.
Thomson Isaac R., 16 Byron, Byron Center.
Thomson Robert, 5 Ada, Grand Rapids
Thorington Smith, 16 Walker, Grand Rapids.
Thurbur Darius, 15 Grand Rapids.
Thurstin S. L., 2 Alpine, Englishville.
Thurston Daniel, Lisbon.
Thurston Daniel B., Lisbon.
Thurston Franklin, Lisbon.
THURSTON JOHN, Lisbon.
Tibbets Henry, 7 Byron, Grandville.
Tibbets Wm. D., 8 Byron, Grandville.
Tierney Michael, 24 Grand Rapids.
Tiffany Alva, 25 Cannon, Cannonsburg.
TIFFANY REUBEN C., 25 Cannon, Cannonsburg.
Tim Charles, 28 Caledonia, Caledonia Station.
Timmersma Derrick, 32 Grand Rapids.
Timpson Joseph, 9 Bowne, Alto.
Tindall Smith, 27 Nelson, Cedar Springs.
Tindall John N., 34 Nelson, Cedar Springs.
TISDELL JOHN S., Cedar Springs.
TITUS NATHAN J., 15 Ada, Ada.

Tobey Albert, 26 Caledonia, Caledonia.
TOBEY GEO. L., 11 Byron, Byron Cen
TOBEY PRINCE W., 26 Caledonia, Caledonia.
TOBEY SAMUEL, 9 Byron, Byron Cen
Tobin William, 34 Walker, G. Rapids.
Tobias Charles, 8 Cascade, Cascade.
Tobias Stephen, 16 Paris, Grand Rapids
Tooley Edward, 11 Grand Rapids.
Tooley Isaac, 15 Paris, Grand Rapids.
Tooley Noah, 15 Paris, Gr. Rapids.
Tole Miss Phebe A., 24 Lowell, Lowell.
Tomlinson Isaac, Sen., 31 Cannon, Austerlitz.
Tomlinson Isaac, Jr., 31 Cannon, Austerlitz.
Tomlinson Stephen, 11 Vergennes, Alton.
TOMPSETT CHARLES, 21 Cannon, Cannonsburg.
Tompsett Henry, 24 Nelson, Nelson.
Tompsett James, 24 Nelson, Nelson.
TOMPSETT JESSE, 24 Nelson, Nelson.
Tompsett Jesse, Lowell.
Tompsett James, 21 Cannon, Cannonsburg.
Tompkins Henry, 15 Nelson, Cedar Springs.
TOWER ISAAC, 29 Oakfield, Oakfield.
Tower Joseph, 15 Grattan, Grattan Center.
Tower Rufus C., 15 Grattan, Grattan Center.
Tower Solomon, 15 Grattan, Grattan Center.
TOWER SCHUYLER, 2 Vergennes, Alton.
TOWER STEPHEN S., 29 Oakfield, Oakfield.
TOWLE JAMES, 22 Plainfield, Austerlitz.
Town Alfred B., 33 Cascade, Alaska.
Towner Samuel W., 21 Byron, Byron Center.
TOWNER SAMUEL S., 21 Byron, Byron Center.
Townes John A., 33 Nelson, Cedar Springs.
TOWNES JOSIAH D., 33 Nelson, Cedar Springs.
Townes Simon, 33 Nelson, Cedar Springs.
Towns John, 30 Paris, Grand Rapids.
Townsend George, 25 Wyoming, Kelloggville.
Tracy Michael, 2 Wyoming, Grand Rapids.

Tompkins William H., 15 Nelson, Cedar Springs.
Toms A. L., 1 Alpine, Englishville.
Toms A W., Rockford,
TOMS A. B., 1 Alpine, Englishville.
TOMS JOSEPH E., 1 Alpine, Englishville.
Toms Oscar, Rockford.
TOPPING R. H., 19 Tyrone, Casnovia.
Torrey Ezra O., Lowell.
TORREY LUCIUS W., Village of Cedar Springs.
Torrey Seymour, 13 Lowell, Lowell.
Totten J. J., 33 Tyrone, Sparta Center.
TOTTEN THOMAS, 26 Solon, Cedar Springs.
Totten Thomas, 30 Nelson, Cedar Springs.
Tower Adelbert A., Rockford.
Tower Charles E., 15 Grattan, Grattan Center.
TOWER CHARLES A., 10 Solon, Cedar Springs.
Tower David, Rockford.
Tower George, 29 Algoma, Rockford.
TOWER ISAAC L., 30 Oakfield, Oakfield.
Train Jarvis C., Lowell.
TRAIN MRS. CAROLINE, 24 Lowell, Lowell.
Tramper J. W., 26 Grand Rapids.
Trauger John, 11 Lowell, Lowell.
Trask Chas. H., 10 Lowell, Lowell.
Trask H. M., 11 Lowell, Lowell.
Traxler Alex,, 6 Algoma, Sparta Cen.
TREADWAY BENJ. S., 19 Tyrone, Casnovia.
Treat B. P., 28 Tyrone, Sparta Center.
Treat Mrs. Elizabeth, 16 Grand Rapids.
Treat Oscar F., Rockford.
Tredenick James, Lowell.
Treust Lurn, 30 Paris, Grand Rapids.
Treiton William, 13 Walker, G. Rapids.
TRILL DAVID P., 22 Nelson, Nelson.
Trill Edward, Rockford.
Trill Samuel, 22 Nelson, Nelson.
Trill Thomas, 9 Courtland, Courtland Center.
Trill William, 22 Nelson, Nelson.
TRIM SAMUEL, Cedar Springs.
Trimmer David, 33 Lowell, Lowell.
Troost Paul, 29 Grand Rapids.
Trowbridge P. C., 21 Tyrone, Casnovia.
Troy Edmund M., 19 Caledonia, Alaska.

Troy James, 19 Caledonia, Caledonia Station.
Troy John C., 19 Caledonia, Alaska.
TROY JOHN M., 8 Caledonia, Alaska.
Truax James, 2 Plainfield, Rockford.
TRUAX JAMES H., 8 Bowne, Alto.
Truax Mrs. Eleanor, 9 Bowne, Alto.
Truax Mrs. Elizabeth, 8 Bowne, Alto.
Trumbull Cassius, 36 Grattan, Alton.
Trumbull Oren S., 36 Grattan, Alton.
Tryon F. E., 13 Algoma, Edgerton.
Tubbs Cornelius, Rockford.
Tubbs Cornelius, 6 Cannon, Rockford.
Tubbs Hosea, 23 Sparta, Sparta Cen.
Tubbs Israel, 10 Walker, G. Rapids.
Tubbs Martin S., 22 Grand Rapids.
Tubbs Nathan, South 7 Walker, Grand Rapids.
Tubbs Mrs. Rebecca, 36 Algoma, Rockford.
Tubbs Tunis, 19 Gaines, Gainesville.
Tucker E. W., 13 Lowell, Lowell.
TUCKER FOSTER, 17 Grand Rapids.
Tucker Henry, 21 Byron, Byron Cen.
Tucker J. B., 9 Byron, North Byron.
Tucker Joseph D., 10 Sparta, Sparta Centre.
TUCKER SOLOMON J., 10 Sparta, Sparta Centre.

Tuttle Abraham S., 26 Nelson, Cedar Springs.
Tuttle Eugene, 35 Cannon, Cannonsburg.
Tuttle George L., 6 Cannon, Rockford.
Tuttle Hiram, 35 Cannon, Cannonsburg.
TUTTLE J. E., 24 Algoma, Edgerton.
Tuttle John, Rockford.
Tuttle Lyman V., 20 Tyrone, Casnovia.
Tuttle Oscar, 24 Algoma, Edgerton.
TUTTLE STEPHEN L., 6 Cannon, Rockford.
Tuthill Jason, 31 Oakfield, Oakfield.
Tuthill Stephen H., 31 Oakfield, Grattan Center.
TUXBURY BENJ. F., 28 Alpine, Gr. Rapids.
Tuxbury Byron S., 19 Tyrone, Casnovia.
TUXBURY JOHN S., 19 Tyrone, Casnovia.
Tuxbury Norton, 28 Alpine, Grand Rapids.
Tyler Asa R., 27 Bowne, Harris Creek.
Tyler Augustus, 33 Bowne, Harris Creek.
Tyler Adon, 13 Bowne, Bowne.
Tyler Alban A., 26 Paris, Gr. Rapids.

Tucker Samuel, 10 Sparta, Sparta Cen.
TUFFELMIRE ABRAHAM, 13 Sparta, Sparta Centre.
Tully Patrick M., 2 Grattan, Ashley.
Turk John W., 26 Grattan, Grant.
Turner Alfred, 11 Grand Rapids.
Turner L. R., 26 Algoma, Rockford.
Turbush Barnard, 12 Cascade, Cascade.
Turner Lewis, 7 Alpine, Pleasant.
Turner Marvin C., 15 Algoma, Rockford.
TURNER MARVIN, 27 Algoma, Rockford.
TURNER SALEM T., 6 Paris, Grand Rapids.
Turner William, 26 Algoma, Rockford.
Turnbull Robert, 6 Ada, Ada.

Tyler Alexander G., 27 Paris, Grand Rapids.
Tyler Edward, 16 Cascade, Cascade.
TYLER HEWITT, 12 Bowne, Bowne.
TYLER JUSTUS J., 25 Paris, Grand Rapids.
Tyler John, 28 Cascade, Alaska.
Tyler Loren B., 13 Bowne, Bowne.
Tyler Oren, 26 Paris, Grand Rapids.
Tyler Roswell F., 15 Bowne, Bowne.
Tyler William, 26 Paris, Grand Rapids.
TYSON ISAAC W., 8 Gaines, Gainesville.
TWADEL JOHN, 22 Plainfield, Austerlitz.
Twiss Loren, 32 Alpine, Indian Creek.
Twohay John, 29 Grattan, Cannonsburg.

U

Umlor Tebolt, 7 Alpine, Pleasant.
Umlor Joseph, 7 Alpine, Pleasant.
UNDERHILL ALFRED, 21 Sparta, Sparta Center.

Underhill George, 19 Courtland, Rockford.
UNGER CHRISTIAN, 3 Vergennes, Alton.
Unger Solomon, 3 Vergennes, Alton.

UNGER WILLIAM, 15 Oakfield, Oakfield.
Upson Jesse, 4 Plainfield, Rockford.
Upson Joseph C., 4 Plainfield, Rockford.
Utter Amos, 33 Wyoming, Grandville.
Utter Franklin, 33 Wyoming, Grandville.
UTTER JOHN B., 6 Byron, Grandville.

V

VALANCE AMOS, 16 Spencer, Spencer Mills.
Vallance John, 9 Solon, Cedar Springs.
Vanamburgh John Nelson, 33 Cascade, Alaska.
Vanamburgh Lewis, 28 Cascade, Alaska
Vanamburgh William, 33 Cascade, Alaska.
Van Antwerp John, 17 Sparta, Sparta Center.
Van Antwerp John, 16 Paris, Grand Rapids.
Van Antwerp Samuel E., 17 Sparta, Sparta Center.
Van Antwerp, Wm. L., 17 Sparta, Sparta Center.
Van Deusen Chauncey B., 1 Plainfield, Rockford.
Van Deusen Elam, 28 Vergennes, Vergennes.
Van Deusen Hiram, Lowell.
Vandeusen Jesse, 4 Lowell, Lowell.
Van Deusen John S., 28 Vergennes, Vergennes.
Van Deusen Ray, 5 Tyrone, Casnovia.
Van Deusen William, 8 Lowell, Lowell.
Vandine Jacob, 29 Grand Rapids.
Van Doren John T., 34 Ada, Ada.
Van Donge Dennis, 19 Walker, Grand Rapids.
Van Donge John, 19 Walker, Grand Rapids.
Vandyke Albert, 8 Bowne, Alto.

VAN AUKEN JAMES, 17 Paris, Grand Rapids.
Van Blaricum Luther, 21 Lowell, Lowell
Van Buren Geo. W., 28 Lowell, Lowell.
Vanderslotpe Engel, 33/ Grand Rapids.
Vanderpool James, 18 Paris, Grand Rapids.
Vanderhoof Simon, 1 Paris, G. Rapids.
Vanderhoof William, Lowell.
Vanderbilt John, 18 Cascade, G. Rapids
Vandermass Martin, 29 Grand Rapids.
Vanderlip John, Lowell.
Vanderstol C., 18 Grand Rapids.
Vanderfliet Martin, 29 Grand Rapids.
Vanderburg Cornelius, 29 Grand Rapids
Vandewerker Henry, 24 Bowne, Bowne
Vandewerker Nelson, 24 Bowne, Bown
Vanderbroeck John, 1 Vergennes, Alton
Vanderbroeck R., 1 Vergennes, Alton.
Van Deusen Austin, 21 Lowell, Lowell.
VAN DEUSEN ALFRED, 28 Vergennes, Vergennes.
Van Deusen A. Delos, 28 Vergennes, Vergennes.
Van Deusen Adam, 24 Vergennes, Vergennes.
Vandyke Alvin, 32 Spencer, Cedar Springs.
VAN EVERY GEO. W., Alaska.
Van Hooven Aaron, 7 Paris, G. Rapids
Van Hoven Edwin, 30 Paris, G. Rapids
Van Hooven Mrs. Nellie, 30 Paris, Grand Rapids.
Vanilen Daniel, Village Cannonsburg.
VAN LEW JOHN, 31 Gaines, Cody's Mills.
Van Lew Oscar G., 31 Gaines, Cody's Mills.
Van Lew Peter, 31 Gaines, Cody's Mills
Van Liew Daniel, 21 Algoma, Rockford.
Van Liew James C., 21 Algoma, Rockford.
Van Liew William, 16 Algoma, Rockford.
VAN LIEW WINFIELD S., 8 Nelson, Cedar Springs.
VAN LOON VOLNEY, 13 Algoma, Edgerton.
VANNEST GEORGE, 5 Byron, North Byron.
Van Nornum Harrison, Lowell.

VANNALSTINE LAMBERT, Ada Village.
Vannalstine Peter L., Ada Village.
Van Order Isaac, 31 Bowne, Harris Creek.
Van Order William, 29 Bowne, Harris Creek.
Van Reen Herman, Grandville.
Van Raalte Ralfee, 3 Wyoming, Grand Rapids.
VAN SCHOTEN GEORGE, 31 Cannon, Austerlitz.
Van Schuyler James, 19 Sparta, Lisbon
Van Schuyler Richard, 19 Sparta, Lisbon.
Van Sickles Alfred, 1 Paris, G. Rapids.
Van Size Simon B., Village Cannonsburg.
Van Sledright Art, 15 Paris, G. Rapids
Van Stolsman Peter, 2 Wyoming, Grand Rapids.
Van Wagner John, 6 Oakfield, Oakfield
Van Winkle Samuel, 25 Spencer, Spencer Mills
Van Wormer James, Rockford.
Van Volkinburg Jonathan, Burchville (Burch's Mills.)
VAN ZANDT JACOB, 23 Spencer, Spencer Mills.
Verlin Michael, 16 Ada, Ada.
Verlin Richard, 17 Vergennes, Vergennes.
Verbanks John, 20 Wyoming, Grandville.
Vincent Benjamin, Sparta Center.
Vincent Michael, 24 Caledonia, Alaska.
Vinkemulder John, Grandville.
VINTON H. H., (Dep'y Sheriff,) Lowell.
Vinton Jerome, 13 Alpine, Grandville.
Vinton Porter, 13 Alpine, Gr. Rapids.
Virgil James E., 1 Wyoming, Grand Rapids.
Vitty John, 7 Grand Rapids.
Vogt Henry, 29 Lowell, Lowell.
Volpert John, 14 Alpine, Alpine.
VOND JOHN, 33 Tyrone, Casnovia.
VOND WILLIAM C., 9 Sparta, Lisbon.
Von Ehrenkrook Charles, Lowell.
VONNEY BICK, 19 Algoma, Sparta Center.
Von Manen Stephen, 16 Wyoming, Grandville.
Vorholick Andrew, 22 Alpine, Indian Creek.
Vorholick Sebastian, 23 Alpine, Alpine.
Vrealand John T., 8 Paris, Gr. Rapids.
VROOMAN JOHN C., 23 Paris, Gr. Rapids.

VAUGHN MALCOMB W., 11 Walker, Grand Rapids.
Vroman William H., Alaska Village.

W

Waddell John, 19 Cannon, Austerlitz.
Waddell William, 30 Cannon, Austerlitz.
Wade John, 13 Grattan, Grattan Cen.
Wade Lawson N., 31 Plainfield, Grand Rapids.
Wadenfellow John, 19 Byron, Byron Center.
Wadsworth A. O., Lowell.
Wagener Christian, 31 Byron, Byron Center.
WAGNER JOHN B., 1 Solon, Sand Lake.
WAIT DeLOSS V., 5 Cannon, Rockford.
Wait Hastings, Sparta Center.
Wait Milo, 27 Cannon, Cannonsburg.
Wait Paine, 13 Grattan, Otisco, Ionia County.
Wait Sanford, Lowell.
Wait Mrs. Susan, Sparta Center.
Waite F. F., 10 Walker, Gr. Rapids.
Waite Joseph, 12 Walker, Grand Rapids.
WAITE L. W., 12 Walker, Gr. Rapids.
WAKEMAN ALFRED, 1 Grattan Grattan Center.
Wakeman John, 28 Spencer, Spencer's Mill.
Wakeman Stephen, 28 Cannon, Cannonsburg.
Walden Lodowic, 16 Gaines, Hammond.
Walden Guy S., 9 Cascade, Cascade.
Walker Albert B., 33 Grand Rapids.
Walker David, 33 Plainfield, Grand Rapids.
Walker Eliab, 28 Vergennes, Lowell.
Walker George, 3 Grand Rapids.

WALKER HUGH, 9 Sparta, Sparta Center.
WALKER ISAAC, 29 Solon, Cedar Springs.
Walker John J., 19 Lowell, Lowell.
Walker John J., Jr., 19 Lowell, Lowell.
WALKER JACOB W., 28 Vergennes, Lowell.
Walker Levi, 21 Vergennes, Lowell.
Walker Melvin, 11 Lowell, Lowell.
Walker Thomas, 11 Lowell, Lowell.
Wall Samuel, 35 Courtland, Bostwick Lake.
WALL WILLIAM, 1 Plainfield, Rockford.
WALLACE MRS. CAROLINE, 26 Sparta, Sparta Center.
Wallace Charles H., 24 Sparta, Sparta Center.
Wallace Corydon, 19 Courtland, Rockford.
Wallace James, 26 Lowell, Lowell.
Wallace John W., 11 Lowell, Lowell.
Wallace Nathaniel, 12 Grattan, Otisco, Ionia County.
Wallace Nathan, 1 Lowell, Lowell.
Wallace Nathaniel T., 11 Lowell, Lowell.
Walton John S., 25 Bowne, Fillmore, Barry County.
Walton Ransom, 25 Bowne, Fillmore, Barry County.
Walz George, 26 Ada, Ada.
Wamsley Edwin C., Village Cedar Springs.
Ward Charles, 20 Grand Rapids.
Ward Hugh H., 15 Ada, Ada.
Ward Horatio G., 36 Ada, Ada.
Ward Henry, 8 Walker, Grand Rapids.
Ward Jonathan, Village Cedar Springs.
Ward John, 5 Vergennes, Cannonsburg.
Ward James, 31 Spencer, Cedar Springs
Ward Jared, 19 Spencer, Nelson.
Ward Michael, 31 Spencer, Cedar Springs.
Ward Silas, 16 Grattan, Grattan Center
Ward Wm. W., 24 Ada, Ada.
WARD WM. D., 14 Grattan, Grattan Center.
Wardwell William, 27 Walker, Grand Rapids.
WARE SAMUEL L., 4 Nelson, Sand Lake.
WARING H. E., 21 Grand Rapids.
Warner Amos W., 32 Bowne, Harris Creek.
WARNER ANDREW, 14 Grand Rapids

WALLACE SAMUEL M., 11 Lowell, Lowell.
WALLACE WILLIAM, 15 Ada, Ada
Waller William A., Rockford.
Wallin Charles, 20 Courtland, Rockford.
WALPOLE JOHN, 11 Paris, Grand Rapids.
Walpole Thomas, 11 Paris, Gr. Rapids.
WALSH HUGH, 32 Walker, Grand Rapids.
Walsh John, 8 Vergennes, Vergennes.
Walsh John, 34 Walker, Gr. Rapids.
Walsh Patrick, 25 Alpine, Mill Creek.
Walsh Thomas, 19 Walker, G. Rapids.
WALTER JOHN, 36 Grand Rapids.
Walter James, 15 Grand Rapids.
Walters George, 17 Tyrone, Casnovia.
Walters Homer P., 34 Ada, Ada.
Walters John, 30 Paris, Grand Rapids.
Walters Niel, 19 Algoma, Sparta Center
Walters Stephen, 36 Wyoming, Kelloggsville.
Walters Townsend, 19 Algoma, Sparta Center.
Walterson John, 26 Cascade, Cascade.
Walton Andrew J., Lowell.
Warner Abijah J., 35 Tyrone, Sparta Center.
Warner Benjamin F., 32 Bowne, Harris Creek.
Warner Calvin F., 35 Cascade, Alaska.
Warner Ezra G., 16 Byron, Byron Cen.
Warner Gilman, 35 Paris, Hammond.
Warner George, 22 Plainfield, Austerlitz.
Warner George W., 26 Plainfield, Austerlitz.
Warner Henry, Rockford.
Warner H. S., 19 Algoma, Sparta Cen.
Warner John W., 12 Caledonia, Alaska
Warner James, 35 Tyrone, Sparta Cen.
Warner Lawson S., Lowell.
WARNER LEWIS, 11 Walker, Grand Rapids.
Warner Lewis W., 14 Paris, Grand Rapids.
Warner Lyman, 20 Bowne, Bowne.
Warner Truman G., 20 Bowne, Bowne.
Warnock William, 17 Spencer, Spencer Mills.
Warner William, 35 Lowell, Lowell.
Warren Chas. H., Lowell.
Warren Francis, 21 Byron, Byron Cen.

Warren Geo. R., Cedar Springs.
Warren G. W., 24 Solon, Cedar Springs.
Warren Ira, 14 Solon, Cedar Springs.
WARWICK MRS. A. A., Lowell.
Washburn Benjamin, F., 33 Ada, Ada.
Washburn Benjamin F., 29 Grand Rapids, Grand Rapids.
Washburn Charles J., 36 Cascade, Al aska.
Washburn Clark D., Ada Village.
Washburn Daniel, 20 Lowell, Lowell.
WASHBURN JAMES A., 1 Cannon, Bostwick Lake.
Washburn Nathan, 20 Lowell, Lowell.
WASHBURN ROLLIN F., 36 Cascade, Alaska.
WASHBURN MRS. ROSETTA, 14 Cascade, Cascade.
Waterbury Dewitt, 2 Wyoming, Grand Rapids.
Waterman Charles, 16 Alpine, Grand Rapids.
Waterman John, 11 Algoma, Edgerton.
Waters B. G., 18 Grand Rapids.
Waters Charles, Lowell.
Waters David L., south 5 Walker, Gr. Rapids.
Waters H., 18 Grand Rapids.
Watson H. C., 30 Cannon, Austerlitz.
WATSON HENRY, 2 Oakfield, Greenville.
WATSON JOSEPH J., 17 Paris, Grand Rapids.
WATSON JOHN S., 2 Oakfield, Greenville.
Watson Montgomery D., 9 Paris, Grand Rapids.
Watson Thomas, 24 Oakfield, Ashley.
Watts James N., 18 Byron, Grandville.
Watts William, 21 Bowne, Bowne.
WATTS WM. H., 18 Byron, Grandville
Weaver Asa, 26 Byron, Cody's Mills.
WEAVER BRADLEY, 35 Byron, Cody's Mills.
Weaver Carlos, 34 Byron, Cody's Mills.
Weaver George, 21 Walker, G. Rapids.
Weaver Josiah, 11 Bowne, Lowell.
Weaver John, 34 Walker, G. Rapids.
Weaver Joseph, 34 Alpine, Indian Creek.
Weaver Martin, 19 Alpine, Alpine.
Weaver Prentiss, 34 Byron, Cody's Mills.
Weaver Randall, 26 Byron, Cody's Mills.
Weatherwax Henry, 11 Lowell, Lowell.
Weber John, 34 Walker, Grand Rapids

Waters Levi, 12 Lowell, Lowell.
Waterson Wm., 20 Lowell, Lowell.
Watkins Adrian, 4 Walker, Indian Creek.
Watkins Charles J., 2 Grattan, Grattan Center.
Watkins E. C., Rockford.
Watkins Joseph, 22 Algoma, Edgerton.
Watkins J. D., 11 Alpine, Englishville.
Watkins Joseph W., 15 Algoma, Edgerton.
WATKINS JOHN, 1 Plainfield, Rockford.
Watkins Jared, 13 Grattan, Grant.
WATKINS JASON C., 23 Grattan, Grant.
WATKINS L. W., 16 Grattan, Grattan Center.
WATKINS MILTON C., 2 Grattan, Grattan Center.
WATKINS OLIVER I., 13 Grattan, Grant.
Watson Andrew, 30 Cannon, Austerlitz
Watson Cyrus P., 29 Cannon, Austerlitz.
Watson Daniel W., 30 Cannon, Austerlitz.
Weber Peter, 13 Walker, Grand Rapids
Webster Charles B., 16 Cascade, Cascade.
WEBSTER ERASTUS W., 9 Cascade, Cascade.
Webster George, 12 Cascade, Cascade.
Webster Hiram, Jr., 12 Cascade, Cascade.
Webster Hiram, 12 Cascade, Cascade.
Webster Henry, Lisbon.
Webster Henry T., 18 Walker, Grand Rapids.
Webster Stephen B., 17 Walker, Grand Rapids.
WEDGE HENRY D., 32 Alpine, Indian Creek.
Wedge Joseph, Sparta Center.
Wedgewood Amaziah, 10 Wyoming, Grandville.
Wedgewood Amaziah, 17 Byron, Byron Center.
Wedgewood Chas. H., 10 Wyoming, Grandville.
WEDGEWOOD GUSTAVUS R., 16 Byron, Byron Center.
Weeks Abel, Lowell.
Weeks John P., 25 Grattan, Grant.

Weeks John J., 30 Nelson, Cedar Springs.
Weeks James H., Lowell.
Weeks Orrin D., 4 Vergennes, Alton.
Weed Sylvanus, 1 Oakfield, Greenville.
Wegell Swen, 5 Sparta, Lisbon.
Weitz George, 34 Gaines, Cody's Mills.
Weiting John, 34 Wyoming, North Byron.
Weiringa Henry, 33 Alpine, Indian Creek.
Wekenmann Henry, 24 Gaines, Caledonia Station.
Wekenmann Stonnas, 24 Gaines, Caledonia Station.
Welch Andrew, 8 Caledonia, Alaska.
WELCH CYRUS S., 12 Gaines, Hammond.
Welch Edward, 25 Plainfield, Austerlitz.
Welch James, 25 Paris, Grand Rapids.
Welch Mrs. Lavina, Grandville.
Welch Patrick, 24 Plainfield, Austerlitz.
Welch Robert, Village Cedar Springs.
WELCH RENSSELEAR J., 5 Nelson, Sand Lake.
WELCH WILLIAM, 8 Nelson, Cedar Springs.
Wells James L., 30 Paris, Gr. Rapids.
Wells Nathan, 31 Courtland, Rockford.
Welton George, 27 Spencer, Spencer Mills.
WELTON MORTIMER G., 36 Caledonia, Caledonia.
Welty Frederick, 2 Gaines, Hammond.
Wells Orville G., 26 Plainfield, Austerlitz.
Wells Robert, 26 Plainfield, Austerlitz.
Wells Robert D., 26 Plainfield, Austerlitz.
Wells T. W., 36 Algoma, Rockford.
Wells Winsor, Rockford.
Welsh James, 11 Lowell, Lowell.
Welsh Wm., Lowell.
Welsh Wm., 31 Solon, Sparta Center.
Wendorf John, 24 Wyoming, Grand Rapids.
Wendover Henry, Lowell.
WENGER ISAAC G., 18 Caledonia, Alaska.
WENGER JONAS G., 7 Caledonia, Alaska.
Werdon Oscar N., 17 Walker, Grand Rapids.
Werdon Mrs., 33 Alpine, Indian Creek.
Wertman Daniel, Alaska Village.
West Charles, 13 Alpine, Englishville.

Welch William, 12 Gaines, Hammond.
Weller Edgar, 16 Cannon, Cannonsburg.
WELLER HENRY N., 22 Cannon, Cannonsburg.
Weller Harvey, 2 Cannon, Rockford.
Weller John P., 13 Plainfield, Austerlitz.
Weller Mirza, 3 Cannon, Rockford.
Weller Morton H., 9 Cannon, Cannonsburg.
Weller Sidney, 8 Cannon, Cannonsburg
Weller Theodore, 4 Cannon, Cannonsburg.
WELLER VIRGIL, 18 Cannon, Rockford.
WELLMAN EUSTICE J., 21 Oakfield, Oakfield.
Welling Henry, 9 Wyoming, Grandville
WELLS ALMERN, 30 Vergennes, Vergennes.
WELLS C. E., Lisbon.
Wells George H., 26 Plainfield, Austerlitz.
Wells Henry, 1 Paris, Grand Rapids.
WELLS JAMES, 30 Vergennes, Vergennes.
WEST H. S., Lowell.
WEST J. C., Lowell.
West Lorenzo, 25 Alpine, Alpine.
West Warren, 13 Alpine, Englishville.
WEST WILLIAM H., 30 Plainfield, Mill Creek.
Westbrook Thomas, 23 Vergennes, Lowell.
Westbrook Haggai, 16 Vergennes, Lowell.
Westbrook John R., 34 Nelson, Cedar Springs.
Westcott Charles, 9 Byron, Byron Cen.
Westcott Dexter, 22 Byron, Byron Cen.
Westcott William B., 22 Byron, Byron Center.
Westerhouse F. J., 34 Walker, Grand Rapids.
Westervelt John, 21 Courtland, Courtland Center.
Westfall Abram, 15 Grand Rapids.
WESTFALL BENJAMIN, 8 Grand Rapids.
Westfall Frederic, 8 Grand Rapids.
Westfall George, 8 Grand Rapids.
Westfall William, 32 Sparta, Lisbon.

Westlake Samuel, 29 Walker, Grand Rapids.
WESTON ADELBERT H., Grandville.
Weston Nathan, 35 Cascade, Alaska.
Weston Horace O., Grandville.
Weston Henry, 21 Algoma, Rockford.
Weston William, 32 Solon, Cedar Springs.
WHALEN KER, 14 Wyoming, Grand Rapids.
Whalen Michael, 11 Wyoming, Grand Rapids.
Whalen Thomas, 31 Walker, Grand Rapids.
Whaley Isaac, 21 Ada, Ada.
Whedon Hamilton, 11 Lowell, Lowell.
Whedon Israel, 11 Lowell, Lowell.
Whelan Andrew, 11 Wyoming, Grand Rapids.
Whelan Mrs. Alice, 20 Wyoming, Grandville.
Whelan Edmund, 11 Wyoming, Grand Rapids.
Whelan Michael, 11 Wyoming, Grand Rapids.
Whelan Thomas, 1 Wyoming, Grand Rapids.
Wheeler Barnes, 14 Grand Rapids.
Wheeler Edward A., 22 Alpine, Alpine.
White Charles, 15 Courtland, Courtland Center.
White Elijah, 31 Cannon, Austerlitz.
White Frank, Lowell.
WHITE GEORGE, 8 Vergennes, Alton
White Isaac N., Lowell.
White Isaac W., 10 Vergennes, Alton.
White James, 32 Ada, Ada.
WHITE JOSEPH, 17 Bowne, Alto.
White John, 16 Grattan, Grattan Cen.
White James M., 10 Walker, G. Rapids
White Mrs. Julia, Lowell.
WHITE JOHN R., 35 Grattan, Alton.
WHITE LEONARD, Lowell.
White Levi, 1 Caledonia, Alaska.
White Otis, 24 Grattan, Grant.
WHITE OTIS, 24 Grattan, Grant.
White Orange, 3 Wyoming, G. Rapids.
White Robert, 8 Bowne, Alto.
WHITE SAMUEL, Jr., 23 Walker, Grand Rapids.
WHITE SYLVESTER C., 15 Courtland, Courtland Center.
White Safford, Alaska.
White Samuel, Sr., 23 Walker, Grand Rapids.
WHITE WM. C., 35 Cascade, Alaska.
WHITE WILLIAM, 16 Caledonia, Alaska.

Wheeler Edward, 22 Alpine, Alpine.
Wheeler John, 14 Grand Rapids.
Wheeler John, 20 Algoma, Rockford.
Wheeler Joseph, 15 Alpine, Alpine.
Wheeler Montsier, 31 Wyoming, Grandville.
Wheeler Martin G., South 6 Walker, Grand Rapids.
Wheeler Nelson J., 8 Cannon, Rockford.
WHEELER WM. W., 22 Alpine, Alpine.
Whipple John, 13 Algoma, Edgerton.
Whipple Wallace, 32 Byron, Byron Center.
Whitbeck Benj., 2 Oakfield, Greenville.
Whitbeck Elizabeth, 2 Oakfield, Greenville.
Whitcomb Riggs, 33 Byron, Byron Center.
WHITE ALBERT C., 34 Wyoming, Grand Rapids.
White Amos S., Lowell.
White Anna, 21 Oakfield, Oakfield.
White Anson, 31 Cannon, Austerlitz.
White Burtis, Lowell.
White Benjamin, 1 Vergennes, Alton.
White William, 32 Grand Rapids.
WHITE WALTER, 10 Vergennes, Alton.
White Zenas B., 15 Courtland, Courtland Center.
Whitebread Lewis, 16 Algoma, Rockford.
Whitehead Thomas, 22 Algoma, Rockford.
Whitfield Henry, Rockford.
Whitford Mrs. Abbey A., 7 Paris, Grand Rapids.
Whitford Henry M., 28 Paris, Grand Rapids.
WHITFORD LINAS, 3 Gaines, Hammond.
Whitford Rufus, 34 Paris, Hammond.
Whitford Silas. 21 Gaines, Gr. Rapids.
WHITING MRS. CATHARINE, Cedar Springs.
Whiting Mrs. Elizabeth, 19 Gaines, Grand Rapids.
Whiting James S., 26 Ada, Ada.
Whitlow J. T., 22 Algoma, Rockford.
Whitmore James, 1 Sparta, Sparta Center.
Whitney Ethel, 16 Plainfield, Belmont.

WHITNEY EUGENE C., 16 Cannon, Cannonsburg.
Whitney Herman E., 16 Grattan, Grattan Center.
Whitney Henry, 8 Nelson, Cedar Springs.
Whitney Job, 2 Byron, North Byron.
Whitney Leonard, 13 Cascade, Cascade.
WHITNEY MINDRUS H., 8 Nelson, Cedar Springs.
WHITNEY M. L., Burchville.
WHITNEY MARTIN, 13 Caledonia, Alaska.
Whitney Solomon, 23 Nelson, Cedar Springs.
Whitney Wm. P., 3 Byron, North Byron.
Whitney William E., 16 Cannon, Cannonsburg.
Whitney Zerah, 16 Plainfield, Belmont.
Whitsell Andrew, Lisbon.
Whitsell Samuel, Lisbon.
WHITWORTH GRORGE, 17 Algoma, Rockford.
Whittall Thomas, 23 Courtland, Courtland Center.
Whittemore Jemima, 22 Plainfield, Austerlitz.
Wightman William, 26 Solon, Cedar Springs.
Wilbur Hiram H., 22 Gaines, Hammond.
Wilcox Ira, 1 Paris, Grand Rapids.
Wild Moses, Lowell.
WILDER HORACE, Grandville.
Wilder Joseph, 4 Walker, Indian Creek
Wilder Marion, Grandville.
WILEY NATHAN W., 22 Cannon, Cannonsburg.
Wilhelm George, Lowell.
Wilkerson Sherwood D., 33 Caledonia, Caledonia Station.
Wilkes George, 22 Oakfield, Oakfield.
Wilkinson Andrew J., 18 Alpine, Pleasant.
Wilkinson Andrew S., 9 Cannon, Rockford.
Wilkinson G. A., Rockford.
Wilkinson James C., 3 Grattan, Grattan Center.
Wilkinson James A., 9 Cannon, Rockford.
Wilkinson L. H., Rockford.
WILKINSON OLIVER, 9 Cannon, Rockford.
Wilkins Almeron, 19 Ada, Ada.
Willard Aaron, 22 Byron, Byron Center

Whitten John, Jr., 7 Grattan, Grattan Center.
Whitten John, 7 Grattan, Grattan Cen.
Whitten William, 33 Oakfield, Grattan Center.
Whitters William, 26 Grand Rapids.
Whitters Robert, 31 Sparta, Lisbon.
WHITTICUS WILSON, 28 Tyrone, Casnovia.
Whittington George, 22 Plainfield, Austerlitz.
Whittington Levi, 22 Plainfield, Austerlitz.
Wickham H. C., Lowell.
Wickham H. S., Lowell.
Wickham William, 25 Vergennes, Lowell.
Wicks Henry, 24 Algoma, Edgerton.
Wicks Wm. E., 3 Lowell, Lowell.
WIDRIG ALLEN, 28 Gaines, Cody's Mills.
Wieland Caleb, 1 Bowne, Alto.
Wieland Christian, 1 Bowne, Alto.
Wiggins Culin, 24 Grattan, Grant.
Wiggins William, 1 Vergennes, Alton.
Wightman David H., 26 Solon, Cedar Springs.
Willard John H., 6 Walker, Berlin.
Willard Warren, 6 Walker, Berlin.
Willcox Gardner, 35 Vergennes, Lowell
Willcoxson James, 34 Ada, Ada.
Willett Lyman C., 18 Cannon, Rockford.
Willett Wm. M., 8 Cannon, Rockford.
Williams Alonzo, Grandville.
Williams Chas. A., 1 Wyoming, Grand Rapids.
WILLIAMS CHARLES, 1 Wyoming, Grand Rapids.
Williams Edmond H., 7 Paris, Grand Rapids.
Williams Eli, 16 Alpine, Alpine.
Williams Egbert, Cedar Springs.
Williams George, 24 Byron, Gainesville
Williams George, 25 Grattan, Smyrna, Ionia County.
Williams Geo. W., Alaska Village.
Williams Gersham H., Alaska.
Williams George B., Alaska.
Williams George, 4 Alpine, Lisbon.
Williams Hiram, 31 Paris, Gr. Rapids.
Williams Jesse B., 23 Byron, Byron Center.

WILLIAMS JACOB C., 23 Byron, Byron Center.
Williams Joel, 6 Byron, Grandville.
Williams James W., 22 Vergennes, Lowell.
Williams Jacob, Alaska.
Williams John C., Lowell.
Williams John J., 5 Gaines, Grand Rapids.
Williams John A., 5 Gaines, Grand Rapids.
Williams Lewis, 16 Alpine, Alpine.
Williams Leonard, 16 Alpine, Alpine.
Williams Orrin H., 16 Algoma, Rockford.
Williams Reuben, 28 Alpine, Alpine.
Williams Smith C., 8 Caledonia, Alaska.
Williams Silas, 26 Oakfield, Ashley.
Williams Sidney L., 23 Byron, Byron Center.
Williams Thomas R., 5 Paris, Grand Rapids.
Williams Worthy A., 22 Vergennes, Lowell.
Williams William, 16 Algoma, Rocktord.
Williams William, 29 Grand Rapids.
Williams Wm. L., 7 Alpine, Pleasant.
Wilson David A., 33 Vergennes, Lowell.
Wilson Daniel, 20 Cannon, Cannonsburg.
Wilson Edwin, 8 Spencer, Spencer Mills.
WILSON GEORGE M., 23 Plainfield, Austerlitz.
Wilson George, 3 Wyoming, Grand Rapids.
Wilson Henry D., 30 Nelson, Cedar Springs.
Wilson Henry, 26 Nelson, Cedar Springs.
Wilson John, 23 Lowell, Lowell.
Wilson John C., 19 Alpine, Pleasant.
Wilson John S., Lowell.
Wilson Mulunox, 28 Caledonia, Caledonia Station.
WILSON R. A., Lowell.
WILSON REUBEN A., 4 Byron, North Byron.
Wilson Thomas, 26 Byron, Cody's Mills.
Wilson William, 26 Plainfield, Austerlitz.
WILSON WM. R., 11 Tyrone, Sparta Center.
Wilson Wm. P., 4 Byron, North Byron.

Williams W. W., 5 Tyrone, Casnovia.
WILLIAMS U. B., Lowell.
Williams Zabin, 8 Caledonia, Alaska.
Williams —, — Alpine, Indian Creek.
Williamson Sylvia, 24 Vergennes, Fallassburg.
Williamson Mrs. S., Lowell.
Willoughby Herbert, 36 Bowne, Fillmore, Barry County.
Willey Franklin, 33 Wyoming, North Byron.
Wiley George E., 22 Walker, Grand Rapids.
WILMARTH DARIUS A., 25 Nelson, Nelson.
Wilson Andrew, 1 Alpine, Englishville.
Wilson A. A., 18 Walker, Gr. Rapids.
WILSON ALBERT E., 19 Alpine, Pleasant.
WILSON ANDERSON, 33 Vergennes, Lowell.
WILSON B. G., Lowell.
Wilson Colvin B., 36 Lowell, Lowell.
Wilson Chester, 12 Plainfield, Rockford.
WILSON CLARK S., 4 Byron, North Byron.
Wilton Thomas, 29 Tyrone, Casnovia.
Wilton William, 29 Tyrone, Casnovia.
Wiltse Benj., 13 Solon, Cedar Springs.
Winans Frank M., Lowell.
Winans John, Lowell.
WINCHESTER CALVIN, 10 Byron, Byron Center.
Winchester Jerome L., 15 Byron, Byron Center.
Winchester Justus J., 4 Byron, Byron Center.
Winchester John L., 14 Byron, Byron Center.
Winchester Laadan, 10 Byron, Byron Center.
Winchester Lorenzo G., Alaska Village.
Winchsel Isaac, 30 Oakfield, Oakfield.
Winchell Justus, 7 Paris, Gr. Rapids.
WINCHELL MONROE, 12 Bowne, Bowne.
WINEGAR ASHBEL, 15 Vergennes, Lowell.
Winegar Isaac, Jr., 28 Byron, Byron Center.
Winegar Milton, 28 Byron, Byron Cen.
WINEGAR R. D., Lowell.
Wingler John, Lowell.

Wingler Joseph, 19 Lowell, Lowell.
Winkler William, 27 Gaines, Cody's Mills.
WINKS CHARLES, 23 Caledonia, Caledonia.
Winks Henry S., 23 Caledonia, Caledonia.
Winslow Peter, 16 Spencer, Spencer Mills.
Winslow Robert, 16 Spencer, Spencer Mills.
WINSOR JACOB W., 32 Grand Rapids
Winter Albert, 5 Grattan, Grattan Cen.
Winters Albert, 26 Spencer, Spencer Mills.
Winters Albert, 11 Cascade, Ada.
Winters Charles, 2 Plainfield, Rockford.
Winters Freeman, 12 Byron, Gainesville.
Winters James, Burchville (Burch's Mills.)
Wirfel Lewis, 22 Paris, Grand Rapids.
WISE ABRAM, 4 Plainfield, Belmont.
Wise Benjamin F., Village Cannonsburg.
Wise Henry L., 9 Cascade, Cascade.
WISE SAMUEL, 27 Algoma, Rockford.
Wise Samuel, Rockford.
Wolcott Philo G., 20 Gaines, Gainesville.
Wolf Alonzo, 30 Wyoming, Grandville.
Wolf Baldasar, 30 Byron, Byron Center
Wolf Jacob, 30 Byron, Byron Center.
Wolf Jacob, Jr., 30 Byron, Byron Cen.
Wolfe Frederick, 4 Oakfield, Oakfield.
Wolfe Mary E., 16 Grattan, Grattan Center.
Wolner Julius, 22 Walker, G. Rapids.
Wolven George E., 29 Algoma, Rockford.
WOLVEN HARVEY H., 24 Algoma, Rockford.
Wolverton John C., 20 Spencer, Spencer Mills.
WOOD AMASA, 24 Paris, G. Rapids.
Wood Abraham, 10 Cascade, Ada.
WOOD BEVERLY B., 1 Alpine, Englishville.
Wood Clinton A., 25 Cascade, Alaska.
Wood Clayton, 5 Nelson, Sand Lake.
WOOD DE ROY A., 25 Cascade, Alaska
Wood Francis, 28 Wyoming, Grandville
Wood Frank A., 25 Cascade, Alaska.
WOOD GEO. D., 22 Grattan, Grattan Center.
Wood Harvey J., Alaska.
Wood Henry, 21 Grand Rapids.

Wiser Joseph, 29 Algoma, Rockford.
Wisinger Alexander, 12 Bowne, Bowne
Wismer Henry C., 11 Gaines, Hammond.
Wisner Byron B., 26 Cascade, Alaska.
Wisner M. L., Lowell.
Wisner Peter S., 26 Cascade, Alaska.
Wite Gilbert N., 18 Tyrone, Casnovia.
Witham Jos. G., 1 Oakfield, Greenville.
Withey Albert, 34 Sparta, Englishville.
Withey Calvin, 25 Wyoming, Grand Rapids.
Withey John H., 3 Cascade, Ada.
Withey James L., 6 Byron, Grandville.
Withey Livius, 24 Sparta, Sparta Cen.
Withey Reuben L., 3 Paris, Grand Rapids.
WITMER HENRY D., 24 Gaines, Hammond.
Witty Jacob, 18 Paris, Grand Rapids.
WOLCOTT ASA, 10 Sparta, Sparta Center.
Wolcott George B., 20 Gaines, Grand Rapids.
WOLCOTT JOHN, 20 Gaines, Gainesville.
WOOD JOSEPH, 7 Nelson, Cedar Springs.
Wood James, Burchville (Burch's Mills.)
Wood Jedediah H., Lowell.
WOOD JOHN, 2 Courtland, Cedar Springs.
Wood Granthan, 2 Courtland, Courtland Center.
Wood Philo, 24 Paris, Grand Rapids.
Wood Philetus W., 33 Gaines, Cody's Mills.
Wood Sylvester, Alaska.
Wood Solomon, Alaska.
WOOD WM. I., 24 Caledonia, Alaska.
Wood Wm. A., Alaska Village.
Woodall Alonzo, 7 Spencer, Nelson.
WOODARD EPHRAIM H., 7 Walker, Grand Rapids.
Woodbeck John, 2 Oakfield, Greenville
Woodbury Samuel, 4 Algoma, Cedar Springs.
WOODBURY THOMAS B., 10 Vergennes, Alton.
Woodcock John, 26 Vergennes, Lowell.
Woodell John, 33 Wyoming, Grandville

Woodin Eleazer, Burchville (Burch's Mills.)
WOODIN RUSSELL H., Sparta Center
Wooding Charles T., Lowell.
Wooding John, 11 Cascade, Cascade.
WOODMAN LEWIS C., 4 Walker, Indian Creek.
Woodman Nathaniel H., Sparta Center
Woodruff Charles, 16 Grand Rapids.
Woodruff F. M., Rockford.
Woodruff Volney, Cedar Springs.
Woods Andrew, 7 Caledonia, Alaska.
Woods John, 7 Ada, Grand Rapids.
Woods John, 1 Wyoming, G. Rapids.
Woods John H., 11 Gaines, Hammond.
Woods John E., 11 Gaines, Hammond.
Woods Thomas, Lowell.
Woodward Daniel, 2 Gaines, Hammond.
WOODWARD GEO. W., 2 Gaines, Hammond.
Woodward R. S., Alaska.
WOODWARD WM. B., 1 Gaines, Hammond.
Woodworth J. H., 32 Grand Rapids.
Woodworth Samuel, 32 Plainfield, Grand Rapids.
Woodworth Thomas, 32 Plainfield, Grand Rapids.
WRIGHT EBER K., 35 Lowell, Lowell
Wright Francis C., 10 Lowell, Lowell.
Wright Geo. E., 12 Lowell, Lowell.
Wright Geo. E., 15 Vergennes, Alton.
Wright Geo. N., 16 Walker, G. Rapids.
Wright Joseph, 4 Lowell, Lowell.
Wright John W., Lowell.
WRIGHT JEREMIAH S., 27 Walker, Grand Rapids.
Wright Leander, 2 Wyoming, Grand Rapids.
WRIGHT N. C., 15 Walker, Grand Rapids.
Wright Patrick N., 13 Walker, Grand Rapids.
Wright Philander B., 25 Byron, Cody's Mills.
Wright Rigdon, 7 Plainfield, Englishville.
WRIGHT SOLOMON, 33 Alpine, Indian Creek.
Wright William, Lowell.
Wright William, 4 Tyrone, Casnovia.
WRIGHTMAN HENRY C., Village Cannonsburg.
Wunsch Anton, South 1 Ada, Lowell.
Wunsch Sebastian, South 1 Ada.
Wurzler Frederick, 11 Walker, Grand Rapids.

Woolever Henry, 20 Cannon, Austerlitz
Wooster August W., 21 Grand Rapids.
Wooster Coonrod, 26 Courtland, Courtland Center.
Worcester Mrs., Lowell.
Worden Annanias, 4 Cannon, Rockford.
Worden David, 17 Grand Rapids.
Worden Henry M., 15 Paris, Grand Rapids.
Worden Silas, Lowell.
Worden Wilson M., 27 Vergennes, Lowell.
Wornica Mrs. Malvina, 31 Paris, Grand Rapids.
Wride Anderson, 32 Ada, Ada.
Wride James C., 6 Cascade, Cascade.
Wride Joseph, 6 Cascade, Cascade.
Wride Mrs. Malinda, 31 Ada, Ada.
Wright Adelbert, 4 Lowell, Lowell.
Wright Anson, 2 Wyoming, G. Rapids.
WRIGHT BENJ. B., 14 Bowne, Lowell
Wright Benjamin, 3 Lowell, Lowell.
Wykes James, 10 Paris, Grand Rapids.
Wykes John P., 10 Paris, Grand Rapids
Wylie George P., 17 Grand Rapids.
WYLIE H. C., 33 Tyrone, Casnovia.
WYLIE HENRY H., 28 Tyrone, Casnovia.
Wylie Wm. D., Sparta Center.
WYLIE WM. M., 17 Grand Rapids.
Wyman Daniel, 24 Solon, Cedar Springs
WYMAN DANIEL G., Cedar Springs.
WYMAN JOHN R., 23 Algoma, Edgerton.
Wyman Lafayette M., 16 Lowell, Lowell.
Wyman O. C., Cedar Springs.
Wyman Samuel J., 27 Vergennes, Lowell.
WYNNE DANIEL, 19 Vergennes, Vergennes.
Wynne Thomas, 19 Vergennes, Vergennes.

Y

Yagle Frank, 27 Alpine, Gr. Rapids.
Yale George W., 8 Paris, Gr. Rapids.
Yale Welcome, 8 Paris, Gr. Rapids.
Yanson Charles, 21 Paris, Gr. Rapids.
Yateman William, 29 Bowne, Harris Creek.
Yates Mrs. Hettie, Cedar Springs.
Yeiter David, 20 Lowell, Lowell.
Yeiter Ered'k 27 " "
Yeiter Fred., jr., 20 Lowell, Lowell.
Yeiter Jacob, 22 " "
Yeiter John, 29 " "
YENORE MOSES, south 4 Walker, Grand Rapids.
Yeomans Elliott, 31 Wyoming, Grandville.
Yeomans Eli, 31 Wyoming, Grandville.
YEOMANS ERASTUS, 32 Wyoming, Grandville.
Yeomans Levi, 32 Wyoming, Grandville.
Yerkes Anthony, 22 Vergennes, Lowell.
Yerkes Edward W., 11 Lowell, Lowell.
YOUELL JOHN, 29 Grand Rapids.
Young Darwin, 36 Gaines, Caledonia Station.
Young Daniel, 27 Solon, Cedar Springs.
Young Elihu R., 30 Courtland, Rockford.
YOUNG GEORGE, 33 Grand Rapids.
Young John, 10 Cannon, Bostwick Lake.
Young John, 32 Byron, Byron Center.
Young Jacob, Lowell.
Young T. E., 32 Grand Rapids.
Young Vachel D., Lowell.
Young ——, 5 Paris, Grand Rapids.
Young William C., 10 Cannon, Cannonsburg.
YOUNG ZEBULON, 30 Courtland, Rockford.
Youngblood Daniel, 8 Algoma, Sparta Center.
YOUNGBLOOD JAMES, 8 Algoma, Sparta Center.

Yerkes William, Lowell.
YODER JOSEPH, 13 Bowne, Lowell.
YODER STEPHEN, 11 Bowne, Lowell.
Yokum P. F., 29 Grand Rapids, Grand Rapids.
Yonge Henry, 10 Wyoming, Grand Rapids.
Yongson Rasmus, 2 Oakfield, Greenville.
Yonkers Andrew, 7 Sparta, Lisbon.
York Joseph, 2 Paris, Grand Rapids.
Yost Jacob, 27 Alpine, Indian Creek.
Youngblood Thomas N., 6 Algoma, Sparta Center.
Youngs Eli, 32 Byron, Byron Center.
Youngs Edward, 22 Solon, Cedar Springs.
Youngs Fayette E., 20 Paris, Grand Rapids.
Youngs James E., 32 Byron, Byron Center.
Youngs James T., 14 Lowell, Lowell.
Youngs Philip, 31 Byron, New Salem.
Youngs T. Newton, 32 Byron, Byron Center.

Z

Zelner Aaron, 25 Bowne, Bowne.
Zelner Aaron, 12 Gaines, Hammond.
ZELNER JOHN, 12 Gaines, Hammond.
Zelner Samuel, 12 Gaines, Hammond.
Ziegenfuss Charles, 21 Oakfield, Oakfield.
Ziegenfuss David, 13 Oakfield, Greenville.
ZIEGENFUSS HANNAH, 13 Oakfield, Greenville.
ZIMMER GEORGE, 6 Byron, Grandville.
Zimmerman George A., 32 Courtland, Rockford.
Zimmerman Paul, 32 Courtland, Rockford.

CLASSIFIED BUSINESS DIRECTORY OF ADVERTISERS

ADA VILLAGE.

BRIDGEBUILDER.

Jared N. Bresee.

DRUGGIST.

Charles K. Gibson.

COOPER.

Bethel Bristol.

GROCERIES.

John R. Robinson.

MASON.

Manson Miller.

MECHANIC.

Andrew G. Livergood.

MERCHANT MILLER.

John R. Bradfield.

MILLERS.

William Bennett.

John Kemp.

WAGON MAKER.

Edward Davie.

ALASKA VILLAGE.

BLACKSMITH.

A. D. Hembling.

BOOTS AND SHOES.

Josiah Irons.

CARPENTERS AND JOINERS.

John L. Hopkins.
Cyrus Hull.

CARRIAGES AND WAGONS—(Manufacturer of.)

B. E. Richards.

DRY GOODS AND GROCERIES.

Beamer & Haviland.

FLOURING MILL.

J. W. Boynton.

FURNITURE MANUFACTURERS.

Van Every & Bellows.

FURNITURE—(Wholesale.)

L. W. Fisher.

GENERAL STORE.

S. T. Colson & Co.

19

HARDWARE AND TIN.

Kniffin & Proctor.

HOTEL.

William H. Lock.

JUSTICE OF THE PEACE.

Hugh B. McAlister.

MASON AND PLASTERER.

Sylvester K. Hickey.

MERCHANT TAILOR.

John Martin.

MEAT MARKET.

Horace S. Newson.

MILLINER AND DRESSMAKER.

Miss E. R. Newson.

MILLWRIGHT AND DEALER IN TURBINE WATER WHEELS.

E. D. Alden.

PAINTING—PLAIN AND ORNAMENTAL.

Daniel R. Fox.

PHYSICIANS AND SURGEONS.

George Fox.
Isaac B. Malcolm.

POSTMASTER.

Warren S. Hale.

PHOTOGRAPHER.

G. F. Hull.

SURVEYOR AND ENGINEER.

Robert S. Jackson.

SAW MILL.

L. W. Fisher, proprietor.

BOWNE TOWNSHIP.

WAGON-MAKER.

Jno. M. Dillinger, at Thomas' Mills.

CANNON TOWNSHIP.

APIARIST.

JAMES PLANK. Section 8. (See Advertisement page 181.)

DAIRY-KEEPER.

Lorenzo D. Hoag. Section 23.

MASON.

Richard Bruner. Section 12.

MERCHANTS.

Ira Ellis, Cannonsburg.

MERCHANT MILLERS.

S. Chase & Son, Cannonsburg.

WAGON MAKERS.

Edward Davie. Section 7.
Loren Brink, Cannonsburg.

CASNOVIA.

GENERAL STORES.

A. C. AYRES. (See Advertisement.)
R. H. TOPPING. (See Advertisement.)
MILON L. SQUIER. (See Advertisement.

HOTEL.

J. Tuxbury.

PHYSICIAN AND SURGEON.

R. H. Colburn.

CEDAR SPRINGS.

DRUGGISTS.

V. Hayes.
H. C. Russell.
Fessell & Hayes.

GENERAL STORES.

Goldsborough & McLouth.
G. M. Stoddard.
Stiles Brothers.

GROCERIES AND PROVISIONS.

Isaac M. Clark.
C. Pelton.

HOTELS.

B. Fairchild.
National, C. W. Denison, proprietor.

LIVERY.

Theodore Phelps.

LUMBER, Etc.

Jacob Cummer.
Morris & Johnson.
C. Pelton.
Salisbury & Co.

NOTARY PUBLIC.

B. Fairchild.

PHYSICIANS.

E. T. Chester.
V. Hayes.
Fessell & Hayes.

SALOON—(Ice Cream and Eating.)

E. A. Straub.

SALOON—(Billiard and Bowling.)

Lewis N. Price.

SHINGLES, Etc.

Goldsborough & McLouth.
Salisbury & Co.
C. Pelton.

STAVES, Etc.

Richards & Sharer.

GAINES TOWNSHIP.

GRAIN MERCHANTS.

Woodward & Buckingham—Hammond Station.

GROCERIES AND PROVISIONS.

W. W. Pierce—Hammond Station.

SAW MILL.

Wm. R. Pursel, proprietor, section 18.

GRANDVILLE.

BLACKSMITH.

D. C. Britton.

BOOTS AND SHOES, HIDES, &C.

C. J. Rogers
J. W. Furman.

BOOKS AND STATIONERY.

A. J. Dunham.

DRUGS.

A. J. Dunham.

FLOUR, FEED, &c.--MANUFACTURER AND DEALER.

H. O. Weston.

GENERAL STORES.

Shoemaker & McCoy.
Silas Powell.
Daniel J. Mull.
Haven & McInroy.

GROCERIES AND PROVISIONS.

J. A. Knowles.

HOTEL.

John Ellis.

HARNESS.

J. W. Furman.

PHYSICIAN & SURGEON.

A. H. Weston.

GRAND RAPIDS TOWNSHIP.

HOTEL.

Delos Drew, (Lake House.)

H. C. STEPHENSON,

Homœopathic Physician & Surgeon,

Manufacturer and Wholesale Dealer in

Stephenson's Patent Trusses and Supporters.

Residence—First House North of Union School. Office—2d Floor, 2d Door East of Bank,

LOWELL, - - - - MICHIGAN.

P. V. & P. N. FOX,

State Agents of the

Mutual Benefit Life Ins. Co.,

OF NEWARK, N. J.,

For Michigan and Wisconsin.

City National Bank Building,

GRAND RAPIDS, MICH.

Merchants Insurance Company

OF CHICAGO.

Cash Assets,
NEARLY
$1,000,000.

SHINKMAN & JENKS,
Agents,
24 Canal St.,
GRAND RAPIDS, - MICHIGAN.

Dwelling Houses and Farm Property Insured against Fire and Lightning for a Term of Years, at Low Rates.

SOLICITORS WANTED.

GRATTAN CENTER.

Cheese Manufacturer.

Cass B. Madison.

Cabinet Maker.

J. A. Adams & Bros.

Miller.

J. A. Adams & Bros.

Wagon Makers.

J. A. Adams & Bros.
Robert Douglass.

KELLOGGVILLE.

Manufacturer and Dealer in Wilkins' & Plumb's Patent Spring Bed Bottoms.

EDGAR M. THOMAS. (See advertisemrnt, page 147.)

LOWELL VILLAGE.

Barber.

John Romig.

Chairs—(Manufacturer of.)

JOHN KOPF. (See advertisement, page 177.

Groceries.

John Giles.
U. B. WILLIAMS. (See advertisement.)
ROBINSON, CHAPIN & CO. (See advertisement.)

Lawyer.

J. M. Mathewson.

Fort's Western Medicine Manufacturing Company.

E. M. FORT, Secretary.

Nursery.

NOAH P. HUSTED. (See advertisement, page 177.)

Physician and Surgeon.

J. Howard Smith.

OAKFIELD TOWNSHIP.

General Stores.

D. V. Emmons, Oakfield Center.
H. A. Rowley, Oakfield Center.
Chester A. Lillie, section 3.

Physician.

Abraham Slaughter.

Shingles.

Chester A. Lillie, section 3.

ROCKFORD VILLAGE.

Clothing.

Peter S. Teller.

Drugs.

H. H. Shackelton.
C. E. Blakeley.

Furniture.

W. B. JOHNSON. See Advertisement.

General Store.

John J. Ely.

Hotels.

AMERICAN HOUSE, SMITH LAPHAM Proprietor. See Advertisement.

Lawyer.

John F. Loase.

Saw Mill.

George French.

Watchmaker and Jeweler.

R. L. Dockeray.

SPARTA TOWNSHIP.

Boots and Shoes.

Thomas Creamer, Sparta Center.

Carriages and Wagons.

Blomstrom & Gramberg, Lisbon.

Drugs.

Drs. C. E. & S. J. Koon, Lisbon.

General Stores.

R. H. Woodin, Sparta Center.
T. D. Barnes, Lisbon.
Chubb & Thurston, Lisbon.

Grist Mill.

Washington Heath, Lisbon.

Harness.

J. J. Smith & Co., Lisbon.

Hotels.

Jno. M. Balcom, Sparta Center.

Notary Public.

Jno. M. Balcom, Sparta Center.

VERGENNES TOWNSHIP.

Blacksmith.

George W. Fullington, Alton.

Farmer.

Orlin Douglass, Fallassburg.

Miller.

Thomas B. Woodbury, Alton.

Drain Tile.

H. LEONARD & SON, 13 Monroe street. (See advertisement.)

Drugs, Medicines, Etc.

E. B. ESCOTT, 57 Canal street. (See advertisement.)

GEO. M. STUART, Bridge street, (West Side.) (See advertisement.)

WILLIAM THUM, 92 Canal street. (See advertisement.)

STEKETEE & KIMM, 67 Monroe street. (See advertisement.)

JAMES GALLUP, 6 Canal street. (See lines.)

Dry Goods.

W. L. WILKINS & CO., 54 Monroe street. [See advertisement.]

VOIGT & HERPOLSHEIMER, 41 Monroe street. [See advertisement.]

C. B. ALLYN, 68 and 70 Monroe street. [See advertisement.]

SPRING & AVERY, 48 Monroe street. [See advertisement.]

D. L. NEWBORG, 46 Canal street. [See advertisement.]

Foundries.

GEORGE STANG, River street, [West Side.] [See advertisement.]

BUTTERWORTH & LOWE, Huron street. [See advertisement.]

Frame Factory.

G. W. LEMON, 71 Canal street. [See advertisement.]

Furnishing Goods.

J. E. & W. S. EARLE, 39 Monroe street. [See advertisement.]

Furniture.

NELSON, MATTER & CO., 29 and 31 Canal street. [See advertisement.]

J. P. CREQUE, 69 Canal street. [See advertisement.]

Groceries.

JOHN E. TOOHER, Coldbrook street. [See advertisement.]

BIRGE & SOMERS, 35 Monroe street. [See advertisement.]

A. J. ROSE, corner Court and Bridge streets, [West Side.] [See advertisement.]

ALBERT & KRUPP, 86 Canal street. [See advertisement.]

P. KUSTERER, 100 Canal street. [See advertisement.]

GEO. H. SOULE, 234 South Division street. [See advertisement.]

PETER C. SHICKELL, corner Front and Leonard streets, West Side. (See Advertisement.)

N. RINGELBERG, 159 Ottawa st. (See advertisement.)

JOSEPH FINCKLER, 104 Canal st. (See advertisement.)

P. SCHENKELBERG, 13 Front st., West Side. (See advertisement.)

S. C. SMITH, 71 Monroe street. (See advertisement.)

Hardware.

W. D. FOSTER, 14 and 16 Monroe street.

TUCKER & ROGERS, 33 and 35 Canal street. (See advertisement.)

FERDINAND SCHEUFLER & SON, Corner Canal and Bridge streets. (See advertisement.)

Harness, Trunks, etc.

C. J. KRUGER & Co., 72 Monroe street. (See advertisement.)

FRANK MATTISON, 67 Canal street. (See advertisement.)

Hats, Caps, &c.

PERRY Bros., 11 Monroe street. (See advertisement.)

Hotels.

National Hotel. (See advertisement.)
Eagle Hotel. " "
Rathbun House. " "
Michigan House. " "

House-builders.

FRANCILLO HALL, Water street, West Side. (See advertisement.)

A. D. BORDEN & Co., Front street, West Side. (See advertisement.)

GRADY & SMITH, Canal street, opposite Kent Woolen Mills. (See advertisement.)

Fire Insurance.

SINCLAIR Bros. & Co., 9 Canal st. See advertisement.

SKINNER & WARD, City National Bank building. (See advertisement.)

CROSBY & SON, 13 Canal street. (See Advertisement.)

S. O. KINGSBURY, corner Canal and Pearl streets. (See advertisement.)

H. E. DEWEY, Leppig's block. (See advertisement.)

Physicians.

Dr. N. J. AIKIN, first stairs north Sweet's Hotel. [See advertisement.]

Dr. E. WOODRUFF, 87 Canal street. [See advertisement.]

Drs. HUNT & HOYT, Monroe street. [See advertisement.]

Dr. E. H. CUMMING, 10 Canal street. [See advertisement.]

Plaster.

G. R. PLASTER CO., 11 Canal street. [See advertisement.]

Printing—Job.

JOHN BOLE, corner Canal and Pearl streets, third floor. [See advertisement.]

Real Estate Agents.

CROSBY & SONS, 13 Canal street. [See advertisement.]

S. O. KINGSBURY, corner Canal and Pearl streets. [See advertisement.]

W. P. INNES, 81 Monroe street. [See advertisement.]

Sewing Machines.

JOHN FOX (repairer) 125 Monroe street. [See advertisement.]

GEO. F. OWEN, 27 Monroe street. [See advertisement.]

G. L. FRETTS, 7 and 9 Monroe street. [See advertisement.]

Stencil Establishment.

A. F. De VINNEY, 57 Canal street. [See advertisement.]

Undertaker.

J. H. FARWELL, 26 Lyon street. [See advertisement.]

Variety Store.

F. LEOTTGERT, 16 Canal street. [See advertisement.]

Wagon Manufactories.

WM. HARRISON, 46 Front street, (West Side), and Mill street, (East Side.) [See advertisement.]

A. WOOD, 33 Waterloo street. [See advertisement.]

CHAS. A. BISSONETTE, 42 Bridge street, (West Side.) [See advertisement.]

JOSEPH EMMER, corner Bronson and Kent streets. [See advertisement.]

FIEBIG & RATHMANN, 221 Canal street. [See advertisement.]

F. OSTERLE & CO., Canal street, three doors north of Bridge street. [See advertisement.]

Wall Paper, Picture Frames, &c.

REID & SMITH, Monroe street, under the Rathbun House. [See advertisement.]

War Claim Agents.

SKINNER & WARD, City National Bank building.

Yankee Notions--(Wholesale.)

TYLER, GRAHAM & CO., 19 Canal street. [See advertisement.]

www.ingramcontent.com/pod-product-compliance
Lightning Source LLC
LaVergne TN
LVHW020224110826
845151LV00003B/822

* 9 7 8 1 4 2 5 5 3 1 5 4 6 *